How China Works

"No better way to judge an action than by effects, no better way to settle arguments than by evidence."

—Wang Chong, Lunheng, 80 AD

"The social process is really one indivisible whole. Out of its great stream the classifying hand of the investigator artificially extracts economic facts. The designation of a fact as economic already involves an abstraction, the first of the many forced upon us by the technical conditions of mentally copying reality. A fact is never exclusively or purely economic; other—and often more important—aspects always exist."

—Joseph Schumpeter, The Theory of Economic Development: An Inquiry into Profits, Capital, Credit, Interest, and the Business Cycle, 1934

"A rigid conceptual framework is no doubt useful in formulating questions, but at all times it evokes the peril that these questions will be mistaken for answers. There is a deep-seated yearning in the social sciences for the discovery of one general approach, one general law valid for all times and all climes. But these attitudes must be outgrown. They overestimate both the degree of simplicity of economic reality and the quality of scientific tools."

—Alexander Gerschenkron, Economic Backwardness in Historical Perspective, 1962

Xiaohuan Lan

How China Works

An Introduction to China's State-led Economic Development

文
景

Horizon

palgrave
macmillan

Xiaohuan Lan
Fudan University
Shanghai, China

Translated by
Gary Topp
Hangzhou, China

ISBN 978-981-97-0079-0 ISBN 978-981-97-0080-6 (eBook)
https://doi.org/10.1007/978-981-97-0080-6

Jointly published with Horizon Media Co., Ltd., a division of Shanghai People's Publishing House
The print edition is not for sale in China (Mainland). Customers from China (Mainland) please order the print book from: Horizon Media Co., Ltd., a division of Shanghai People's Publishing House
ISBN of the Co-Publisher's edition: 978-7-208-17133-6

Cover credit: DuKai photographer

This Palgrave Macmillan imprint is published by the registered company Springer Nature Singapore Pte Ltd.
The registered company address is: 152 Beach Road, #21-01/04 Gateway East, Singapore 189721, Singapore

Paper in this product is recyclable.

For My Parents

Foreword

This book tells the economic story of China. From the rapid economic growth that makes Chinese people proud, to the sky-high house prices that cause so much suffering. The book is written for students and readers who are interested in economics or China, and who hope to better understand some of the phenomena that they read about in the news or learn about when visiting the country. It seeks to break the issues down in a simple way, the complex political and economic system that's too often hidden by a screen of boring government documents.

The main protagonist of this book is neither the market-driven micro economy, nor the business cycle-driven macro economy, rather it is the government and government policy, areas that are currently not well understood or written about in Western literature. The material from my book comes mainly from lectures that I give to my students at Fudan University in Shanghai and at the Chinese University of Hong Kong. In writing the book, I removed the technical details and attempted to discuss the concepts that drive China's economy in a plain language. In China, the government not only affects the distribution of the economic pie, but also plays a far deeper role in the production process than we are used to in the West. It's therefore impossible for us to talk about the Chinese economy without talking about the government. A deep understanding of how the political and economic spheres work together is therefore necessary before we can make any judgments or assertions. When studying China, it is therefore important to avoid misusing theories imported abroad and reducing them to preconceptions and biases. When the reality does not conform to the theory, we need to try hard to observe what actually happens instead of jumping to conclusions, otherwise we will lose our chance of empathic understanding.

The political and economic phenomena that drive China are extremely complex and we need to piece together different theories and different information to understand the complete picture. For those readers who work in finance, business or in economic policy, I hope the book can help them to understand the broader political and economic context that impacts their daily business. For students majoring in economics or business, the book can help to apply a framework different from mainstream (neoclassical) economics that can be used to analyze China. By using the Chinese government as the main protagonist for the book, I hope to build a bridge between mainstream economic theories and the reality on the ground in China. For students or readers working in different areas, I hope the book can help them better understand China and put more meaning to the stories that they might read in the news.

The book focuses on describing reality and explaining the what and the why. When it's necessary to explain how, the book focuses on explaining the policies and reforms that are currently in place at the time of writing. It is more important for readers to know what the Chinese government is thinking and behaving rather than my opinions and advices on what the government should do.

Organization of the Book

The investment and financial decisions made by local governments in China are the core concept that runs throughout the book. Divided into two parts, the first part will explain details and microeconomics including the basic responsibilities of Chinese local governments, their sources of revenue and main expenditures, as well as discussing the use of land to generate income and the debt that comes along with it. The second part will look more broadly at some of the key macroeconomic challenges facing China, which are consequences of the micro-behavior discussed in the first part, including excessive levels of debt, economic imbalances and inequality, as well as international trade and conflicts. The final chapter refines and summarizes the content of the book.

The book strives to be concise, highlighting the main logic and key facts without going into too much detail. Readers who are interested in going deeper can refer to the recommended further readings at the end of each chapter.

This book uses a lot of data, and if I mark data source in each case, there would be way too many footnotes. For commonly used data, such as GDP figures or population numbers, I have used the China Statistical Yearbook or the Wind database. I have not marked these sources in the text, but readers should be easily able to cross check the numbers. I only cite the sources of data that are either uncommon or quoted from other people's research. Although this book is written for a general audience, it strictly follows academic norms and uses a large number of cutting-edge research results that can be found in the references.

Expressions of Gratitude

I never intended to translate this book in English until I met Mr. Gary Topp. He had been working in China for five years and he knew China very well. He was concerned that the images of China in western media were so different from his experiences. He read my book and contacted me to offer to translate it in English. I was a bit hesitant because I knew the translation would be a huge workload, and I was not sure that Gary could finish it given his already-packed work schedules. But after we met and talked about the project, I was convinced that he was very serious and determined. The translation took him a whole year of weekends and night-time. Without his efforts and tenacity, this English version would not exist.

I started to study seriously about Chinese economy after I joined the School of Economics at Fudan University in 2014. I learned tremendously from my colleagues, particularly from Lu Ming and Chen Zhao. Many of my colleagues and friends read the manuscript of this book and offered valuable comments and advices, and I particularly thank Chen Shuo, Chen Ting, Dong Feng, Liu Zhikuo, and Wu Lemin. I also thank my students Bai Minyang, Ding Guanzu, and Li Song for their outstanding research and teaching assistance.

The publication of this English version was not possible without the enthusiastic and patient support of my editor at Palgrave Macmilan, Jacob Dreyer. I also thank Isabella Weber for her help during the publication process. Of course, my outstanding Chinese editors, Jia Zhongxian and Cao Dihui, are absolutely instrumental in every stage of this work. I take full responsibility for any mistakes.

Translator's Note

It was summer of 2021, I'd been living and working in China for exactly five years. Being part of China's booming internet sector, I had got used to the hard-charging, ever-changing environment that had turned companies such as the one I worked for, Alibaba, into some of the world's most valuable. But something was amiss, from the start of that year, and even as early as 2020, things had started to change. The Chinese government was playing an ever more active role in the internet sector and new regulations were coming thick and fast. I suddenly realized that during the 5 years I'd spent in China, I had learned about many things, the language, the food and the 996 work environment. By all accounts, I was a 中国通 or a China expert. But I realized that during all my travels, all my conversations, I had learned relatively little about the Chinese government. How it's structured, how does it operate, where does the money come from, why does it do the things it does? I struggled for answers.

At first, I searched for books in English to try and fill the gap in my knowledge. I found it hard to find material that got into the nitty gritty of how this notoriously opaque organization works, instead finding more material on international politics and economic relations or books looking at what the rise of China might mean for the world. I therefore turned to my Chinese friends, including journalists from Chinese state media, and my then boss at Alibaba. To my surprise, nearly everyone recommended me the same book. *"If you want to understand the way China's government works and how it links to the economy in a simple way, you should read 置身之内"*. The book had become a bestseller in China due to its simple and no-nonsense language and lack of political bias when describing China's economic and political situation. By focusing on the facts and the nitty gritty of how China's government operates, and by clearly linking its work to the broader micro—and macroeconomic trends that we read in the news, Professor Lan Xiaohuan was able to breakthrough to a non-academic audience, gaining great acclaim in the process.

After giving it some thought, I decided that such a guide was severely lacking in the English literature about China and decided to contact Xiaohuan and offer to translate the book. Fortunately for me he was open to the idea and after many evenings and weekends working on the translation and with great patience from Xiaohuan, I am delighted that we are able to bring a version to foreign audiences. Whether we like it or not, the rise of China and the country's relationship with the West will be one of, if not the defining theme of the years leading up to 2030. Yet too little is known about China in the West, and information that is available is often skewed or biased or overlaid with a Western perspective that doesn't represent the facts on the ground. At the same time, given its secret nature, it can be hard for Westerners to really get into the details of how the government operates. In this book, Xiaohuan has provided a simple and detailed introduction to the business of government in China. He starts by examining how the government is structured and financed, and the responsibilities it holds, before examining the role it plays in different industries. Finally, in the second section of the book, he goes on to discuss some of the major internal and external challenges that are facing China, such as house price affordability, debt levels and inequality, as well as structural imbalances both domestically and internationally.

I hope the book will become required reading for businesses dealing with China, and for policymakers thinking about how to deal with today's China, as well as for those students of economics or international politics who want to gain a different perspective on the world's second largest economy. But above all, I hope the book can serve as a primer for those non-academic readers who are curious about China and want to know more than what they read in the news, the book will provide an excellent primer on how the Chinese political and economic environment works. As Xiaohuan mentioned in his foreword, when thinking about policy in China, we need to know what the Chinese government is actually thinking about rather than what we think it should be thinking about, the book can help us to do just that.

Gary Topp, Hangzhou (2022)

Gary Topp has lived and worked in China for over 7 years. He holds an M.B.A. with concentrations in economics and finance from the University of Chicago.

Contents

List of Figures

Microeconomic Environment

Local government plays a pivotal role in China's economic development, with a large and complicated scope of work. Its level of authority and autonomy in decision-making is also high. The first chapter of this book discusses the factors that determine exactly what Chinese local governments are responsible for. Since these factors do not change frequently, the work done by local governments and the amount of money they need to spend do not change greatly from year to year. If the amount of revenue accruing to local governments were to change suddenly, the gap between income and expenditure would quickly lead to changes in their behavior. Chapter 2 therefore discusses the 1994 tax reforms that changed the way tax was distributed between central and local government. These reforms had a profound impact on local governments' finances, which gave rise to their land finance as the major source of funding and as a tool to drive rapid urbanization and industrialization. Chapters 3 and 4 discuss in more detail the logic, mechanisms, and specific case studies of this development model. The associated risks such as the huge amount of debt of the local government, as well as reforms to tackle these risks, are also discussed. Overall, these four chapters form a microeconomic basis for understanding the macroeconomic phenomena in later chapters of the book.

CHAPTER 1

The Roles and Responsibilities of Local Government

There is one thing I always remember from my time in middle school: if you took California out of America, it would be the sixth largest economy in the world! At the time, I thought to myself, if the US is made up of 50 states, it must be wealthy beyond imagination. It was only later that I found out California alone makes up 15% of America's total GDP, a larger share than any other state. I also learnt, that this kind of comparison is very easy for people to remember and today I have incorporated this technique into my teaching. For example, Guangdong province and Jiangsu province are the equivalent of the 13th and 14th largest economy in the world, producing more GDP than Mexico and Australia. Shandong province, Zhejiang province and Henan province if counted alone would each have a place in the top 20 world economies. Henan's annual GDP is equivalent to that of the Netherlands.

A few years ago, a team of young startup entrepreneurs from MIT were thinking about how to enter the Chinese market. They had already developed a sizable automobile parts business and things were looking good. The two 20 something founders had an open mind and came to China looking for strategic investors who might be interested in their next funding round. Back then, I was working on a consulting project for Hubei province's investment fund and gave the two founders an introduction to Hubei's automobile industry. It was their first time to come to China, and obviously they had no idea about Hubei, so I used the above

X. Lan, *How China Works*,
https://doi.org/10.1007/978-981-97-0080-6_1

method "Hubei's GDP is the same size as Argentina, so Hubei province's state investment fund is like the Argentina's sovereign wealth fund". I still remember how, upon hearing this information, the entrepreneur's eyes lit up. A few years later, in 2019, I checked the data again. Hubei's GDP had nearly caught up with Switzerland's, and at the same time, Argentina had fallen into another recession, the country's total economic output accounting for only 70% of Hubei's.

China's scale is immense. From a population, land mass and economic perspective, it is the equivalent of a large continent. Each province, if treated separately, is the size of a medium-sized country. Moreover, there is also a lot of diversity between the provinces, for example, Xinjiang's land mass is 47 times the land mass of Hainan. Likewise, Guangdong's population is 33 times the population of Tibet. Beijing's GDP per capita is 5 times that of Gansu. This scale of difference in terms of economic development is much greater than in the US, where New York State, the wealthiest state, has a GDP per capita that is only 2.3 times that of Mississippi, the poorest state.[1] What's more, China's provinces display a huge variation in terms of customs, geography and culture. There are more than 100 local dialects. All of this makes for a country that's not easy to govern.

In order to understand the way China's government administers and runs the country, we need to first understand the allocation of power and resources inside the administration. This includes the internal hierarchy within departments, as well as the horizontal relationship between different departments at the same level. This chapter introduces the basic framework necessary to understand the allocation of responsibilities within China's government. The first section explains some key characteristics of China's administration. The second to the fourth sections introduce the three key principles determining the allocation of responsibility: the principle of externalities and boundaries between public goods, the principle of complex information and the principle of incentive alignment.[2] The fifth section introduces the way in which local governments attract outside investment. Since economic development is one of the key responsibilities of local government, there are many different resources

[1] Washington DC, the capital is omitted in calculations here. Its GDP per capita is very high only because its population is tiny.

[2] For a brief discussion of these principles, please see the book by Lou Jiwei, former Chinese Minister of Finance (楼继伟 2013).

and methods that can be used to attract investment that go far beyond the textbook definition of a government's responsibility as a provider of "public services" and "public goods". Understanding the ways in which local governments attract investment is the first step to developing a deeper understanding of the role they play in China's economic development.

Section 1: Government with Chinese Characteristics

In Fig. 1.1, we can see the 5 levels of the government administrative system in China: Central, Provincial, City, County and Township. This system evolved from the original 3-level system present in China's history: Central, Provincial and County. After the People's Republic of China was established in 1949, a prefecture or regional level was added under a province. From the 1950s onwards, the government begun to try a new model of administration, with (prefectural) cities taking responsibility from provinces for managing counties (以市管县). Due to the increasing pace of industrialization and urbanization of China, from 1983 onwards, the model of city managing county was applied across the country, and many regional-level governments were changed to prefecture-level cities, in doing so the number of administrative cities increased to over 600 (Fig. 1.1's prefecture-level cities and county-level cities combined) from about 200.[3] Most regional governments that are still in place today can be found in China's borderlands, such as Inner Mongolia and Xinjiang in western China, that tend to be very scarcely populated. On county and township levels, the historical precedent of local elites self-governing ended alongside the collapse of the Imperial system. With the arrival of the Republic of China in 1912 and later the People's Republic of China in 1949, the state's authority gradually extended below county level to include township level and also below city level to include neighborhood level. At the same time, anything beneath township level, such as

[3] In 1959, the Standing Committee of the National People's Congress passed the "Decision that Municipalities and Large Cities Can Lead Counties and Autonomous Counties", which opened up the process of cities leading counties. In 1982, the Central Government issued the notice on "Reforming the Regional System and Implementing the System of Cities and Counties" which began to be piloted in 1983. More details can be found in this textbook (景跃进, 陈明明, 肖滨 2016).

local village governance, put in a place a standardized practice of villager self-autonomy, thereby reducing the administrative burden that would increase exponentially with one more level of government.

The actual situation is of course much more complicated than the simple five-level framework outlined above. For example, even if both are classified as prefecture-level cities, the status and resources of a provincial capital are much greater than that of a regular city. Equally, even though they are all classified at the county level, county-level cities, counties and municipal districts are very different. For example, with regard to economic and land-related matters, county-level cities have a higher authority than counties, while counties have higher authority than municipal districts. The five-level framework is also subject to constant evolution, such as the recent policies to fold counties into municipal districts (撤县设市), folding townships into towns (撤乡设镇) and giving more authority from cities to provinces over county affairs (省直管县). From

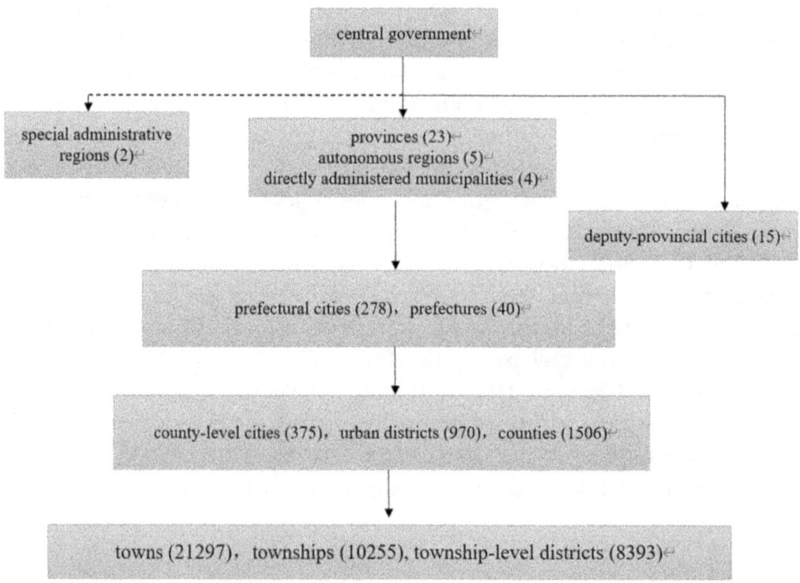

Fig. 1.1 Administrative divisions of China, 2018 (*Notes* The numbers in parentheses are the numbers of divisions. *Source* Ministry of Civil Affairs of the People's Republic of China)

time to time, there are also significant changes on provincial levels, such as the creation of Hainan province in 1988 or the creation of the Chongqing Municipality in 1997. Further, in recent years, the country's development strategy has called for the creation of the Yangtze River Delta Economic Zone (centered around Shanghai, Jiangsu province and Zhejiang province in Eastern China) and the Big Bay area (centered around Hong Kong, Macau and Guangdong province in Southern China). These policies will also have an impact on the future allocation of power and resources inside the government system.

China's government system has a long history and a deeply engrained culture, not only is it constantly changing, but it's also extremely complicated. There are many studies on the subject, and the additional reading at the end of the chapter provides some more detailed reading materials. This chapter will concisely introduce some characteristics of the government system that are key to understand China's economic development model.

Central and Local Government: The relationship between central and local government has been studied extensively in Chinese history. On the one hand, maintaining a unified country needs strong leadership from the central government; on the other, the vast scale and diversity in China's geography means that the daily business of administration must be taken care of at the local level. Historically, the balance of power between central and local government required many effective institutes to maintain stability, once those institutes broke down, a dynasty may split or collapse in the ensuing instability. One of the most famous novels in Chinese literature "Romance of the Three Kingdoms" begins with a philosophical take on the world *"if the world is divided for a long time, it must be united, if it is united for a long time, it must be broken"* that reflects on the difficulty of keeping the balance of power in check. According to statistics compiled by historian Ge Jianxiong (葛剑雄), from the Qin Dynasty in 221BC right through to the end of the Qing Dynasty in 1911, China was unified for only 45% of the time, meaning 55% of the time the territory was split between competing authorities or at war.[4] From these statistics, we can see that maintaining a unified China is not easy. As of today, the importance of the relationship between central and local government is reflected in the Chinese constitution (originally

[4] The data are from the work by historian Ge Jianxiong (葛剑雄 2013).

adopted in 1982). Articles 1 and 2 of the Constitution stipulate the state system and the political system, whereas Article 3 stipulates the underlying principle of the relationship between central and local government: "The division of responsibility and power between the central and local government is governed under the unified leadership of the central government, while fully encouraging the principle of local government initiative and proactivity". This is a highly abstract and flexible principle that will be discussed in more detail during later chapters.

Party and Government: The absolute leadership of the Chinese Communist Party over the government is a key topic when discussing the Chinese political system. In simple terms, the party makes major decisions and key personnel appointments, whereas the government is responsible for the day-to-day implementation of policies; however in terms of organization, the two are closely related. There is a high degree of overlap between the two in terms of personnel, and it's often difficult to strictly define the boundary. In fact, since this book is about economic development, there is no need to distinguish between the party and the government for three reasons: Firstly, local economic development relies on local governments, and the local party secretary is essentially a local official whose power only applies locally.[5] Secondly, the factors that restrict the division of power within the government are the same as those that restrict the division of power between different levels of party committees. For example, the transmission of information is a problem that exists both at all levels of government and also at all levels of the party organization. Therefore, when discussing the principle of the division of powers, there is no need to make a distinction between party and government. Finally, local economic affairs are implemented inside local government departments. Even though each department is led by a party committee, there is no permanent party committee in place to lead the daily economic work. However, this indistinction between party and government would be inaccurate if this book was about the legal system, and the role of key party committees, such as the Political and

[5] There is an exception in that the secretaries of certain locations are also members of the higher-level party standing committee, for example the party secretary of the provincial capital is a member of the provincial-level standing committee, so his power would reach beyond the capital city.

Legal Affairs Commission or the Commission for Discipline Inspection, would be missed.[6]

Matrix Organization and Multi-Level Leadership: A key feature of China's political system is the tendency to replicate the same structure at all levels of government. The main structures of the central government, i.e. party committees, administrative government, the National People's Congress and the Chinese People's Political Consultative Conference, are essentially replicated at each level of the government, creating the commonly referred to "four teams" (四套班子) organization. The key ministries and commissions of the central government also have replicas at lower levels of government, with a few notable exceptions such as the Ministry of Foreign Affairs. For example, the central government has the Ministry of Finance, the provincial government likewise has a finance department and the city and county government has a finance bureau. This hierarchical relationship between departments is known as " 条条" which we may roughly translate to vertical strips. Similarly, the horizontal relationship between departments at the same administrative level is known as "块块" which we may roughly translate as horizontal blocks. Most local government departments have to accept dual leadership from both stripes and blocks. As an example, a county-level education bureau needs to accept the leadership of both the city education bureau vertically and the leadership of the county-level party committee and county government horizontally. Under normal circumstances, the vertical relationship between strips is more of a business relationship whereas the horizontal relationship between blocks is more of a leadership relationship, since the local party committee and local government have the right to appoint and remove personnel. In many ways, we can understand this structure as similar to the matrix organization that we see in operation in many businesses.

[6] The institutions under direct control of the Provincial Party Committee or the Municipal Party Committee, but a part of the administrative government, include the General Office, the Disciplinary Committee, the Political and Legal Committee, the Organization Department, the Propaganda Department as well as policy research departments. In fields related to personnel, politics and law, communication and education, the party committee has functional departments separate from the government; however in the fields of economics and finance, the distinction between government and party is usually not important. At the central level, there are some groups under the party leadership which directly formulate economic policy, such as the Central Financial and Economic Affairs Commission.

Upward Management and Coordination: In such a complex administrative system, power is spread across various departments, and there is often no clear legal boundary. Therefore, whenever there is a requirement for cross-department or cross-functional coordination, things become complicated quickly, with different departments often in possession of confusing or conflicting information. At the same time, there is often bickering between departments, and as long as one department opposes an idea, it can be enough to torpedo a whole project. On issues where there is no clear precedent on how to proceed, government officials from different departments tend to pass the buck to each other, or simply escalate the decision to a superior, so the concentration of power naturally moves upward inside the administration. A major task of organization design is to avoid concentrating too much power in the hands of senior organization members, both to reduce the burden on senior members (allowing them to spend time on more important tasks) and to enhance the organization's overall efficiency. Therefore, one of the most important principles of the Chinese government administration is to allow a decision to be made at the lowest level possible.[7] If it's a departmental matter, then the head of the department has the authority to make the decision. If it's a frequently occurring cross-departmental matter, then a high-level leader or leadership group can be given authority to decide. As an example, economic affairs often require the coordination of multiple departments such as the Ministry of Finance, the Ministry of Industry and Commerce, the Taxation Bureau, and the National Development and Reform Commission. Since economic development is one of the key tasks of local government, most government usually appoint a high-level official as the de facto leader in charge of economic affairs, for example an Executive Vice Mayor who is also a member of the Standing Committee of the City's party committee.

Bureaucracy: In the end, all rules and regulations have to be implemented by people. Put different people in place, and the same system might bring about very different results. So, whether running a country or a company, the system of people management is one of the core parts of the organization. China was the first country in the world to develop a professional, specialized bureaucracy. Even before the Qin

[7] This observation comes from Kenneth Lieberthal of the Brookings Institute whose work is very enlightening on the functioning of Chinese government and politics (Lieberthal 2003).

Dynasty unified the Six Kingdoms around 221 BC, each kingdom had begun to recruit people based on their military capability and scholarly knowledge, and official positions could not be inherited, which weakened any hereditary system based on blood ties. After the Tang Dynasty (618-907AD), the imperial examination became the basis for a unified bureaucratic system that became one of the most important pillars for ensuring China's political and social stability.[8] The bureaucrats recruited through the imperial examination quickly became political leaders as well as moral role models for society at large. They also became key vessels for keeping Chinese society culturally and ideologically unified. The three key characteristics of the system are still present today: firstly, officials must learn and work to a unified ideology, secondly, officials can only be appointed by their superiors, and finally, local government leaders must rotate between localities. With the aim of maintaining unity, these characteristics demonstrate the way in which the people management system is used to maintain a power balance between China's central and local governments.

To summarize, China has a political system that is built on its own long history and culture. As in all political systems, the realities in practice differ from the rules and regulations that are drafted in statutes, but nothing is arbitrary. In any organization, the execution of power is subject to two constraints, the ability and the willingness to get things done. The ability depends on the resources and capability at hand, whereas the willingness depends on the initiative and incentive system in place. Next, we will discuss the impact of these constraints in more detail.

[8] Francis Fukuyama expounds on the cornerstones of three cornerstones of the modern political order, namely government, the rule of law and democracy. The idea of government as a management system run by special talents and not by blood relations, originated in China (Fukuyama 2011). Jin Guantao and Liu Qingfeng (金观涛, 刘青峰 2010) used the term "hyper-stable structure" to describe ancient Chinese society undergoing dynastic changes. This structure comprised three parts: economy, politics and ideology. Bureaucrats and Confucian scholars who share a unified ideology were key to the day-to-day functioning and also critical in avoiding ruptures caused by dynastic collapse, which could explain why China can survive numerous dynastic collapses over 2000 years and still maintain its continuity in culture. This point is well described in Henry Kissinger's book on China (Kissinger 2011).

Section 2: Externalities and Economies of Scale

The geographical scope and authority of China's local government is determined by administrative districts, and the extent of local power is bound together with the administrative district in question (属地管理). So, to start with, we will examine the division of power from the perspective of administrative districts. One of the main concepts influencing the division of administrative districts is the concept of "externalities", an important concept in economics, which, put simply, means a situation where one person's behavior has an impact on another person. For example, if you smoke in public it means that other people have to breathe your smoke, having a negative impact not just on your health, but also on the health of other people. We call this a negative externality. Likewise, getting a flu vaccine both reduces the risk that you will catch flu, but also reduces the risk that you will spread the virus to other people. We call this a positive externality.

We can use this externality framework to discuss whether or not something should be within the scope and authority of a local government. If the matter only affects the local area, and does not have any externalities crossing over to other administrative districts, it can be handled locally. If the matter contains externalities that cross into other administrative districts, the government level above should enter the fray to coordinate between the districts. For example, if a primary school is built in the city, and only recruits students from that city, then the city government has authority to make decisions. However, if a factory in the city releases pollution that affects another city (a negative externality), then the province needs to be involved in decision-making. If the pollution also spreads to a neighboring province, then the central government may also need to be involved. Therefore, the size of the local administrative district should be consistent with the scope of policy influence that the local government has. If the district is too small, and too often requires coordination and input from a higher level, then the whole government structure becomes pointless. Conversely, the district also helps to limit the scope of local governments' policy influence and the amount of resources it has at hand.

The Boundary of Public Goods and Services

According to classical economic theory, the core role of government is to provide public goods and services, such as defending the country or providing public parks for recreation. Once these kind of goods or services are produced, everyone can use them. For example, a defense service protects all people in a country and a park is open to everyone. What's more, the more people that use the service, the more cost-effective it gets, since the cost of construction and upkeep is spread across more people. This is what we call an "economy of scale". However, in reality, most public goods can only serve a limited number of people. Although a park is free, it will be crowded if too many people use it and the quality of service will be degraded or even ruined (something economists call a tragedy of the commons). At the same time, one park is not enough to serve a whole city, since many people live far away making it inconvenient. A city is divided into different districts and counties, and the boundary between districts is dependent on the scope of public services to be provided. In some respects, due to economies of scale, it is more cost-effective to have more people in one district, so the larger the district the better. In another respect, the size is limited by the cost that people are willing to incur to acquire the services, for example traveling a long way to a park or school, therefore the size of the administrative district is restricted.[9]

This logic may seem too obvious, but it can help us to understand many different situations the government faces, including those ranging from small, such as school district zoning, to large, such as how to reduce the country's carbon emissions or pollution. Even in ancient times, when the dynasty wanted to expand territory, the emperor had to consider the limits of expansion and ask the question: Is bigger necessarily always better? Would the administrative capacity be stretched too thin? Would people far away be difficult to govern? During the Han Dynasty reign of Emperor Wu (ruling from 141 to 87BC), territorial expansions through military were vast, which greatly expanded geopolitical influences of Chinese civilization. Emperor Wu was henceforth acclaimed as one of

[9] The theory upon which this section is based was developed in a series of seminal papers by Alberto Alesina and his collaborators. Relevant mathematical models, empirical evidence, and historical and real-world cases are included in the book written by Alesina and Spolaore (2003).

the greatest emperors in Chinese history. However, these achievements also consumed a lot of resources. When his son, Emperor Zhao, came to throne, he held the famous debate on various state policies during his father's reign. The debate was recorded in the well-known book, "Discourses on Salt and Iron". Chapter XVI of this book is about territorial expansion. Scholars who opposed the expansion, called the Literati, argued: "The Qin dynasty (*the short-lived dynasty right before the Han Dynasty, which was considered a failed government model by the emperors of the Han Dynasty*) assuredly went to extremes in waging wars. Meng Tian (*a famous general of Qin Dynasty*) certainly extended the boundary to a great distance. Now, we have far overreached the barrier set up by Meng Tian, and have established administrative areas in the land of the raiding nomads. As the land extends to greater distance, people suffer from a greater burden...Zhang Qian (*a famous diplomat of Emperor Wu, who expanded the Central Asian parts of the Silk Road*) penetrated to strange and distant lands, but brought in only useless exotics. Thus the reserves of the treasuries flow to foreign countries..." In other words, remote areas are not worth expanding to. They lack good land for growing crops, and the people are savage, administering them from a long distance will be difficult and expensive, so there is no need to continuing expanding the empire to these areas. This argument made a lot of sense, and it was difficult to provide a strong counter-argument, so its opponents resorted to personal attacks on the Literati' character.[10]

[10] This personal attack is quite famous and is a common routine used around the world to attack academics and intellectuals: "He who possesses the wisdom of Guan Zhong (*a famous ancient prime minister*) would not take up the offices of an underling. He who possesses the acumen of Tao Zhu (*a famous ancient rich man*) would not remain in poverty. The Literati are capable of speech, but incapable in action. They occupy a low position, and yet blame their superiors. They remain poor, while criticizing the rich. They make extravagant speeches, without following them up. They are high sounding, but their conduct is low. They criticize, praise, and discuss, in order to gain a name and the favor of the time. Those who earn salaries of not more than a handful, are not qualified to talk about government. Those who at home possess less than a load or shih [of grain] are not qualified to plan things. All the scholars are poor and weak, unequipped with necessary clothes and hats. What do they know about the affairs of the state or business of the officials? What do they know about military expansion and state building in distant land?" These quoted English translations of the "Discourse on Salt and Iron" come from the Institute for Advanced Technology in the Humanities at the University of Virginia, available online.

According to our theory, it's not necessary to resort to personal attacks to fight back. If you want to provide a counter-argument in favor of expanding, you can talk about the economies of scale that can be achieved. At the end of the American Revolutionary War, the 13 victorious states had to decide whether to create a centralized, federal government. Understandably, many people were against the idea. The British rulers had just been overthrown, did they really want to create a new set of rulers straight away? Those who supported the idea had to find a way to convince people of the benefits of creating a federal government. In order to do so, they wrote many articles, which later became the Federalist Papers, a classic text in American history. Among them is Article 13, written by Hamilton, where he put forth the argument that a federal government is more cost-effective than 13 small governments, precisely due to the scale economies it provides: "When the dimensions of a State attain to a certain magnitude, it requires the same energy of government and the same forms of administration which are requisite in one of much greater extent".

The scope of coverage provided by public services also depends on the infrastructure and technology available. For example, when discussing news provided by public broadcasters, we should ask whether every household has a television set or internet connection necessary to watch? Is everyone able to understand Mandarin Chinese? Is it possible for people of all education levels to understand the basic content? These hard and soft technological requirements play an extremely important role in decisions related to public services. One well used example comes from the Qin Dynasty (221-206BC). After unifying six Kingdoms, the emperor set about to standardize the rules for both hard and soft technology across China, including standardized wheel tracks, currency, weights, measures and a uniform system of writing, in this way people across the country could communicate with each other, and, from a government perspective, public services could benefit from the economies of scale.

Using the framework of scale economies and boundaries of public goods can also help us to understand the way central and local government splits work in China. For example, defense spending is mainly covered by the central government, since the military protects the whole population and there no provinces are left out. Conversely, a primary or middle education depends on teachers and facilities which can only cover a small area and can only serve local people. The economies of scale are therefore limited. So, teacher spending and school building maintenance is mainly covered by local governments. However, the content of school textbooks is not limited by physical distance and has strong externalities. For example, if everyone across the country is able to recite or be familiar with the works of Du Fu (a poet, 712–770), Li Bai (a poet, 701–762) and Sima qian (a historian, c. 145 or 135BC to c.86BC), then it is not only good from an educational perspective, but it also helps provide a common language, a common set of knowledge and the basis for forming consensus on a set of basic cultural and political issues. This process of nation building is common to all major countries in the world.[11] So, the daily spending on education is controlled by the local government, whereas compiling textbooks is the responsibility of the central government, where the Ministry of Education invests a lot of resources. Toward the end of 2019, the Ministry of Education issued a new regulation aimed at strengthening the unification of teaching materials for primary and middle schools across China in key areas such as history, language and politics.

So, we may ask, if the content and scope of public services provided by local governments across the country is all the same, and the level of infrastructure doesn't differ materially between places, should the area covered by each administrative district be of the same size? Or course not, is the answer. Since there are many other factors which also impact the effective provision of public services.

Population Density, Geography and Cultural Differences

The first important factor is population density. China covers an enormous amount of land, over which the population is not evenly spread. If we were to draw a straight line between Aihui in Heilongjiang province (in the northeast) and Tengchong in Yunnan province (in the southwest), and split the land into 2 parts, the eastern side would contain only 43% of China's land but would contain 94% of the population, while the western side would contain 57% of the land, but only 6% of the population.[12] The population density is much lower in the west, and as a result the area

[11] There are many great works on the topic of national building and nationalism. From the perspective of cultural anthropology, a classic reference is Anderson (2006).

[12] The line was originally proposed by the late population geographer Hu Huanyong, therefore it is also called the Hu Line.

covered by western administrative districts is much larger. It's no coincidence that the four largest provincial administrations, Xinjiang, Inner Mongolia, Qinghai and Tibet, are all in the west and cover roughly 50% of China's total land area. Some administrative regions in Xinjiang have a larger area than an entire eastern province, but less population than some eastern counties.[13]

The method of dividing administrative districts by population density is quite natural. Providing public goods and services incurs costs, and with more people comes more revenue, as well greater economies of scale. In densely populated areas, enough people can be served within a small area to achieve economies of scale, so the administrative area can be smaller. In less densely populated areas, the administrative area needs to be larger in order to reach any kind of scale economy. As early as the Qin and Han dynasties (221BC-220AD), the most important administrative unit was the county, and counties were divided according to population density. If the population density increases, then the size of administrative districts should decrease and the number of districts should increase. In ancient times, as the center of economic activity, and hence population, moved from northern China to southern China, the old adage of the north being densely populated and the south sparsely populated completely reversed. Taking Jiangxi province in southern China as an example, during the Western Han dynasty (206 BC-06 AD), Jiangxi had a total of 19 counties, by the time of the Tang dynasty (618–907 AD), that number had already increased to 34. By the time of the Southern Song dynasty (1127–1279AD), Jiangxi had become a major grain producing region with 68 total counties. The number further increased to 81 by the time of the Qing dynasty (1636–1912).[14]

The second important factor is geography. In ancient times, moving from place to place was inconvenient and natural barriers, such as rivers or mountains became the natural boundary for administrative districts. At the start of the Tang Dynasty (618–907 AD), China was divided into 10 regions (十道), and the most divisions were made along the natural

[13] There are dozens of county-level units with a population of more than 1 million in Guangdong Province, any of which is larger than the total population of Xinjiang's Altay or Hami regions.

[14] These numbers come from the book by Zhou Zhenhe (周振鹤 2014). The next paragraph is also based on the book.

boundaries of the Yangtze River, Yellow River and the Qinling Mountains. By the end of the dynasty, it had evolved into 40 Fangzhen (方镇), also divided by natural boundaries. For example, Jiangxi province and Hunan province were bounded by the Luoxiao Mountains, and the boundary still exists to this day. Indeed, there are still many natural barriers in today's provincial boundaries. Hainan, of course, as a standalone island is bounded by the South China Sea. Shanxi and Shaanxi are separated by the Yellow River. Sichuan, Yunnan and Tibet are separated by the Yangtze River. Chongqing and Hubei are bounded by Wu Mountains and Guandong and Guanxi are separated from other northern provinces by the Nanling Mountains.

The third important factor is language and cultural differences. Standard Mandarin Chinese contains many dialects, and there are significant differences between them. Likewise, many languages of China's 55 ethnic minorities may bear little resemblance to Mandarin. If the languages of one district are not the same, then government services maybe also need to be multi-language, which increases cost and reduces economies of scale, thereby affecting the division of administrative districts. Of course, there is a high correlation between linguistic and geographic differences. The very formation of dialects is mainly due to natural boundaries between peoples, such as rivers or mountains, that limit communication in ancient times. This pattern is seen around the world; if a country tends to have a highly differentiated topography or a wide diversion in the spread of arable farmland, then the variation in the country's language is more apparent.[15]

The dialect of each province in China is different, and this language difference affects the drawing of provincial boundaries. Cities and counties within a province also often have different accents or different ways of saying the same thing; this also impacts the boundaries of these administrative districts. Zhejiang province is famous for the Wu dialect, known for its complexity, the Wu dialect has a large variation between places and the spread of different dialects has a high correlation with administrative districts. For example, the cities of Taizhou, Wenzhou and Jinhua have distinct dialects and the administrative district of each roughly covers the area over which the dialect is used. Distribution of language and culture within a city may also affect the administrative districts within the city.

[15] The relationship between geographic and linguistic diversity comes from research by Michalopoulos (2012).

Indeed, it is interesting to compare the maps of China's administrative districts with the *Language Atlas of China* to see the overlap.

Once we understand these key factors, many policies and reforms can also be understood. For example, with the concentration of dense populations around certain metro areas, and the resultant growth in economic activity, it is sometimes necessary to break up existing administrative districts and provide integrated public services at a larger scale. Some of these strategies take on national importance, for example the integration of the Yangtze River Delta (around Shanghai), the creation of the Greater Bay Area (around Guangdong, Hong Kong and Macau) and the connection of Beijing, Tianjin and Hebei province are examples of such policies. Another example is the breaking of geographic barriers. With today's high-speed rail, internet and road network, many of the traditional geographic barriers can be overcome and administrative districts that were once separated can be simplified and brought together. In addition, understanding the differences between dialects and cultures across China helps us to understand the necessity for promoting a unified language, in the form of Mandarin Chinese, as well as unified teaching of history and culture.

Of course, these factors of population density, geographical and cultural differences only provide a general framework for understanding the division of administrative districts and cannot cover all possible cases. For one, people can move easily and population density can change quickly, but administrative districts take time to redraw. Areas of population inflow can merge counties and establish districts to expand the city, however areas of population outflow rarely abolish administrative districts, preferring instead to merge facilities to save cost (e.g., merging two schools together). Secondly, some administrations, for the sake of political stability, may see fit to draw administrative districts that cross natural barriers for fear that plotting forces or separatists may form. A good example is the Yuan dynasty (1271–1368) which was ruled by Mongols and resisted by Han rebels. The rulers went to great lengths to break up natural barriers, forming huge provinces that crossed rivers and mountains, however it was not successful. Thirdly, dialects and cultures may be separated by administrative regions. For example, the region where the Hakka dialect is spoken as the main language is split between 3 provinces, Guangdong, Jiangxi and Fujian. Another example is Jiangsu province; cities in southern Jiangsu, such as Suzhou, Wuxi and Changzhou, speak the same Wu family of dialects found in Zhejiang. However, they are administered together in Jiangsu province with northern cities such as Huai'an and Yangzhou where Jianghuai Mandarin is the main dialect.

The Economics of Administrative Boundaries

There is a common phenomenon in the Chinese economy; regions located at the boundary of administrative districts tend to be underdeveloped. This is particularly apparent at the boundary of provinces. Across China, there are 66 provincial land boundaries covering a total length of 52,000 kilometers. If we count any land within 15 kilometers of a border as a "borderland" then the total land mass would cover 1.56 million square kilometers, accounting for 1/6 of the country's total land mass. However, of 592 counties named in 2012 as being important targets for poverty alleviation, more than half are located within the borderlands and the incidence of poverty is much higher than counties located in other areas of the province.[16]

This phenomena, known as "三不管地带" roughly translated as "anarchic regions", can also be explained using the framework of scale effects and boundaries of public goods. To start with, the provincial capital is the political and economic center of any province. The population there is most dense, and the scale economy effect of public goods is most significant. However, on closer examination, we can see that there are very few provincial capitals located at provincial boundaries (exceptions include Nanjing in Jiangsu province and Xining in Qinghai province) and this geographical distance from the capital limits public resources in border areas. Furthermore, as learned in the section above, the division of provincial boundaries is related to geographic conditions. As such, many counties on the provincial boundary are located in mountainous areas, and the land has an average gradient 35% higher than non-boundary counties, which is not conducive to economic development. Good examples include the Taihang Mountains on the border of Shanxi and Hubei province, the Wuyi Mountains on the border of Jiangxi and Fujian province, and Dabie Mountains located between Anhui, Hubei and Hunan province. Thirdly, although the division of provincial boundaries is correlated with the location of languages and cultures, it doesn't completely overlap. The mainstream culture of a province is

[16] The geographic data are from the book of Zhou Li-An (周黎安 2017), and the data of poverty-stricken counties are from Tang Wei (唐为 2019).

typically located around the provincial capital, while the borderlands are often home to diverse languages that are not the same as the provincial capital. For example, the Hakka language found at the border of Jiangxi, Fujian and Guangdong province is not the same as the Gan, Min and Cantonese dialects spoken within each province. These borderlands are distinct in culture and language from the remainder of the province, while exchanges or cooperation with the same culture in neighboring provinces is restricted by administrative boundaries, this is not good for economic development.[17]

These issues already existed in the Republic of China period (1912–1949), so these "anarchic regions" provided a fertile space for the Communist Party during the revolutionary period (1921–1949). Indeed, many important revolutionary sites are located in the borderlands, for example, Jinggangshan (井冈山), located in the Luxiao Mountains on the border of Hunan and Jiangxi province. Other well-known revolutionary bases are also at the provincial boundary, for example Gansu-Ningxia-Shaanxi border region, Shanxi-Inner Mongolia-Hebei border, Hubei-Henan-Anhui border and Hubei-Hunan-Jiangxi border. The well-known battle of the Communist Red Army's long march, known as the "Four Crossings of Chishui", occurred on the Chishui River at the boundary of Guizhou, Sichuan and Yunnan province.[18]

From the perspective of public goods, China's borderlands first have to cope with a lack of infrastructure, for example road networks. In the 1980s and 1990s, dead end roads at provincial borders were still common. For example, in 1992, I took a car ride from Inner Mongolia to Beijing, passing through Shanxi and Hebei province. The road condition was good in the inner province, but became poor quickly as we reached the provincial boundary and we often had to take a detour. By 2012, this "boundary effect" in provincial road networks still existed albeit in a better state than 20 years before, with lower road density and less road traffic found at the provincial boundary. Even after excluding

[17] The data for the slope in this paragraph comes from the work of Tang Wei (唐为 2019). Gao Xiang and Cheryl Xiaoning Long (高翔, 龙小宁2016) pointed out that the economic development of provincial boundaries with cultures different from the provincial mainstream falls behind.

[18] Content about the location of revolutionary bases comes from the book by Han Maoli (韩茂莉 2015).

factors such as economic development, population density and geography, the boundary effect still exists, but it is limited to roads and expressways invested by the provincial government, not national roads and railways invested by the central government. The existence of this effect demonstrates that provincial governments are not so willing to invest their limited resources at the borderland.[19] However, as of today, with the rapid economic development of China, and huge sums invested in infrastructure, the "boundary effect" is no longer a major problem.

Another problem that has long plagued borderland areas is environmental pollution, especially the pollution of rivers or lakes which cross provincial borders—for example, the Huai River, Yellow River and Lake Tai. Environmental pollution is a textbook example of a cross-district externality problem. It was not until 2003 that the central government put forward the proposal named "A Scientific Outlook on Development" (科学发展观) and clarified specific targets for reducing water pollution in the 10th and 11th Five-Year Plans, that water quality begun to improve significantly. However, issues at provincial borders are still not completely resolved. Some provinces choose to locate factories and businesses that have a high level of water pollution on downstream provincial borders, in doing so the pollution released mainly affects the downstream province and the average level of pollution in the polluting province may actually decrease.[20]

Cross-district externalities are best managed by appointing a supervisor with authority over all affected districts to help coordinate and make decisions. This is why, the Chinese government operates the matrix organizational structure that we discussed before. Once this kind of cross-district problem arises, it is necessary to escalate it to the level above, for example provincial to central, in order to reach a resolution. Likewise, as we discussed before, all authority within the government is granted by superiors, and specifically which issues the lower-level government has authority over is linked closely with the existence or not of externalities. While in principle, a superior official can intervene in any matter, the reality is that the existence of externalities, economies of scale and cross-district coordination difficulties vastly restrict the likelihood and the

[19] Research on road network density comes from work by Tang Wei (唐为2019).

[20] The phenomenon that industrial water pollution is concentrated in downstream provincial areas comes from the work of Cai, Chen and Gong (2016).

extent of intervention. After all, the capacity of superior officials is limited, how would they know their intervention would lead to a satisfactory instead of embarrassing result?

The boundary of administrative districts affects economic development, and regional protectionism and market segmentation still exist today, this is especially the case when considering the market for factors of production such as land, labor and capital. Land use quota and China's famous Hukou (户口) system of household registration have a great impact on land use and population mobility. Over the longer term, eliminating these barriers to mobility requires even deeper market-orientated reforms. However, over the short to medium term, adjusting administrative districts, expanding cities and creating new metropolitan districts can help to more efficiently allocate resources. Many of the current administrative districts are inherited either from ancient times or at least from the time of a planned economy, and cannot fully adapt to the rapid development and agglomeration of modern service industries. Moreover, given China's huge scale, the integration of national markets for factors of production inevitably requires time and it makes sense to first integrate regional markets.

The first place to start thinking about regional integration is cities. And one of the first steps taken is often to integrate rural areas into the city, in effect changing them into urban sub-district areas under city government rather than county government. City sub-district areas typically rely on industry and services for economic growth, whereas counties rely on agriculture. This leads to different preferences and demand for public services that is diverging widely over time. Reconciling the different needs and making optimal use of finite public resources has become a major problem. There are two proposed directions of reforms: firstly, increase the independence and autonomy of the county areas by weakening their links with cities and urban areas. The second chapter of the book will discuss reforms in this area, which include expanding the authority and power of the counties, upgrading counties into cities and changing the reporting structure, so that counties directly report to provincial governments, bypassing the city. The second reform direction is to expand the city and turn counties into sub-districts of the city. In fact, from 1983 to 2015, a total of 92 prefectural cities expanded and merged with 134 counties or county-level cities.[21] For example, Beijing originally had only 8 districts, but has now increased to 16. The incremental eight were all created by turning neighboring counties into districts of the city. For example, current Tongzhou District was formerly Tong County and Fangshan District was formerly Fangshan County. In Shanghai, it's a similar story with Songjiang, Jinshan, Fengxian and other new districts created from the merger with neighboring counties.

Turning counties into city districts expands urban areas and turns rural residents and farmers into city residents, which gives them full access to the public goods and services available in the city, increasing economies of scale.[22] In turn, many of these counties turned city districts also act as a magnet for migrants, further expanding the urban populations and driving economic development. What's more, the change also provides cities with more land resources that can be used for urban construction, for commercial purposes or for housing. This further stimulates the city's economic development. However, given the vastly different system of land use between urban and rural areas, this process gives rise to many problems which we shall discuss in later chapters.

Section 3: Complex Information

There is an old Chinese saying "the mountains are high, and the emperor is far away" (山高皇帝远). It is often used to describe unscrupulous or even predatory behavior of local authorities, who being far away from the Imperial Court, are hard to control and can therefore avoid being caught. This example demonstrates the influence of information on power. Effective administration and management require access to key information. However, information is constantly changing and information collection and monitoring is very costly. As a result, the party that has access to key information or who can obtain information at a lower cost has a decision-making advantage.

[21] The data come from a paper by Shao, Su and Bao (邵朝对, 苏丹妮, 包群 2018).

[22] A paper by Tang and Wang (唐为, 王媛 2015) found that folding counties into city districts increases the migrant population.

Information and Power

At nearly all levels of Chinese government, the superior has the final decision-making power and authority over the subordinates' work. It means that a superior can overturn any decisions that a subordinate makes. However, it is impossible for a superior to have access to and understand all the information in every situation, so many decisions are delegated to subordinates. Even if supervisors feel the need to intervene, they still need to rely on information provided by subordinates. For example, when a superior inspects work, he must rely on reports from a subordinate and it's hard to know whether the information provided is accurate or not. If there is no access to a reliable third-party information source, then it's easy for a subordinate to mislead a superior.

So, although supervisors have the right to make the final decision, or so-called formal authority, given that information is often complex and costly to process, subordinates still have great autonomy and what we call "real authority". Maintaining a balance between the two types of authority is vital for maintaining an effective government. If subordinates are in possession of better information and incentives for the consequences of making the decision are aligned correctly, then the subordinates should be free to make their own decisions. If the lower-level subordinate has an information advantage, but the project at hand is very important to the higher-level superior, then the superior may still choose to intervene. However, as we all know, too much micromanaging from superiors may reduce the motivation of subordinates and therefore may not produce the best results.[23]

Take the reform of China's State-Owned Enterprises (SOEs) as an example. Which level of government should be responsible for regulating SOEs? Should the SOE be a central SOE, a provincial-level SOE or a city-level SOE? From a "formal authority" perspective, a government department manages SOEs at its own level and all those SOEs at levels lower down the chain. However, in "real authority" terms, those SOEs at lower levels are actually managed by the lower-level government. So, the difficulty in obtaining information is an important factor in SOE reform. If the SOE is located far away from the higher-level government, and information is not so easy to come by, or if the business among SOEs

[23] The theory of "formal authority" and "real authority" comes from a paper written by Aghion and Tirole (1997).

varies a lot and is difficult for higher-level government to manage, then it's not possible for the higher-level government to make effective decisions regarding the SOE. The task is therefore more likely to be delegated to a lower-level government department. Unless, in some cases, the SOE is strategically important to the supervisor, then the supervisor will be able to overcome the location problem or be willing to bear a higher cost to obtain and process information.[24]

In the real world, there is no clear delineation between supervisor inference and subordinate autonomy, it's more a question of to what extent. In the end, work must be executed by the subordinate, so it's not possible to operate without some degree of autonomy. At the same time, subordinates' performance is evaluated by the superior, so it's also not possible to ignore the supervisor completely. But in all cases, access to superior information is always an important factor in the operation of power. Subordinates usually have the information advantage, so as long as the superior does not explicitly reject, a thing can be done if the subordinate want it done, one way or another. Conversely, if the subordinate doesn't want to do something, they can raise the issue to a senior with limited information or ask frequently for guidance, thereby passing the decision-making risk to a supervisor and also slowing down the process until the issue eventually disappears. Even if the superior really wants a project to be done, the subordinate can usually find a way of delaying or even sabotaging the project if he does not agree. This situation gives rise to the common Chinese saying "the leaders have policies and the staff have ways of getting around them" (上有政策, 下有对策).

As shown above, real authority derives from information and the same logic applies within the same department. Although unit leaders have formal authority and decision-making power, most work requires specialized knowledge and professional experience, so the front-line staff have strong discretion and bargaining power. For example, in ancient China, there was a big difference between scholar-officials (Guan,官) and local government clerks (Li,吏). After the Tang Dynasty (618-907AD), most officials were selected from the imperial examination and were assigned to work in a local government for a few years, which was usually not located in the officials' hometown. Being unfamiliar with the local administrative area, and lacking trusted connections to provide information, these

[24] The relationship between information and state-owned enterprise classification comes from a paper by Huang et al. (2017).

scholar-officials had to rely heavily on information provided by the indigenous government clerks. Although they lacked "formal authority" these indigenous clerks were the backbone of the local government and exercised a great deal of "real authority". Not only were they unaffected when new officials transferred into the area, but they could also survive a change of dynasty. One indigenous clerk in Qing Dynasty (1636–1912) once said: government is like a horse coach, the people are the passengers; we, the clerks, are the coachman, the superior scholar-official appointed from above are the horse, driven by us.[25]

In fact, complex information and its relation to the distribution of power is a universal issue, and not one solely found in the Chinese system. In many governments, senior technocrats have more information and are more powerful than their ministerial leaders, who frequently change. For example, Cabinet Minsters in the British government may change as the result of an election or as the result of a cabinet reshuffle, which involves demoting and promoting ministers as well as switching ministers across departments. However, a permanent secretary, as the most senior technocrat in a given department, may work in the same department for many years and often has more real power. The renowned British political comedy, "Yes, Minister", refers exactly to this situation. With newly appointed Minister Jim Hacker being held hostage by Sir Humphrey, his permanent secretary.

Many of the factors that limit the effectiveness of public services discussed in the previous section, such as population density, geographic boundaries and different cultures and dialects, can also be understood as barriers to collecting information. So, information asymmetry and the cost of information collection and processing can help us to understand the need for decentralization of governments, both at different levels and within the same level. The division of administrative districts is therefore not only impacted by economies of scale, but also by the comparative advantages in accessing information.

[25] Since the Jin Dynasties (226–420AD), there had been a separation between scholar-officials and indigenous government clerks in China. Although they work together in the bureaucracy, they are isolated from each other in terms of recruitment, promotion and salary. For an analysis and description of this institutional change and its implications for understanding the current bureaucracy, readers may refer to the excellent articles by Zhou Xueguang (周雪光 2016) and Zhou Li-An (周黎安 2016).

Acquisition and Concealment of Information

It takes a lot of time to acquire and transmit information. Superiors must manage downwards, and subordinates must report upwards, likewise officials at the same level need to spend time coordinating between peers. Therefore, a major part of working within the Chinese government is vast amount of time that needs to be spent on meetings and corresponding documents. In Chinese, this is described using the phrase "文山会海" which refers to mountains of paperwork and endless meetings that swamp cadres. Over time, this system of meetings and documentation has also become a crucial vehicle in the execution of power.

The division of authority between Chinese government departments is usually not written in law and therefore relies on a complex internal set of rules and regulations that are enshrined in various documentation. In order to reduce distortion or error when transmitting information, and also to reduce the cost of transmitting information, there are clear distinctions between document types, as well as strict specifications for document formats, and various rules around document submission. According to the most recent regulations on the handling of government and party documents issued by the State Council in 2012 (which I will refer to here as "the regulations"), there are 15 types of official document. These include "Decisions" and "Orders" which must be strictly implemented by lower levels, those that can be handled relatively flexibly, such as "Opinions" and "Notices", as well as those which have less information content such as "Letters" and "Minutes". There are strict regulations on which agency can issue and send each type of document, as well as guidelines regarding the urgency and confidentiality. In order to prevent a flood of documentation, the process for initiating and submitting an official document must also follow a strict procedure. For example, the regulations stipulate that matters involving multiple departments may not be documented unless the departments have reached a consensus through discussion. This is also to prevent an endless stream of endless documents from being generated.

Similar to the documentation system, the system of meetings is also equally complicated. For example, which topics should be discussed at which meetings? Who are qualified to attend the meeting? And whether the purpose of the meeting is for discussion only or in order to reach a decision? At all levels of government, there is a set of rules of organizing various meetings. For example, at the central level, there are meetings of the Standing Committee of the Political Bureau (otherwise known as the Politburo), meetings of the Politburo itself, as well as plenary meetings of the Central Committee and the National Congress of the Party.

Because the consequences of certain information can be large, key stakeholders may have an incentive to distort or withhold certain information. A good example is local GDP figures. Economic development is one of the key objectives of the government and every year the State Council (of the central government) sets a national target for GDP growth which is also passed down to local governments, for example at the provincial level. This in turn is used as an important criteria when measuring the performance of local officials.[26] The growth targets of most provinces are usually set higher than the central target. Likewise, the growth targets of cities and prefectures are usually higher than the provincial target. For example, in 2014, the target set by the central government was 7.5%, but the target of all provinces was set higher than 7.5% with an average of 9.7%. At the city level, nearly 90% of targets are above the provincial level, with an average of 10.6%.[27] While this might seem strange to an outsider, there are reasons behind this "target inflation" at every level of government. Partly, it is due to the pressure of superiors to ensure that they achieve their own target, and partly it is a proactive desire on behalf of subordinates to achieve high targets in order to demonstrate their competence and enhance their standing within the government. But are these goals really achievable? In 2017 and 2018, some provinces such as Liaoning and Inner Mongolia made a "correction" of their past GDP figures, which turned out way too inflated.

Since subordinates may have a tendency to conceal information, supervision and auditing by superiors is necessary. However, effective monitoring is also constrained by information. Below are two examples, firstly, the system for land inspection. Due to the rapid pace of urbanization in China, the value of land has soared and certain illegal behaviors have cropped up as a result. For example, farmland may be incorrectly labeled as being available for urbanization. Many of the culpable parties are local governments or entities related to local governments, over which local land management agencies usually have no authority. In 2006, the central

[26] In 2020, due to the outbreak of COVID 19, the State Council did not set a GDP growth target, which was the first time in more than 20 years.

[27] For a detailed discussion and data behind the phenomenon of increasing GDP targets at every level of government, see the papers of Li et al. (2019).

government established a national land inspectorate. The Ministry of Land and Resources (now changed to the Ministry of Natural Resources) established a National Land Supervision Inspector (now changed to National Natural Resources Inspector) and set up several regional Land Supervision Bureaus to monitor local governments. This mechanism has had a significant effect on curbing land violations, however there are still problems. The central government has only appointed 9 regional-level inspectorates, and the cities where they are located in tend to have lower land violations than other cities. This reflects the fact that the inspector has better information about the city where he or she is resident and hence is better able to stop violations.[28]

The second example relates to water pollution. Compared with GDP numbers, water pollution numbers are much easier to measure and information collection is simpler. As early as the 1990s, central government had established the National Environmental Quality Monitoring Network-Surface Water Monitoring System, setting it up in various rivers and lakes. Once a water monitoring station had been put in place, it automatically reported data directly to the central government. However, back in the 1990s, goals related to GDP growth far outweighed those related to environmental protection, so the data were mainly used for scientific research rather than actively measuring and improving the environment. By 2003, the central government developed the "Scientific Approach to Development" concept and water pollution targets begun to be incorporated in five-year plans (starting with the 10th and 11th five-year plan). The target had to be met by the local government. Even though the data are directly reported (so it cannot be modified) to the central government, it is still susceptible to distortion. Due to the natural flow of water, a monitoring station can only measure water coming from upstream. Therefore, a local government can improve the reading by focusing specifically on reducing pollution from firms upstream from the monitoring station. As a result, pollution from upstream firms reduced by 60% more than that from downstream firms. Even though the overall pollution level has surely been reduced, upstream firms need to bear higher pollution

[28] The resident cities of these nine regional inspectors are: Beijing, Shenyang, Shanghai, Nanjing, Jinan, Guangzhou, Wuhan, Chengdu and Xi'an. Regarding the "resident effect", please see the paper by Chen Xiaohong, Zhu Lei and Wang Yangjie (陈晓红, 朱蕾, 汪阳洁 2018).

reduction costs, and the overall distribution of pollution is uneven, which distort the efficiencies of pollution reduction.[29]

Given that information is complex and subject to constant change, the fact that ambiguities exist, and that the boundaries of each government departments scope is not clearly defined in law, the real execution of power within the Chinese government is highly personalized. I will use an analogy to demonstrate this. There are generally two ways for university professors to assess their students, either through exams or essays. If an exam is full of multiple-choice questions, the professor has the right to set the questions, but cannot decide the final score. However, if the exam is full of subjective questions, the professor has more freedom in terms of how to distribute marks. In the case of a graduate thesis, there is no objective standard for the answer, and the professor has even more power. So, the graduate students develop the habit of calling their thesis supervisor "boss", something they wouldn't consider with other professors.

If all aspects of a situation are clear and the outcome can be objectively measured, then the distribution of power is simple. All parties involved can make a contract and the rights and responsibilities of each party can be clearly defined, once everything is agreed upon, then everyone can get on with their respective role. Just like the case of the multiple-choice exam paper, there is no fuzzy space when everything is clear, and a machine is doing the review. 100 correct answers are equal to 100 points and there can be no argument had. Once the questions are set, the professors have no further say on the final grade. But most things are not so simple, especially government work with many tasks at hand and information hard to come by. There are always many often ambiguous questions that need to be answered: should the work be done? If it is to be done, how thoroughly? What constitutes doing well?And who should take credit for the work? Or who should take the blame in the case of failure?And since there are usually no set answers to these questions, if things remain unclear or disputed, who should have the final say? So, the execution of power can actually be understood as "whoever gets to make a decision when things are not clear".[30] If many situations are unclear, then the execution of

[29] Discussion on water quality monitoring stations and the discharge behavior of nearby firms comes from the paper by He, Wang and Zhang (2020).

[30] From the perspective of the contract theory in economics, it is impossible for a contract to clearly state all the circumstances in advance, so the essence of power is the right to decide what to do in these unspecified circumstances, which is called "residual

power will inevitably be concentrated in individuals, which is one of the root causes of "the responsibility in the hands of the leader" system (一把手负责制) that is present across Chinese government departments. However, this natural concentration of power into the leaders' hands, if not managed well, can lead to corruption and autocracy.

Given the complexity of information, untrustworthy information abounds, and power and responsibility are highly personal, rules and regulations cannot completely replace personal trust. When superiors are promoting subordinates, aside from looking at capability, they must therefore also consider if it's someone they can trust.

Section 4: Incentive Compatibility

If one party wants to do something, and a counterparty has both the ability and willingness to do it, we can call this incentive compatibility. In the Chinese government system, incentive compatibility is required between superiors and subordinates, as well as between work goals and officials' own personal interests. This section discusses the former, while later in Chapter 3 we will discuss the later.

Broadly speaking, there are two types of tasks that a higher-level government might assign. The first is very specific, with clear and measurable goals that are easy to evaluate. The other category is more abstract, such as economic growth or employment stability. The supervisors only have general goals and the subordinates need to take the initiative and mobilize resources to achieve them. For these two types of situation, the division of power is different.

Vertical Management

In highly specialized departments, with standardized processes, many matters are very clear and specific. In this scenario, the department is more suitable for vertical management. For example, the customs department is mainly under the vertical leadership of higher-level customs officials

control rights". The theory of analyzing power in this light began with Nobel Prize-winning economist Oliver Hart (1995). He uses the concept of "residual control rights" to analyze "property rights", that is, the right to dispose of property when the contract is incomplete. Broadly speaking, power or authority can be regarded as the right to decide in various ambiguous situations.

and the local government has less influence. This division of authority conforms to the principle of incentive compatibility: since the work is mainly organized by supervisors, evaluation is also carried out by supervisors. Likewise, promotion and work-related benefits are also under the control of the vertical supervisor.

For some other departments, although the nature of the work is relatively specialized, they are closely linked to the local economy and much of the work requires cooperation within the local government. If vertical management is fully implemented, then problems may arise. For example, in a 1999 reform, the State Industry and Commerce Bureau adopted a vertical management system, which removed the authority of local (i.e. city or county) governments over local bureaus and shifted it to provincial-level bureaus. The reform was designed to reduce the influence of local governments on business registration and administration, in order to reduce local protectionism and to promote a unified national market. However, with the fast development of the market economy and the increased diversity of interests, the effectiveness of this vertical provincial administration became weaker and weaker, and problems with incentive compatibility also started to arise. Industrial and commercial issues are inseparable from the region where they are located, but due to the vertical management structure, local governments had limited power to control or influence the Industry and Commerce Bureau in their administrative district. After a series of serious scandals, especially the infamous "poisoned baby formula" incident that shocked China in 2008, the central government decided to reform again, and, in 2011, restored a local government-based management system for Industry and Commerce Bureau below the provincial level. The promotion for and management of staff members became the dual responsibility of local government and higher-level bureaus, led by local government.[31] And in 2018, the Industry and Commerce department was finally merged into the State Administration for Market Regulation (SAMR), and this new department is controlled and managed by local government.

[31] See the Notice of the General Office of the State Council on "The Issues Concerning the Adjustment of the Administrative System of Industry and Commerce and Quality Supervision at the Provincial Level and Below to Strengthen Food Safety Supervision" in 2011. This document expires after the introduction of the new State Administration for Market Regulation (SAMR) in 2018.

All departments with a dual leadership structure encounter an incentive compatibility problem: which leader is the main decision-maker? Who is responsible for the work? If the incentives of all parties were completely aligned and everyone had the same goals and interests, then none of this would matter. In the rigid planned economy era, there was no major conflict of interest between departments, so ideological education was relatively effective in facilitating communication and execution of work, as well as placing restraints on cadres' behavior. However, after the onset of market-based reforms, individual interests have become larger in scope and more diverse in their nature. Conflicts of interest between departments or between superiors and their subordinates have become increasingly common. Although a political training system focused on "unified thinking" and taking a "big picture view" are still valuable, it's not enough to smooth out conflicts of interest. A more complex incentive system is required. At the very least, the supervisor who sets the content of the work, the supervisor who evaluates and rewards performance, and the supervisor who bears the main consequences of the work should be one and the same.

When a conflict arises between superiors and subordinates, reforming the management system of the entire department is only one possible solution, and fine tuning might be more appropriate. Take environmental protection as an example, for a long time, although superiors paid attention to the quality of the environment, subordinates worried about the impact of environmental controls on economic development. The incompatibility of the incentives led to lackluster policy implementation and degradation of the environment.[32] However, with the advancement of technology, the central government can directly monitor polluting firms. In 2007, the central government initiated a program called National Specially Monitored Firms, which directly monitor some heavily polluting firms, including 3,115 water-polluting firms, 3,592

[32] In addition to environmental protection, there are similar conflicts in other fields: superiors pay attention to quality while subordinates pay attention to cost, and subordinates will not hesitate to compromise quality in order to reduce costs. Such conflicts are not always due to information asymmetry between the two parties. Even if there are no information problems, there are capacity problems. This conflict can occur as long as the superior does not have the ability to completely replace the subordinate. In this case, delegating power will reduce quality, and taking power will reduce work efficiency. This dilemma requires compromise and balance. A paper by Hart, Shleifer and Vishny (1997) explores such issues in detail.

air-polluting firms and 658 sewage treatment plants. These firms were required to install a real-time monitoring system that transmitted data to the national environmental monitoring system. This system increases data accuracy, strengthens supervision and greatly reduces pollution. Moreover, it does not require a fundamental change to the management system for environment protection, and local governments are still responsible for day-to-day enforcement of laws and policies.[33]

As the central government began to place a higher priority on environmental protection, more and more cross region coordination work is required and the power of environmental protection departments has also been expanded. In 2016, reporting lines for environment agencies below the provincial level were switched to the provincial level, putting in place a vertical leadership structure. This change greatly reduces the influence of the local government on the local environmental protection agencies. This reform also incorporated some lessons learned from the case of the Industry and Commerce Bureau reform discussed above. During the period that the Industry and Commerce department operated a vertical leadership structure, both city- and county-level officers reported directly to the provincial leadership. So the city bureau has no authority over the county bureau. This led to a lack of communication and coordination between the city and county level. Therefore, in the reform of the Environmental Protection Bureau, county-level officers are assigned by the city level and also report directly to city management, effectively becoming an extended part of the city government.[34] This system is different from the US, where regional environmental agencies are under the direct control of the Federal Environmental Agency.

Local Management

In many areas of government work, such as economic development, a success requires coordination between many parties and mobilization of

[33] The research on firms monitored at the central level comes from the papers by Zhang, Chen and Guo (2018). In 2016, the number of these firms has increased to 14,312.

[34] For details, please refer to the "Guiding Opinions on the Pilot Reform of the Vertical Management System for Monitoring, Supervision, and Law Enforcement of Environmental Protection Institutions Below the Provincial Level", jointly issued by the Central Committee of the Party and the State Council in September 2016.

various resources. The principle of incentive compatibility requires delegating power to local governments: they need to be held accountable for success or failure, and credit must be shared when things go well. Local governments should be sufficiently motivated to do well but also not to overdo. Everything has a cost, and the optimal outcome needs to maximize a cost–benefit ratio, not to succeed at all costs. Without some form of constraint in place, it's not difficult for local governments to achieve a splendid short-term GDP goal, however doing so may have negative side effects, such as excessive use of debt, inefficient allocation of resources or achieving growth today in a way that is costly in the future (e.g., by degrading the environment).

The first step to align incentives involves clarifying what should be the role and responsibility of local government. A major feature of the division of power in China is that power and territory are related. Whoever is responsible for a given area also has authority over that area, and the boundary of that authority is defined by the administrative division of territory. This is different from the Soviet-style planned economy with its top-down allocation of resources and strong central government control. Management based on local territory accounts for the issue of boundaries between public services and also for problems related to information availability. At the same time, it also delegates a lot of power and responsibility to local governments which gives them a strong motivation to get things done. In 1956, Chairman Mao Zedong laid out this point in his famous article "On the Ten Major Relationships". Mao noted that given the vast scale of China, the size of its population and the ensuing complexity, it was better to have both central and local governments strongly motivated, rather than just a strong central government. He went on to observe that China shouldn't be like the Soviet Union where centralized decisions got stuck with the central government and were not flexible enough for local governments to operate.

The second consideration with regard to incentive compatibility involves the institutionalization of power structures. The allocation of power and resources should be institutionalized and shouldn't be subject to overnight change. For both the superior and the subordinate, the institutes should be clear in order for both to form clear expectations. Institutional reform relies on reform of the administrative system (such as the reforms of the industry and commerce department and the environmental protection agency mentioned above) and the improvement of the legal system. Similarly, it also needs reform of the fiscal system. The division of revenues and expenses should be clarified, money should be used responsibly, and debt burden should be restricted. Budget constraints therefore must be "hardened" that put absolute limits on spending and borrowing.

External competition can also restrain local governments. If the factors of production (labor and capital) are able to flow freely and vote with their feet, places that deliver poor returns will not be able to attract much resource. Although a local government is not a firm and rarely goes bankrupt and quits the competition, reducing resources available to inefficient governments can still improve the overall efficiency.

Summary: The Three Principles of Government Power Allocation

Sections 1.2–1.4 discuss the three principles guiding the division of power inside the Chinese government administration: economics of scale in providing public services, complex information and incentive compatibility. These three principles each offer a different perspective on the division of power and help to illuminate different sides of the same question. They are not mutually exclusive and should be seen as complementary with each other. The drawing of administrative districts, for example, is related not only to economies of scale in providing public services, but also depends on the availability and cost of processing information, and helps to set the boundary for power and responsibility across which incentives need to be aligned. Another example is building new infrastructure, which can not only expand the service scope of existing public services but can also improve the efficiency of information transmission and the mobility of factors of production such as labor and capital. This in turn increases competition between local governments and incentivizes them to work harder in order to attract more resources.

Underlying the three principles is a common theme dealing with conflicts of interest that exist between groups. From the perspective of public services, and the area that needs to be covered by them, people value public services differently and the price they are willing to pay is different. Therefore, public service delivery needs to be divided by administrative districts. From the perspective of complex information, people in possession of different information hold different opinions and come to different judgments, so decision-making power should be handed over to those with the best information. When it comes to incentive compatibility, the objectives and abilities of supervisors and subordinates may be different, so a mechanism is needed to ensure that subordinates work toward the correct goal. In a perfect world, there would be no differences or conflicts between groups and it would matter little how power is divided since the outcome would be the same regardless. Of course, in the real world, it's not possible to completely eradicate conflicts, but if different parties' evaluation of the costs and benefits could be aligned, many conflicts can be resolved and mutual trust can increase. As a result, the Chinese state places a high importance on educating citizens in a common set of values. Likewise, from ancient times until today, China goes to a great effort to cultivate a set of common values among government officials.

Although the three principles outlined above are not enough to explain every situation that might occur in reality, they help to provide an analytical framework for understanding the division of power and the related reforms underway. In 2013, the Third Plenary Session of the 18th Central Committee of the Communist Part of China (CCCPC) passed the "Decision of the CCCPC on Some Major Issues Concerning Comprehensively Deepening Reform", in which the explanation on the reform of power division was in line with these principles *"appropriately enhance the authority of office and responsibility of expenditure of the central government, over those concerning national defense, foreign affairs, national security,* ***and unified national market rules and management****. The authority of office over some social security programs, and* ***the construction and maintenance of major trans-regional projects*** *will be shared by the central and local governments, and the authority of office will be gradually clarified in this regard. Regional public services are the responsibility of the local government"*.[35]

In 2016, Guiding Opinions of the State Council on Advancing the Reform of the Division of Financial Powers and Expenditure Responsibilities between the Central and the Local Governments was released, further refining the earlier decision from the Third Plenary of the 18th CCCPC. Here the three principles discussed in this chapter can be seen more clearly: *"It is necessary to progressively move the provision of basic public services to the responsibility of the central government, such as*

[35] The emphasis in the citation is added by the author, which applies all the cited government documents in this book.

national defense, diplomacy, national security, major national highways, border and immigration management, national defense highways, border rivers and lakes, the prevention and control of major countrywide infectious disease, and strategic natural resource use and protection...Likewise, it is necessary to progressively move the provision of basic public services ***with strong regional effects, complex information, and which are closely related to local residents*** *to the responsibility of the local government, such as social security, municipal transportation, rural roads, and local community affairs. Finally, for provision of basic public services* ***which reflect central government overall strategic planning, involve strong cross regional collaboration, but have local information advantages in management****, such as compulsory education, higher education, scientific research and development, public culture, basic pension insurance, basic health care and medical insurance, employment, food security, major inter-province (or inter-district/city) infrastructure projects, and environmental protection, the central government and the local government will have joint responsibility and the specific responsibility of each party should be clearly defined".*

Since reform is still underway, there are still many problems in the system. For example, matters involving security and national defense, in principle, should mainly be the responsibility of the central government. However, management of rivers and lakes, which border other countries (mainly in the southwest and northwest of China), is still under the management of the local government. Another example is pension and medical insurance, which is very important to a unified national labor market, and should therefore be administered by the central government, however the current system is still very fragmented. For now, migrants may have to go through a complicated process to transfer their pension contributions across provinces. As for powers that should belong to local government, while the central government should maintain the right to intervene, intervention should not be excessive, otherwise the local government may lose motivation and the intervention may lead to a worse result. So, the question of how to restrict excessive intervention still requires further reform and clarification.

Section 5: Attracting Investment

In China, the power of local governments is very broad and, especially in the area of economic development, the resources that can be utilized and the actions taken often go far beyond providing public services or public goods that is emphasized in mainstream economics. Local governments can not only create an environment which is conducive to economic development, they can also thoroughly participate in the process, especially when it comes to the task of attracting investment. With economic development set as the core job of local government, attracting investment requires the local government to mobilize all the resources at its disposal and therefore is not simply the responsibility of some investment promotion office. Many local governments require all government departments to participate in the investment promotion process, which means that even department such as health and education should understand local investment policies and consider how to attract more investment in their daily work, maybe through officials' social network.

The local government needs an industrial park or a manufacturing complex to host outside investment, which involves a lot of work including construction, industrial planning and project management. Chapters 2 to 4 will go into more detail on this process. Concisely summarized, since the local government is the owner of urban land, it will often transfer the land to a firm at a very favorable price. Before the firm moves in, the local government will make some initial investments in the area, including providing electricity, transport links, heating, ventilation, supplying water, drainage and communication networks, and the land must be leveled as well. (a process known in Chinese as "七通一平" which translates to "7 openings and 1 leveling").

For large firms, local governments will often provide additional support in finance. For example, government-owned investment firms may become shareholders, local state-owned enterprises may promise to jointly invest, and state-owned banks may offer cheap access to capital. Local governments will also provide legal and regulatory support for those enterprises operating in complex or highly regulated industries. For example, the electric vehicles manufacturers that have sprung up in China in recent years (such as Nio, X-Peng or Li Auto) may not have a license to manufacture cars. Obtaining one is not easy, which may require communication and permission from central government departments such as the Ministry of Industry and Information Technology or the National

Development and Reform Commission. Since the local government are better connected and more familiar with central government, they often help firms coordinate and smooth the process, which greatly reduces the burden on the firm itself. Another example is the network security and communication services industry that has developed fast in recent years. Both are regulated by the state and require various permits and licenses, which usually needs help from local governments. Some other industries may have restrictions on foreign capital, and the local government have to help foreign companies work around these restrictions.

Local governments can also provide tax incentives or subsidies for certain businesses. Examples may include tax credit for research and development or subsidies on export. One common tax incentive involves businesses paying no corporate income tax for the first three years of operation and paying half the rate for years 3 to 6 (known as the "three tax-free and three half-tax" or "三免三减半").[36] Aside from enterprises, individuals may also benefit from preferential tax policies. For example, for large firms, local governments may offer rebates on the personal income tax of executives. The top marginal tax rate on high income earners in China is 45% for the portion of income earned over 960,000 RMB, so personal income tax rebates could be attractive. For high-level talent, the local government may also provide subsidies for their family's schooling or medical expenses.

Job creation is also one important task of local government, and employment is of course crucial to maintaining social stability. For newly established large and medium-sized enterprises, local government may assist in recruiting staff, such as providing dormitories and public transportation services. Many cities also operate housing subsidies for or direct cash transfer to highly educated talents.

Local governments are generally in a strong position to intervene in the allocation of factors of production. Land is owned by the local government, and much capital is provided by local government-owned banks and investment firms. In terms of labor, governments control the residency

[36] China implements a tax sharing system between central and local governments. According to the tax sharing ratio between the central government and the province, 60% of the corporate income tax goes to the central government, and the rest is divided by the provinces, cities, districts and counties. Corporate income tax deductions are generally reduced or exempted from the local retained portion of the company's location. However, for some state-supported industries, such as integrated circuits, 100% of corporate income tax can be subject to the "three tax-free and three half-tax" model.

(户口) system, as well as the supply of basic services such as education and healthcare, and the supply of land which of course affects housing. In addition, for the factor of technology, a large portion of scientific research and investment comes from public universities and research institutes. Finally, local governments have control over their tax and industrial policies, as well as policies related to international trade. All of these may have a significant impact on the success of an enterprise.

This mix of public and private resources in the task of economic development is not the simple division of tasks between the government and the market that is found in economic textbooks, where the government is responsible for providing public goods and the market takes care of resource allocation. Instead, it is a model in which government and its' related entities (state-owned enterprises and banks, various public institutions, etc.) are deeply involved in both the production process and also the allocation of economic resources. In China, it is impossible to understand the economy without understanding the government.

Summary

This chapter introduces three theories for the division of power and authority within Chinese government: economies of scale and boundaries in the provision of public goods, information complexity and incentive compatibility. These theories provide a general framework for the division of labor within government. Although they are different, the three theories are complementary. Social phenomena are very complex, and it helps to use different perspectives to analyze the same issue, and only by integrating the common points from different theories can we get a more complete and deeper understanding.

Local governments in China not only provide public goods and services, but they are also deeply involved in the process of production and the allocation of economic resources. The costs and benefits of this model will be discussed in more detail in the following chapters. However, if we ignore this complex reality and simply apply mainstream economic models and ideology of "limited government", it will lead to distortions and misunderstandings when analyzing questions related to China. Economic topics cannot be isolated from the government, which is a basic principle for understanding China's economy. Only by understanding and thinking deeply about the facts, we could use reality to adjust and refine theory, instead of using theory to distort reality. In this way, we can also begin to think more deeply about the role that government has played in China's economic development over recent decades.

The division of power and authority discussed in this chapter provides the basis for understanding the allocation of financial resources within government. The government must first decide what to do, before then deciding how much money is needed. Therefore, the division of Chinese government financial power and financial resources will be the topic of the next chapter, which is based on the discussion in this chapter about who does what. Despite frequent reforms in terms of financial power, the overall division of administrative power is relatively stable. The main reason is that the key determinants of administrative power discussed in this chapter, such as geography, language and culture, are relatively stable over time, so are information and incentive issues.

Further Readings

For a good introduction to Chinese government and politics, interested readers may want to look up the book of Kenneth Lieberthal, a senior expert at the Brookings Institute, *Governing China: From Revolution through Reform* (2nd edition). This highly readable book explains the basic historical context for Chinese politics and its evolution. For a more comprehensive and textbook-style description on current Chinese politic system, *China's Political System,* edited by Sebastian Heilmann, is a standard reference.

Information complexity and incentive compatibility are crucial for understanding any complex organization, including Chinese government. *The Logic of Governing China: An Organizational Approach*, by Xueguang Zhou, a Stanford sociologist, is a great book in this field. Also particularly relevant is the work of the late Harvard historian, Philip A. Kuhn. His book, *Soulstealers: the Chinese Sorcery Scare of 1768*, tells the story of an absurd incident during the prosperous years of the Qin Dynasty Emperor, Qianlong. The incident, which started as random scams in certain places, was interpreted by the emperor as a plot to overthrow the Imperial Court and led to nationwide investigations and executions. Panic prevailed among authorities and citizens. Countless people were falsely convicted. Eventually, this witch hunt proved nothing and had to be ended abruptly. This book cited many imperial court reports and the emperor's comments and orders. From this constant back and forth of communications, we could see how the information is distorted and misunderstood, sometimes accidentally and sometimes intentionally, eventually leading to great chaos.

References

Aghion, Philippe, and Jean Tirole (1997). "Formal and Real Authority in Organizations." *Journal of Political Economy* 105.1: 1–29.

Alesina, Alberto, and Enrico Spolaore (2003). *The Size of Nations.* MIT Press.

Anderson, Benedict (2006). *Imagined Communities: Reflections on the Origin and Spread of Nationalism (revised edition).* Verso.

Cai, Hongbin, Yuyu Chen, and Qing Gong (2016). "Polluting Thy Neighbor: Unintended Consequences of China's Pollution Reduction Mandates." *Journal of Environmental Economics and Management* 76: 86–104.

Fukuyama, Francis (2011). *The Origins of Political Order: From Prehuman Times to the French Revolution.* Farrar, Straus and Giroux.

Hart, Oliver (1995). *Firms, Contracts, and Financial Structure.* Clarendon Press.

Hart, Oliver, Andrei Shleifer, and Robert W. Vishny (1997). "The Proper Scope of Government: Theory and an Application to Prisons." *Quarterly Journal of Economics* 112.4: 1127–1161.

He, Guojun, Shaoda Wang, and Bing Zhang (2020). "Watering Down Environmental Regulation in China." *Quarterly Journal of Economics* 135.4: 2135–2185.

Huang, Zhangkai, Lixing Li, Guangrong Ma, and Lixin Colin Xu (2017). "Hayek, Local Information, and Commanding Heights: Decentralizing State-Owned Enterprises in China." *American Economic Review* 107.8: 2455–2478.

Kissinger, Henry (2011). *On China.* Penguin Press.

Li, Xing, Chong Liu, Xi Weng, and Li-An Zhou (2019). "Target Setting in Tournaments: Theory and Evidence from China." *Economic Journal* 129.10: 2888–2915.

Lieberthal, Kenneth (2003). *Governing China: From Revolution through Reform* (2nd edition). W.W. Norton & Company.

Michalopoulos, Stelios (2012). "The Origins of Ethnolinguistic Diversity." *American Economic Review* 102.4: 1508–1539.

Zhang, Bing, Xiaolan Chen, and Huanxiu Guo (2018). "Does Central Supervision Enhance Local Environmental Enforcement? Quasi-experimental Evidence from China." *Journal of Public Economics* 164: 70–90.

Translated References (in Chinese)

Chen, Xiaohong, Lei Zhu, and Yangjie Wang (2018). "Government Station Effect: Empirical Evidence from the State Land Supervision in China." *China Economic Quarterly* 1: 99–122. (in Chinese)

Gao, Xiang, and Xiaoning Long (2016). "Does Cultural Segmentation Caused by Administrative Division Harm Regional Economic Development in China?" *China Economic Quarterly* 2: 647–674. (in Chinese)

Ge, Jianxiong (2013). *Unification and Division: Enlightenment from Chinese History*. The Commercial Press. (in Chinese)

Han, Maoli (2015). *Fifteen Lectures on Chinese History and Geography*. Peking University Press. (in Chinese)

Jin, Guantao, and Qingfeng Liu (2010). *The Cycle of Growth and Decline on the Ultrastable Structure of Chinese Society*. Law Press · China. (in Chinese)

Jing, Yuejin, Mingming Chen, and Bin Xiao (2016). *Contemporary Chinese Government and Politics*. China Renmin University Press. (in Chinese)

Lou, Jiwei (2013). *Rethinking of Intergovernmental Fiscal Relations in China*. China Financial & Economic Publishing House. (in Chinese)

Shao, Chaodui, Danni Su, and Qun Bao (2018). "Growth Performance Evaluation of County Merger under the Chinese Style Decentralization." *The Journal of World Economy* 10: 101–125. (in Chinese)

Tang, Wei (2019). "Decentralization, Externalities and Border Effects." *Economic Research Journal* 3: 103–118. (in Chinese)

Tang, Wei, and Yuan Wang (2015). "Administrative Boundary Adjustment and Urbanization of Population: Evidence from City-county Merger in China." *Economic Research Journal* 9: 72–85. (in Chinese)

Zhou, Li-An (2016). "Organizational Boundary of Administrative Subcontracting: An Analysis of 'the Separation of Officials and Local Staff and Stratified Mobility'." *Chinese Journal of Sociology* 1: 34–64. (in Chinese)

Zhou, Li-An (2017). *Local Governments in Transition: Officials' Incentives and Governance* (2nd ed.). Truth & Wisdom Press. (in Chinese)

Zhou, Xueguang (2016). "Between 'Officials' and 'Local Staff': The Logic of the Empire and Personnel Management in the Chinese Bureaucracy." *Chinese Journal of Sociology* 1: 1–33. (in Chinese)

Zhou, Zhenhe (2014). *History of China's Local Administrative System*. Shanghai People's Publishing House. (in Chinese)

CHAPTER 2

Finance, Taxation and Government Behavior

There are two Chinese television series that I like very much, one is *Ming Dynasty in 1566* and, the other, *Towards the Republic*. These two shows have something in common, during the first episode of each series, some of the most famous characters in Chinese history are displayed, not in a state of impassioned ecstasy or insidious plotting, rather they are doing the most mundane thing in the world—accounting. The imperial chancellors of the *Ming Dynasty in 1566* were calculating the debts of the treasury and making a budget for the new year. Likewise, in the first episode of *Towards the Republic*, Qing Dynasty Emperor Guangxu, Empress Dowager Cixi and General Li Hongzhang were worrying about money, should it be spent on building the navy or the Summer Palace? However, through these mundane calculations of silver taels, the audience could sense plotting and fighting. All those political conflicts and personal schemes are hidden in the budget.

To truly understand government behavior, we must understand taxation. The reason is simple, doing things costs money, and no matter how good a plan is, if there is not enough money available, it will be hard to execute it. Moreover, to understand the objectives of a government, it's not enough to read documents or listen to speeches, instead we must examine where the government chooses to spend its money. So public finance can never be treated as a purely economic issue, it is also driven by politics. In 2013, the third plenary session of the 18th Central

X. Lan, *How China Works*,
https://doi.org/10.1007/978-981-97-0080-6_2

Committee of the Communist Party of China (CCCPC) adopted "The Decision of the CCCPC on Several Major Issues Concerning Comprehensively Deepening Reform" which clarified the role of public finance: "*Public finance is the foundation and an important pillar of state governance. Good fiscal and taxation systems are the institutional guarantee for optimizing resource allocation, maintaining market unity, promoting social equity, and realizing enduring peace and stability*".

I have always been interested in the relationship between government and finance. During my PhD study in the US, I took a full year course on public finance. In the first semester, we studied fiscal revenue, which includes theories related to government tax revenue. In the second semester, we studied fiscal expenditure, that is the design and effect of government expenditure programs. In my PhD class, the split of American and non-American students was roughly 50/50, however I was the only non-American to take the public finance class. The reason being that the class teaches the many intricacies of the US political system and it is both difficult for non-Americans to understand and also of little relevance to their later work. This course helped me to develop a deeper understanding of the US, but when I returned to work at Fudan University in Shanghai to teach a course on Public Finance, I found it difficult to prepare the course, since the things I learned in the US had little relevance in a Chinese context. Textbooks that I had studied were of little use and I ended up preparing my own lecture notes. The US and Chinese governments play different roles in the economy and have different priorities, and the public finance systems reflect these differences. So, it's not possible to simply use American theories to analyze China. What's more, China has been continuously reforming for decades, and since government affairs have also undergone significant change, the fiscal and taxation system is naturally also changing fast. Moreover, reforming one part of the system has an impact on the system as a whole, adding extra complexity. I have spent years teaching and studying the system, and now I am finally able to put some pieces together.

The first chapter of this book introduced the division of powers within Chinese government and any kind of authority naturally also needs financial support, otherwise they cannot get things done. Therefore, from the perspective of spending money, the principle of aligning "administrative power with financial power" is not controversial. However, from the perspective of collecting money, the question of whether Chinese local governments should also have the power to collect money commensurate

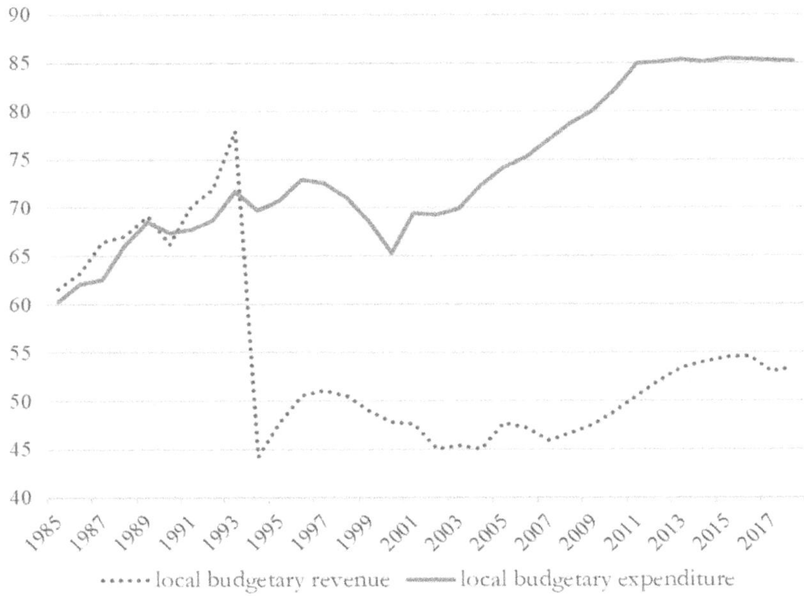

Fig. 2.1 Percentage of local budget in the national budget (*Source* WIND)

with their administrative power is a highly controversial one. If we do not consider these controversies and simply consider facts, the reality is that there is a large mismatch between the level of expenditure needed and the amount of revenue available to China's local governments. As shown in Fig. 2.1, since the implementation of a tax sharing system in 1994, local government expenditure has accounted for nearly 85% of China's total government spending, but revenue collected directly by local governments only accounts for 50%–55% of the total government revenue. The gap between expenditure and revenue is covered by fiscal transfers from the central government.

The reform of the tax sharing system in 1994 had a profound impact on government behavior and also on China's economic development. The first section of this chapter goes into more detail on this reform and seeks to deepen our understanding of the relationship between central and local governments. The second section seeks to analyze the impact of the reform on local economic development and also introduces the concept of "land finance" that was developed by China's local governments as a response to financial pressure. This section is also the basis for understanding urbanization and local government debt in China. The third section discusses the financial pressure on local governments and regional imbalances brought about as a consequence of the tax sharing reform, and it also introduces later reforms in the area.

Section 1: Tax Sharing Reforms

Strong finances are necessarily the foundation of a strong nation. Since the founding of the People's Republic of China in 1949, the fiscal system has gone through many arduous and complicated reforms. This section is not intended to document the entire reform process and starts only from 1985. In the period from 1985 and 1993, the income and expenditure of local governments was relatively in sync (Fig. 2.1). This period of matching administrative power with financial power had a great impact on economic development, but also caused many problems, thereby acting as the impetus for the 1994 tax sharing reform.

Fiscal Contracting and Its Consequences (1985–1993)[1]

If we were to use one word to sum up the character of China's economy in the 1980s, it would be "contracting". Land in the rural areas was contracted out to farmers, public enterprises were contracted out to managers, and fiscal revenues were contracted out to local governments. At the start of the reform and opening up period in the 1980s, many people still couldn't accept the idea of private ownership or private property. After all, the planned economy and the public ownership of properties had been in place for decades, so no immediate change could be made to the fundamental ownership structure of properties. The contracting system, however, could be used to incentivize work efforts and improve economic efficiency, while leaving the nominal ownership intact. The fiscal contracting arrangements started in 1980, known by its nickname "eating from different stoves" (分灶吃饭). The period from 1980 to 1984 was a period of experimenting, and after 1985 the

[1] This section relies heavily on the book of Zhou Feizhou (周飞舟 2012), which is an excellent reading on the process and logic of fiscal reform after the founding of the People's Republic of China.

system was fully implemented. Essentially, this is a revenue sharing system negotiated between the central and provincial governments.

The exact sharing arrangements vary across provinces. One popular scheme was the "incremental increase contract". Take Beijing's government revenue in 1988 as an example, the revenue of the previous year, 1987 was used as a base and a fixed annual growth rate was set, in this case 4%. If the fiscal revenue from Beijing grew more than 4% in 1988, then the portion above the 4% level belonged to the Beijing government and the portion of revenue below this level was split 50/50 with the central government. So, if Beijing's revenue in 1987 was 10 billion yuan and by 1988 it had increased 10% to 11 billion, then the extra 600 million would wholly belong to the Beijing government and the remaining 10.4 billion would be split equally between the central government and Beijing.

In Guangdong province, the scheme was simpler. In 1988, Guangdong agreed to remit 1.4 billion yuan to the central government and agreed to increase the amount by 9% each year. Any remaining revenue should be kept by the Guangdong provincial government. In 1988, Guangdong's revenue was 10.8 billion yuan, so the 1.4 billion remitted to the central government only accounted for 13%. Moreover, Guangdong's revenue increased much faster than 9% per year (e.g., in 1989, revenue increased by 29%), so the share paid to the central government was actually decreasing year over year. Of course, Guangdong was happy about this scheme and when the fundamental tax sharing reform was later proposed in 1993, Guangdong was in strong opposition. In contrast, Shanghai's burden was much heavier. Shanghai must remit a fixed amount of revenue, 10.5 billion yuan, to the central government each year, no matter what. In 1988, Shanghai's budgetary revenue totaled 16.2 billion yuan, meaning 65% had to be paid to the central government. As a result, Shanghai's financial pressure was much greater than Guangdong.

Under this contracting system, whatever left after the remittance to the central government belonged to local governments, so they had a strong incentive to promote economic growth as a means to increase their own revenue.[2] One way to do so was to set up a township or village enterprise (TVE). These enterprises could contribute to local government revenue in two ways: the first is value added tax (VAT), which had to be paid regardless of whether the enterprise was profitable or not. The

[2] Jin et al. (2005) discuss this incentive effect.

amount of VAT depends on the total sales, so larger enterprises pay more. After the mid-1980s, the number and scale of TVEs grew quickly, and local government tax revenue increased accordingly. By 1995, the peak of the TVEs, the number of their employees stood at 60 million. The second potential government revenue contributed by TVEs came from their after-tax profits, which were typically handed over to the local village collectives and township governments as non-tax revenue. At that time, TVEs enjoyed preferential tax rates and the income tax paid on profits was very low. In 1980, the profit tax was only 6% and by 1986 it had risen to 20%. Therefore, the after-tax (net) profit of TVEs was substantial, meaning that substantial amounts were available to turn over to local governments.[3]

The 1980s was the start of the reform and opening up period. Many fundamental changes had still not been made to the economic system, and this method of contracting was useful in terms of motivating people, pushing them to move outside of the rigid structure of the planned economy and letting them experience some income growth for the first time. However, it was precisely because of the experimental nature of the reform that many contracting arrangements were not able to sustain. The fiscal contracting system led to a continual reduction in two key proportions: firstly, the percentage of total revenue paid to the central government was steadily decreasing, and secondly, total tax revenue as a percentage of GDP was also decreasing (Fig. 2.2). Not only was the central government becoming continuously poorer, but the overall government finances were also getting poorer.

The reduction in the share of revenue going to central government is easy to understand. Local economies grew rapidly in the 1980s and prices also rose rapidly, so local government tax revenue grew much faster than the fixed amount initially agreed with the central government, as a result the share of revenue going to the central government continuously declined. However, the reasons for the decrease of total tax revenue as a percentage of GDP are more complicated. On the one hand this is due to the incentives built into the system. The remittance paid by the local government needs to be renegotiated every few years, if local tax revenue grows too rapidly, then the local government may be at a disadvantage in the next round of negotiations: they may have to accept both

[3] Data on taxation and employees of TVEs come from Kung and Lin (2007). Data on township business profit tax rates come from Naughton (2018).

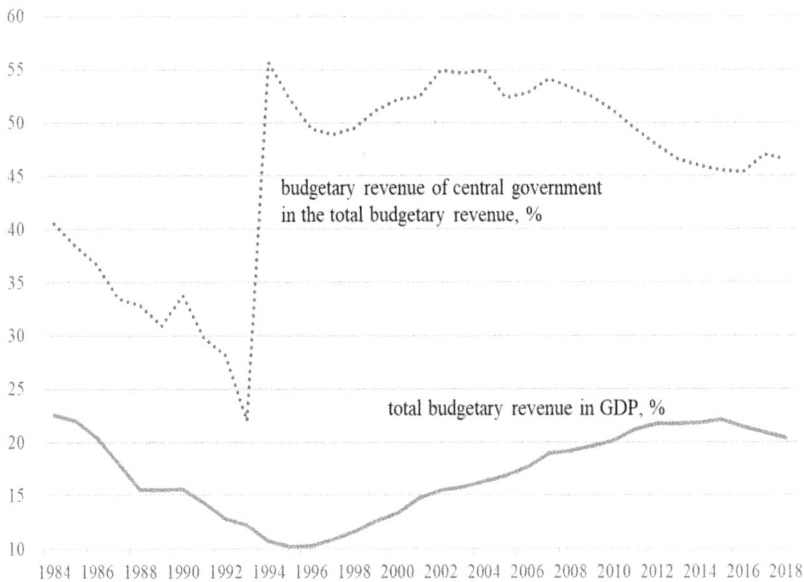

Fig. 2.2 Declining percentages of budgetary revenues (*Source* WIND)

a higher base and a higher percentage of remittance. In order to avoid this "rachet effect", the local government may deliberately avoid letting revenue grow too fast. On the other hand, the decline is also related to the growth of extra-budgetary or non-tax revenue during the period. While budgetary revenue needs to be shared with the central government, extra-budgetary revenue can be wholly retained by the local government. Local governments could cut tax for enterprises first, then they could harvest the money through various non-tax means, such as administrative fees, fundraising, sponsorship or appropriation. This extra-budgetary revenue doesn't need to be shared with the central government and also doesn't contribute to an increase in the baseline tax revenue. As a result, local governments often cut taxes arbitrarily for businesses and weakly enforce tax collection. As a result, budgetary revenue hardly grew while extra-budgetary revenue grew rapidly. From 1982 to 1992, the annual growth rate of extra-budgetary revenue was 30%, far exceeding the 19% annual growth rate in budgetary revenue. By 1992, local government extra-budgetary revenue amounted to 86% of budgetary revenue, essentially becoming a second system of public finance.[4]

The decline of these two proportions seriously weakened the governments' overall financial situation and their capacity to implement necessary reforms. To start with, economic reform damaged the interests of many people and the central government needed resources to compensate them. Many people had lost their jobs as a result of reforms to the state-owned enterprises, likewise army veterans needed to be compensated if the military was to be reformed and the army size was to be cut. Moreover, in a country as huge and complex as China, the development of different regions (rural vs. urban, the coastal east and the inland west, etc.) needed to be treated differently. In order to create a stable internal environment, the disparity of public services between different regions needed to be reduced, which also required significant investment from the central government. Otherwise, even to provide some basic public service all over the country, such as a compulsory education, would be difficult. If the central government is poor or even has to borrow money from local governments, the capacity of rebalancing and control on the national level would be insufficient. The finance minister of the time, Liu Zhongli, described the poor financial conditions of the central government[5]:

> Chairman Mao once said, "if you don't have rice, even the chickens won't come", if the central government's overall finances are in such a bad shape, it would be detrimental politically. The fiscal situation must be reformed...
>
> ...in the decision of the fiscal reforms at the time, there was an important sentence, "to secure the long-term stability of the country". Many theoretical discussions at the time advocated that financial power formed the basis for the government's administrative capacity. Its ability to get things done depended on the financial resources at its disposal. Without

[4] Wang (王绍光 1997) discusses the prisoner's dilemma game that exists between central and local governments: local governments were reluctant to try to collect taxes in anticipation of the rachet effect in the renegotiation, however this is purely theoretical and is difficult to verify conclusively. The logic of converting tax revenue into nom tax revenue is supported by data, see the paper by Li et al. (李学文, 卢新海, 张蔚文 2012).

[5] The citation is from the "Memoirs of Fiscal Reform" edited by Liu Kegu and Jia Kang (刘克崮和贾康 2008).

money, compulsory education or disaster relief or other promises are nothing but empty words. Therefore, this sentence of "to secure the long-term stability of the country" has a very deep connotation.

Tax Sharing Reform and the Resistance of Local Governments

The 1994 tax sharing reform split taxes into 3 categories: central government taxes (such as customs duties), local government taxes (such as business taxes) and shared taxes (such as value added tax). At the same time, separate central and local government tax agencies were created, and they were separated from the Ministry of Finance or local finance departments. Below the provincial level, the tax agency operated on a vertical management system with the provincial tax bureau being responsible for appointment of personnel and payment of wages. The aim of this structure was to reduce the interference of local governments on taxation and to protect central government tax revenue. But there were disadvantages: the number of tax workers almost doubled, increasing the administrative cost of tax management, at the same time, companies now needed to deal with both the national tax bureau and local tax bureau, the cost of compliance also increased significantly. In 2018, after 24 years, the dual tax bureaus were reformed again and gradually consolidated into one bureau.

The most important tax included in the tax sharing reform was value added tax (VAT), which accounted for a quarter of total tax revenue. Before the tax reform, VAT revenue was attributed only to local governments and formed the largest share of local tax income. After the reform, it had to be shared with the central government. According to the new law, the central government received 75% of VAT income and the local government kept 25%. As an example, if in 1993 the total VAT income for a province was 10 billion, and in 1994 it increased to 11 billion, then according to the new tax system, the provincial government kept only 25% and its income dropped from 10bn to 2.75bn. In order to prevent such a sharp decline in local tax revenue, the central government introduced a "tax refund" mechanism. This mechanism ensured that local tax revenue didn't decrease after the reform, with tax sharing applying only to the incremental portion of revenue. Therefore, in our example, the local government would keep 10.25 billion in 1994, while the central government would receive only 750 mn. As a result, the proportion of

VAT in local revenue didn't experience a sudden drop, rather it decreased gradually each year (Fig. 2.3).

The reform of the tax sharing system faced a great deal of resistance from local governments. For example, Guangdong province had a favorable arrangement under the fiscal contracting system and expressed strong resistance to the new reform. Getting the agreement of Guangdong would be absolutely necessary to push forward the tax sharing reform. The memoirs of the finance minister of the time, Liu Zhongli, and the later finance minister, Xiang Huaicheng, paint vivid portrait of the situation at the time:

> From Xiang Huaicheng, "*Implementing the tax sharing reforms is much more difficult than just making a plan because there are many conflicting interests. At the time, revenue accruing to the central government accounted for less than 30% of total government revenue. After the reform, this increased to 55%. A huge difference! To implement the reform, we needed the support of senior leadership. Premier Zhu Rongji personally led the effort.*

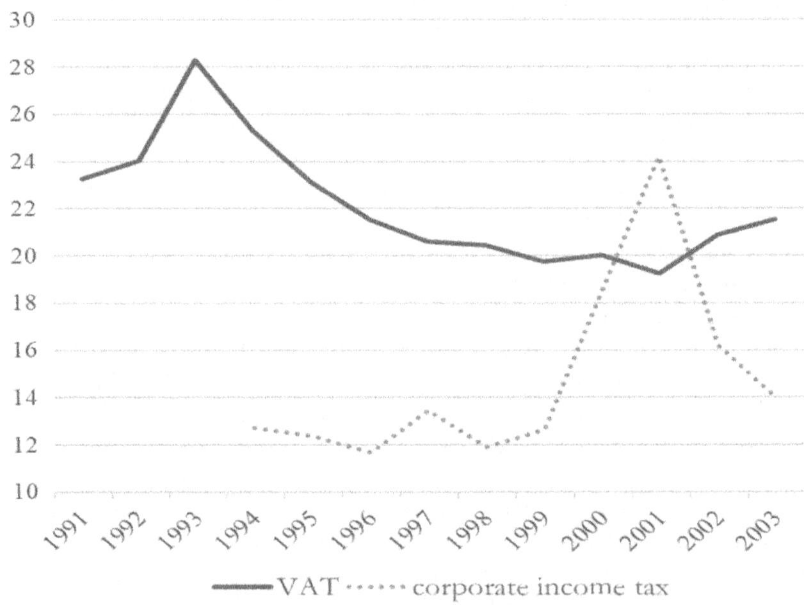

Fig. 2.3 Percentages of different taxes in local tax revenue (*Source* WIND)

He spent more than two months traveling to over 12 provinces across the country to make face to face deals with provincial leaders... We may ask, why did it take so much effort? Why should such a senior member of government, a member of the Standing Committee of the Central Committee and Executive Vice Premier of the State Council spend so much time to lead a team and talk to each province one by one? Because only when Premier Zhu makes the trip can we be assured to speak with the provincial Party Secretary and local governors, and to exchange frank views. Sometimes the provincial leaders can't make up their mind, they have to consult with some elder and retired secretaries and governors whose opinions must also be respected. If we go alone without the Premier, we might not even get to meet with the key decision makers".

From Liu Zhongli, "*The atmosphere when talking to the local governments was very tense. The Ministry of Finance alone was not powerful enough, and the Politburo must come as well. In the negotiations with Guangdong Province, Xie Fei (the party secretary of Guangdong) did not speak, and every point his colleagues had just finished making, Premier Zhu Rongji immediately rebutted them. Suddenly, a member of the Provincial Party Committee of Guangdong (Fu Rui) spoke up: "Premier Zhu, if you speak like that, then there's no way we can negotiate, you are the Premier and we have no way to answer back to you". The Premier replied, "That's right, and what about Xie Fei, he is a member of the Politburo too, as soon as he speaks, Liu Zhongli also has no way to answer back. It must be me who takes the lead". The situation was tense and vivid, but it must be said, Xie Fei understood the overall situation and Guangdong eventually endorsed the reform. But they put forward two requirements, firstly to use 1993 as the base year for future calculations and, secondly, having a transition period for the reform".*[6]

I often retell this story in my university classes, but many students are unable to understand why the negotiation was so torturous, if the central government decides something, shouldn't the local government just follow? It's not difficult to understand that Generation-Z would think like this. Decades after the tax sharing reform, the central government now is indeed much stronger than in the 1980s and 1990s. Likewise, the public usually could only observe the decisions and consequences, but not the process of decision-making. Particularly, unsophisticated young people tend to confuse decisions that must be obeyed, with the decision-making process that is full of negotiations and compromises. Even today,

[6] The quote comes from Liu Kegu and Jia Kang (刘克崮和贾康 2008).

new policies introduced by the central government may require rounds and rounds of consultation and negotiations, and may experience many revisions before announcement. Behind any successful policy always lies rounds and rounds of negotiation and compromise. A simple model of "order and obey" does not work well in the world of policy making. Therefore, understanding the interests of different parties and the process for resolving them is the foundation for understanding policy.

During the negotiations, one of the requirements of Guangdong was to set the base year for the tax reform as 1993. This may seem like a small request, however the VAT revenue in the base year is a crucial factor in how much tax rebate the local government can receive from the central government in future years. Given negotiations between Guangdong and the central government took place in September 1993, the Ministry of Finance naturally wanted to set the base year as 1992. The data were already in place and there was no turning back time to fake the data. However, if the base year were to be set as 1993, then there would still be 3 months until the end of the year. In that case, the local government may find a way to inflate the tax revenue in 1993, for example by adding new taxes or by collecting in advance tax owed in future years, thereby inflating the base level and greatly increasing the tax rebate in future years. Initially the Ministry of Finance did not agree with Guangdong's request, however in order to get the policy implemented, they finally compromised and agreed to set the base year as 1993 for all provinces. This decision immediately sparked a tax collection frenzy in the final quarter of 1993. According to the memoirs of Xiang Huaicheng and Liu Kegu:

> Xiang Huaicheng: "*In fact, this kind of situation started to occur after September. In that year, taxes that had been owed for many years were all successfully collected. Some local government and party leaders even asked banks to make special loans so firms can pay them to the government as tax. This resulted in a surge in tax revenue during the last 4 months of 1993*".
>
> Liu Kegu: "*...there was a year over year increase (in local government tax collection) of 60% in September, 90% in October, 110% in November, and finally 150% in December. This led to an increase by 50% - 60% in the total local tax revenue for the whole year*".[7,8]

[7] Liu might remember this number wrong. Local tax revenue in 1993 actually increased by 38% from 1992.

[8] The quote once again comes from Liu Kegu and Jia Kang (刘克崮和贾康 2008).

As shown in Fig. 2.3, there was an abnormal spike in the percentage of VAT in local tax revenue in 1993. This led to trouble in 1994, with the fiscal rebate due from the central government delayed due to the sharp increase in the amount. This issue could only be resolved by another round of compromise and negotiation. However, despite this experience and lesson, a similar situation reoccurred in 2001 when a reform relating to the sharing of income tax was introduced (Fig. 2.3).

Corporate income tax is the second largest source of tax revenue in China, accounting for 23% of total tax revenue in 2018. Prior to the reform in 2002, corporate income tax was paid according to the administrative relationship of each company. Central state-owned enterprises (SOEs) paid taxes to the central government, and local companies and local SOEs paid taxes to the local government. Given there are more local companies than central companies, 60% of corporate income tax was allocated to local governments. This arrangement incentivized local governments to create large local enterprises that could produce a lot of profits and income tax. Since tobacco and liquor are highly regulated and super profitable, local governments would set up tobacco or liquor companies and block outside companies from the local market, so people could only consume the local brands. This local protectionism was not conducive to creating a unified national market and also made it difficult to close economic disparities between regions.

In the 2002 income tax reform, all corporate income tax would be split 60/40 between central and local government. Only certain special central SOEs would be exempt, paying all tax to the central government. In order to avoid a sudden drop in local government tax revenue, a tax rebate mechanism similar to the earlier VAT tax reform was put in place with the corporate income tax level in 2001 being used as the base for calculations. As a result, local governments pushed to collect incremental tax in the last two months of 2001 in order to inflate the base revenue, and the Ministry of Finance and State Council had to intervene and announced that "members of government at all levels must adhere strictly to the rule of law when collecting taxes. Tax fraud is prohibited. In January 2002, the State Council will organize a special investigation, and punish those falsifying or artificially inflating tax income. For those governments that are found to have acted inappropriately, the level of tax rebate from the central government in the next year will be reduced, and the people who are involved and local leaders will be held accountable."[9] However despite these actions, we can see in Fig. 2.3 that the level of corporate income tax in 2001 was still abnormally high.[10]

The tax sharing reform was one of the most important reforms made by the Chinese government in the 1990s and also one of the most successful. The reform managed to successfully reverse the trend of the two declining proportions (Fig. 2.2). The central governments' share of tax revenue jumped from 22% to 55% as a result and has been stable at this level for a long time. Moreover, the tax income as a percentage of GDP increased from 11% to more than 20%. The reform greatly enhanced the central government's ability to enact macroeconomic policies, which proved valuable during the 1997 Asian Financial Crisis, the 2008 Global Financial Crisis, and the 2008 Sichuan earthquake. It has also provided the financial resources necessary to execute a series of major reforms, including the SOE reform, national defense modernization, and the implementation of key infrastructure and construction projects. The tax sharing reform also led to a fundamental change in the economic development model of local governments.

9 "The General Office of the State Council forwarded an urgent notice from the Ministry of Finance reporting on the abnormal growth of local corporate income tax in November and the first half of December 2001".

10 As shown in Figure 2.3, corporate income tax began to rise sharply in 2000, which may be due to statistical changes. Before 2000, corporate income tax statistics included only state-owned enterprises and collectively-owned enterprises, after 2000, all enterprises were included. One way to eliminate the impact of this statistical adjustment over time is to compare the original budget with the realized final amount within the same year. Normally, there should be little difference between the two numbers. According to the 2002 China Fiscal Yearbook, 104.9 billion yuan was budgeted to be collected from corporate income tax, but the realized final amount collected was actually 168.6 billion, an increase of 61%. This abnormal surge is not found in other taxes. For example, business tax, which was not involved in the reform at that time, budgeted to collect 183 billion, with an actual amount collected of 184.9 billion; while value added tax, which had already been reformed, budgeted to collect 122.9 billion and with a final amount collected of 134.2 billion. Another example is the central enterprise income tax, which underwent the reforms of income tax but without any incentive for local governments to inflate the base amount collected. The budgeted amount was 93.7 billion, and the final amounted collected was 94.5 billion.

Section 2: Land Finance

The tax sharing reforms did not change the responsibility of local governments to drive economic development, but did reduce the financial resources at their disposal. Central government transfers and tax rebates can help somewhat to fill the budget deficit, however many essential activities for developing the economy, such as attracting investment or developing local land, require significant additional investment. One option for local governments is to try to increase the amount of tax revenue, even if a portion needs to be shared with the central government, the bigger the cake, the more that will be available for everyone to eat. The other option is to increase non-tax revenue and the most important way of doing this relates to land and real estate.

Attracting Investment and Taxation

If the tax rate cannot be increased, the only way to increase tax revenue is to either expand the tax base or to enforce tax collection more efficiently. After the tax sharing reform, the proportion of tax revenue to total GDP gradually increased (Fig. 2.2). One reason is an improvement in the enforcement of tax collection, but the main reason is the expansion of the tax base.[11]

Before the reform, corporate tax was charged according to the affiliation of the company (either with the central or local government), but after the reform they were paid based on the location of the company. This change incentivized local governments to attract more companies to their region. Local governments have a strong preference for asset-heavy manufacturing industries. These industries involve a lot of investment, so have a strong impact on local GDP figures. Moreover, VAT is collected from producers instead of consumers, and it is based on total sales instead of profits. In other words, lager producers pay more VAT. Finally, these industries could also provide lots of jobs for attract low-skilled workers who are leaving the agricultural sector. More industries and workers could help to stimulate the development of service industries, which once again increases the tax base.

[11] Fang Hongsheng and Zhang Jun (方红生和张军 2013) summarize research on the enforcement of tax collection after the tax sharing reform.

Because the vast majority of taxes are collected from enterprises, local governments put a higher emphasis on providing services to enterprises as opposed to people. Likewise, they put a higher importance on production as opposed to household consumption. Taking VAT as an example, even though VAT is eventually paid by consumers in the final product price, this tax is typically collected on producers during the production process, this means governments care more about the location of the producer rather than the location of the consumer. This tax system that relies heavily on production has stimulated large-scale investment in manufacturing and promoted the development of the manufacturing industry in China. Put together with factors such as the outsourcing of western supply chains and an abundant supply of willing labor, China has become the world's largest manufacturer in a space of only 20–30 years. However, this rapid industrialization also comes with a price. For example, the competition for tax revenue and large investment projects between local governments placed a lower priority on the environment and also led to excess production capacity. From the years 2007 to 2014, over half of industrial tax revenue came from industries with excess production capacity. Those local governments with financial stress tended to attract more polluted industries.[12]

Not only is 90% of tax revenue in China collected from enterprises, but the source of most non-tax revenue is also collected from enterprises. These include land transfer fees, and profits and dividends from state-owned enterprises. The proportion of social security contributions made by enterprises is also greater than that made by individuals. So, in the initial years after the tax reform, local governments' investment in areas such as infrastructure and corporate tax subsidies, which mainly benefits enterprises, were far larger than the investment in areas such as medical care, education and environmental protection, which mainly benefits people.[13] In 2003, the central government launched the "*Scientific Outlook on Development*" policy which required "*bringing*

[12] The evidence that financial pressure on local governments leads to worsening industrial pollution and pushes up excess capacity comes from the research by Xi et.al (席鹏辉, 梁若冰, 谢贞发 2017a; 席鹏辉等人 2017b).

[13] After the tax sharing reform, there is a lot of evidence that local government's public spending focused more on production rather than people's livelihood. For example, Fu and Zhang's research on provincial expenditure (傅勇和张晏 2007), Ma et al.'s research on prefecture-level city expenditure (马光荣, 吕冰洋, 张凯强 2019), and Yin and Zhu's research on county-level spending (尹恒和朱虹 2011).

together economic and social development and ensuring a harmonious balance between man and nature". This also required more expenditure on the quality of people's lives. Due to the economies of scale and information complexity discussed in Chapter 1, these kinds of expenditures are typically borne by local governments, so from 2002 onwards, the proportion of local government expenditure in total expenditure has grown rapidly from 70% to 85% (Fig. 2.1).

In sum, after the tax sharing reform, the resources available for local governments to carry out economic development were squeezed in many ways. To start with, budgetary expenditure started to shift focus from infrastructure and manufacturing to public services and public welfare. In the mid-1990s, so-called economic construction expenses accounted for 40% of fiscal expenditures and "science, culture and education" (including spending on science, education, culture, health and social security) expenses accounted for only 26%. By 2018, these "science, culture and education" expenses accounted for 40%, while "economic construction" expenses accounted for a much smaller share.[14] Next, before the reforms, enterprises not only paid tax but also paid many other fees to local governments (these might include administrative fees, sponsorship and fundraising), and this non-tax revenue was greatly reduced after the reforms. In the later part of the 1990s, township and village enterprises were restructured and the income available to be turned over to local government was also vastly reduced. Finally, after the income tax reform of 2001, the central government took 60% of any incremental income tax revenue, intensifying the pressure on local government finances. Local governments needed to find another way to raise revenue and "land finance" begun to play an increasingly important role in China's public finances.

Land Finance 101

China operates under a public land ownership system. Urban land is owned by the state and rural land is owned by collectives. To make rural land available for urban development, the land must be acquired by the state and converted into state-owned land, only then can it be used for

[14] In 2007, China adjusted the classification of government revenue and expenditure, so there is no way to directly compare the proportion of government spending used for economic construction before and after 2007, but it has undoubtedly declined.

industrial, commercial or residential development (in 2019, this rule was changed by the newly revised "Land Administration Law of the People's Republic of China", and Chapter 3 will explain in more detail). Given the fact that state-owned land can be used for urban development, it tends to have a much higher value than rural land that is used for agriculture. Why does China operate such a system that separates urban and rural land? Actually, the system is the result of an accumulation of changes that have been made since the "Constitution of 1982" was passed, each change being made to solve a specific issue, rather than being part of a systematic design. Even though every change made during the process can be justified in terms of the specific problem it solved at the time, the result has been to create a system with huge disparities between rural and urban areas, as well soaring urban house prices and other serious problems. In 2020, the Central Committee of the CCP and the State Council issued the "*Opinions on Building a More Complete System and Mechanism for Market Based Allocation of Factors*", one of the main areas mentioned in the text was to "*promote a more market based allocation of land as a factor of production*" and the first proposal for reform was aimed at decreasing the divide between rural and urban land by "*establishing a unified market of rural and urban land for construction*". The policy direction demonstrates that policy makers are well aware of the problems embedded in the current system, and the relevant reforms will be discussed in more detail in Chapter 3.

After the tax sharing reforms of 1994, local governments were left with control over the transfer of land ownership and related profits. However, at the time, the portion of local government income from this source was very small. Firstly, although village and township enterprises were still common at the time, they mostly occupied rural land owned by the rural collective, so they did not have to pay to the government for using urban land. Secondly, even though the local government could sell the use rights of urban land for profits, most of the land sales were priced very favorably in order to attract investment (especially foreign investment). So the income earned from land sales was limited.

However, in 1998, two significant changes occurred, and the true value of urban land began to emerge. The first change is that government and state-owned enterprises (SOEs) stopped building housing for their workers, and instead paid money to the workers in the form of a housing subsidy. The era of commercial housing and real estate development therefore started in earnest. From 1997 to 2002, the average annual growth rate of newly constructed residential areas reached 26%, and the absolute number increased 4x in 5 years. The second change is that the implementation of the revised "Land Administration Law of the People's Republic of China" which stipulated that rural land could only be used for non-agricultural construction purposes if it is first transferred to state-owned land, thereby giving city governments a monopoly over urban land construction.[15]

By 1999 and 2000, the income generated from land sales was still not high (Fig. 2.4), because the system of auctioning land had still not been fully implemented. Land deals were still opaque and relied heavily on developers taking advantage of the system. For example, some developers took advantage of the SOE reform to obtain land from SOEs, later securing a development permit from the local urban planning department, often paying only a small fee for the land transfer, then they could build houses and sell them at market price. This process allowed those involved to make a great deal of money, and inevitably involved a lot of corruption.

By 2001, with corruption in the real estate development more and more evident, the State Council proposed to "Promote Bidding and Auctions" as a means to deal with land sales. In 2002, the Ministry of Land and Resources clarified that the four types of business land use (commercial, tourism, entertainment and real estate) must adopt the auction system. As a result, local governments begun to expropriate land from farmers, transfer it to state-owned urban land and sell the use rights. Income from land finance therefore started to expand rapidly. By 2003, income from land sales already equaled to 55% of local government's budgetary revenue. And after the global financial crisis of 2008, China launched a large fiscal stimulus and favorable credit policies, driving income from land sales to 68% of local government budgetary revenue in 2010, a new high. Although in recent years, this share has begun to

[15] Although the law stipulates that collectively-owned land can also be used for the construction of township and village enterprises, as these enterprises started to reform one after another in the 1990s, there were fewer and fewer real township and village enterprises in existence, so this provision is actually of little significance. Furthermore, since 1997, the total amount of land use in a province must be permitted by the central government. Naturally, a provincial government wants to allocate the scarce land quota to the provincial capital or to the urban areas of other cities, instead of using them in counties, where most rural areas and collectively-owned lands are located. For a more detailed introduction in this regard, please refer to Chapter 8 of the book by Liu Shouying (刘守英 2018). The numbers used in this paragraph are also from that book.

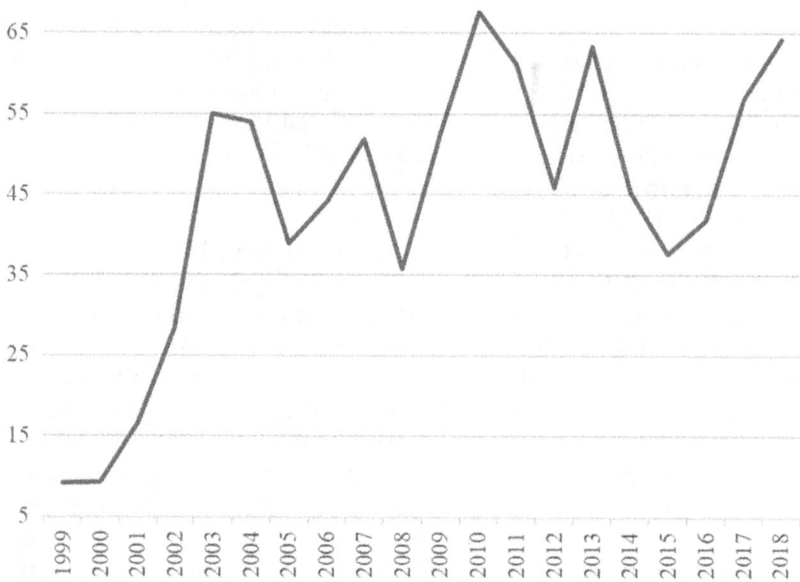

Fig. 2.4 Transfer fee of state-owned land, as a percentage of local budgetary revenue (*Source* China Land and Resources Statistical Yearbooks)

decline, the absolute value of the revenue from land sales is still increasing, reaching 6.29 trillion yuan in 2018, 2.3x higher than in 2010.

So called "land finance" doesn't only consist of revenue made by converting rural land to urban land and selling it, there is also a stream of tax revenue related to land use and development. The tax base for most of these taxes is the value of land instead of the size of land, so tax revenue increases as land prices increase. These taxes can be divided into 2 categories, the first is directly related to land, including land VAT, urban land use tax, arable land occupation tax and deed tax. All the revenue earned from these taxes belongs to local governments. In 2018, income from these four types of tax revenue totaled 1.51 trillion yuan, accounting for 15% of local governments' budgetary revenue, a significant amount. The second category of tax is related to real estate development, mainly VAT and corporate income tax levied on real estate developers. For these taxes, local government only gets to retain a portion of the income (50% for value added tax and 40% for corporate income tax) and the two combined accounted for 9% of local budgetary revenue in 2018.[16] These two categories of taxes, added together with the revenue from land sales, were equivalent to 89% of local government's budgetary revenue in 2018. So outside of the normal tax revenues, this land finance is really large enough to be called "the second public finance".

Although land transfers and sales can bring in significant income, local governments also have costs to bear in the process. These might include the cost of acquiring land, developing land and also investing in the infrastructure necessary to attract investment, including the 7 openings and 1 leveling discussed in Chapter 1. In recent years, the expenditure related to land transfers is generally equal to the income generated, and in some cases may even exceed it. In 2018, income from the transfer of state-owned land use rights equaled 6.29 trillion yuan, but the expenditure was equal to 6.82 trillion, so the government loses money in the process. Of course, the real aim of local government is not to make money by selling land, rather it is to stimulate economic activity through industrial and commercial activities taking place on and around the newly developed land.

If we examine the data over time, we can see that large-scale fiscal revenue related to land finance started to develop from the early 2000s. After the income tax reform in 2001, the central government further centralized power and took away 60% of corporate income tax from local governments. Since that time local governments' strategy of driving economic growth has changed from simply relying on industrialization, to relying on a combination of industrialization and urbanization. On the one hand, local governments continue to supply low-cost industrial land to attract investment. On the other hand, they monopolize and restrict the supply of land available for commercial and residential investment, thereby ensuring that land prices continually rise. In recent years, land used for industrial purposes accounts for around 50% of the urban land sold, however the price is usually extremely low, in 2000 the average price was 444 yuan per square meter, by 2018 it had risen to 820 yuan,

[16] Before the reform that replaced business tax with value added tax in 2016, real estate development and construction enterprises mainly paid business taxes, which is a 100% local tax and did not need to be shared with the central government, so the proportion of local government tax revenue was even higher. In 2013, for example, the business tax and the income tax attributable to the local government paid by real estate development and construction companies accounted for 16% of local government tax revenue. The figures in this paragraph are all from the China Taxation Yearbooks.

an increase of only 85%. In comparison, the price of commercial land has increased 460% and the price of residential land has increased 740% during the same period (Fig. 2.5).

So, although commercial and residential land accounts for only 50% of the sold urban land, they account for almost all the income. Therefore "land finance" can more simply be understood as "real estate finance". On the one hand, all regions subsidize industrial land in order to attract outside investment, which has helped to promote rapid development of the manufacturing industry. On the other hand, the process of industrialization and urbanization has led to rapid inflows of migrants into newly developed areas, increasing the local population, but since the supply of residential land is limited, house prices naturally skyrocket, driving up prices of land sold for residential and commercial land use. The problems inherent in this process and the attempts at reform will be discussed further in Chapter 3 of the book.

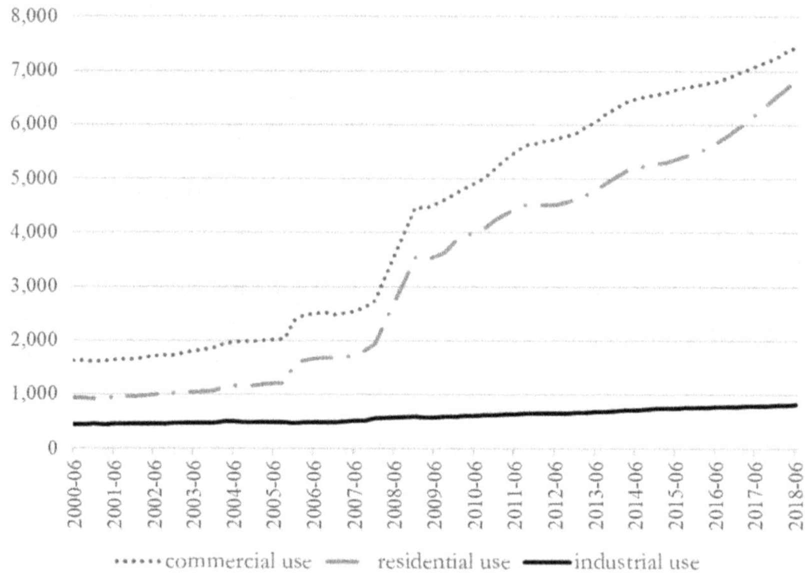

Fig. 2.5 Quarterly average price of land in 100 main cities, yuan/square meter (*Source* WIND)

Taxation, Ground Rent and Local Government Competition

Let's take a moment to step back and examine the bigger picture about what exactly local governments are doing. Economic development in its purest form is simply about using existing resources more efficiently and making the best use of the talent and resources at ones' disposal. China is a country with relatively poor natural resources. In the first stage of development, the resources that can be used are just labor and land. Many major reforms over the recent decades have involved reforming and improving the way these two resources are used. Land is more easily capitalized than labor, and future revenues derived from using land can capitalized into a high land price today, which could be used by the landowners, i.e. local governments. So, although "land finance" has many drawbacks, it has still been a major source of funds driving China's industrialization and urbanization over the recent decades.

As we have already seen, local governments will use all resources at their disposal to attract investment and drive urbanization. Tax revenue, as well as land finance, needs to be balanced to ensure that the government maximizes the overall amount of funds at its disposal. Local governments proactively drive down the price of industrial land, because attracting investment in industry plays a crucial role in developing the economy, nurturing the development of local industry clusters, bringing in VAT and other taxes, and also creating jobs. In addition, industrial productivity can continuously be increased. It could modernize the local economy, promote the development of service sectors and drive up the prices of commercial and residential land. In industrial production, the upstream and downstream chain of is very long and the effects of agglomeration and economies of scale are remarkable. If an industry cluster (the ceramics industry in Foshan in Guangdong province as an example) is successfully nurtured, it provides a competitive advantage to the region and is a stable source of tax revenue. As a result, the competition for investment between different local governments is fierce. Although local governments monopolize the supply of industrial land, their monopoly power is very limited since enterprises could choose their location. So local government has little incentive and capacity to raise the price of industrial land. However, commercial and residential land is different. It only supplies local residents to whom the moving cost could be high, so the monopoly power of local government over the sales of commercial and residential land is stronger, making it much easier to raise prices.

Chinese economist Steven Cheung once made a very apt metaphor. Local governments are like shopping malls and attracting outside investment is similar to attracting shops to the mall. Shops only need to pay a low upfront fee (similar to the land transfer fee paid to the local government when acquiring industrial land), but the operating revenue must be shared with the mall as ground rent, no matter whether the shop is profitable or not (similar to VAT). Shopping malls aim to maximize overall income, so it is necessary to balance the upfront fee and rent, as well as to balance the influence of different shops. Some shops are more famous and attract more customers to the mall, so they should be given a big upfront discount or even subsidies in order to incentivize them to set up shop in the mall.[17] Similarly, local governments could charge a very low land price or even offer subsidies in order to attract big companies.

The model of "contracting" responsibility for economic development to local governments, who use taxation and land finance as a means to attract investment, while sharing the benefits at all levels of governments, has been one of the key reasons why China's economy has achieved rapid economic growth after the tax sharing reforms. However, over time the negative side effects of this development model have become more and more evident. Many areas need to be reformed. The first is the high debt level of local governments. The capitalization of land essentially involves using future revenue streams as a collateral to pay a high price for land today. If the land owner is prudent, and only invests the borrowed money in profitable projects with high future cash flows, then debt is not a problem. However, the limited term length typically served by local government leaders inevitably leads to short-sighted behavior. They tend to over-borrow and invest in huge projects to drive up the GDP figures, get promoted for their seemingly outstanding performance and leave the huge debt burden to their successors. If these projects fail to deliver the promised returns, debt repayment can become a serious problem (more on this in Chapter 3).

The debt problem per se is not too hard to alleviate. A series of financial and fiscal reforms have been implemented in recent years, which have effectively reined in the rapid growth of debt. However, the economic growth has also slowed down, suggesting that the efficiency of resource

[17] For a detailed explanation, see the paper by Cheung (2014).

use is still low. Taking land as an example. Although there is an incentive for local governments to allocate land efficiently and balance the use of industrial and residential land, it is hard to ensure a nationwide balance and efficiency since land cannot simply move between regions to where efficiency is highest, no matter how fierce the competition between regions is. The economies of the Pearl River delta around Shenzhen and the Yangtze River delta around Shanghai have grown rapidly, and millions of migrants have moved to these two regions. However, there is simply not enough land quota available for urban development, which has restricted both economic growth and population growth. In Shanghai, where every inch of land is highly valuable, there are still large areas of unprofitable farmland (193,000 hectares as of 2020). Meanwhile, in central and western China, there are many industrial parks that either sit idle or have been abandoned. Given the vast amount of land available and sparse population in the west, this loss in efficiency might not be as huge as the media usually exaggerates. But if the land quota in urban development could be traded across provinces, the efficiency could be improved significantly. After all, if competition is not able to move resources to the most efficient places, this competition would not improve efficiencies continuously. Once the flow of investment stops, there will be an immediate impact on economic growth.

If the system has always been like this, then why have problems only started coming to light recently? The answer is that the stage of economic development has changed. In the early years of industrialization and urbanization, since the efficiency of the traditional agricultural sector was low, transforming farmland into more profitable industrial or commercial land would greatly improve efficiency. However, as the market economy continues to develop, competition is getting fiercer and technical requirements are getting higher. Enterprises need not only land to succeed, they also need investment in R&D, industry and supply chain agglomeration, financing and logistic access, some of which may not be available in all places. For many underdeveloped regions, cheap land is not enough to attract outside investments anymore. The direction of recent reform is clear. In 2020, the Central Committee of the CCP and the State Council issued the "*Opinions on Building a More Complete System and Mechanism for Market Based Allocation of Factors*", which placed introducing the "*market-based allocation of land*" as its top priority. The reform requires local governments to break down market barriers between urban and rural land within a province, a city and a county, to establish a unified land local land market and to improve the allocation efficiency of local land reserve. Moreover, the central government is also looking to "*establish a national market and a cross-regional trading mechanism for construction land*". The aim is to improve land use efficiency nationwide.

Section 3: Horizontal and Vertical Imbalances

After the tax sharing reforms, the majority of tax income now flowed to central government, but the majority of spending stayed with local governments. The deficit between spending and income was made up by transfer payments from the central government. Judging by the total value of transfer payments made by the central government, these transfers should have been enough to make up the local deficit experienced.[18] However, even though the total transfers might be sufficient, it does not mean that every local government received sufficient money. Sufficiency to a provincial government does not imply sufficiency to every county government within the province. Sufficiency to a coastal city does not imply sufficiency to a western city. These vertical and horizontal imbalances between places have created many conflicts and contradictions and have also spawned many reforms.

Financial Troubles in Lower-Level Governments (Vertical Imbalances)

After the tax sharing reform, tax revenue was shared between the central government and the provinces, and the provinces also need to share with cities and counties. However, since in the Chinese government system, higher levels have a higher authority, the lowest levels often receive the least amount of money but a large amount of work. As a result, a few years after the reforms, many lower-level governments begun to encounter serious financial difficulties. In the 1990s, there was a popular saying that went as follows "The central treasury is booming, provincial treasury is

[18] Starting from the tax sharing system reform in 1994 until 2008, the total amount of central government transfer payments made each year was higher than the gap between local government revenue and expenditure, generally around 10%–20% higher. After the huge "4 trillion" fiscal and financial stimulus in 2009, local governments could issue bonds to finance themselves, and the gap between local revenue and expenditure grew larger than the central government transfer payments (after the new Budget Law in 2015, provincial governments could issue bonds directly. Between 2009 and 2014, the Ministry of Finance could issue bonds on behalf of provincial governments).

steady, municipal treasury is shaky, county treasury is weeping, and the township treasury is empty!"

On average, tax revenue plus transfer payments from the higher-level government were only sufficient for the local government to pay salaries to their staff, but there are also great differences between regions. In the coastal east of China, where industrialization and urbanization were progressing rapidly, land finance provided a large source of non-tax income. The tax revenue could be used to pay expenses and the land finance revenue could be used to drive economic growth. However, in many parts of central and western China, land is not valuable and the money received from tax and transfer payments may not even be enough to cover officials' wages. The financial pressure on maintaining basic operations and investing in new economic opportunities was high and constant.[19] Once lower levels of government run out of money, they must find ways to make money to maintain operations. From the 1990s to the 2000s, many arbitrary charges begun to appear in villages and townships around China, making life difficult for farmers and resulting in a tense relationship between government cadres and the local people. Local governments struggled to make various payments, leaving workers short on wages, triggering complaints and even protests. In early 2000, Li Changping, Party Secretary of a township in Hubei province, wrote a letter to Zhu Rongji, then Premier of the State Council. One sentence became a sensation nationwide: "*The farmers are suffering; the countryside is poor, and the agricultural industry is in grave trouble*". These three rural issues would later become the focal points for many policy reforms in the early twenty-first century.

The tax sharing reforms, as well as other reforms such as the reform of the SOEs and reforms to the housing market, intensified social conflicts throughout the 1990s. These provided the backdrop for an era in which the 16th National Congress of the Communist Party of China (in 2003) proposed the "harmonious society" and "scientific outlook on development" policies. Among the "Five Coordinations" that corresponded to

[19] Tian and Zhao's book (田毅和赵旭 2008) and Wu's book (吴毅 2018) have vivid records and in-depth analysis of the "suspended" state of finance and various difficulties experienced by lower-level governments.

the "Scientific Outlook on Development", the first one was "coordination of rural and urban development".[20] Starting from 2000, a reform of rural government taxes and fees begun, preventing local governments from arbitrarily collecting fees or apportioning money, and canceling most fees and corvees born upon the peasants.[21] On January 1, 2006, the agricultural tax was completely abolished. This was an event with major historical significance, since farmers had paid such a tax for millennia. These reforms to tax and fee helped to increase farmers' incomes and also reduced the gap between the haves and the have nots in rural areas.[22] An important factor in allowing these reforms to be carried out is the entry of China into the WTO in 2001, which led to rapid growth in industry and commerce, reducing the government's reliance on taxes from agriculture. Between 2000 and 2007, agriculture's share of Chinese GDP fell from 15% to 10%, while the overall level of tax revenue increased 3.6x.

The reduction in rural taxes and fees made life easier for farmers, but it put further pressure on lower-level government's finances. Therefore, subsequent reforms focused on increasing the coordination between different levels of government to ensure adequate transfer payments were made.

The first step was to include the expenditure on basic public services in rural areas into the scope of the national public finance guarantee, which is the joint responsibility of central and local governments. For example, the reform of the compulsory rural education guarantee begun in 2006, and as of 2011, the central government had provided a total of

[20] The Third Plenary Session of the 16th Central Committee of the Communist Party of China held in 2003 proposed "five coordinations" in line with the "Scientific Outlook on Development": these included coordination of urban and rural development, coordination of regional development, coordination of economic and social development, coordination of the harmonious development of man and of nature, and coordination of domestic development and opening to the outside world.

[21] Rural taxes and fees before the reform can be roughly divided into three categories: "taxes", "fees" and "corvees". The tax part includes five types of agricultural taxes: agricultural tax, agricultural special product tax, slaughter tax, agriculture-related deed tax and cultivated land occupation tax. The fee part includes the three types of fees retained by the village collective (village cadre management fee, village provident fund, village public welfare fund) and five types of fees retained by the township government (education surcharge, family planning, special care, militia training, rural road construction). The corvee part includes unpaid labor used for afforestation, flood control and school building repairs.

[22] See a study by Chen Binkai and Li Yinyin (陈斌开和李银银 2020).

330 billion yuan to exempt 130 million rural students from costs related to compulsory education, such as the expenditures on textbooks and various costs of school administration.[23] Another example is government funding of the New Rural Cooperative Medical System, which started in 2003, and the New Rural Social Endowment Insurance, started in 2009. Both the programs are jointly funded by the central government and local governments at all levels.

The second step was to add an incentive mechanism into the transfer payment system, setting specific goals and targets for lower-level governments and rewarding them if the targets are met. For example, launched in 2005, the "three rewards and one subsidy" ("三奖一补") rewarded lower-level governments for streamlining their operations and personnel.[24] Overstaffing had been a perennial problem of local governments ever since the tax sharing reforms were implemented, and a significant portion of the transfer payment was often used to maintain operations and pay staff wages. If there are more staff needing to be paid, then there is a greater chance of receiving a larger transfer payment, a perverse incentive that naturally increases the size of the local government. From 1994 to 2005, the number of local government support staff (including those retirees who worked in government and whose pension were stilled paid by the government) soared by 60% from 29.81 million to 47.78 million people. After the new incentive mechanism was introduced, the number dropped by 3.18 million before rising again and finally stabilizing around 46.31 million in 2008, the last year when data were published.[25]

[23] Figures are from the book by Lou Jiwei and Liu Shangxi (楼继伟和刘尚希 2019).

[24] "Three rewards and one subsidy" included: increasing county and township tax revenue for county and township governments with financial difficulties, and providing incentives for provincial and municipal governments to increase financial transfer payments to counties with financial difficulties; rewarding county and township governments for streamlining institutions and personnel; subsidies are given to places that have done a good job in alleviating financial difficulties in counties and townships.

[25] The data come from an edited volume by Li Ping (李萍 2010), former director of the Budget Department of the Ministry of Finance. If we extrapolate the average annual growth rate of 1.8% from 2006 to 2008, the number of personnel supported by local government in 2018 should be around 55 million. According to the data of Lou Jiwei (楼继伟 2013), 94% of all the civil servants worked in the local government in 2011. If this ratio also applies to all people who are supported by the government, then in 2018, the total number of national financial support personnel (incumbent and retired) should be about 58.5 million.

The third step was to coordinate finances of lower-level governments with those of higher-level governments. For example, township finances began to be integrated with county finances in 2003. After the reform of rural taxes and fees, the amount of revenue and the scale of expenditures made by township government decreased significantly, and problems with overstaffing and debt became more prominent. Merging township budgets and expenses to the county and transferring township financial decision-making power to the county helped to monitor spendings of township governments, and also helped to equalize public service delivery in different places. According to data from the Ministry of Finance, by the end of 2012, 86% of rural townships had merged their finances with the corresponding county.

Merging township finances with the county may seem like a good idea, but what about the problems with the county finances? Under an administrative system where cities are responsible for managing counties, county-level income and expenditure should be shared with the city, but the city always has a bias toward urban districts and prioritizing expenditure and investment in these districts, instead of in those larger rural areas located in counties. As a result, urban districts in cities prospered at the expense of rural areas in counties, and the urban–rural inequality continued to widen. Moreover, many cities were themselves underdeveloped, providing little scope to drive economic development of counties under their jurisdiction. In the early twenty-first century, China started many policies to strengthen counties, giving them authority similar to many cities, for example those related to land sale and construction approval, while at the same time moving the reporting line of county finance departments directly to the provincial level, bypassing the city. This helped to balance the needs of the county and the city in terms of expenditure and investment, removing the urban bias previously inherent in the system. These reforms helped to increase the financial resources available to the county and reduce the urban–rural gap.[26]

Giving management of townships to counties, and moving the county reporting line directly to provinces, effectively restructured the five-level administrative management system that we discussed in Chapter 1. The

[26] There are many studies on the reform moving "county finances directly under the provincial control". Interested readers can refer to research by Tan et al. (谭之博, 周黎安, 赵岳 2015).

five-level administrative management structure, Central-Provincial-City-County-Township, was combined with a three-level finance management structure, Central-Provincial-City/County. However, although counties now had a lot of financial power, it was not necessarily conducive to long-term economic development. The reform of "province managing county" began in eastern Zhejiang province during the 1990s with positive results, but Zhejiang may be a special case. The counties in Zhejiang are economically strong and many counties and townships have developed specialized industry clusters, such as the world's largest manufacturing cluster of socks. In 2019, 18 of Zhejiang's 53 counties were among the wealthiest 100 counties in China. However, in other provinces this may not be the case and after the reforms at least two difficulties started to emerge. The first related to provincial management capability. Prior to the reforms one province on average had to manage 12 cities, but after the reform this increased to an average of 52 cities and counties. This lack of supervision capability meant that many counties used the money and power they had been given to engage in land-related corruption. The second major issue relates to the relationship between the county and the city. Under the old system, though counties had to share fiscal revenues with their managing cities, cooperation was more common than competition between cities and counties. However, after the reform, counties were essentially separated economically from the managing city, and cities and counties became competitors and collaboration was limited. In economically underdeveloped areas, cities were not strong and without the support of surrounding counties and districts, it was already hard to achieve the agglomeration or scale effects necessary to drive industry development and economic growth. After the reform, instead of gathering around urban city districts, economic activities tend to be more scattered in many separated small towns, and it became even harder to achieve the agglomeration or scale effects. According to existing research, after provinces became responsible for directly managing counties, despite more financial resources available for counties, the growth rate of per capita GDP on the county level has slowed.[27]

[27] Corruption associated with land and economic slowdown caused by the reform of "province managing county", and the number of administrative units managed by the provincial government before and after the reform, all come from the research of Li et al. (2016).

To summarize, the tax sharing reforms resulted in many difficulties at lower-level governments and follow-up reforms have been aimed at resolving these. One result has been to flatten the hierarchy of the financial and taxation system. However, the results are still not conclusively positive and there is still ongoing debate about the effectiveness of the reforms already implemented, and also about which direction future reforms should take. For example, should China implement a three-level finance manage system (Central-Provincial-City/County) in every province, like the system in the US (federal-state-county/independent city)?

Regional Inequality (Horizontal Imbalances)

The gap in terms of economic development between different regions in China began to widen in the latter half of the 1990s. Rapidly growing export industries naturally located near the coast in Eastern China to reduce freight and logistics costs. This result is a consequence of economics and is not related to tax policy. However, with the benefits of this industry agglomeration accruing to coastal provinces, regional gaps in terms of economic development and financial development quickly started to emerge. One of the main objectives of public finance is to redistribute financial resources and balance the level of per capita public services (such as medical care, schooling and public transport) in different regions, so the central government begun to make large-scale transfer payments to regions in central and western China. Between 1995 and 2008, the total amount of transfer payments increased from 66.5 billion yuan to 6.17 trillion, equivalent to 93 times and much higher than the growth rate in local tax revenue, and the value of transfer payments as a share of total GDP also increased from 1% to 7%.[28] The central and western regions of China receive more than 80% of the total transfer payments, helping to ensure that the per capita level of public spending remains balanced between regions.[29] Although today there may still be salient differences

[28] The transfer payment data in 1995 come from the "National Financial Statistics of Prefectural Cities and Counties in 1995", and the data in 2018 come from "the Report on the 2018 Final Financial Accounts of the Central Government" published on the website of the Ministry of Finance.

[29] According to the "the Report on the 2018 Final Financial Accounts of the Central Government" released by the Ministry of Finance, 85% of the transfer payments that year

in the level of public services between eastern and western China, the difference would have been markedly larger without the help of transfers from the central government.

Figure 2.6 shows the gap between per capita tax income and public expenditure of the richest three provinces (Jiangsu, Zhejiang and Guangdong) and the poorest three provinces (Guizhou, Yunnan and Gansu). Taking 2018 as an example, the per capita tax income and per capita GDP of the richer provinces was equivalent to 2.7 times that of the poorer provinces, however due to the effect of fiscal transfers from the central government, the per capita public spending of these provinces is more or less the same and the situation has been the same for the past 20 years. Starting in 2005, the gap in per capita public spending narrowed further, this was due to the "three rewards and one subsidy" program mentioned in the previous section. However, even though the spending may look balanced on a provincial level, the gap between individual counties in different regions may be large. Taking 2009 as an example, the top 1% of counties with the highest per capita spending, on average, spent 19 times more than the poorest 1% of counties.[30] The disparities experienced by those at the bottom of the government pyramid is related more to the vertical distribution of funds within the province, i.e. lower-level governments receive less money, and this may help to amplify cross-regional disparities among lower-level governments.

Transfers from the central government to local government can roughly be divided into two categories: general transfer payments (which were renamed as balance transfer payments after 2009) and special transfer payments.[31] In simple terms, the former has limited conditions attached and can be used more or less as the local government likes, while the latter will typically have to be used in specific projects with conditions attached.

were made to the central and western regions. According to the calculations of Miao Xiaolin et al. (缪小林, 高跃光, 王婷 2017), from 1995 to 2014, more than 80% of the transfer payments were allocated to the central and western regions.

[30] The currently available county-level fiscal expenditure data are available only up to 2009, from the 2009 National Fiscal Statistics of Prefectural Cities and Counties. I only included counties and county-level cities in the calculation, excluding urban areas, and did not include the 4 municipalities directly under the Central Government control nor the Tibet Autonomous Region.

[31] Generalized transfer payments should also include tax rebates, but the rebates here originally belong to local governments and are not included in the statistics in this paragraph.

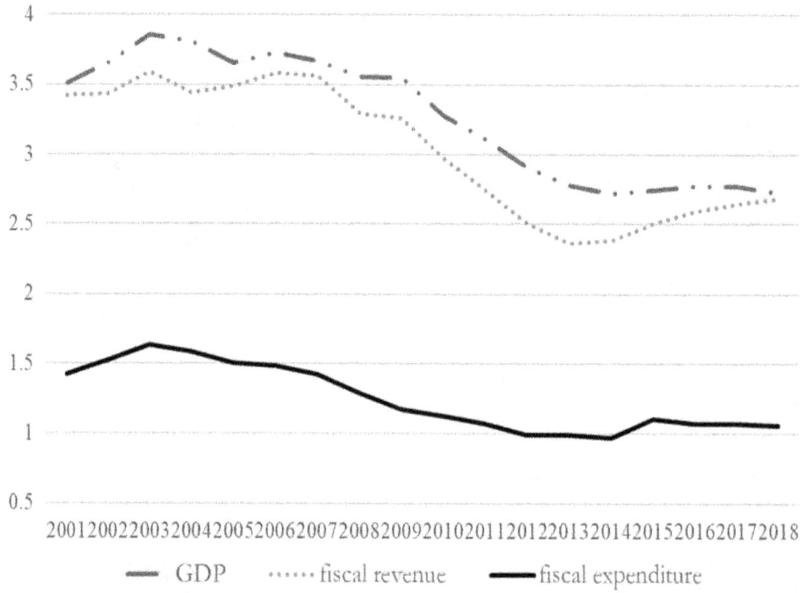

Fig. 2.6 Pubic finance per capita: the ratio of the three richest provinces to the three poorest provinces (*Notes* The three richest (highest GDP per capita) provinces are Guangdong, Jiangsu and Zhejiang, while the three poorest provinces are Gansu, Guizhou and Yunnan. I do not include the 4 provincial-level municipalities and Tibet, which are special cases in terms of economic data. *Source* WIND)

What would be the reason for specifying the use of funds and not allowing local decision-making? Since unconditional or balance transfer payments are aimed at equalizing per capita spending across regions, the poorer a region gets, the more money it gets. This leads to a perverse incentive where the region has less incentive to increase its income since doing so would reduce the amount of transfer payments received. Moreover, the balance transfer payment is used to ensure government operations run smoothly, and that government officials' wages are paid, so there is an incentive for local governments to either run their operations inefficiently or overstaff.

Special transfer payments account for roughly 40% of total transfer payments and they are generally allocated according to a specific project.

By attaching conditions to the special transfer payments, the central government can ensure that the money is spent on projects that align with their goals. But in fact, this type of payment can lead to a worsening of regional inequality, since regions with better economic conditions and stronger financial resources are likely to receive more special transfer payments.[32] There are three reasons for this: firstly, superiors like to concentrate financial resources in large projects, making success more likely, at the same time they also look for regions with the capability to execute on such projects. Secondly, prior to 2015, special transfer payments had to be co-funded by the region receiving the transfer, and only those regions with the financial capability to co-fund could receive funds.[33] Thirdly, personal connections played a pivotal role in the fund allocation process. The Ministry of Finance typically allocated money to individual ministries who then took responsibility for allocating down to the different regions. Developed regions often have stronger connections to the central ministries and commissions and are therefore better able to influence the allocation.[34]

An important function of public finance is to achieve equality in terms of public service across the realm. Although China continues to make improvement on this issue, there is still more to do. As of today, there are still large differences between the level of public service provision between eastern and western provinces, between urban and rural areas within the same province, and between those carrying a city resident registration (户口) and those not carrying one within the same city. Chapter 5 will continue to examine these regional imbalances and inequalities between people in more detail.

[32] Special transfer payments actually increase the difference in local per capita financial resources. There is a lot of evidence for this, such as the research by Wang Ruimin and Tao Ran (王瑞民和陶然 2017).

[33] In February 2015, the State Council issued the "Opinions on Reforming and Improving the Central-Local Transfer Payment System", specifying that "the central government shall not require local governments to co-fund when arranging special transfer payments".

[34] Personal connections with central ministries and commissions play an important role in the allocation of special transfer funds, see the research by Fan Ziying and Li Xin (范子英和李欣 2014).

Summary

To understand any government in depth, one must have a thorough grasp of taxation. This chapter introduces the reasons behind the tax sharing reforms in China and also their consequences. Figure 2.7 helps to summarize the main framework in this chapter. Any government must constantly adapt to new situations and new challenges that arise, and we cannot simply judge and guide reforms based on some theoretical or philosophical standard, instead, to fully understand and evaluate the effectiveness of a set of reforms, we must understand the detailed background and constraints, as well as the specific conditions in the country at the time. Only by examining the necessities and success of the tax sharing reforms can we understand which parts of the new system would fail to adapt to new situations and need to be reformed again.

The type of land finance that emerged after the tax sharing reforms has provided local governments with an annual income of around 5–6 trillion yuan from transferring land use rights. Although this is indeed a considerable sum, it is still not sufficient to fully support China's rapid urbanization and industrialization. Each year China requires a huge amount of investment in infrastructure, for example the high-speed rail network that has been built at light speed over the past 10 years takes a lot of money to construct. Where does it all come from? Likewise, cities around China have been rapidly building high-rise commercial districts, parks and roads. Districts across the country are being reshaped day by day, where does all the money come from? The real power of "land finance" is not the high sales value of land use rights, but its ability to use land as collateral to mobilize capital markets and leverage up more funds for investment. It snowballs in size, leading to more and more investment, but also more and more debt for local governments, which has become a significant problem for China's economy in recent years. This topic has been very popular in both Chinese and Western media over recent years, with commentators concerned about the level of debt held by China's local governments. In the next chapter we will examine the financial system that supports land finance in more detail, exploring how exactly local governments finance investment and some of the problems it causes.

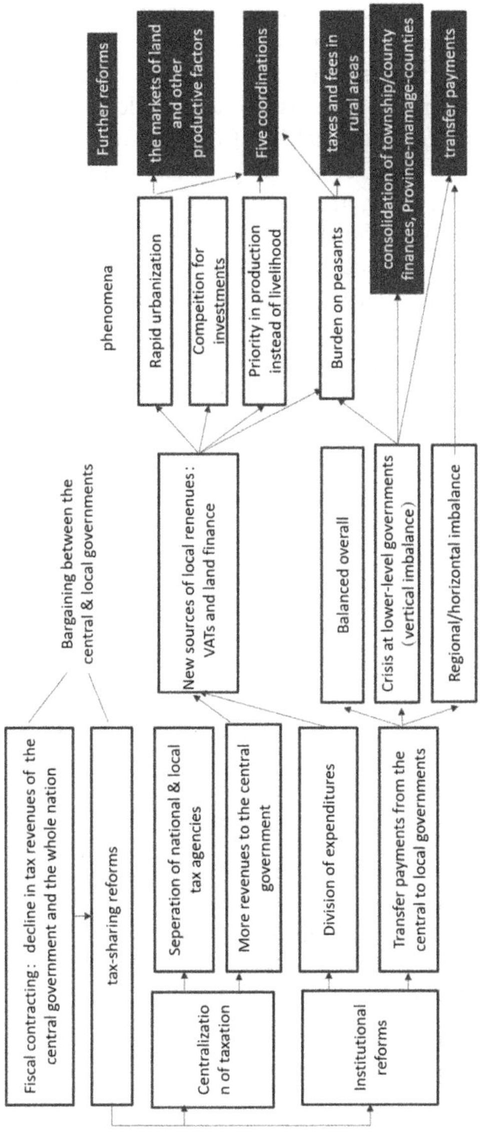

Fig. 2.7 Summary of this chapter

Further Readings

I am not aware of an English book that introduces the complex fiscal system in China, particularly viewing its role in economic development. So I will recommend two research articles here, both are easy to read. Chenggang Xu's long article (Xu 2011) is an excellent and comprehensive introduction to those fundamental institutions under China's economic growth, including the fiscal contracting system and the following tax sharing reforms. Particularly, the combination of the sharing of VATs and the state ownership of urban land transformed the behavior of local governments and shaped the competition between them. Steven Cheung's paper (Cheung 2014) articulates how and why.

For those who are interested in the large gap between the rural and urban development in China, Scott Rozelle and Natalie Hell's book, *Invisible China: How the Urban-Rural Divide Threatens China's Rise*, is a good place to start.

References

Cheung, Steven N.S. (2014). "The Economic System of China." *Man and the Economy* 1.1: 1–49.

Jin, Hehui, Yingyi Qian, and Barry R. Weingast (2005). "Regional Decentralization and Fiscal Incentives: Federalism, Chinese Style." *Journal of Public Economics* 89.9–10: 1719–1742.

Kung, James Kai-Sing, and Lin Yi-min (2007). "The Decline of Township-and-Village Enterprises in China's Economic Transition." *World Development* 35.4: 569–584.

Li, Pei, Yi Lu, and Jin Wang (2016). "Does Flattening Government Improve Economic Performance? Evidence from China." *Journal of Development Economics* 123: 18–37.

Naughton, Barry J. (2018). *The Chinese Economy: Adaptation and Growth* (2nd edition). MIT Press.

Xu, Chenggang (2011). "The Fundamental Institutions of China's Reforms and Development." *Journal of Economic Literature* 49.4: 1076–1151.

Translated References (in Chinese)

Chen, Binkai, and Yinyin Li (2020), "The Influence of Redistribution Policy on Rural Income Distribution—An Empirical Research Based on the Tax and Fee System Reform," *Social Sciences in China*, 2:70–92+205–206. (in Chinese)

Fan, Ziying, and Xin Li (2014). "Political Connection of Ministers and the Allocation of Fiscal Transfer." *Economic Research Journal* 6: 129–141. (in Chinese)

Fang, Hongsheng, and Jun, Zhang (2013). "Grabbing Hand, Helping Hand and Tax-Exceeding-GDP Growth." *Economic Research Journal* 3: 108–121. (in Chinese)

Fu, Yong, and Yan Zhang (2007). "The Chinese Decentralization and Fiscal Expenditure Structure Bias: The Cost of Competition for Growth." *Journal of Management World* 3: 4–12+22. (in Chinese)

Li, Ping (2010). *A Concise Illustration of the Fiscal System*. China Financial & Economic Publishing House. (in Chinese)

Li, Xuewen, Xinhai Lu, and Weiwen Zhang (2012). "Local Government and Extra-Budgetary Revenue: Issues in China's Economic Growth Model." *The Journal of World Economy* 8: 134–160. (in Chinese)

Liu, Kegu, and Kang Jia (2008). *A Review of China's Thirty years of Fiscal and Tax Reform*. Economic Science Press. (in Chinese)

Liu, Shouying (2018). *Land System Reform and Economic Development in China*. China Renmin University Press. (in Chinese)

Lou, Jiwei (2013). *Rethinking of Intergovernmental Fiscal Relations in China*. China Financial & Economic Publishing House. (in Chinese)

Lou, Jiwei, and Shangxi Liu (2019). *70 Years of Public Finance and Taxation Development in the People's Republic of China*. People's Publishing House. (in Chinese)

Ma, Guangrong, Kaiqiang Zhang, and Bingyang Lv (2019). "Tax Sharing and Local Fiscal Expenditure Structure." *Journal of Financial Research* 8: 20–37. (in Chinese)

Miao, Xiaolin, Ting Wang, and Yueguang Gao (2017). "The Effect of Fiscal Transfer on the Gap Between Urban-Rural Public Services Based on a Grouping Comparison of Different Economic Catching-Up Provinces." *Economic Research Journal* 2: 52–66. (in Chinese)

Tan, Zhibo, Li-An Zhou, and Yue Zhao (2015). "'County Administrated by Province' Reform, Fiscal Decentralization and People's Welfare: A Difference-in-Differences Estimation." *China Economic Quarterly* 3: 1093–1114. (in Chinese)

Tian, Yi, and Xu Zhao (2008). *Township Tax: Thirty Years of a Town, a 'Secret' Financial History of a Country*. China CITIC Press. (in Chinese)

Wang, Ruimin, and Ran Tao (2017). "The Equalization Effect of China's Intergovernmental Fiscal Transfer: An Empirical Assessment Based on County-Level Data." *The Journal of World Economy* 12: 119–140. (in Chinese)

Wang, Shaoguang (1997). *Bottom Limits of Decentralization*. China Planning Press. (in Chinese)

Wu, Yi (2018). *Noisy Town: The Deduction and Interpretation of the Political Operation of a Township*. SDX Joint Publishing Company. (in Chinese)

Xi, Penghui, Ruobing Liang, and Zhenfa Xie (2017a). “Tax Sharing Adjustments, Fiscal Pressure and Industrial Pollution.” *The Journal of World Economy* 10: 170–192. (in Chinese)

Xi, Penghui, Ruobing Liang, zhenfa Xie, and Guocan Su (2017b). “Fiscal Stress, Excess Capacity and Supply-Side Reform.” *Economic Research Journal* 9: 86–102. (in Chinese)

Yi, Heng, and Hong Zhu (2011). “A Study of Productive Expenditure Bias in County-Level Finance in China.” *Social Sciences in China* 1: 88–101+222. (in Chinese)

Zhou, Feizhou (2012). *Interest for Interest’s Sake: Fiscal Relations and Local Government Behavior*. Shanghai Joint Publishing Company. (in Chinese)

CHAPTER 3

Government Investment, Financing and Debt

There is a place called "Shipai Village" (石牌村), located near Jinan University in Guangzhou, it is one of the largest urban villages in Guangzhou and overall is a very prosperous place. A few years ago, a food television show visited a small shop located in the village, no doubt tempted by its reputation for having the best duck and rice. The rice was said to be delicious and also very cheap, costing only 12 yuan per bowl. During the course of the show, the host asked the middle-aged, ingenuous-looking owner how he was able to make a living selling his food so cheaply. The owner replied: "Yeah, I don't make much money. But I'm still happy. Because I…I can tell you, I have…not much, but I have 10 houses rented out". "10 apartments!" The host laughed, "no wonder you can sell your dish for 12 yuan and still have a smile on your face". The owner stayed calm and corrected the host, "No, not 10 apartments. It's 10 houses and each house has 7 floors". The laughter on the hosts face froze realizing that this man owned the equivalent of a 70-story building.

Many people in China have fantasies, if only their house could be moved to Beijing, Shanghai, Guangzhou or Shenzhen, or so-called first tier cities, then it would be worth so much more. After all, it's only land, why does it become so expensive when it's turned into housing?

Even the poorest countries have a large amount of land, but the land in and of itself is not worth anything. It's the economic activity that takes

X. Lan, *How China Works*,
https://doi.org/10.1007/978-981-97-0080-6_3

place on the land that has value. If the land is used to grow wheat crops, then it's value will be limited, but if the land can attract commercial and industrial investment, as well as skilled workers, then its value will start to increase. In such a case, the advantages of land will also start to come to the fore. Given land will not suddenly disappear or move to another place, it is naturally suitable to mortgage and to use as collateral for all types of loans and financing transactions, which leads to soaring value. The magic of land lies in its ability to break free from its physical self, to combine past savings, as well as future income together into an abstract promise of what can be developed in the future. The resulting energy, as powerful as technological progress, drives huge investments into urbanization and industrialization. One of the great wonders of economic development is the ability to transform tangible assets into intangible capital, which can congregate money and resources across space and time.[1]

The previous chapter explained how city governments balance the use of industrial land with commercial and residential land, thereby driving industrialization as well as urbanization. At the same time, they also derive extra income from the transfer and sale of land use rights. However, these transactions do not capture the full value that land provides to local governments. They can also use land to obtain loans or other types of financing. Land, therefore, moves from simply being a secondary form of local government revenue, to playing a critical role in capital markets.

The first section of this chapter uses examples to explain how local governments use land to raise capital for investment. The second section introduces one of the key drawbacks of this model, namely the increased debt burden placed on local governments. There have been various reforms related to local government debt, which also involve reforms of the incentive mechanism for local government officials. The third section will therefore analyze the role and behavior of local government officials in the process of local government financing and investment.

[1] Peruvian economist Hernando de Soto's classic book, *The Mystery of Capital: Why Capitalism Triumphs in the West and Fails Everywhere Else* (2003), contains an excellent discussion of the properties of capital.

Section 1: Urban Investment Corporations and Land Finance

Industrial investment is much more complicated than simple financial investment. In addition to considering basic factors, such as the holding period for the investment, prevailing interest rates and potential risks, it is necessary to also deal with many unforeseen and complex situations that arise in the process of executing a project. Just as fund managers may buy thousands of stocks from retail investors, real estate developers may buy land use rights from thousands of homeowners. Both cases involve the purchase of assets for investment, but the related operating difficulty is not comparable, and land purchase would not be possible without government intervention. Industrial investment is a continuous process that requires constant input and management. Each stage may have a different objective and requires different skills and resources, and different kinds of relationships need to be managed. A mistake at any stage may affect the whole process. Take building a shopping mall as an example, land demolition is the first stage, followed by construction and later operation of the mall, as well as promotion of the mall to merchants, and later consumers. Each stage requires a different skill set and may be executed by different entities. It is therefore necessary to have a thorough understanding of the whole project while also dealing with any specific difficulties occurring along with the way.

The Chinese government not only owns urban land, but it also has control over the financial system, it's only natural that it should play a large role in industrial investment. In fact, without the participation of government, most projects would not be able to proceed. However, industrial investment is not the same as buying and selling stocks of companies, it's not possible to exit an investment at any time and investment decisions are often irreversible. For any project that is abandoned or fails to complete on time, the initial investment may be completely lost. Therefore, once the government enters a project, it is very hard to get out and each project requires a high level of commitment. For a long time, the main driving force of Chinese economic growth has been investment, which necessarily requires the government to have a deep involvement in the economy. In the second part of the book, we will discuss whether this model is efficient or not from an economic perspective, and the answer to this question depends on the stage of economic development. However, we must first take time to understand how the government invests. This chapter will explore land and infrastructure investment more deeply, with the next chapter focusing on industrial investment.

Local Government Financing Vehicles: Starting in Chengdu

Before 2015, Chinese law stipulated that local governments were not allowed to borrow money from banks and were not allowed to issue bonds, therefore if a local government wanted to borrow money, it had to set up a special company.[2] Most of these companies are wholly state owned and are referred to, by media and economists, as Local Government Financing Vehicles (LGFVs). The name highlights the role these entities play in financing and when they are discussed in the media, LGFVs are almost always associated with local government debt problems. However, the official name of these vehicles does not contain the word "financing", rather most of them use words such as "investment and development" or "construction", which emphasizes the company's role in investment rather than financing. So in China, these vehicles are also collectively referred to as Urban Investment Corporations (城投公司). Some examples include Wuhu Construction Investment Co. (also the main shareholder of Chery Automobile Co.) and Shanghai Urban Construction Investment and Development Corporation, both of which are wholly owned by the local government through the State-Owned Assets Supervision and Administration Commission. There are also companies specializing in the development of tourist attractions, which generally have "tourism development" in their name. For example, Chengdu Culture & Tourism Development Group (CDCT) is a state-owned enterprise of the Chengdu City Government, and the company develops a famous tourist site called Kuanzhai Alley (宽窄巷子).

The Kuanzhai Alley project has a relatively simple financing and investment structure. From start to finish, the project has been completely executed by the local government and associated state-owned enterprises. Given Kunzhai Alley is located in a historic area that benefits

[2] The General Rules for Loans formulated by the People's Bank of China (the central bank of China) strictly limit the qualifications of borrowers, explicitly excluding local governments. The 1995 version of the Budget Law prohibits local governments from issuing bonds, while the 2014 revision allows provincial-level governments to issue bonds.

from cultural protection, the work was extremely complex, requiring preservation, demolition, repair and reconstruction. The initial investment required was large, with a long and uncertain investment cycle and there was no certainty that the project would ever turn a profit. These factors make it difficult for private enterprises to take on such a project. As a result, since the project was launched in 2003, it has been managed by two state-owned enterprises: Chengdu Urban Investment Group before 2007 and CDCT after that. While the tourist site officially opened in 2008, it continued to be developed while already in operation and the first phase of development was only officially completed in June 2019. The first development stage therefore required a total of 16 years to complete. Since CDCT took over the project, a total of 650 million yuan has been invested, including bank loans, government subsidies and reinvested income from operations.

CDCT has a typical profile for a LGFV. First, it has land use rights granted to it by the government. These assets are valuable and when combined with operating income and government subsidies, they can be used to access bank loans and other forms of financing. When it was established in 2007, the company's registered capital was only 500 million yuan and its primary business was to develop the Kunzhai Alley project. By 2018, the registered capital had reached 3.1 billion yuan and total assets were 20.4 billion yuan. The company had 23 subsidiaries and many projects ongoing.[3]

The second typical characteristic is that the company's profitability relies on government subsidies. From 2015 to 2016, the net profit of CDCT was more than 66 million yuan, but the total amount of subsidies received from various government agencies exceeded 200 million yuan. In other words, without government subsidies, the company would have suffered net loss. There are various types of subsidies, such as tax rebates or other special subsidies included in the public budget. For example, in the budget of the Chengdu City government, there is a special fund to support the local tourism industry. From 2012 to 2015, the annual subsidy from this fund to CDCT exceeded 100 million yuan. Local governments can also transfer land use rights to a LGFV for a fee and

[3] The data come from information and statements disclosed by the company when issuing bonds. Readers can download it from the website of Shanghai Clearing House.

then return the fee to the LGFV as a form of subsidy.[4] In 2015, the new Budget Law required local governments to end many subsidies. From 2017 to 2018, the net profit of CDCT increased to 140 million yuan, with subsidies dropping to 40 million yuan.

Is it inefficient for a company such as CDCT to rely on government subsidies for profitability? It's not possible to generalize an answer to this question. Most of the projects operated by LGFVs are related to infrastructure and the underlying profitability of the projects is not strong. If there was a strong profit motive related to the projects, there would be less need for the government to be involved since private companies would invest. More importantly, the return of projects often depends not only on the underlying profitability of the project per se, but also on the economic and social benefits derived from the project. However, calculating these benefits is often controversial. Borrowing a framework of welfare analysis from economics can be useful in terms of logic, but the estimated numbers are not reliable. At the beginning of 2009, I went to Kuanzhai Alley for the first time. At that time, it was still a relatively new attraction and there were not many people. By the summer of 2016, when I went for a second time, the place had become a famous tourist destination and was teeming with people. According to financial data published by the CDCT, Kuanzhai Alley now receives 20 million visitors a year and the groups' revenue is 80–90 million yuan. Net profit stands at 20-30million and is still growing. The profitability of the project is good, but what if there was no profit or even a loss? Would the project necessarily have failed? It's hard to say. Even if the 20 million visitors, on average, spend 50 yuan on site per person, then the total spending is 1 billion yuan. This is a prosperous economic cluster that sustains many jobs in retail, restaurants and transportation, and it generates sizeable tax revenues. In terms of the projects' value to government and to local people, these social benefits may be more important than the profitability of the project itself.

Thirdly, implicit government guarantees allow LGFVs to access capital and borrow heavily. Open credit lines for CDCT total 17.6 billion yuan and bonds issued by the group are able to achieve an AA + rating.

[4] For example, at the end of 2009, the Chengdu City Finance Bureau returned a land transfer fee of 37.69 million yuan, initially collected from the Kuanzhai Alley historical and cultural protection project, to CDCT as a form of subsidy. The subsidy is targeted toward advertising the Kuanzhai Alley as a tourist attraction.

Whether the company deserves to have such a high credit rating is open to debate. However, it is the market consensus that there is an implicit government guarantee behind debt issued by LGFVs. The guarantee is "implicit" because the Guarantee Law stipulates that governments cannot provide guarantees to financing vehicles. However, in reality the government continues to inject various assets into LGFVs and the market believes that the government will not allow them to go bankrupt, so the actual risk is very low.

The Kuanzhai Alley project is quite special. Most similar urban leisure and entertainment projects do not involve the repair and protection of historical buildings and the development process can be completed by private companies. For example, Xintiandi in Shanghai or the numerous Wanda Plazas all over China are all based on land use rights granted by the local government, with the projects being developed and operated by private enterprises. In these projects, LGFVs generally only participate in the demolition of existing buildings and the consolidation of land. To use some Chinese terminology, a piece of "raw land" (生地) that has been marked for development, can turn into "ripe land" (熟地) ready for development, only after the land is leveled and cleaned up. This process of turning raw land into ripe land is called primary land development, which is not very profitable but highly complex because it often involves demolition of buildings and relocation of existing residents. It is typically completed by LGFVs, then the ripe land is sold to real estate companies for so-called secondary land development and operation.

Industrial Park Development: Suzhou Industrial Park vs China Fortune Land Development

Looking at the way it operates, CDCT has all the typical attributes of a LGFV. However, the main business of LGFVs is not tourism development, but development of industrial parks and other urban infrastructure. Industrial parks are developing rapidly all over China. In 2018, there were 552 national-level industrial parks, 1,191 provincial-level industrial parks and even more below the provincial level.[5]

[5] The data are from the "2018 China Development Zone Review", which is jointly released by six ministries of the central government, including the National Development and Reform Commission and the Ministry of Science and Technology.

Suzhou Industrial Park is one of the largest and most successful industrial parks in China. It covers a land area of 278 square kilometers. In 2019, the GDP arising from economic activities inside the park totaled 274 billion yuan, and tax revenue accruing from the park was 37 billion. This economic output generated within the industrial park was larger than many prefecture-level cities.[6] The development and operation of such a large industrial park is necessarily more complicated than the Kuanzhai Alley example we discussed above. There are many participating companies, and in the case of Suzhou Industrial Park, two SOEs lead the project. Zhaorun Group is responsible for the primary land development, including consolidating land and building infrastructure. Zhongxin Group, a company listed as recently as 2019, is responsible for secondary land development, including construction, attracting investment and companies to move to the industrial park, and the daily operation of the park.

Zhaorun Group (which has the full name of "Suzhou Industrial Park Zhaorun Investment Holding Group Co., Ltd) is a typical LGFV. The company is 100% owned by the local government and its' registered capital was 16.9 billion yuan in 2019. Zhaorun runs a typical "land finance" operation. The government grants land to the company, which becomes its capital. The company carries out work on the land, for example "7 openings and 1 leveling", turns the "raw land" into "ripe land" and then resells it back to the government ready for auction to real estate developers. Zhaorun Group can use the land as collateral to secure loans or can secure pledge loans using the revenue from future land sale as collateral. It can also issue bonds, which can be repaid once the land is sold back to the government or can be repaid with government subsidies. Zhaorun has a lot of land assets at its disposal, and at its peak in 2014, the group had a total of 20 billion yuan in long-term collateral loans and 10 billion yuan in pledge loans.[7]

Compared with projects such as Kuanzhai Alley in Chengdu or Xintiandi in Shanghai, the development of industrial parks is more similar

[6] Figures are from the website of the Suzhou Industrial Park Management Committee. My hometown, the city of Baotou, has a population of 2.9 million people. Its GDP in 2019 was only 272 billion yuan, and its tax revenue was only 15 billion yuan.

[7] The data are from the prospectus and related rating announcements issued by Zhaorun Group. In addition to developing industrial parks, Zhaorun also develops real estate.

to an infrastructure project, requiring large investment and with low profitability. Most industrial parks are thus developed by state-owned LGFVs before being handed back to local governments to attract outside investment into the park. The ease of attracting companies to invest in the park depends on the business environment and economic development in the region. In places like Shanghai and Suzhou, where the economy is strong, it's more a case of attracting the best of the best to their industrial parks. The local government wants to better agglomerate companies in similar industries to achieve economies of scale. I have visited Suzhou Industrial Park on several occasions and I am always impressed by its green and clean environment, not something one would associate with a manufacturing park. In 2019, the total volume of import and exports associated with the park reached 87 billion US dollars. Although the rapid development of the park has benefited from its location in the Yangtze River Delta, the local government and several major state-owned enterprises have also played a critical role in its success.

Conversely, in many cities and counties in Western China, it is much harder to attract investment. The geographic location is not convenient, and the economy is less developed. The local government's financial and human resources are limited, and except for some land there is not much to offer. Therefore, some governments choose to simply outsource an entire development package to private enterprises: granting them a piece of land, allowing them to develop and operate an industrial park, and requiring them to attract outside investment in the name of government.

An archetype of this type of private enterprise is China Fortune Land Development. The core business of this listed company could be described as "integration of industry and city", which means building and operating industrial parks and real estate at the same time. The local government often allocates a huge piece of land to China Fortune, measured by square kilometers, who then conducts primary development, and later also secondary development of the industrial park. One famous example is Gu'an High Tech Park, which is located in Hebei province, northern China, where the local county government handed over a 170 square kilometer piece of land to China Fortune. In 2017, Caixin Weekly (a major newspaper on Chinese economy and politics) described China Fortune as a "city maker", which, given the scale of the development, is no exaggeration.

It's not easy to make a profit developing industrial parks. Convincing companies to move to the park is hard and for a park to be successful, it needs a large number of companies to move together. It could take many years for an industrial park to generate meaningful profits for its owner. China Fortune therefore primarily relies on real estate to make money. By bringing industrialization and urbanization together under one umbrella, money made from selling houses can be used to support the operation of the industrial park, which in turn provides jobs to the houses' new residents. According to the typical process, the local government grants land to China Fortune for primary development, later purchasing it back for land auction and secondary development by a real estate company. If China Fortune fails to win the bid for the secondary development, which is much more profitable than the primary development, then it won't be able to make a profit from the project. So, according to Caixin Weekly, in practice, for projects where China Fortune is the primary developer of the industrial park, the relationship between the company and the local government is very close, and it is nearly impossible for other real estate companies to win the secondary land auction bid.

Using profits from real estate development to fund industrial park sounds similar to the "land finance" model used by local governments that we discussed in Chapter 2. With one hand, the government supplies cheap industrial land that, once developed, can generate tax income and employment. With the other it supplies expensive residential land that can be sold to generate non-tax revenue. However, a local government can justify losing money on industrial parks in order to create employment and tax revenue. As a private business, China Fortune doesn't have these justifications. So, what does it stand to gain from developing industrial parks? The simple answer is that the company can also share tax benefits with the government. Tax income paid by enterprises located in the park (after subtracting park operating expenses) can be shared between the local government and China Fortune according to some pre-agreed proportion. According to Chinese law, the government cannot share tax revenue directly with enterprises, however it can pay the agreed share by purchasing services from the developer.

Governments paying to use infrastructure, such as industrial parks, developed by private companies is not a new idea. The model, called "Public Private Partnership" (PPP for short), originated in the West well before it was imported to China. However, if we want to look for ways that the model has been adapted specifically for a Chinese context, then there are two things we can refer to. The first is that there are many PPP projects, and that the projects are generally of a large scale. As of

May 2020, there were a total of 9,575 PPP projects across China, with a total value of nearly 15 trillion yuan, however only 40% of the projects had started construction. The second feature is that most of the "private partners" are actually state-owned enterprises including LGFVs, such as CDCT or Zhaorun Group discussed above. By the end of 2019, only 30% of PPP projects in construction or in operation involved private enterprises, and most of them were small independent projects such as sewage works or garbage facilities.[8] There are not many private enterprises involved in large projects such as Gu'an High Tech Park undertaken by China Fortune. And this project is a "National Demonstration PPP Project", awarded by the central government. In recent years, policy regulations on the real estate and land development have become much stricter, and some traditional real estate companies have also begun to explore this model of integrating industrialization and urbanization, however we are yet to see how far this exploration can go.

Chapter 2 posited that Chinese local governments' attempts to attract investment can be likened to a shopping mall operator, who needs to attract different shops with different rents in order to maximize overall income. In this section, we have discussed how the government can completely outsource the entire operation to private enterprises, allowing them to participate deeply in the process of attracting investment and developing local economy.

As early as in 1930s, Ronald Coase, who received the Nobel Prize in Economics, asked the question "*where is the boundary between the firm and market?*" and "*if the market is so efficient, why do firms exist?*" These questions are not easy to answer, and we could also ask, where is the boundary between the firm and government. On paper, the various entities seem to be distinct, but from the perspective of actual behavior, we can see that LGFVs seem to be a combination of both governments and firms. Private developers such as China Fortune are also responsible to attract investment to the region in the name of government, while also carrying out basic infrastructure construction. In the real world, there is no clear boundary or definition, only interlocking rights and obligations. As Steven Cheung, a Chinese economist and a protege of Coase, says,

[8] The data related to PPP come from the website of the China Public Private Partnerships Center (www.cpppc.org).

there is only a series of contractual arrangements.[9] In order fully understand these arrangements, it is necessary to investigate the constraints faced by different parties, including the resources and capabilities at their disposal, policies in place and information available. A simple dichotomy of government vs. market is useless in the real world.

Section 2: Local Government Debts

Figure 3.1 summarizes the logic behind China's land and real estate finance. After the reform of the tax sharing system in 1994, most tax revenue accrued to central government, but with tax rebates and transfer payments, local governments had little trouble balancing the books. However, economic development remained a crucial task for local governments, they needed to attract investment and invest themselves in infrastructure and land development, all things that require extra money. With China's ongoing urbanization and housing boom, the value of land has continuously soared. Local governments not only received revenues from selling land use rights, but also captured the future value of land in mortgages and other forms of borrowing. Unlocking this investment has helped to propel China's rapid industrialization and urbanization, but in the process, it has also created a large amount of debt. The key variable in this model is the price of land. Provided that continuous investment and construction can drive sustained economic growth, cities will continue expanding and land prices will continue to rise, and debts can be safely repaid with interest on top. However, if land prices fall and revenue from land sales starts to decrease, then the debt accumulated over years of rapid development will become a heavy burden and LGFVs, as well as local governments themselves may be overwhelmed.

Liabilities of local government started to increase rapidly from 2008 to 2009. In response to the global financial crisis that originated in the US, the Chinese government quickly issued a 4-trillion-yuan stimulus package. The central government invested 1.18 trillion (including investment necessary for rebuilding after the Sichuan earthquake), and local government invested 2.82 trillion. In order to ensure the fiscal stimulus was implemented effectively, and in order to make it easier for local governments to raise funds, the central government eased restrictions

[9] Steven Cheung develops a general theory of contract in Volume 4 of his book (张五常 2019).

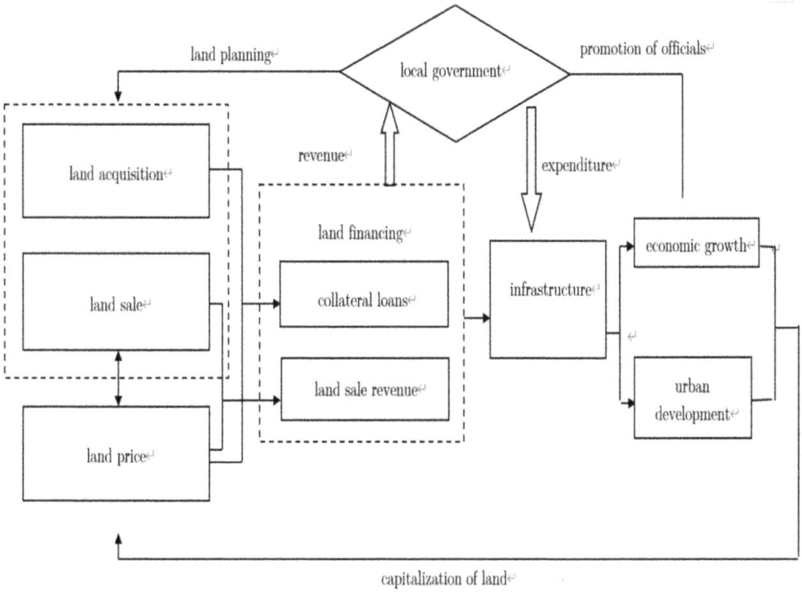

Fig. 3.1 Land finance of local government (*Source* Zheng et al. [郑思齐等 2014])

on LGFVs, making it easier for them to access credit. In 2008, there were roughly 3,000 LGFVs in China, however by 2009, the number had increased to over 8,000, with more than 60% being set at the county level. Large stimulus was necessary to save the economy, but with so much money released at once, many of the investment projects were bound to fail. Financially distressed locations could suddenly borrow freely, and projects with a low probability of being profitable were able to access finance. In just 3–5 years, local governments accumulated a huge amount of debt and to this day, these debts still present risks for China's financial system.

Financing Development: China Development Bank and Urban Investment Bonds

Industrial investment is a complex and lengthy process. It is not like financial investment, whereby a series of financial indicators can be used to decide whether to invest or not. Industrial investment requires continuous work and there can be many unforeseen challenges at each stage. It is therefore important to choose the correct partners at each stage. Investment in large-scale infrastructure projects in China almost always involves the direct participation of the government. This may come from various entities, for example LGFVs, government-sponsored scientific research and design institutes, as well as other state-owned enterprises. Under China's existing financing system, it is easier for projects involving local governments or state-owned enterprises to receive financing. This section focuses on investment and financing of infrastructure projects. Chapters 4 to 6 will discuss industrial projects, as well as debt risks arising from government credit.

In the 1980s and 1990s, most funds used for urban construction relied on fiscal budget. After the reform of the tax sharing in 1994, local government finances were inevitably tight. While urbanization was accelerating, funds available for urban construction remained very limited. If a city could rely on limited fiscal revenues for urban development, it will never be able to meet the construction demand of rapid urbanization. It had to find a way to borrow more money from banks. However, in order to introduce more bank funds into urban construction and development, three technical problems needed to be solved. First, there needs to be a cooperation that is able to borrow money because the government is not able to borrow directly from banks. Second, urban development and construction projects are complex, including tap water pipelines, roads, parks, flood control as well as many other things. Some of them make money, some of them don't, and it is difficult to ask banks to finance the latter projects. So it's better to bundle various projects together and use profitable projects as a means to finance unprofitable projects. Third, tax revenue alone is not enough to repay debt, so income from "land finance" also needs to be used.

The urban investment and development corporations (UDICs), or from the perspective of financing, LGFVs, were formed to solve the above three problems. The model was originally conceived by China Development Bank (CBD). In 1998, CBD partnered with Wuhu City in Anhui province, to bring 8 urban construction projects together into one company, called Wuhu Construction Investment Co., which was a specially created UDIC. The company acted as a single borrower for the 8 projects and borrowed 1.08 billion yuan from CDB. The amount was very significant for a city such as Wuhu at the time, and it provided the groundwork for a lot of construction in the city. At the time, land finance had still not been developed and the city government could only use tax revenue as a source to repay debt. From 2002, China began to operate the land auction system and the Wuhu government allowed Wuhu Construction Investment Co. to pledge the proceeds from any land sales as a repayment guarantee. In 2003, in an agreement with the city of Tianjin, CDB begun to allow the proceeds from land appreciation to be the source of loan repayment. This later became the standard model across the country.[10]

CDB is the world's largest development bank, with total assets exceeding 16 trillion yuan by 2018, about 5 times the size of the World Bank.[11] Before 2008, CDB was the main source of loans for UDICs, however after the 4 trillion government stimulus in 2008, various commercial banks, including the "Big 4" national banks (Industrial and Commercial Bank of China, Bank of China, China Construction Bank and Agricultural Bank of China) and city-level commercial banks, also began large-scale lending to UDICs. By 2010, among all the loans granted to UDICs, CDB accounted for 2 trillion yuan, the "Big 4" accounted for 2 trillion, city banks accounted for 2.2 trillion, and other banks and rural cooperative financial companies accounted for roughly 1 trillion yuan. We can see that in terms of financial to UDICs, city banks had reached the same level as both CDB and the "Big 4".[12]

City commercial banks are mainly controlled by local governments. As of 2015, the largest shareholder of about 70% of city commercial banks was the local government.[13] In the process of competing for attracting investment among city governments, being able to provide financing is one of the core advantages. So, city governments typically control at least one bank to facilitate loans for investment vehicles and infrastructure construction. However, there are two key risks that arise when city banks provide funds to UDICs. First, infrastructure and construction projects

[10] For the ins and outs of the "Wuhu Model", please refer to *A History of China Development Bank (1994-2012)* (编委会 2013).

[11] Assets of CDB and World Bank are from their respective annual reports. World Bank assets only include the International Bank for Reconstruction and Development (IBRD) and the International Development Association (IDA).

[12] Data come from an article by Dang and Wang of the Risk Management Department of Postal Savings Bank of China (党均章与王庆华 2010).

[13] The data come from the article of Hong et.al. (洪正, 张硕楠, 张琳 2017).

have a long lifecycle and require long-term loans to match, while commercial banks often rely on highly liquid short-term debts or deposits for funding, which leads to a maturity mismatch and liquidation risk. China Development Bank, on the other hand, relies on long-term bonds for funding and is therefore better suited to financing infrastructure projects. Second, the Big 4 national banks have large and stable deposits and are therefore better able to withstand mismatch risks. City banks have less stable deposits and less capital, and they rely on various short-term debt instruments on the capital market, thereby making them more prone to risks. Taking Baoshang Bank as an example, it was taken over by regulators in 2019 and filed for bankruptcy in 2020, the first time for this to happen in the banking industry for over 20 years. Regular deposits only accounted for less than half of the bank's total liabilities and almost all of the remaining funding came from debt instruments on interbank markets.[14] Although this example is extreme, in the 10 years following the stimulus of 4 trillion yuan, small and medium-sized city banks across the country relied heavily on interbank financing. If liquidity were to suddenly tighten, it could cause a cascade of failing banks.

The primary financing method for UDICs is bank loans, followed by issuance of bonds, which are commonly referred to as urban investment bonds. Theoretically, there are two benefits to issuing bond instead of loans. Firstly, whereas bank lending consolidates risks in the banking system, bonds can be sold to a wider range of investors, which helps to diversify risks. Secondly, bonds can be traded, and prices and yields fluctuate over time reflecting the markets' perception of the bonds' risk. Risky bonds will be cheaper and have higher yields, reflecting the markets' perception of the risk. This flexible price mechanism can help allocate bonds to different investors with different levels of risk tolerance, this improves the efficiency of the market.

But in the case of urban investment bonds, these two theoretical benefits don't matter much. First, the vast majority of urban investment bonds are issued in the interbank market and the holders are mainly commercial banks. The liquidity is low, which means the risks are still concentrated in the banking system. Second, investors assume that these bonds are implicitly guaranteed by government and hence very safe. Bonds from poorer

[14] The data come from an article in the 21st issue of Caixin Weekly in 2019, titled "The Full Record: the Central Bank, Banking and Insurance Regulatory Commission Jointly Takes Over Baoshang Bank".

cities or provinces naturally carry a higher risk, however a slightly higher interest rate can make them very popular in the market.[15] This market perception of low risk has been proved rational. Urban investment bonds exploded in popularity after the 2008 stimulus, and although the market has undergone several regulatory reforms, the default rate has been very low. These low-risk but high-yield bonds have distorted the development of the bond market, and the implicit risks are not small.

Risks of Local Government Debts

No-one knows the total amount of Chinese local government debt. In addition to the part displayed on official accounts, there is also much hidden debt that's hard to calculate. UDICs account for the majority of this hidden debt. Many researchers have done a lot of work to estimate the exact amount of local government debt, with the estimated total standing at around 45 trillion yuan in the period of 2015 to 2017, roughly 50–60% of Chinese GDP. And 30–40% of them are hidden debts.[16]

Although the level of local government debt is not low, it is not particularly high either. Even if it accounts for 60% of GDP, together with the debt of the central government, the total government debt accounts for only 80% of GDP. In contrast, by 2018, US government debt accounted for 107% of GDP and Japan's was as high as 237%.[17] Moreover, the money borrowed by local governments in China is not used for operating expenditure, nor is it used to pay for social security benefits like in some European countries such as Greece, instead it is used for infrastructure investment which produces valuable physical assets. Although the rate of return on these assets could be very low, perhaps less than 1% on average, if we calculate the benefits of better infrastructure to citizens and to the long-term economic development, then the aggregate economic

[15] From 2010 to 2012, the central government tightened bank loans issued to UDICs and other financing channels such as trusts. In order to circumvent these regulations, UDICs began to issue a large number of urban investment bonds, at the expense of paying higher interest rates.

[16] There are many estimates of the level of hidden debts, and most of them use similar data sources and reached similar figures. The figures are from three sources: two papers by Bai, Hsieh and Song (2016) and by Zhang and Xiong (2019), and one research report from Haitong Securities (姜超, 朱征星, 杜佳 2018).

[17] The data for the US and Japan are from the Global Debt Database maintained by the International Monetary Fund, see Fig. 6.3 in Chapter 6 for details.

and social returns could be much higher than the financial returns calculated from the book.[18] In addition, China has very limited amounts of debt held by foreign entities. According to the State Administration of Foreign Exchange in its 2019 balance of payments report, the external debt balance of the entire government by the end of 2019 was 307 billion US dollars, accounting for only 2% of China's GDP.

However, when analyzing debt risks, it's necessary to look not only at the global risks, but also at local risks. A debt of one billion is not a big deal from the perspective of a nation's GDP, but it could easily overwhelm its borrower, whether it is a firm or a local government. The national debt burden cannot be used to sugarcoat risks that may occur at the local level. Looking between the different levels of the government, the lower the level, the heavier the debt burden and the higher the risk. The debt burden at the county level is much higher than that at the provincial level because counties have a less developed economy and therefore less fiscal revenue. Looking between the governments at the same level, debt burdens are greater in the central and western areas where the economy is weaker than the east.[19]

Although from the perspective of economic analysis, infrastructural projects invested by the government have many spillover benefits into the economy and the society, in the real world, debt repayment requires hard cash and, in this respect, non-cash benefits do not matter much. The cash return on investment of UDICs is low and it can be difficult to repay debts. With the backing of local governments, they can roll over and extend debts by using new borrowing to pay for existing debt, as long as they can pay the interest and have enough cash in hand to pay the principal when it is due, they can survive. However, most UDICs have little income of their own and need to rely on government subsidies to pay off interest. In 2017, aside from 6 provinces and cities, Beijing, Shanghai, Guangdong, Fujian, Sichuan and Anhui, the average income of these UDICs, if deducting government subsidies, would not be enough to

[18] Zhang and Xiong (2019) calculated the rate of return on assets of 1,109 UDICs, and the median was just 0.8% in 2016.

[19] A book by Lu (陆铭 2016) shows that poorer provinces have greater debt burdens.

cover debt interest payments.[20] These government subsidies come from the income generated by land finance, so if the economy cools and land price drops, interest payments may overwhelm local governments as well.

Policies and Reforms on Local Government Debts

Regulations and reforms on local government debts started around 2010, and over the past 10 years, 4 important reforms have taken place. The first is debt replacement, which started in 2015, right after the implement of the new budget law, and was essentially completed by 2019. In simple terms, the reform allows some bank debt and bonds issued by local government financing vehicles (LGFV) to be replaced by bonds issued by local governments. The replacement has 3 benefits. Firstly, the interest rate can be lowered from roughly 7% to 8% to around 4%, which reduces the interest payment expense and the cash flow pressure. Lower interest rates also help to improve the efficiency of the financial markets. Bank loans and bonds issued by LGFVs are assumed to be implicitly guaranteed by local governments, but the interest rate charged to these "safe assets" is high, around 7–8%. Banks love these low-risk yet high-yield assets and are willing to purchase a large amount, which could crowd out their lending to other borrowers. This means other companies need to offer higher interest rates to attract funds and the overall market interest rate is higher than would be in an efficient market. The interest rates are distorted so much that they could not efficiently allocate the funds and risks, and this therefore requires the government to step in and carry out reforms. Secondly, the maturity of local government bonds is much longer than those of urban investment bonds of bank loans issued to LGFVs. Infrastructure projects are usually long term in nature and switching to local government bonds reduces maturity mismatch and related liquidity and refinancing risks. Thirdly, at least in theory, local governments are more creditworthy than LGFVs that are companies, so the debt replacement helps increase the credit rating applied to the debt.

One of the objectives of debt replacement is to limit debt growth and to regulate borrowing, so the amount of replaceable debts issued by local governments is regulated. The central government has an overall cap on

[20] Zhang and Xiong (2019) calculated the "interest coverage ratio" of 1,109 UDICs, which is the ratio of company EBITDA or EBIT divided by interest expense. If this ratio is greater than 1, then the company has the ability to repay its interest.

the amount of replaceable bonds, and the amount is controlled by the State Council and needs to be approved by the Standing Committee of the National People's Congress. Under this overall cap, each province has its own cap set by the Ministry of Finance, according to local financial situation and risks. The advantage of this kind of cap is that it sets a hard limit and can't be exceeded. On the flip side, such a cap is rigid and inflexible, a province that have high-quality projects may not be funded because it has reached its debt cap, while another province can borrow more money to fund low-quality projects when under the cap.

The second reform was aimed at transforming the LGFVs, clarifying the relationship between them and the local government, removing their role as a borrowing vehicle for local governments and removing the implicit guarantee provided by local governments. A typical LGFV manages many projects, and some projects with a strong public service component can be passed directly to the local government to handle. The related debt could either be replaced by local government bonds, or be restructured to a PPP project. However, many LGFVs are heavily indebted and even local governments are only able to replace a small portion of their debts. If the remaining debts cannot be stripped away, it will be difficult for any transformation to succeed. Moreover, in order to turn a LGFV into an ordinary company, its business and governance structure must be transformed too. It must be able to make some profits and generate sufficient cash flow to survive, and it cannot be managed by local officials. So the transformation of LGFVs is not easy and still an ongoing project. During this reform period, in order to control debt growth, it's necessary to break the implicit debt guarantees from local governments. In a number of recent court cases, the guarantee letters provided by local governments have been rejected as invalid. In 2017, the Ministry of Finance investigated several cases of violations of the guarantee rule by local governments. For example, the finance bureau of Qianjiang District in Chongqing once issued a letter to guarantee the principal and interest payment of a debt instrument issued by a LGFV, as a result the associated people from both the government and the LGFV were punished.[21]

The third reform aimed to put constraints on banks and other financial institutions, preventing them from lending money to LGFVs. The

[21] For details, please refer to the article "Re-examination of Local Hidden Debts" in the 21st issue of Caixin Weekly in 2017.

difficulty in this reform is not related to supervising the banks themselves, rather to supervising various shadow banking businesses. Chapter 6 will discuss the relevant reforms in detail, including the "New Asset Management Regulations" introduced in 2018.

The fourth reform aims to hold local government officials to account for over-borrowing. This reform started in 2016. In 2018, the General Office of the Central Committee of CCP and the General Office of the State Council jointly issued the "Measures for Accountability of Local Government Hidden Debts". The new rule required local officials to understand that political achievements should not be measured by grandiose investment projects, and an increase in local debts must be controlled. The new rule also made local officials accountable for their over-borrowing. In recent years, some officials have indeed been held responsible, and the cases typically involve explicit debt guarantee documents issued by local governments, such as the case of QianJiang District government mentioned above. Such blatant violations of the rules are easy to identify and deal with, but those that are less obvious, such as following the book but eventually investing money in unprofitable projects, are difficult to supervise. Further reforms should be targeted at restricting and altering the impulse of officials to over-borrow and over-invest, but what are the institutional foundations of such an impulse?

Section 3: The Role of Local Officials in Attracting Investment

A few years ago, I attended a government meeting in central China aimed at pushing local officials to attract more investment to the region. A government official with a good track record of attracting investment shared some wisdom: "You must be sensitive to opportunities, be persistent and not give up easily. To be successful, you need to have a copper head, iron mouth, all-hearing ears, a rubber waist, teapot belly and rabbit legs". Having a copper head means being daring and able to push hard and create opportunities, while an iron mouth means someone who speaks well and can hold an argument. The having all-hearing ears and rabbit legs part refers to the need to be well informed and to travel a lot. The teapot belly refers to the need to be able to drink a lot to socialize and make deals. These descriptions are very vivid and easy to understand. However, I didn't quite understand what the "rubber waist" meant at the time, and the official explained to me as follows: "You must respect our guest businesspeople and be ready to bow down when necessary, but you shouldn't make too many concessions in the negotiation process. When it's time to straighten your waist (and stand firm) you must do so". These characteristics of the official reminded me of a salesman, whereas what he said next reminded me more of a customer service officer: "We must pay attention to etiquette, pay attention to details and do four things. First, we must keep our promises. Second, we must remember to return calls and reply messages from businesspeople in time. Third, we must deal with issues at the fastest speed and with the highest efficiency. Fourth, we should be a careful person and prepare in advance when visiting businesspeople".

Of course, when someone is speaking on stage, it's easy to speak as though everything makes perfect sense, but the reality is often a different story. Later in the trip, I had more interactions with the city's investment promotion officials. They were indeed very proactive and frequently made calls to their potential clients. Even if some firms or investors had already indicated that they were not willing to invest in the area, the officials would call again offering new or improved terms. They constantly tested new ideas and did not give up easily. During the trip, I learned that the city government has developed and streamlined its investment promotion process and designed a series of effective incentive mechanisms (money and promotion to officials). Even though this particular city does not have much resources and endowments for economic development, it does a good job in terms of attracting investment.

China has a huge and complex bureaucratic system that has been one of the backbones of both politics and society since ancient times. It is a tradition that social elites work for the government, and the bureaucratic system has abundant human resources available. According to the sixth census in 2010, roughly 22% of the urban population aged 22–59 had a college degree, but this percentage was over 50% among government workers. Among those aged 25–40, more than 70% of government workers hold a college degree, compared to only 30% of the total urban population of the same age.[22] Although in today's diversified Chinese society there are many different opportunities available for bright young

[22] The educational attainment data of the urban population come from the "China 2010 Population Census Documents" published by the National Bureau of Statistics. The data of government workers come from micro-data of the Chinese General Social Survey from 2006 to 2013.

talent, the tradition and values associated with becoming an official still exist today. The government is still the most influential and resourceful organization in the country, so the yearly civil service entrance exam is extremely popular and competitive. Only those with a college degree or above can take the exam, and the admission rate is extremely low.

This section focuses on local government officials. In terms of population, local officials compose the largest part of China's bureaucracy. In the total number of civil servants, the central government accounts for only 6%, and if various other public institutions affiliated to government (*shi ye dan wei*) are counted, the central government workers account for only 4%. This is an anomaly among major countries. Central government officials account for 19% in the US, 14% in Japan and 11% in Germany. In fact, the OECD average is as high as 41%.[23]

Local Officials Performance Management and Incentive Mechanism

People are the core of any government system and how to choose the right people, and how to incentivize them to do the right things is a key determinant of government efficiency. To put it simply, an incentive mechanism is nothing more than offering carrots and sticks. What's the reward if something is done well? And what's the punishment if something is done badly? Since economic development is the core task of local government, individual gains and loss need to be linked closely to the local economy, both for government leaders and for ordinary workers.

From the perspective of "carrots", economic development is the main priority of local governments, and a leader's performance in driving economic growth plays an important role in their promotion and reputation. For ordinary government workers, there are few opportunities for promotion, but their salary and compensation are still closely related to the local fiscal revenue and to the performance of their individual department, which in turn are all related to the state of the local economy. From the perspective of "sticks", on the one hard there is discipline inspection from the party and anti-corruption laws from the state; on the other hand there is fierce competition between regions to attract investment and business. In order to prevent the loss of industry and investment to

[23] These figures are from an article by former Minister of Finance Lou (楼继伟 2018).

competing regions, officials need to improve the local business environment and government efficiency. If a department harms the local business environment in pursuit of its own goals, or if disputes between departments reduce government efficiency, the top leaders would intervene to maintain the overall performance.

The term of local leaders is limited, and in order to boost economic growth during their tenure, leaders have little choice but to increase investment and launch some expensive projects. Taking the Party Secretary and Mayor of a city as an example, the average tenure in one city is around 3 to 4 years, but even with the most optimistic estimate, any large industrial or infrastructure projects will take 2 to 3 years to complete. Therefore, in the first two years of a term, industrial or infrastructural investment and local fiscal expenditure tend to rise rapidly. On average, around 30% of cities need to replace their mayor or party secretary every year, meaning there will be continuous boosts to investment happening across China, and there are salient political business cycles in macroeconomic data.[24] Investment requires capital, and land finance and real estate development plays a critical role in providing this capital. Therefore, in the first years after leaders take office, land sales tend to increase. Most of the new land supply is necessarily located in suburbs around the city, leading to a situation of urban sprawl that increases commuting times, makes city traffic more crowded and costly, and has an overall negative effect on the environment.[25]

Although leaders' motivation for being promoted does not conflict with economic development and can even be used to explain a large portion of regional economic growth, this investment-heavy growth

[24] Yao and Zhang (姚洋和张牧扬 2013) collected data on 1,671 mayors and party secretaries of 241 cities from 1994 to 2008, and they found that their average tenure in a city was 3.8 years, and the median was 3 years. Yang et al. (杨海生等 2014) collected data on the mayors and party secretaries of nearly 400 prefecture-level cities from 1999 to 2013, and found that on average, nearly 30% of these cities have at least one leader shift every year. A large number of studies have shown that regional economic indicators vary with the tenure of local leaders. Readers can refer to the summary of these studies in Chapter 6 of Zhou's book (周黎安 2017).

[25] Wang, Zhang and Zhou (2020) found that there is a positive relationship between the promotion of city leaders and the expansion of the urban area they manage.

model can have many adverse consequences.[26] Before 2016, leaders were no longer accountable for debts created in office after being promoted or transferred to a new place, and new leaders usually continued to borrow and invest on top of predecessors' debt, so government debt was continuously rising. Beyond a certain stage of economic development, the number of low-risk and high-return industrial projects will decrease, and the benefits accruing from more urban infrastructure will also start to decrease. Continuing to invest heavily will lead to overcapacity and lower overall efficiency. In addition, due to performance assessment considerations, local leaders often focus on highly visible infrastructural projects such as roads, bridges, parks or subways, while paying relatively little attention to invisible projects such as underground pipes. As a result, when it rains heavily, many cities are susceptible to flooding.[27]

Since the incentives for local leaders significantly affect local government investment, major structural reforms of recent years, including deleveraging, capacity and inventory reductions, have also been accompanied by a change in the performance assessment for local leaders. In 2013, the Organization Department of the Central Committee issued the "Notice on Improving the Performance Evaluation of Local Party and Government Leaders", which emphasized that "Regional GDP growth cannot be the only major indicator for assessing political performance. The regional ranking of GDP and GDP growth should not be used. Relevant central departments should not simply measure the effectiveness of provincial development based on the level of provincial GDP and the growth rate of GDP. Local party committees and governments at all levels cannot simply evaluate and rank lower-level leaders by GDP performance". After this change in performance assessment metrics, and after a series of fiscal and financial reforms related to local debts, growth rates of regional GDP and fixed asset investment begun to decline.[28]

[26] There are many studies on the relationship between the promotion of leaders at province, city or county levels and local economic performance. Zhou's book (周黎安 2017) summarizes this literature.

[27] Xu and Ma (徐业坤和马光源 2019) studied the relationship between official turnover and overcapacity of local industrial firms. Wu and Zhou (吴敏和周黎安 2018) studied the relationship between the promotion of officials and the investment in visible urban infrastructural projects.

[28] After 2013, growth rates of GDP and investment at province and city levels started to decline. For this phenomenon and explanations, please refer to the paper by Zhang et al. (张军等 2020).

In 2019, the General Office of the Central Committee of the Chinese Communist Party issued the "Regulations on the Assessment of Leading Party and Government Officials", which clearly stated that when assessing performance of local party and government leaders, a more holistic set of criteria should be considered, including "economic development, political development, cultural development, social development, as well as environmental protection, solving problems related to unbalance and inequality, and better serving people's need for a better life".

Although political and economic performance is important in the evaluation and promotion of local leaders, personal connections and relationships are also important. Whether it be a company or a government, so long as work performance cannot be 100% quantified, then the subjective evaluation and impression of a supervisor will always be important, and the relationship with the supervisor will be important. These subjective relationships and objective performances may be mutually reinforcing: the supervisor values good performance, and support from the supervisor also helps to deliver good performance. However, if some leaders use cronyism to appoint subordinates that help expand their personal power and influence, instead of rewarding performance, it may dampen the work incentives of their subordinates. In places where cronyism is prevalent, the bureaucratic system would try to restrict the leaders' irresponsible decisions. It might put more weights on seniority in promotion, since age and tenure of service are objective and transparent that can't be modified. But this change will also reduce work incentives and overall government efficiency.[29]

Although human relationships will have an impact on a local region's political and economic environment, I am skeptical that it has a big enough impact to explain overall national economic development. On the one hand, there is a competitive between different regions, which puts some hard constraints on officials' behavior. On the other hand, political connections rely on some core people in the network, and the uncertainty related to these key players' career would spread to the whole network.

[29] When officials are considered for promotion in China, both political achievements and personal connections are important, and in fact they are complementary (Jia, Kudamatsu and Seim 2015). For some economic theories of human relationships and work performance in organizations, see Prendergast and Topel (1996), as well as Chen, Fan and Zhu (2020).

Once key person succeeds, cronies would be lifted into powerful positions; but once he fails, so would his cronies. But regardless of whoever behind the helm, government works continue, and leaders must continue to focus on developing the economy.

Being recognized for political achievements and promotion are undoubtedly important for members of local government leadership teams, but they are not sufficient to motivate the vast majority of government workers. For the average worker, day-to-day work bears little relation to political performance and chances for promotion are slim. County-level or above leaders account for only 1% of the total government workforce. Therefore, the most important incentive for most government workers is not promotion, but rather the income and perks. These include salaries, bonuses, allowances, subsidies, free food and comfortable offices, etc. These income and perks are closely linked to the local economic and fiscal conditions and can vary widely between regions and even between different departments in the same region. Most government workers can see the extra benefit of working for a thriving region and thriving department, and this helps to remind them of working to develop the economy. If some departments harm the local business environment, they will be subject to supervision and criticism.

Economists typically pay attention to tangible rewards and punishments, emphasizing external incentives and the institutional environment, but in reality, intrinsic motivation is also very important. No organization, whether it be government or business, can motivate employees solely through external rewards and punishments. External rewards and punishments necessarily require work performance to be highly visible and measurable, but most work cannot be clearly measured, so it needs a sense of mission, vision and values related to inner feelings to motivate staff. "Remain true to original aspiration", "patriotism" and "serve the people" are all mottos devised to capture the emotions of government employees. The selection and promotion of officials emphasizes "both integrity and ability, with priority given to integrity", which also emphasizes the importance of intrinsic motivation and self-discipline.[30]

[30] David Kreps at Stanford University is a leading economist on economic theories of incentive. However, in his popular little book on incentives (Kreps 2018), the "external incentive" (incentive) emphasized in economics is only a small piece of the puzzle, the major part of the book discusses "inner drive" (motivation) emphasized in psychology and management science.

Corruption and Anti-Corruption

A major drawback of the land finance development model is the corruption that it spawns. Transactions related to land are often large in size and concentrated in the hands of a few officials, which provides a fertile breeding ground for corruption. Most of the major corruption cases investigated in recent years have been related to land. From 2008 to 2013 nearly 50% of the corruption cases reported by the Supreme People's Procuratorate were related to land transfer and sales.[31] With the rise of local government financing vehicles, funds from corruption can more easily be hidden via financial transactions and various financing instruments, making the whole corruption process more secretive and difficult to discover. Since the Communist Party's 18th National Congress, "anti-corruption" has become one of the key themes of Chinese politics and the campaign has maintained its momentum ever since. As of the end of 2019, a total of 156,000 officials at the county-level and above leadership had been investigated, including 18,000 at the city-level leadership and 414 top officials directly affiliated with the center of the party.[32]

From an economic development perspective, corruption in China has two notable characteristics. First, corruption and rapid economic growth have co-existed for a long time, something that conflicts with the oversimplified narrative that corruption hampers economic growth. Predictions that corruption will lead to fall of China's economy have also repeatedly failed to come true. Second, with reforms going forward, the relationship between the market and the government is constantly changing, which means the forms of corruption also evolve. Most of the corruption cases in the 1980s were related to the downfall of officials who took advantage of the loopholes in the dual price system and made illegal deals. Cases in the 1990s were mainly related to the reform of state-owned enterprises and the loss of state-owned assets. Since the twenty-first century, corruption cases related to land transfer and sale have become more and more prevalent.[33]

[31] The data come from Chen and Zhu (陈硕和朱琳 2020).

[32] The data are from the website of the Central Commission for Discipline Inspection and State Supervision Commission.

[33] For detailed data and analysis of various forms of corruption since the reform and opening up, please refer to the works of Chen and Zhu (陈硕和朱琳 2020) and Ang (2020).

The key to understanding the relationship between corruption and economic development is to understand the effect of different types of corruption has on the economy. Roughly speaking, there are two types of corruption. The first type can be labeled as "predatory corruption" and relies on extorting people or private enterprise, taking bribes or embezzling public funds. This type of corruption hurts economic growth and lowers trust in the protection of property rights. With the continuous improvement of political and legal institutes in China, and with the development of supervisions techniques, this type of corruption has become much less common. As an example, in the 1980s and 1990s, there were many irregular fines and arbitrary charges made by local government. As a common response, people might pay cash bribes to officials as a way to avoid higher fines or charges. Nowadays, this kind of situation is much less common. Any such government fine must now have related documents and evidence, and the payment should be made at a bank or via mobile phone to a specific government account. This transparent process leaves little room for corruption. In China, there is little petty corruption that might be found in some other developing countries, for example police asking for money when stopping someone, or passengers placing money inside passports when going through immigration clearance. In recent years, China's environment of doing business has greatly improved. According to the Ease of Doing Business Index published by the World Bank, China has risen from 89th place in 2010 to 31st in 2020. The foreign direct investment (FDI) entering China has remained high, at around 130 billion USD per year during recent years.

The second type of corruption can be labeled as "crony capitalism", a mutually advantageous relationship between government officials and businesspeople. For example, officials might grant licenses for projects to business friends. In return, the businesspeople must not only finish the projects that contribute to the official's political achievements, and they also pass a lot of the benefits to officials in private. This type of corruption occurs in the process of investment and these investments can stimulate local economic growth, so corruption can co-exist with economic growth for a period of time. However, from the perspective of the long-term sustainable development of the economy, this type of corruption can do four types of harm. First, officials always want to invest more, which has distorted the economic structure, with a high proportion of income accruing to owners of capital at the expense of workers. As a result the growth of household income and consumption has been slow. Chapter 7 will discuss this distortion. Second, it distorts the allocation of investment and credits, wasting a lot of money on projects with a low return. This pushes up the overall level of debt and risk in the economy. Chapter 6 will discuss this debt risk. Third, this cronyism widens inequality between rich and poor. Chapter 5 will analyze the impact of this inequality on economic development. Fourth, local interest groups may not only corrupt the local economy but also corrupt the local politics, and could potentially lead to political instability. Since the Communist Party's 18th Congress, the party's Central Committee has emphasized over and over that gangs, factions and interest groups are not allowed to exist within the party. A close but clean relationship between the politics and business must be established.

The anti-corruption campaign since the 18th Party Congress is part of a broader system of reforms, these include not only structural economic reforms such as "deleveraging" and reducing financial risk, but also reforms related to the markets of various factors of production, especially to the land markets. The goal of these reforms is to move China away from its old economic development model, so it's necessary to remove interest groups that formed under the old model. Before the reforms are completed, anti-corruption pressures will remain high. In 2020, researchers from Harvard University released the results of an independent poll of urban and rural residents in China. The survey begun in 2003 and interviewed more than 30,000 people. The survey results show that the anti-corruption achievements since the 18th Party Congress have been widely appreciated. In 2016, about 65% of respondents believed that local officials were relatively clean, up from 35% in 2011.[34] Overall satisfaction with central government has been high for a long time, at around 83%. The satisfaction with local governments is lower, around 78% for provincial governments and 70% for county and township governments.

However, before the transformation has been completed, local government officials who are used to working under the old model may tend to shirk from their duties for fear of making mistakes and being labeled corrupt. In 2016, the central government begun to emphasize that "shirking or slackness" is also a form of corruption, and that an official must take his job seriously and work hard. In 2018, the General Office

[34] Data are from the report by Cunningham, Saich and Turiel (2020).

of the Central Committee of the Communist Party issued the "Opinions on Further Incentivizing Officials to Take New Responsibilities and Actions in the New Era" emphasizing the need to "establish a more failure tolerant system, that tolerate mistakes made in the process of reform and innovation, encourage officials to more proactively try new ideas and learn from mistakes, while not being held back by a lack of experience. Mistakes that occur in the process of trial and error should be distinguished from knowing violations of party discipline. Mistakes that occur in experiments when rules are not clearly defined should be distinguished from those where clear legal and political boundaries are intentionally broken. Accidental mistakes that occur during pushing development should be distinguished from those deliberate violation of laws and disciplines in pursuit of private benefits". It remains to be seen what the impact of this new system will be.

With 40 years of astonishing economic development, social wealth has grown rapidly, and corruption is inevitable. In the so-called Gilded Age that ran from the late nineteenth to early twentieth century in the US, various types of corruption were also commonplace. Nepotism was common, and the economy corrupted politics, which in turn further corrupted the economy, resulting in systemic corruption. Only after decades of improvements to both the political and legal systems did the corruption start to gradually ease.[35] From a long-term perspective, removing corruption is part of government capacity building. In addition to building institutions that can root out corruption, more fundamental measures are needed such as delegating power to other market entities and reducing intervention in the market. Or in other words, the role of government in the economy must be transformed. As put forward in the 19th Party Congress in 2017, "the government needs to transform its functions, further streamline administration and delegate powers, develop new ways of regulation and supervision, and strengthen its credibility and administrative capacity, building itself into a service-oriented government able to satisfy the needs of the people".

[35] On corruption and governance in the US during this period, please refer to an excellent paper by John Wallis (Wallis 2006).

Summary

After the 1994 tax sharing reform, financial power was increasingly concentrated in the hands of the central government, but through tax rebates and transfer payments, local governments had sufficient funds to maintain operations. But almost all provinces, regardless of fiscal revenue, are all experiencing rapid expansion of debt. Therefore the root of the debt problem is not insufficient fiscal revenue, rather too much investment expenditure, on which local governments rely to boost economic development. Therefore, the debt problem is not a simple "soft budget constraint" problem that can be fixed by changing fiscal budget rules and laws, but a fundamental issue that has more to do with the role that local governments must play in China's economy. The way of reform lies in reducing government tasks and further delegating power to other market entities. At the same time, the government needs to transform from a production/investment-orientated government to one focused more on providing public service to the people.

Debts and assets are the two sides of the same coin. After understanding the debt problem of local governments, it's also necessary to know the assets produced from government borrowing and investment, including both infrastructure and other industrial firms. Regarding to infrastructure investment, it's better to calculate not only the project-level financial returns (which may be low), but also the overall benefits brought to the economy and to society (which may be much higher). However, there is no consensus on how to evaluate these social and macroeconomic benefits, so the values of many infrastructural projects are always open to debate. In the end, population density and utilization rates always play a big role when evaluating infrastructure. Building a subway in a small city, building multiple huge new urban districts in a medium-sized city or building industrial parks well away from critical supply chains is obviously questionable and makes little economic sense, regardless of the promised benefits. As for the government investments in industrial firms, excess capital can lead to over-expansion and excess production capacity, leading to oversupply of products and collapsing prices. However, on the other hand, the large flow of capital can help industries grow rapidly and even become world leaders, which also boosts economic growth and technology advancement. Some examples are high-speed rail, photovoltaics and LCD/LED/OLED displays. I will tell these industrial stories in the next chapter.

Further Readings

The topics discussed in this chapter, including demolition work, attracting investment, local government debt, household registration and urbanization, etc., all can be found in an excellent documentary film called *The Chinese Mayor* (中国市长) by director Zhou Hao (周浩). The film traces the story of Geng Yanbo, the ex-major of Datong city, through his process of rebuilding the city. In 2013, Geng Yanbo was transferred away from Datong and nearly 10 years have passed since that day. Today if you look on the internet, the comments about the rebuilding process and about Geng himself are mixed. Comparing these current comments with the past stories and conflicts presented in the film is very thought provoking.

Yuen Yuen Ang's book (Ang 2020), *China's Gilded Age, the Paradox of Economic Boom and Vast Corruption*, discusses various types of corruption in China in recent years. It also has a comparison of corruption in China, with that carried out in the US both in the past and during the present day. It explains why corruption and economic growth can co-exist in China. This book is also a comprehensive review of the current literature on corruption.

Land is rarely emphasized in mainstream economic textbooks. With regard to production and income distribution, generally only labor and capital are analyzed as factors of production and land is simply considered as one kind of capital. In classical economics, including Marxist economics, land and capital are treated separately and landlords and capitalists are two types of people. This change in emphasis is related to the stage of economic development: modern economies are dominated by industry and services, and agriculture plays only a minor role, so land, which is the most important factor of production for agriculture, has been merged into a more general concept of capital. However, land has some crucial differences from typical capital goods, its supply is fixed and generally doesn't depreciate in value. Indeed land, in the form of real estate, has become one of the most important components of national wealth across countries. It deserves to be treated more seriously by mainstream micro- and macroeconomics, instead of being isolated as some "field topic" in urban economics. The book by a group of Britain economists (Ryan-Collins, Lloyd and Macfarlane 2017), *Rethinking the Economics of Land and Housing*, is a useful start.

References

Ang, Yuen Yuen (2020). *China's Gilded Age: the Paradox of Economic Boom and Vast Corruption*. Cambridge University Press.

Bai, Chong-En, Chang-Tai Hsieh, and Zheng Song (2016). "The Long Shadow of a Fiscal Expansion". *Brookings Papers on Economic Activity*, Fall: 129–165.

Chen, Shuo, Xinyu Fan, Zhitao Zhu (2020). "The Promotion Club," *Working paper*.

Cunningham, Edward, Tony Saich, and Jesse Turiel (2020). "Understanding CCP Resilience: Surveying Chinese Public Opinion through Time." *Harvard Kennedy School Ash Center Policy Report*.

De Soto, Hernando (2003). *The Mystery of Capital: Why Capitalism Triumphs in the West and Fails Everywhere Else*. Basic Books.

Jia, Ruixue, Masayuki Kudamatsu, and David Seim (2015). "Political Selection in China: the Complementary Roles of Connections and Performance." *Journal of the European Economic Association*, 13.4: 631–668.

Kreps, David (2018). *The Motivation Toolkit: How to Align Your Employees' Interests with Your Own*. Findaway World, LLC.

Prendergast, Canice, and Robert Topel (1996). "Favoritism in Organizations." *Journal of Political Economy* 104.5: 958–978.

Ryan-Collins, Josh, Toby Lioyd, and Laurie Macfarlane (2017). *Rethinking the Economics of Land and Housing*. Zed Books.

Wallis, John J. (2006). "The Concept of Systematic Corruption in American History." *Corruption and Reform: Lessons from America's Economic History*. University of Chicago Press: 23–62.

Wang, Zhi, Qinghua Zhang, and Li-An Zhou (2020). "Career Incentives of City Leaders and Urban Spatial Expansion in China." *The Review of Economics and Statistics* 102.5: 897–911.

Zhang, Zhiwei, and Yi Xiong (2019). "Infrastructure Financing," *Working paper*.

Translated References (in Chinese)

Chen, Shuo, and Lin Zhu (2020). "Market Transformation and Governance Corruption: Based on Individual Evidence of Officials," Fudan University School of Economics Discussion Paper. (in Chinese)

Dang, Junzhang, and Qinghua Wang (2010), "Analysis on the Risk of Local Governments' Financing Platform." *The Chinese Banker* 4: 11–16+6. (in Chinese)

Editorial Board (2013). *The History of China Development Bank: 1994–2012*. China Financial Publishing House. (in Chinese)

Hong, Zheng, Shuonan Zhang, and Lin Zhang (2017). "Economic Structure, Fiscal Capacity and the Local Government's Financial Holding Pattern of City Commercial Bank." *Journal of Financial Research* 10: 83–98. (in Chinese)

Jiang, Chao, Zhengxing Zhu, and Jia Du (2018). "The Scale of the Potential Debt of Local Government," Haitong Securities. (in Chinese)

Lou, Jiwei (2018). "On the Reform of Intergovernmental Function Assignment and Fiscal Responsibility." *Comparative Studies* 4. (in Chinese)

Lu, Ming (2016). *Great State Needs Bigger City*. Shanghai People's Publishing House. (in Chinese)

Wu, Min, Li-An Zhou (2018). "Political Incentives and City Construction: The Visibility of Public Projects." *Economic Research Journal* 12: 97–111. (in Chinese)

Xu, Yekun, and Guangyuan Ma (2019). "Local Officials 'Turnover and Enterprises' Overcapacity." *Economic Research Journal* l5: 129–145. (in Chinese)

Yang, Haisheng, Shaoling Chen, Luo Danglun, and She Guoman (2014). "Between the Policy lnstability and the Economic Growth: The Empirical Evidence from China's Change in Her Local Officers." *Journal of Management World* 9: 13–28+187–188. (in Chinese)

Yao, Yang, and Muyang Zhang (2013). "Performance of Officials and the Promotion Tournament: Evidence from Chinese Cities." *Economic Research Journal* 1: 137–150. (in Chinese)

Zhang, Jun, Haichao Fan, Zhiwei Xu, and Longfei Zhou (2020). "Structural Decline in the GDP Growth Rate: The Impact of the Official Assessment Mechanism." *Economic Research Journal* 5: 31–48. (in Chinese)

Zhang, Wuchang (2019). *Economic Explanation (2019 updated version)*. China CITIC Press. (in Chinese)

Zheng, Siqi, Weizeng Sun, Jing Wu, and Yun Wu (2014). "Infrastructure Investment, Land Leasing and Real Estate Price: A Unique Financing and Investment Channel for Urban Development in Chinese Cities." *Economic Research Journal* 8: 14–27. (in Chinese)

Zhou, Li-An (2017). *Local Governments in Transition: Officials' Incentives and Governance* (2nd ed.). Truth & Wisdom Press. (in Chinese)

CHAPTER 4

The Role of Government in Industrialization

At the beginning of 2019, I visited Taipei and met a local executive of an American company who exclaimed: "The economics on your mainland (China) is different from what I studied at Harvard Business School - markets, competition, supply and demand – your mainland companies receive government subsidies and support, how can we be expected to win such competition? You cannot do that all the time, otherwise our companies will die!" I was a little taken aback by the dramatic turn of phrase and replied: "Mr. X, companies are not human beings, companies do not really die. It's not a matter of life and death, it's simply a case of resource reallocation and reorganization. Now, the wages given to Taiwanese engineers on the mainland are higher than before, and the product quality of mainland companies is higher than before, and the price is also cheaper. Shouldn't it be considered a good thing? Last year your company started to build a new factory in Wuhan, and the project needed an investment of 10 billion yuan. When your colleagues asked for subsidies from the local government, they were very tough negotiators, and I didn't hear any talk of it not being a market economy then!" The manager replied: "Who wouldn't try to take more subsidies? Hey, don't go back to the government and tell them not to subsidize us".

In the real world, away from textbooks, there is no clear demarcation between the government and the market, only various forms of interconnected interests and relationships. The starting point for China's

X. Lan, *How China Works*,
https://doi.org/10.1007/978-981-97-0080-6_4

economic reform was a planned economy, so governments own a lot of resources including land, finance intermediaries and state-owned enterprises, it's therefore inevitable that governments play a major role in the industrialization process. As we learned in Chapter 3, industrial investment is much more complicated than simple financial investment. It is a continuous process that requires constant input and management, and a mistake at any stage may damage the whole project. As a result, the Chinese government's involvement in the economy is deep, and its relationships with various firms are close and complex, it's therefore not easy for the government to just step aside and watch the market play.

In each specific industry, factors such as technology, resources, as well as historical development path, all affect the way that governments interact with enterprises. What happens in the steel industry won't be the same as what happens in the chip industry. It's therefore unconvincing to abstract the analysis of government intervention in the economy and industrial policy from industrial specifics, otherwise it would be easy to reach conclusions which prove to be too general. Social phenomena are complex and changeable, and for any theories, there are always many counterexamples or counterarguments. There are always many other variables not included in the theory, not least people, but also geography, weather and pure luck. Uncertainty has a great impact on real-life results, and these results almost always dominate the final evaluations and judgments of related theories and practices. Only the final success can justify certain industrial policies, and even in that case, these policies are usually only successful in the eyes of their beneficiaries. Just like anything else in a market economy, successes and failures are both common in industrial policy. If we simply use market successes to criticize policy failures, or we use policy successes to criticize market failures, the debate would be endless.

The focus of this chapter is therefore on specific case studies. How can industries and enterprises in China use the government to help in their development? What specific policies have been implemented? How does government invest and exit, and how do they affect the rise and fall of industries as well as the adoption of new technologies? To start with we must understand the basic facts and underlying experiences before we can judge any results. Mathematical models and statistics may be popular in economics, but they are not the only form of reasoning nor are they always the best form available. Concrete stories or case studies may be more powerful than an abstract mathematical model.[1] When researching industries, case studies often contain a lot of information that is missing in an abstract theory, especially the information of leading companies. Statistical analysis often relies on data from financial statements, and it tends to focus on averages. But the conclusions we can draw from averages are limited. Most industries operate on an 80/20 basis, and what applies to the bottom 80 has little relation to the top 20. Financial data also fail to accurately capture the complexity of large enterprises, which are often standard setters for the industry, drivers and platforms of technological innovation and adoption, and the center of supply chains. Their relationships with government are always deep and complex, even in market-driven economies such as the US.

The first two sections of this chapter are specific industry case studies: LCD displays and the solar power industry. The starting point for the case studies is again the financing and investment of local governments. Readers will once again be able to see the critical role of local government financing vehicles or urban investment corporations, as well as the role of governments in attracting investment and the role of land finance in providing funds. However, this time, the targets for investment are not industrial parks or infrastructure, but rather specific industrial firms. The third section of the chapter will introduce the model of government industrial investment funds that has started to emerge in recent years. This kind of fund is not only a new way of attracting investment and a new tool of industrial policy, but also an innovative method of using fiscal funds in a more market-orientated way.

Section 1: The Story of BOE and Government Investment

During the annual Singles Day sale in 2020, Dell's 27-inch high-definition LCD screen sold for 949 yuan on Alibaba's TMall shopping platform. Back in 2008, Dell's 27-inch monitor sold for 7,599 yuan and it was not high-definition. In 2020, you can buy a 70-inch high-definition LCD TV for 3,000 yuan from various domestic Chinese firms. Back in 2008, however, only Samsung and Sony had the capability to produce

[1] For a more detailed explanation, please refer to the paper of Nobel Prize winner George Akerlof (2020) or the book of another Nobel Prize winner, Robert Shiller (2020).

such a large LCD screen. At the time, the price was close to 400,000 yuan, more than 100× the price today. In fact, at that time, 400,000 yuan could buy half a small apartment in Shanghai or Beijing.

Behind this huge drop in price are two key factors, firstly technological progress and secondly, substitution for domestic supply. For monitors and TVs, nearly 80% of hardware costs come from the LCD panel. In 2008, industry was dominated by Japanese, Korean and Taiwanese firms and mainland Chinese company's share of the market was negligible. In 2012, the total value of LCD panels imported to China was 50 billion USD, behind only integrated circuits, oil and iron ore in terms of import volume. However, by 2020, China had become the world largest producer of LCD panels, and the market share of Chinese companies in the global market had risen to 40%, completely reducing the need to import. Several world leading firms emerged in China, such as BOE, TCL-CSOT, TIANMA and Visionox. The development of a domestic Chinese LCD panel industry not only drove down the prices of monitors and TVs, but also helped to lower the costs for domestic mobile phone producers such as Xiaomi and Huawei, thereby helping contribute to the rise of many Chinese consumer brands relying on LCD screens.

Local governments in China have played a key role in enabling the development of the LCD industry. If we take BOE, the largest and most important company in the industry, as an example. Its sales of LCD screens in mobile phones, televisions, tablet computers and notebook computers have consistently ranked first in the world in recent years.[2] According to BOE's financial report from the third quarter of 2020, the top 6 investors are all state-owned investment companies located in Beijing, Chongqing and Hefei. Combined, these state-owned investment companies own a 23.8% stake of BOE. Among them are general investment groups (Beijing State-Owned Capital Operation and Management Co. Ltd), industrial groups in specific industries (Beijing Electronics Holding Co. Ltd), and also local urban investment corporations discussed in Chapter 3 (Hefei Construction Investment Co. and Yufu Holdings in Chongqing). Different funds may employ different investment methods, for example purchasing equity directly from the company or investing indirectly through third-party funds (see Section 4.3 of this chapter).

[2] The data come from an industry analysis report by Yuan Jiancong et al. at CITIC Securities (袁健聪等人 2020).

The Story of BOE and Local Government Investment

In the late 1990s and early 2000s, the TV industry in China was still fighting various price wars. At the time, most factories in China were still making bulky (CRT) TVs. A large number of factories were built and their products flooded the domestic market. However, in the international market, the technology had already upgraded to focus on flat-screen LCD TVs and the trend was irreversible. At the time, mainland China lacked the capability to produce LCD display panels, which accounts for roughly 70–80% of the flat-screen TVs, and therefore relied entirely on imports. It had taken nearly 20 years for China to localize the 95% of the value chain for colored CRT TVs, but now falling behind in LCD technology, the country once again had to rely on imports for 80% of the value chain.[3] At the time, the major manufacturers were located in Taiwan, Japan and South Korea, and they jointly manipulated prices and sales. From 2001 to 2006, six major companies, including South Korea's Samsung, held 53 special meetings in Taiwan and South Korea to manipulate prices, and at times the LCD panel reached 80% of the production cost of a flat-screen TV. In 2013, the National Development and Reform Commission fined the six companies 350 million yuan in accordance with the Price Law (at the time of the price manipulation, there was no anti-monopoly law in China, which only went into effect after 2008). The European Union and US also fined these companies 650 million Euros and 1.3 billion dollars, respectively.[4]

With this market context as background, BOE Technology Group, a company that possesses independent R&D capability, has gradually come to the fore of the industry. The predecessor of BOE is an old state-owned enterprise called Beijing Electron Tube Factory. After continuous reforms and constant struggles, by the beginning of the 2000s, the company had developed the capability to make small LCD display panels. Most of these capabilities originated from the 5th generation production line built in 2005 in Beijing's Yizhuang Special Development Zone. This was only

[3] The data come from the masterpiece of LCD industrial history written by Lu Feng (路风 2016). Unless otherwise specified, the history of BOE's development in this section mainly comes from his book.

[4] See the report published by Caixin.com on January 4, 2013, "Development and Reform Commission Answers Questions about Samsung and Others Monopoly LCD Panel Prices", and the report from China Trade on August 2, 2016, "Chinese Enterprises Face Three Challenges and Four Risks on Anti-monopoly".

the second 5th generation line built in China, and at the time it was very advanced, only 3 years later than the first 5th generation line in the world, built by LG in South Korea.[5] The production line had been purchased from a Korean company, and the related investment was large. The original plan had been to finance the investment through a public market listing in Hong Kong, however the transaction fell through. The construction of the production line had already started, and many orders of equipment had been placed. Therefore, the Beijing city government and China Development Bank put together a consortium of 9 banks, led by the Beijing branch of China Construction Bank, that loaned 740 million USD to BOE. In addition to this loan, the Beijing city government also loaned 280 million yuan to BOE. And this loan was operated through the Beijing Industrial Development Investment Management Co. Ltd, a wholly owned subsidiary of the Beijing State-Owned Assets Supervision and Administration Commission. The government loan was later converted to shares of the company, and it proved to be profitable when the stake was later sold on the secondary market. During the construction of the 5th generation line, the Beijing city government also subsidized interest payments of the loan, with a value totaling 180 million yuan, and the city finance bureau provided a special subsidy fund worth 53.27 million yuan.[6]

But things did not work out as planned. BOE's 5th generation line didn't work out well. The timing couldn't have been worse, investment was at the peak of the industrial cycles, but production only started after the demand fell. The price of BOE's flagship product, a 17-inch display, dropped from 300 dollars per piece when the construction of the production line started, to 150 dollars per piece by the time BOE had reached mass production scale. In 2005 and 2006 alone, BOE lost 3.3 billion yuan and the Beijing government was no longer able to help. If the syndicated bank loan of 740 million USD had to be repaid on time, without extension to the term, BOE would have faced a huge risk of bankruptcy. However, any extension to the term of the loan required the approval of

[5] To explain in simple terms, the higher the X number in the "X generation line", the larger the screen the line can produce. For example, the flagship product of the 5th generation line is a 17-inch screen, and the main product of the 6th generation line is a 32-inch screen.

[6] The figures regarding loans and subsidies come from Caixin.com's article "Crazy LCD" published on April 16, 2007.

all 9 participating banks. In initial discussions, the smallest bank with the lowest capital contribution disagreed with extending the loan, and only after multiple rounds of negotiations was an agreement finally reached. The difficulties and risks experienced during this struggle led BOE to change its financing strategy. The construction of several future production lines used equity financing. When BOE plans to build a new factory in a city, it would first secure sufficient capital from the local government, before seeking commercial loan financing.

In 2008, BOE decided to build a 4.5th generation production line in Chengdu, using it to test a new model of financing for the first time. The total investment in the production line was 3.4 billion yuan, of which 1.8 billion yuan was from selling newly issued equities privately to two Chengdu urban investment corporations. The remaining 1.6 billion yuan was financed through a syndicated loan from a group banks led by China Development Bank. The two urban investment corporations were Chengdu Industrial Investment Group, a wholly owned subsidiary of the Chengdu city government, and Chengdu High-Tech Investment Group, a wholly owned subsidiary of Chengdu's High-Tech Development Zone. These companies not only run a large number of businesses related to land development and financing (such as the businesses discussed in Chapter 3), but are also among the most important local state-owned vehicles of industrial investment. Compared to the 5th generation line built in Beijing, the Chengdu production line had a much better supply of capital and the construction timing also proved to be better. This new production line focused mainly on small sized LCD screens and was ready just in time for the boom in smartphones.

However, at the time, the most lucrative LCD market was still the TV market, especially for 27 and 32-inch screens. For these sizes China still mainly relied on imports. To construct a 6th generation production line capable of producing large LCD screens of this size required an investment of over 10 billion yuan, and where to find the money was a big problem. Between 2005 and 2006, a group of Chinese TV producers, such as Skyworth, TCL, Konka and Changhong, decided to solve the import problem jointly, starting a project jointly with BOE to build a 6th generation line in Shenzhen, with the help from the financially resourceful city government of Shenzhen. After news of the project leaked out, a Japanese company, Sharp, immediately began to lobby the Shenzhen government, promising to build a 7.5th generation line with a total investment of 28 billion yuan. Since Sharp's capability and experience was vastly superior to BOE, the Shenzhen government signed an agreement with Sharp in 2007, and the joint project with BOE was canceled. But just one month later, Sharp terminated the agreement with the Shenzhen government. At the same time, Shanghai Radio and Television and Investment Co. Ltd was also planning to build a 6th generation line with BOE in Kunshan near Shanghai. Sharp once again came to meddle with the deal, promising and later reneging on a commitment to build a more advanced line with Shanghai, only to kill the chance of BOE.

Sharp's interferences helped to delay the development of China's first high specification production line, but it also provided Hefei (the capital city of Anhui province) an opportunity to collaborate with BOE. In 2008, Hefei's total tax revenue was 30.1 billion yuan, of which only 16.1 billion yuan could be kept by the local government. Building a production line at the cost of 17.5 billion yuan would be almost unthinkable, and the political and economic risks associated were too huge. However, at the time Hefei desperately needed to upgrade its industrial capability and promote economic growth. The local government leaders acted with great political will to move forward with this 6th generation line, and rumor has it that the construction of Hefei subway could have been delayed if BOE had needed more money. The financial plan utilized the same model that BOE had used in Chengdu, selling newly issued equities privately to Hefei government. But since Hefei's government lacked resources to finance the whole project, the newly issued equities had to be sold to some other private investors as well. The Hefei government itself promised to invest 6 billion yuan and would increase to 9 billion if the participation from other investors was not sufficient. During the process, Sharp once again tried to disrupt, however BOE had already learned from the previous examples and convinced the Hefei government to stand firm in face of Sharp's lobbying.

As we discussed in the previous chapter, during the early stages of economic development, capital markets are less developed and credit allocation may be inefficient. In this case, it makes sense to utilize government entities which have high credit ratings, backed by governments' fiscal capacity, as the main vehicles for financing and investing. This applies not only to land-related debt financings that we learned about in previous chapters, but also to equity-related financings. In the case of the 6th generation line in Hefei, the city government used two urban investment corporations to purchase BOE's newly issued equities, Hefei Construction Investment Co (a subsidiary of the city government) and Hefei New

City Co. (a subsidiary of the high-tech development zone).[7] The participation of the two state-owned companies also helped to attract third-party capital: this round of private placement raised a total of 12 billion yuan, with the two urban investment corporations contributing only 3 billion yuan, the remainder was contributed by eight third-party institutions. Similar to Chengdu, in addition to the private placement, BOE also raised a syndicated term loan of 7.5 billion yuan from a group of banks led by China Development Bank.[8]

Hefei's 6th generation line is China's first high specification production line, and it is the largest investment on a single industrial project in Anhui province since 1949. This line produced the first 32-inch LCD screen in mainland China, which Hefei made a great leap to become a high-tech manufacturing base. The success of Hefei government's investment attracted lots of attention. Many national leaders from Beijing, as well as leaders from more developed neighboring provinces (Jiangsu, Zhejiang and Shanghai), visited Hefei to learn their industrial investment practices. The great reputation of Hefei and Anhui province paid off. BOE later built two more lines in Hefei, an 8.5th generation line (operated in 2014) and a 10.5th generation line (operated in 2018), which attracted the whole supply chain to move to Hefei and formed a huge industrial cluster. Hefei has become one of the centers of China's LCD screen and optoelectronics industry.

After the onset of the global financial crisis in 2008 and China's 4 trillion-yuan stimulus investment, BOE entered a stage of rapid expansion. At the beginning of 2009, the central government included the manufacture of "new digital displays" as one of the industrial areas earmarked for policy support for the first time.[9] In June 2009, construction of the 6th generation line in Hefei officially started. In August, the foundation stone was laid for BOE's 8.5th generation line in Beijing's

[7] Hefei Construction Investment Co. participated in the issuance through its wholly-owned subsidiary, Hefei Lanke Investment Co., Ltd.

[8] The data come from BOE's 2009–2011 annual reports. It's actually not so easy for BOE to raise a large amount of funds through private placement, since it needs to find sufficient institutional investors to meet the supply. Had the Hefei government been financially strong enough, BOE could have saved the trouble and raised all the money from the government.

[9] In 2009, the State Council issued the "Plan on Adjusting and Revitalizing the Electronic Information Industry".

Yizhuang District. These two events finally broke the stranglehold that Japanese, Korean and Taiwanese companies had held over the LCD display manufacturing industry. Watching the developments, foreign manufacturers realized they could not sit still and begun to move more quickly with their own development plans in mainland China. Sharp started a joint venture with Panda Group in Nanjing to develop new production lines, LG signed a deal with Guangzhou to build a new 8th generation line, and Samsung signed a deal with Suzhou to build a 7.5th generation line. LCD panel makers in Taiwan also begun to call on the Taiwanese government to loosen policy restrictions and allow them to open new factories on the mainland. However, these new joint ventures didn't immediately receive approval from the Chinese government, and BOE was handed some time to get ahead.

In this stage of rapid expansion, BOE's basic financing model was equity financing plus syndicated bank loans. The local government owned urban investment corporations could either purchase more shares through new private placements, or use land as equity contributions. In the case of BOE's factory in Ordos City, the local government even offered the rights to mine 1 billion tons of coal as equity contributions. In addition, urban investment corporations could also lend money to BOE in the form of entrusted loans through local commercial banks, usually with low or even zero interests. For example, during the construction of the Yizhuang 8.5th generation line in Beijing, Beijing Yizhuang State Investment, a wholly state-owned investment company once entrusted Bank of Beijing to loan 200 million yuan to BOE with an annual interest rate of only 0.01%.[10] As another example, when BOE built a production line in Chengdu's high-tech development zone in 2015, a company owned by the local government, Chengdu High-tech Investment Group, offered an entrusted loan of 4.4 billion yuan with an annual interest rate of 4.95%, however the local government completely subsidized the interest payments, making the loan effectively interest free for BOE.[11]

[10] See BOE's 2009 Annual Report.

[11] This part of the interest payment is paid by the High-Tech Zone government to Chengdu High-tech Investment Group, and is counted as the non-operating income of this investment company, and is therefore not counted in BOE's account, although it is BOE that is subsidized. These financial details come from the bond market prospectus of Chengdu Hi-Tech Investment Group.

In 2014, BOE made the largest private placement in its history, 44.9 billion yuan, and it was used for the construction of production lines in Beijing, Hefei and Chongqing. The top three participants in this private placement were all local government financing vehicles, with 8.5 billion yuan invested from Beijing, 6.2 billion yuan from Chongqing and 6 billion from Hefei.[12] After 2015, as investment necessary to build more advanced production lines became larger and larger, BOE stopped issuing private placements. Instead, it let local government financing vehicles raise necessary capital through syndicated loans or other methods. As an example, the 10.5th generation line in Hefei started construction in 2015 and need a total investment of 40 billion yuan: 22 billion yuan was provided through outside investment, and the remaining 18 billion yuan came from syndicated bank loans. Among the 22 billion yuan of outside investment, Hefei Construction Investment Co, the largest local government financing vehicle helped to raise the 18 billion yuan, with the outstanding 4 billion yuan raised by BOE itself. During the fundraising process, a new method of government industrial investment funds was also used. This will be discussed more in Section 4.3 of this chapter.[13]

In fact, the development process witnessed by BOE is not an exceptional case. TCL-CSOT, which ranks second in China in terms of LCD panel display production is a private enterprise, but it also benefited from government investment while developing. As early as 2007, after the above-mentioned plan of jointly building 6th generation line in Shenzhen fell through, Li Dongsheng, the chairman of TCL attempted to introduce new generation production lines to China through joint ventures with overseas companies, but all failed. So he decided to independently build a 8.5th generation line, with the help from the Shenzhen government. The project required a total investment of 24.5 billion yuan and was the largest single industrial project in Shenzhen's history. The upfront investment required was 10 billion yuan with TCL raising 5 billion yuan through third-party investors, and the Shenzhen city government invests 5 billion yuan through Shenzhen Investment Holdings Co. Ltd, a company owned by Shenzhen's State-Owned Assets Supervision and Administration Commission. The project was very risky, mainly because

[12] See BOE's 2014 Annual Report.

[13] Details about the capital investment made by Hefei Construction Investment Co. during the construction of the 10.5th generation line come from the "Memorabilia" section of its company website.

TCL lacked the technical resources and experiences that BOE possessed, instead relying on a team of engineers it had poached from Taiwan. To hedge some of the risks, the Shenzhen government even sold 15% of its stake to Samsung. Later these shares were acquired by Hubei province's investment fund to support the construction of a new TCL-CSOT production line in its capital city, Wuhan. From 2013 to 2017, the annual operating income generated by TCL-CSOT nearly doubled, rising from 15.5 billion yuan to 30.6 billion yuan, and net profit rose by an even larger proportion, from 320 million yuan to 4.9 billion yuan. Thanks to the success of TCL-CSOT, the TCL Group has been able to transform itself from a losing player in the market of home appliances to a new giant of LCD panel producers. It officially changed its name to TCL Technology in 2019.[14]

Economic Lessons

The economies of scale witnessed in the modern industrial economy are very large. Investing in a production line for the LCD display panel industry costs tens of billions of yuan and only through mass production can the average cost be reduced. As a result, the entry threshold for new enterprises is very high, not only because the upfront investment required is extremely large, but also because the technological knowhow takes time to acquire. If a new company is able to achieve scale in production, it can reduce its own average cost and seize market share from incumbents, in turn weakening their economies of scale and pushing up their production costs. As a result, incumbents are likely to respond strongly to any attempt to entry, and Samsung's price wars and Sharp's lobbies are just two examples.

Textbook market competition usually implicitly focuses on the domestic market instead of the global market. On the domestic market, new entrants may try many methods in order to break an incumbents' advantage, these might include poaching technical teams or mergers and acquisitions to acquire capability. If the incumbent uses too harsh a means to suppress the new entrant, then anti-monopoly laws might come into play. However, when we consider the international market, there are many other distortions caused by national borders and politics. Tariffs

[14] The data on TCL-CSOT and TCL Group come from the article "Li Dongsheng Breaks Through", published in the second issue of Caixin Weekly in 2019.

or other non-tariff-related barriers to trade are just conventional means of inhibiting competition, and price manipulation, restrictions on foreign investment, or blocking technology transfers are also common practices. For example, a Chinese company may want to acquire an overseas company at a premium to the market price, the share price rises as a result and the target company's shareholders are happy, but the foreign government may reject the takeover due to political reasons. If resources cannot flow freely, traditional economic reasoning such as market competition, survival of the fittest and comparative advantage may lead to unrealistic conclusions.

Distortions caused by politics or policy can often only be resolved through changes to policy or other political means, but this does not mean that government should necessarily support domestic companies to enter a certain industry. One key consideration is the size of the domestic market. In a small country with only a few million people, companies find it hard to reach economies of scale in the domestic market and must necessarily rely on exports. In this case, subsidies spent by the national government are essentially a subsidy to foreign consumers. However, this is not the case in China. With a population of 1.4 billion, China has the world's largest consumer market for products that use LCD screens, such as TVs and mobile phones. Therefore bringing LCD production home to China has a strong spillover effect on many other products. If domestic producers can produce LCD panels at a lower cost than overseas companies, then the price offered by international manufacturers can also be reduced. In this situation, the government may well consider supporting domestic firms to enter the industry since success will both break the monopoly of international producers and help to lower the cost of downstream products, promote the development of downstream industries.[15]

There are many examples where the government invests in upstream industries and at the same time stimulates the development of downstream industries. In the 1970s, the US retreated from Vietnam and readjusted its Asian strategy. President Nixon announced that the US

[15] The links between industries are close and complex, like a giant spiders' web. Some industries have strong spillover effects, and if the government supports these industries, it can have a positive impact on the entire economy. There is a lot of research on this topic, see the paper by Ernest Liu (2019) and references there.

would no longer offer direct military support for Asian allies. The President of South Korea at the time, Park Chung-hee, moved to adjust his national industrial strategy to focus on heavy industry, in order to consolidate South Korea's own national defense capabilities. Since 1973, the government used to two entities, the National Investment Fund and Korea Development Bank to support this strategic shift, and they invest large amounts of money into "six strategic industries": steel, non-ferrous metals, shipbuilding, industrial machinery, electronics and petrochemicals. At the time, this industrial strategy was often questioned. For example, in 1974, the World Bank made it clear in a report that it had serious reservations about whether South Korea's development goals could be achieved, arguing that these industries were not tied to the nation's comparative advantages. The report advised that the textile industry, with low technological and financial barriers to entry, should be the key driver of industrialization.[16] Fortunately, the Korean government didn't listen to the World Bank. Later in the century, these strategic industries would not only incubate some world leading companies such as Samsung Electronics and POSCO (a world leading steelmaker), but also help to reduce the input costs for production in downstream industries. South Korea therefore also became more competitive in industries such as automotive manufacturing, with world leading companies such as Hyundai developing as a result. In 1979, Park Chung-hee was assassinated and Korea's industrial policy begun to evolve, and much of the original policy support was removed. However, the original foundation given to these industries was solid and they have continued a good development trend for a long time.[17]

The rise of companies such as BOE and TCL-CSOT has helped to drive development of the whole optoelectronics industry in China. This is also a manifestation of economies of scale. When the size of an industry is small, there is not enough incentive for upstream and downstream players

[16] The World Bank report and related questions come from Studwell's book on Asian development (2013).

[17] There are many studies on Korean industrial policy in the 1970s, and the basic process and facts are clear. However, rigorous micro-data analysis, especially the estimation of the impact on prices and output of upstream and downstream industries, has only recently been available. For more details, please see the paper of Lane (2019). Of course, government support is not a sufficient condition for industrial development, and there are many other factors at play, but government support and a large amount of capital investment are undoubtedly necessary conditions for these industries to develop rapidly.

to cluster together. However, once a certain scale is reached, different players in the supply chain will start to move together and what are called agglomeration effects will start to take hold. Not only will the volume of production reduce average production costs, but by agglomerating together in one place, transportation and communication costs can also be reduced. The optoelectronics industry has a long and complex supply chain. Up to this day, many upstream parts of the supply chain, such as chemical materials and equipment used in the production process, are still dominated by non-Chinese firms, and their profit margins are higher than those now seen in LCD panel manufacturing. Regardless, the development of domestic LCD panel manufacturers such as BOE has spurred many domestic companies to enter other parts of the supply chain. And the technologies and materials produced can also serve other industries, such as semiconductors, thereby helping to drive the development of other industries. Furthermore, the work of BOE and its partners has also attracted overseas companies to set up factories in China, helping the development of domestic upstream industries.[18]

Economies of scale and industry agglomeration effects are crucial to stimulate technological innovation. The larger the size of a market, the larger the profit motive, which in turns supports larger investment in R&D. Industrial agglomeration also brings spillover effects in terms of technology and knowledge sharing, which promotes innovation. According to a report by the World Intellectual Property Organization (WIPO), from 2016 to 2019, BOE and Huawei were among the top 10 companies worldwide in terms of number of patent applications.

Innovation is of course the driver of long-term economic development, but innovation cannot simply be bought with money. In order to innovate, it takes dirty hands and on the ground experience that leads to an accumulation of knowledge and skills. This learning-by-doing process can never be replaced by textbooks or theories. Only by doing something yourself, rather than simply copying or importing, can we truly learn the technical knowhows, learn to communicate more effectively

[18] There have been many reports on the localization of the optoelectronic display industry chain, since many of the Chinese companies involved have become significantly large and publicly listed, such as Sunnypol Optoelectronics and Jingce Electronics. In the field of international economics, there are also many studies on the positive effect of foreign direct investment (FDI) on domestic companies in the local supply chain, which is almost a consensus. Readers can refer to Havranek and Irsova (2011) for more details.

with suppliers, to revise product design to satisfy the demand of local customers, as well as to innovate independently. If an industry solely relies on imports, without any opportunity to take part in the production process domestically, it will be difficult for domestic technologies to progress, and the crucial skills and knowledge will be controlled by others. Such an international division of labor is not conducive to long-term economic growth.[19] Many documentaries on Chinese industrialization have recorded in detail the difficulty experienced by scientists, engineers and innovators in China as they tackle new production processes. It's like a student who attempts to finish a dissertation only by reading the work of others, not by trying to do his own research and write the paper himself. His understanding would remain superficial, and he would stay at the level of knowledge consumption and not be able to reach the level of knowledge production. Even with all the academic papers and books in the world on hand, one does not automatically become a scientist.

Emphasizing domestic independence in critical supply chains is not the same as advocating for a closed economy. In the real world, it's not necessary to do everything by oneself and being open to trade also helps an economy to learn, which is not contrary to independence.[20] In most modern, industrialized economies, a significant share of R&D spending and technological innovation comes from large and domestic manufacturing firms.[21] And this is exactly what we see from the story of BOE. A big country like China needs to grasp more core technologies and product types than smaller countries. Chapter 7 will discuss this topic in further detail.

An important feature of the East Asian economic miracle is that governments help companies to enter into highly complex industries, making full use of any learning effects, scale economies, and spillover effects to rapidly upgrade local technical capabilities. This leads to increased competitiveness internationally for domestic manufacturing industries. In 1970, if South Korea had done its industrial planning based

[19] International trade is not an unconditional win-win situation. After introducing dynamic economies of scale and learning-by-doing effects, free trade could harm a country's economic growth and social welfare. Readers could refer to works by Krugman (1987), Young (1991) or Gomory and Baumol (2000).

[20] Regarding independent innovation in Chinese contexts, there are many wonderful and unique analysis done by Lu Feng (路风 2016, 2019, 2020).

[21] For detailed data, see Cherif and Hasanov (2019).

on the comparative advantage model proposed by the World Bank, it would have invested in the textile industry. But in spite of the World Bank's advice, the Korean government decided to pursue industries which didn't exist (let alone having a comparative advantage) in the country at the time. By 1990, South Korea's top 10 export categories with the most comparative advantage in the global market, such as ships and computer electronics, did not exist at all in 1970.[22] We can therefore see the huge uncertainty associated with the concept of comparative advantage. The advantage could clearly be created from scratch, and it can change over time. In essence, comparative advantage means doing something with a lower opportunity cost. However, for things that have never been done before, it's difficult to *ex ante* calculate opportunity costs in the long run, so sometimes maybe the best strategy is simply to have a try.

The Chinese story is similar, with the government and private sector joining forces to enter new and complex industries. These industries had no comparative advantage historically, but after years of development, they are now competitive in international markets.[23] From 2000 to 2018, the product complexity of China's exports rose from 39th in the world to 18th.[24] This not only reflects the improvement in hard factors such as technical capabilities and infrastructure, but also reflects improvements in soft factors such as the business and legal environment. Since complex products and supply chains involve many different entities and the ensuing business relationships, the business environment as well as the legal environment is paramount to ensuring contract enforcement, economic stability and trust between partners. In fact, the complexity of a country's manufacturing products is directly related to its legal and

[22] South Korea's export data come from Cherif and Hasanov (2019). Justin Yifu Lin of Peking University's theory on comparative advantage and industrial upgrading is called "New Structural Economics", readers can seek out his books (Lin 2012, 2014). These books also include many scholars' discussions on this theory and Professor Lin's response. These conversations and arguments are fascinating and can help understand and clarify many issues.

[23] Liu Shouying and Yang Jidong (刘守英和杨继东 2019) calculated the "explicit comparative advantages" of 1,240 Chinese export products. There are 196 products considered to have international comparative advantages in 2016, but not in 1995. Many of these new products come from more complex industries, such as machinery, electrical appliances and chemicals.

[24] Data on product complexity come from the "The Atlas of Economic Complexity", a project of the Harvard Center for International Development.

business environment.[25] According to the World Bank's "ease of doing business" ranking, between 2010 and 2020, China rose from 89th to 31st.

Local Government Competition

During the course of BOE's development, local governments across China have offered very favorable terms to attract the company to settle in their area. As we discussed in the previous chapter, infrastructure investment made by urban investment corporations should not be simply evaluated by financial return directly generated by the projects, their effects on local economic growth must be considered as well. This principle also applies to industrial investments. BOE not only invests a lot in itself, but also drives investment from other companies in its supply chain. These enterprises can help to drive a significant amount of GDP growth, tax revenue and employment. A spokesperson for Hefei city government once refuted doubts about its investment in BOE in the following way: *"to think that we can't make a balance of the books is wrong; the government's calculation is indeed very careful and thorough. A BOE production line can immediately drive 30 billion yuan in industrial investment when the construction starts, and after it comes into operation, the annual output can be at the level of 100 billion yuan. Although it takes five years to build the production line, once it's done we have a ready-made high-tech cluster here in Hefei, generating hundreds of billion yuan. That makes the investment very effective and efficient"*.[26]

The agglomeration effects of manufacturing industries are strong since clustering production together can help to save on the transportation costs of raw materials and intermediate inputs. Companies gathering together in the same place are also conducive to knowledge and technology spillovers which helps to raise the capability of the whole supply chain. Therefore, once an industrial cluster has been formed it acts as a center of gravity, pulling in companies and knowledge from other areas. Once the cluster is developed in a given location, it's not easy to break

[25] Levchenko (2007) analyzes the relationship between institutional quality and product complexity.

[26] The quote comes from a 2013 *Global Entrepreneur* article "BOE, the money-burning machine: the political and business logic behind CDB's 20 billion financing" https://m.sohu.com/n/364543762/.

up by economic forces. However, during the early investment and development phase, many accidents can affect which exact city would host the clusters' formation.[27] Most modern manufacturing industries do not rely heavily on natural resources or specific natural conditions, so it is usually not tied to certain geographic areas. Moreover, China has a well-developed logistics network, which means that inland cities, while not being as convenient as coastal cities in terms of access to ports, can still compete. Inland cities such as Hefei and Zhengzhou are therefore able to attract industry leaders such as BOE and the Apple manufacturer Foxconn, which in turn enable them to attract the whole supply chains to the city. These inland cities have earned a chance to develop new-tech industries and succeeded remarkably.

Given the huge upfront investment required, it's natural for a company such as BOE to first seek cooperation with a city such as Shanghai or Shenzhen, which have vast financial resources. However, in this case, Sharp disrupted both processes, which presented an opportunity for Hefei and Chengdu to step in. In 2001, after China joined the WTO, coastal provinces such as Guangdong, Jiangsu, Zhejiang and Shanghai all developed rapidly, while Hefei, Chengdu, Wuhan and other inland cities were in urgent need of industrial investment to boost their development. These cities were therefore quite willing to take risks in order to attract industries to relocate. BOE has built three production lines in Hefei, which has also attracted a large number of supply chain industries to the city. This has turned Hefei into one of the main centers for the optoelectronic display industry in China. Many technologies in this sector are also related to other industries, such as semiconductors or computer chips, so the Hefei government used the foundation it had built through investment with BOE to attract leading companies in the semiconductor industry. Hefei also supported the establishment of the chip industry in the city,

[27] In the theory of "new economic geography" or "spatial economics", once an industry has been formed in a given location, economic forces will accelerate geographic agglomeration. However, the initial location of an industry is usually uncertain, and the "initial conditions" have a great influence. A small change to the initial conditions may affect the final industrial geographic pattern. Whether it is China or the US, if we trace the historical roots of many industrial agglomeration areas, we will find that some accidental factors have played a key role. For example, in the case of BOE, it was the strong support of the leaders of Hefei at the time. Krugman (1992) describes many examples of the impact of this combination of contingency and economic forces on the geographic distribution of industries.

becoming one of the biggest manufacturers of memory chips (DRAM). From 2008 to 2019, Hefei's real GDP (inflation-adjusted) grew 3.4x, which was higher than the national real GDP growth rate of 2.3x. By 2020, Hefei's annual GDP exceeded 1 trillion yuan, making it the newest member of "the trillion-GDP club" that includes only 23 cities in China.

The success of Hefei naturally leads to imitation in other regions. Many other cities also launched LCD production lines, and government support for the industry encouraged other companies without the technical prowess of BOE to enter the industry, leading to concerns of overcapacity.[28] The LCD display industry is highly cyclical and when prices are high, many companies choose to enter the industry, which causes supply to increase and prices to plummet. As a result, many companies may go into bankruptcy and require restructuring. The lower price also serves to increase demand, which may cause prices to rise again and the cycle continues. Overcapacity in the industry has wiped out many companies, and the center of production has gradually moved from the US to Japan, Taiwan, South Korea and later to mainland China. The future is hard to predict; maybe in the future screens will be everywhere and demand will increase, or an alternative technology may come along and completely wipe out the industry in the same way that LCDs wiped out the CRT TV technology. No-one can accurately predict the future, but overcapacity and investment caused by competition are common, especially in industries with low technological requirements and small upfront investment, such as the solar power industry.

Section 2: Solar Industry and Government Subsidies

Photovoltaic (PV) technology is used to convert solar energy into electricity. In 2012, many photovoltaic companies in China shut down as the industry entered a prolonged downturn. The industry became a byword for the failure of state-led industrial policies and government subsidies, with many in academia, the media and government taking aim at the policies which led to the downturn. However, if an investor had purchased the stocks of solar companies such as LONGi during the period, they

[28] See the article "Overcapacity of LCD Panels, Hidden Worries over Local State Investment Manias", on 2019s 44th issue of Caixin Weekly's.

would have received a return worth multiple times their initial investment. In fact, after the restructuring that occurred during 2012, China's solar industry has become a global leader and 80% of the world's production is made by Chinese companies or their overseas subsidiaries. Almost all the key sections in the supply chain, including polysilicon, silicon wafers, batteries and PV modules are dominated by Chinese firms.[29] Driven by economies of scale and advances in technology, the price of PV modules fell by 85% in the decade up to 2020, while total installed capacity has increased by 16 times. Moreover, China's domestic market has become the largest market for solar panels, with one-third of the world's capacity installed here.[30] Like high-speed rail, the solar industry has become one of the major success cases of "Made in China".

The Story of the Solar Industry

In the 1970s, the Arab world placed an embargo on oil and the resulting oil crisis encouraged the US government to begin investing in new energy industries. The Carter administration heavily subsidized research in photovoltaic technology and sought to commercialize the industry. By the early 1980s, the US solar market accounted for more than 85% of the global market. However, later Reagan came to power and oil prices fell, most of the supportive policies for the solar industry were removed. The industrial supply chain gradually begun shifting to Germany and Japan where government subsidies were more generous. During the period, Martin Green, a professor at the University of New South Wales, developed many new technologies which greatly enhanced the efficiency of solar power generation, later he became known as the father of the modern solar industry. Many of his students later became the backbone of China's solar industry, including Dr. Shi Zhengrong.[31]

In 2001, Shi Zhengrong founded Suntech with the support of the Wuxi city government in Jiangsu province, which held a 25% share of

[29] Data on the scale of China's solar industry come from a report by Gong Yongfeng and Lin Jie of CITIC Securities (弓永峰和林劼 2020).

[30] Estimated decline in global PV module prices is from the work of energy expert and Pulitzer Prize winner, Daniel Yergin (2020). The data on the total installed capacity of China and the rest of the world come from a report by the global renewable energy industry think tank REN21 (2020).

[31] For a history on the early development of solar industry, see Sivaram (2018).

the company. Three local government financing vehicles in Wuxi and five local state-owned enterprises invested a total of 6 million USD into the company, which accounted for roughly 75% of shares of the company. It's not an exaggeration to say that the Wuxi government acted as an angel investor for Suntech. In 2005, Suntech became the first "private" Chinese enterprise to list on the New York Stock Exchange, with all state-owned shares being acquired prior to the listing, by private and foreign investors such as Goldman Sachs. Shi Zhengrong's share of the company reached 46.8% and he became the richest man in China after the listing. The stellar wealth created acted as a strong demonstration effect and local governments across China soon begun to invest in the solar industry. In 2005, with significant support from the local government, a company called LDK was established in Xinyu city in Jiangxi province. The company later became the first company from Jiangxi province to be listed on the New York Stock Exchange in 2007, and its founder, Peng Xiaofeng, became the richest man in Jiangxi. By 2010, there were already more than 20 Chinese solar companies listed on stock exchanges either in China or abroad.[32]

In 2008, with the fiscal stimulus after the global financial crisis, local governments in China significantly increased investment in infrastructure and industrial projects, including in the solar industry. The main policy tools involve cheap land, tax incentives and subsidized loans. With the support of local governments, companies such as Suntech and LDK begun to take on significant amounts of debt. By 2011, the scale of Suntech was already quite large, but the Wuxi government was keen to continue expanding and determined to build a "second Suntech" within 5 years. The government gave land to Suntech to build a new factory with a scale of 50,000 workers and help the company get bank loans. By 2011, LDK had become the largest contributor to Xinyu's tax revenue, creating 20,000 jobs and contributing 1.4 billion yuan per year in tax, equivalent to 12% of the total fiscal revenue of the city.[33]

Unlike the LCD panel industry, which was mainly developed to serve domestic markets, products produced in the solar industry in the first decade of this century were mainly exported to the US and Europe,

[32] The number of listed solar companies is from an article "Solar Energy: China-style Leap Forward" published in the 4th issue of *China Reform* in 2010.

[33] The data come from the article "LDK: An Example of Bankruptcy and Reorganization" published in the 37th issue of Caixin Weekly in 2017.

especially Spain and Germany. Within China, electricity made from solar power was much more expensive than that made from fossil fuels or hydro, thereby limiting domestic demand. By 2011, 57% of solar exports were made to Europe and 15% were made to the US. Although some government subsidies were later introduced to try and drive solar energy use in China, the total amount of subsidies was too small to create significant demand. In 2010, the domestic market accounted for only 6% of the total sales of China's solar industry.[34]

Since the cost of producing electricity from solar energy is much higher than from traditional sources of energy such as coal, overseas demand also depends heavily on government subsidies. Subsidies in Europe are especially generous. Germany not only subsidies installation of solar capacity, the government also introduced feed-in tariffs (FiT) in 2000, which later became a global model of government subsidy in solar industry. Since PV technology relies on energy from the sun, electricity can't be generated at night. This unstable supply of electricity puts extra pressure on power grids, therefore grids are often reluctant to connect to solar based power plants. However, under the FiT system, power grids must purchase solar power at a fixed price for 20 years, and the price is higher than the production cost of solar power. This price subsidy is added to the bill for energy consumers, and this higher energy price is therefore shared by consumers. Over time this fixed purchase price is gradually lowered to encourage technological innovation and efficiency improvement of solar power producers, otherwise their profit margins would decline. In fact, the rate of decline in the price was slower than the decline in costs due to rapid technological progress, and it is therefore profitable to invest in solar power generation. As such, China's solar industry benefits widely not just from domestic government policies, but also from those of other countries, such as Germany, Spain and Italy. Chinese firms took advantage of scale effects, government subsidies, and the benefits of industry agglomeration, their low-cost products flooded the European and American markets.

From 2008 to 2011, the global financial crisis quickly morphed into the Eurozone debt crisis and European governments cut their spending on solar subsidies. Moreover, in response to the impact of Chinese products, the US and EU governments successively launched anti-dumping

[34] The data on solar firms and exports are from a report by Zhu Yue (朱玥 2019). The data on the share of domestic market come from Sivaram (2018).

and anti-subsidy investigations to Chinese firms, and tariffs surged. However, during this period, the actual number of subsidies provided by the Chinese government were quite limited and most were just routine policies of attracting investment by local government, such as cheap land or subsidized loans, and they were not specific to the solar industry. Only Jiangsu province, where the solar industry is large, took the lead in 2009 in enacting a pricing mechanism similar to the FiT system in Germany, stipulating that electricity produced via solar power should be priced at 2.15 yuan per kilowatt hour, which was much higher than 0.4 yuan per kilowatt hour for coal-fired electricity. The funding for the subsidy came from a surcharge to electricity consumers in the province (excluding households and agricultural use), with any excess money earned being kept in a fund used to support the development of the solar industry in the province. In order to encourage firms to increase efficiency and lower costs, the Jiangsu government lowered the purchase price to 1.7 yuan per kilowatt hour in 2010 and 1.4 yuan per kilowatt house in 2011.[35]

In the years' leading up to the 2008 financial crisis and the aforementioned anti-dumping investigations, Chinese firms had built a vast amount of production capacity and accumulated a lot of debt in the process. With foreign demand suddenly plummeting, a large number of firms went bankrupt, including the industrial leaders, Suntech and LDK. With the entire industry entering into a hard winter, the focus started to turn to how to stimulate and expand consumption in the domestic market.

In 2011, the central government began to phase in FiT pricing, requiring power grids to purchase solar generated electricity at a fixed price of 1.15 yuan per kilowatt hour. By 2013, the government shifted to regional pricing system, dividing the country into three types of area.[36] Type 1 includes northwestern regions that have strong sunlight, Type 2 includes central and western regions, and Type 3 is mainly eastern regions. The price paid by power grids for solar power varied by region, with prices of 0.9, 0.98 and 1 yuan per kilowatt hour respectively. Compared with

[35] See the "Opinions on the Promotion of Solar Power Generation in Jiangsu Province", published by the Jiangsu government in 2009.

[36] In July 2011, the National Development and Reform Commission issued the "Notice on Improving the On-grid Pricing Policy for Solar Photovoltaic Electricity", and the on-grid price was fixed at 1.15 yuan per kilowatt-hour. In August 2013, the National Development and Reform Commission issued the "Notice on Using Pricing to Promote the Healthy Development of the Photovoltaic Industry", and the regional on-grid pricing system began to operate.

the average price of coal-fired electricity at the time of 0.4 yuan per kilowatt hour, the subsidy amounted to roughly 0.6 yuan. For the funding source, a surcharge was once again levied on end users of electricity, which was then turned over to the central treasury and placed in a renewable energy development fund. In addition to this price subsidy offered by the central government, many provincial and city governments also offered local subsidies. For example, Shanghai set up a special fund for the development of renewable and new energy, which offers an incremental fixed subsidy of 0.3 yuan per kilowatt hour. And the subsidies are financed by Shanghai's government budgetary revenues and revenues from the local progressive electricity tariff system.[37]

Like other countries around the world, the subsidies offered by Chinese governments have gradually reduced over time to encourage firms to reduce production cost. From 2016 to 2017, the central government reduced the FiT in the three types of regions to 0.65, 0.75 and 0.85 respectively, a decrease of 28%, 23% and 15%. In fact, the efficiency improvement and cost reduction occurred much faster than the reduction in subsidies. The price of solar PV modules was dropping by as much as 30% per year. It was therefore profitable to operate solar power plants and the overall production capacity increased rapidly. In 2016 and 2017, China's production of solar PV accounted for 73% of the global production, and China's installed capacity accounted for 51% of the global market, making China both the world's largest producer and largest consumer of solar electricity.[38]

However, the rapid increase in installed capacity has led to a serious shortage of subsidy funds and arrears in terms of subsidy payment. In June 2018, the total amount of unpaid subsidy stood at 120 billion yuan (including wind power subsidies). Many solar plants are built in the sunny northwest of China where lands are cheap. But this region is sparsely populated and the economy is underdeveloped, meaning electricity consumption is insufficient to absorb all electricity generated by local solar plants. Long-distance transferring electricity between provinces is costly, and there are many policy distortions in the inter-province power

[37] Shanghai implements a progressive pricing system for electricity consumption. Subsidies for offshore wind power and solar power plants are specified in the "Measures for the Support of Special Funds for the Development of Renewable Energy and New Energy in Shanghai".

[38] The data come from a report by Zhu Yue (朱玥 2019).

distribution network. As a result, grid companies often refuse to pay solar power plants for electricity, on the grounds that they have not received the subsidies owed by the government. This has led to the abandonment of many solar power plants, particularly in western provinces such as Gansu and Xinjiang.[39]

Against this background, the "531 new deal" was introduced on 31 May 2018, which greatly reduced the subsidized electricity price and set a cap for the amount of solar power capacity that could receive a subsidy. Any newly installed solar capacity that exceeds this cap is not eligible for subsidy. The new policy had an immediate big impact on the industry, even bigger than the impact of the previous anti-dumping investigations in Europe and the US. By the end of the year, policy turned favorable once again. Meanwhile, the EU canceled anti-dumping and anti-subsidy policies, and trade with Europe returned to normal. The EU's anti-dumping campaign proved unsuccessful in saving European companies, and except for upstream providers of silicon materials, European companies have more or less withdrawn from the solar industry. From 2019 onwards, China begun to gradually remove the subsidized fixed pricing system and introduce a market-based bidding mechanism. With many years of investment, technological advancement and increasing economies of scale, the cost of solar electricity is now approaching the cost of coal-fired electricity. During 2020, the stock prices of solar power companies listed in China and abroad soared, reflecting optimism about the future of the industry.

Economic Lessons

If we accept that climate change and global warming exist, and we care about the future of the planet, then renewable energy must be developed. Even if we do not accept the existence of climate change, then breaking a reliance on imported fossil fuels and securing energy independence can also be an important argument in support of renewable energy. However, traditional energy sectors have benefited from many decades of technological advancement and investment, and new energy sources are not competitive when they first enter the market. Considering solar power

[39] The data on the total amount of outstanding subsidies come from the cover article of the 25th issue of Caixin Weekly in 2018. There are many related reports on the conflicts between power grids and new energy power plants.

as an example, two decades ago the cost of solar-powered electricity was many times higher than coal-fired electricity. If we only rely on market and price-based mechanisms, solar power would never be used. The technological advancement and economies of scale necessary to reduce costs in new energy can only happen with large-scale production in real markets, and theoretical and laboratory breakthroughs alone are not sufficient. Entire supply chains must be optimized in order to achieve economies of scale. R&D and innovation are never just activities conducted in an ivory tower, and they are inseparable from real-world market environment and from companies that can only learn by doing.

New energy technology must therefore start to operate in the real market even it does not have any initial competitive advantage over traditional energy sectors. There are only two ways that they can survive. First, government can levy a heavy carbon tax on the traditional sectors, raise their price significantly and create some chances for new energy firms. Second, government can directly subsidize new energy firms. Obviously, the first method does not make economic sense because in the early stage of development of new energy, the traditional energy sectors account of over 90% of the market, and they are very cheap. To levy a heavy tax on them would significantly increase the burden of taxpayers, and the resulting distortions would be huge. A more reasonable method therefore would be subsidizing new energy firms, accelerating the process of technological innovation and cost reduction. When the market share of new energy grows, its costs would converge to the traditional energy, then government could gradually reduce subsidies to new energy as well as start to tax traditional energy use, which would further reduce the market share of traditional energy.[40]

So be it Europe, the US, Japan or South Korea, the demand for solar energy all first come from government subsidies. When China first entered the market, nearly all key factors were outside of its control: demand came from overseas, key raw materials came from overseas and key production equipment also came from overseas. Meanwhile, given the stage of China's economic development at the time, the cost of solar power was too high for the domestic market. The support of local government subsidies, such as cheap lands and loans, enabled Chinese companies conducting price wars in overseas markets, flooding markets with cheap

[40] Acemoglu et al. (2016) model such a dynamic transition from traditional energy to new energy, and discuss the optimal combination of tax and subsidy policies.

products. In order to gain an advantage over fierce competition, many producers upgraded technology and moved into more complex upstream sectors. However, since the demand came from overseas, once the anti-dumping and anti-subsidy policies took effect in the US and Europe, demand plummeted, and many companies had to close down.

However, companies are not human being. They do not pass away with death, the accumulated technology, talents and industry knowhows survive. Once market demand picks up, these resources can quickly be reorganized. Starting from 2013, the domestic demand quickly picked up steam and China's solar industry thereby entered a new stage of development. Since the entire supply chain is located in China, the cost of communication among partners is low and more collaborations throughout the supply chain begun to take place. Different links in the supply chain worked together and led to further cost reduction and optimization of the entire chain, which further increased the competitiveness of Chinese solar producers. After 2018, not only European policies changed, but the cheap and efficient PV technology also stimulated the global demand. Chinese suppliers were ready to capture this opportunity, and their prior experience in overseas markets proved to be valuable helping them to ride a wave of growth.

The experiences of the solar industry do not demonstrate a clear causal relationship between government subsidies and the success of businesses. In advanced economies, such as Europe, Japan and the US, the PV industry not only started early and received government subsidies early, but it also had advantages in key technologies, raw materials and production equipment. When competing with Chinese companies, their governments resorted to trade protectionism through anti-dumping and anti-subsidy measures, but eventually they still lost the battle and withdrew from the market. Whether it is subsidies or trade protectionism, governments can at best only help firms reduce certain financial and market risks, but they cannot help them to develop sufficient capabilities and competitive advantages to survive in the everchanging market. Without these competitive advantages, subsidies and protectionism can eventually encourage rent seeking among companies looking to capitalize on governments. This logic applies in China, as it does in Europe or the US, but it's not a sufficient argument to abandon industrial policy altogether. Industrial development, with or without government intervention, has no surefire successes or failures. As for the solar industry, although subsidies may not be able to guarantee business success, the industry certainly couldn't survive without subsidies, let alone getting rid of the dependence on subsidies bit by bit over its development.

Looking at the development of the solar industry, we can see another key feature of the East Asian Industrial Policy model, which is an emphasis on exports. When domestic demand is limited, overseas markets can help to enhance competition and encourage innovation. Subsidies and preferential policies inevitably lead to many inefficient companies, but these companies are unlikely to receive orders from international customers with high requirements. The companies that manage to export a lot therefore tend to be those that are more efficient. If these efficient companies increase their market share, it can help to squeeze out inefficient players and improve the overall efficiency of the industry.[41] Of course, a big country like China also needs to deal with an everchanging global environment, and relying heavily on external demand can be risky, development of the domestic market is therefore necessary to ensure the long-term prosperity of the industry. However, if local governments act to inhibit market forces, preventing losing companies from going out of business, then it will be hard to improve the overall efficiency and exacerbate the problems of overcapacity.

Local Government Competition and Overcapacity

Preferential policies offered by local governments in order to attract investment help to lower barriers of market entry, which may result in excess investment and production capacity. This is one downside of China's industrial policy that is often mentioned in policy debates, and the solar industry is often cited as a textbook example. Having a period of overinvestment and overcapacity is nothing surprising in itself and would likely occur in a market economy even without government interventions. Since investment is tied to the future and the future is always uncertain, the amount of investment chosen by the free market is unlikely to match exactly the future market demand. Industrial investment, given

[41] Entering the global market improves the efficiency of domestic firms, not only because the international division of labor based on comparative advantages could improve efficiency, but also because a larger global market could increase the market share of efficient firms and reduces the market share of inefficient firms. This is the core idea of the "Melitz model", a classic model in trade theory. Melitz and Trefler (2012) introduce this idea and present a simplified model.

its long-term nature, is hard to reverse once the investment is made, therefore it is almost always too much or too few. When markets are optimistic, investment tends to overshoot, leading to excess capacity and falling prices. Many companies would go bankrupt, but the falling prices would stimulate more demand, which can once again stimulate a cycle of overinvestment. Periods of overcapacity are therefore normal as a supply and demand respond to each other in an everchanging market economy. It is precisely because of this overcapacity, companies have to work hard to increase their competitive advantage and survival chance, leading to continuing technology progress and efficiency improvement.[42]

In China, there are at least three more factors that can lead to overdevelopment of a given industry. To start with, a developing country, such as China, can see trends in developed countries. Certain products that become everyday items in developed countries first, such as color TVs, refrigerators or washing machines, are surely to catch on in developing countries later. The demand for such products will be huge and certain, and relevant production technology can be easily imported and copied. Meanwhile, the domestic market just begins to grow, and everyone has an opportunity, investment therefore floods into these sectors. Secondly, many preferential policies and subsidies from local governments in order to attract new investment, such as cheap land and loans, are often provided during the construction phase of a project. It takes time to build factories but local government leaders change frequently, if construction is not started quickly then these preferential policies and subsidies might be changed. Even worse, these preferential policies and subsidies might be given to a firm's competitors. Even if the market situation changes after the factory has been built, it is always possible for firms to find some room to adapt by adjusting production volumes or prices. But if firms do to invest fast and early, many opportunities would be lost. The third reason is that local governments tend to follow industrial policies of central government. Even if a region is not suitable for a given industry, the local government may still try to invest in it because the investment

[42] The impact of uncertainty on investment and the economic cycle is one of the important topics in economics. The related literature is vast. Readers can refer to Bloom (2014) for an excellent introduction to the topic.

would be politically correct, which would contribute to drive investment in overcapacity.[43]

Overinvestment may not always be a bad thing. In the early stage of economic development, overinvestment supported by local governments has at least two benefits. Firstly, local factories not only provide employment, but they also help to serve as training grounds for local workers, helping local peasants' transition to industrial roles. Turning peasants into factory workers is a core part of industrialization, which requires a complete change in lifestyles and mindset. This transition cannot happen automatically and requires learning and training that can only be done in the factory. In the 1980s and 1990s, when township and village enterprises were growing quickly, a unified domestic market had still not formed. Countless small factories were built under the stewardship of local governments across the country, and their overall production efficiency and technical capability were very low. But these small factories provide local peasants with factory jobs, effectively a chance of "leaving the soil without leaving home". In this way, peasants across the country became familiar with the operation of factories, and a huge force of industrial workers was trained. This process laid the foundation for China to take advantage of its labor force and become the world's factory after entry into the WTO in 2001. From this perspective, the factory essentially assumed an educational function for the industrial economy and had a strong positive externality on the economy, and it should be subsidized and supported.

The second benefit of overinvestment is that it increases competition. Overcapacity has made price wars a norm for many products in China. Therefore, for a long time, innovation in cost reduction was the main type of innovation pursued by Chinese companies. In the West, this is often mocked as "copycat behavior". However, functional simplification and cost innovation are very important. Many products in the west, such as automobiles or home appliances, have been upgraded over many years to satisfy the requirements of western and richer customers, so the

[43] The first factor is called the "tidal wave phenomenon", as detailed in the paper by Lin et al. (林毅夫, 巫和懋, 邢亦青 2010). The second factor is known as the "Oi-Hartman-Abel" effect, that is, companies can benefit from expanding (in this case, building factories) and control risks by shrinking (in this case, reducing production volume after factories started to operate), see Bloom (2014) for an introduction. The third factor, or the phenomenon that local industrial policies are converging with industrial policy of central government, can be found in the paper by Zhao and Chen (赵婷和陈钊 2019).

functionality tends to be complex and the price higher. But when these products are introduced to Chinese consumers for the first time, they are too fancy and too expensive. If sacrifices in terms of certain features and product quality can help to bring the price down, then it would expand the market demand. As consumers become more familiar with the products, and as they become richer, they will increase their demand for higher quality and more additional functionality. Therefore, it is not surprising that many industries in China have gone through the copycat and price war stages. And it is exactly in this stage of brutal competition that the industry is developing quickly, numerous small firms rise and fall fast, and resources and technologies are quickly concentrated in the hands of leading companies. Both technology and product improve rapidly. Take the home appliance industry as an example, domestic Chinese products start from being cheap and low-quality, upgrade fast to become high-quality but still cheap, with reliable service and beautiful design. In a short period of about two decades, domestic brands started from scratch but managed to dominate the Chinese market. The same is true for many other consumer products.[44]

So, whether there is government support or not, the key is not overinvestment itself but to maintain competition. The fundamental advantage of a market economy is not an improvement in individual decision-making per se. No-one can precisely predict an uncertain future, and in a free market there will be much more failures than successes. The advantage of a free market is that it ensures competition and through a process of trial and error, only the fittest or best adapted companies survive.[45] Therefore, industrial policies that are designed to support competition, rather than supporting specific companies, tend to be more effective at stimulating development.[46] However, in practice it is difficult to avoid policies that only support specific companies. Even if an industry policy advocated by the central government is designed to target the entire industry and maintain competition among firms, when it is implemented at the regional

[44] Yip and Mckern (2016) analyze many cases of cost innovation by Chinese enterprises.

[45] The idea that the core advantage of a market economy is not decision-making but the survival of the fittest comes from the late economist Alchian (1950). His article from seven decades ago is still wonderful to read today.

[46] China's industrial policies that are competitive in nature, such as industry-wide subsidies, tax breaks and low-interest loans, have a positive effect on improving technology and efficiency of an industry, see Aghion et al. (2015).

level it necessarily benefits specific local companies. Local governments may choose to protect local companies from bankruptcy. But if these "zombie companies" cannot be eliminated, then the benefits of competition will be limited, and many resources will be misallocated and wasted. This is the main reason that many economists oppose industrial policy. In China, local governments have a strong preference for big industrial projects which stimulate investment and GDP growth. These big companies employ lots of people, and it becomes much harder to allow them to go bankrupt without disrupting social stability. So local government have strong incentives to intervene bankruptcy cases once big companies are involved, which could lead to inefficient and unfair results. In the bankruptcy case of LDK, a former solar giant in Xinyu city of Jiangxi province, this problem is salient.

As mentioned earlier in the chapter, by 2011, LDK became the largest contributor to Xinyu's public finances, paying 1.4 billion yuan in taxes which was equivalent to 12% of the city's annual tax revenue. At the same time, the company created 20,000 jobs in the city. With the support of the local government, LDK received a large amount of credit from banks, far more than the total assets of the company. Starting from 2012, the company begun to default on many of its debts. But local governments repeatedly injected funds into the company, and help persuade banks to rescue the company. In spite of all these efforts, the debt problem only got worse. By 2016, the total assets of LDK were valued at 13.7 billion yuan, but the total debt was as high as 51.6 billion yuan, and the company was bankrupt. However, the bankruptcy procedure was led by the local government, harming the interests of creditors. When creditors rejected the debt-restructuring proposal because the repayment offered is too low, the local court adjudicates in favor of the proposal against the will of the committee of creditors. This clearly violated the guidance from the Supreme People's Court regarding legal practices in firm bankruptcy, and it received a great deal of attention in media, law communities and financial industry.[47]

Industrial policies must therefore have an exit mechanism. Such a mechanism can have two meanings. The first is that a subsidy policy itself needs an exit mechanism. For example, the solar electricity FiT subsidy mentioned above gradually declines over time, and all companies are

[47] For details, refer to an article from the 37th issue of Caixin Weekly in 2017, "Bankruptcy and Restructure of LDK".

aware that the subsidy will eventually be removed, therefore they need to continually reduce costs and improve efficiency to be competitive in the market. The second meaning is that there needs to be a channel for inefficient companies to go bankrupt. If inefficient firms cannot be driven out of the market, competition would be distorted. This involves not only industrial policy but also reforms of bankruptcy and restructure laws. In essence, it requires fundamental and market-oriented reforms of the allocation of production factors. However, enforcing efficient bankruptcy procedures has been a chronic problem for China's economy. Creditor banks are reluctant to go through bankruptcy procedures because it will bring to light non-performing loans and losses. Local governments are reluctant to see firms, particularly big ones, go through bankruptcy procedures because the conflicts with unemployed workers and various creditors could be hard to control. In coastal areas of China where market economy is more developed, bankruptcy procedures are relatively easier and more transparent. For example, in the industry of solar power, the bankruptcy and restructuring cases of Wuxi Suntech and Shanghai Chaori proved to be more market orientated and creditor friendly than that of LDK. These two cases were listed by the Supreme People's Court in the "top 10 bankruptcy model cases for 2016". However, in general, China still has a long way to go in terms of reforming its bankruptcy liquidation and reorganization laws.

Section 3: Government Industry Guidance Funds

Industrial upgrading and technological innovation have become hot topics in China during recent years. When it comes to funding for high-tech companies, Silicon Valley style venture capital investment is often the first thing that comes to mind. However, an American style venture capital system cannot be directly replicated in China. Instead, venture capital investment was adapted to the Chinese political and economic context and mixed with funds from local government, creating "government industry guidance funds". This new tool of equity investment in high-tech sectors was born out of the traditional model of local government investment and financing. But the old model is associated with a huge debt problem and cannot continue growing fast. With reforms increasingly focused on reducing excessive debt and reducing industrial overcapacity, these new "government guidance funds" more than doubled in size from 2014 to 2019. According to data from Zero2IPO, as of June 2019, there were 1,686 "industry guidance funds" already established in China, with total funding of 4 trillion yuan in place, and according to separate data from ChinaVenture, there were 1,311 funds with total funding of 2 trillion yuan.[48]

Government industry guidance funds not only provide a new tool to attract investment and to drive industrial policy, they also represent a more market-orientated way of using government money. Understanding such funds could help us understand the industrial development in China. At the same time, it is also an excellent example of "China's gradualism in economic reform". Government guidance funds are closely related to private equity funds, and therefore we must first understand how private equity funds work.

Private Equity Funds and Industry Guidance Funds

Put it in the simplest terms, private equity funds (PE) involve a group of people who give money to another group of people to carry out and manage investments. The two groups then share in any returns from the investments. It is called private in order to distinguish it from mutual funds that are available for anyone to buy on the public market. PEs have special regulations governing investor qualifications, fundraising and exit methods, and they are not like the shares of mutual funds which can be bought and sold on a daily base. Figure 4.1 depicts the basic operational structure of PE. The person who contributes the money is known as a limited partner (LP), and the person who manages the money and investments is called a general partner (GP). The LP hands money to the GP in order to carry out investments, and pays fees to the GP in return for their services. Typically, these fees include a management fee, typically 2% of the LP's contributed money. This fixed fee should be paid regardless of the GP's investment returns, even if the GP loses money. The second type of fee is performance-based, known as "carry". If the investment makes

[48] Zero2IPO and ChinaVenture are two domestic research firms focusing on private equity funds. The information disclosure of private equity funds is usually incomplete and opaque, so different estimates can vary widely. The figures here are quoted from the cover report of Caixin Weekly, 39th issue in 2020, "Supervision of 10 Trillion Private Equity Funds". In the private equity fund industry, the target size of the fund is usually not important, and the actual fundraising and funds in place are generally much smaller than the target size. The astronomical numbers on the target size of government guidance funds often seen in the media therefore do not matter much.

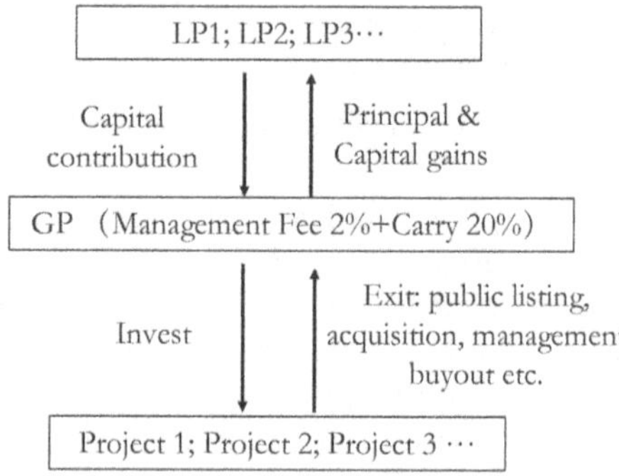

Fig. 4.1 Basic operation model of private equity funds

money, the GP must first repay the principal to the LP along with any pre-agreed baseline return (typically 8%). If there is any profit above this baseline return, then the GP can earn commission of around 20% on it.

To give a simple example. A LP invests 1 million and the fund is active for 2 years, then the GP receives 20,000 in management fees every year. If the fund were to lose 500,000 in two years, then the GP would earn a total of 40,000 in management fees and the LP would receive only 460,000 back, recognizing a loss. If the fund were to earn 500,000 over 2 years, then the GP would still earn 40,000 in management fees. Given the return is now positive, the GP would return to the LP 1 million in principal plus the pre-agreed baseline return of 8% per year or 160,000. For the remaining extra profits of 300,000, the GP would take 20% "carry" or 60,000, and return 240,000 to the LP. In total the GP earns 100,000 for his service and the LP gets back 1.4 million in principal and profits.

GPs could invest in publicly listed companies or in the equity of unlisted companies, it may also involve private placements of publicly listed companies. If the investment is an unlisted company, there are many ways to exit, for example selling shares after IPO (initial public offering), selling shares back to the company's management, or alternatively, allowing the company to be acquired.

The legal structure under which LPs and GPs cooperate is known as a limited partnership. Compared with corporations and joint stock companies, a limited partnership is more flexible. Joint stock companies require an equal number of shares to have an equal number of votes and to have an equal claim on profits. Regardless of the number of shares held, the voting rights and dividend rights attached to each share are the same. Therefore, the more shares you hold, the more rights you have. However, in a limited partnership, the LP pay the money but only enjoy quite limited rights, it is the GP who makes the investment and management decisions. Not only that, the GP can share 20% of the profits without making any initial investment into the fund.[49] A further difference involves life of the company. Whereas corporations are supposed to operate into perpetuity, PE funds typically have a fixed duration of 7–10 years. During this time, the fund needs to pass through 4 stages, fundraising, investment, management and exit. After the duration, the fund should be liquidated and all the money should be distributed.[50]

Under this model, it is natural that the GPs take the spotlight, since they are the ones who invest and manage the money. Many GP institutions and their star partners can become famous with a strong track record. Their investment portfolio not only earns high returns, but may also include some famous and influential companies. These star GPs are highly sought after and can raise large funds, sometimes over 10 billion yuan. In contrast, the LPs who provide the money are much more low key. Most of the world's largest LPs are institutional investors, such as large pension funds. In the US, many top LPs are pension fund, such as the California Public Employee Retirement System (CalPERS) and the Pennsylvania Public School Employee's Retirement System (PSERS). Another type of institutional LPs is sovereign wealth funds, such as Singapore's Temasek and GIC or Norway's Sovereign Wealth Fund. In China, the largest type of LPs are government industry guidance funds, these can

[49] In practice, LPs will design various mechanisms to supervise and motivate GPs so that they act in the interests of LPs. For example, major LPs may participate in the GP's investment decision-making, have a vote or veto in the GP's investment committee, or send observers to monitor the GP. For another example, when forming a fund, LPs may ask the GP to contribute some money, perhaps 1–2% of the total investment of the LP, to show that it is bound to the interests of the LP.

[50] The rise of private equity funds in the US is closely related to the rise of "leverage buyouts" in the capital markets. The rise of this financial instrument has a complex economic and social background, including changes in the perception of the role of companies in society, changes in labor-capital relations after globalization, and financial deregulation. Appelbaum and Batt (2014) make a wonderful analysis and introduction to the background and logic of the era of private equity funds and leverage buyouts.

include funds from the central government, such as the National Integrated Circuit Investment Fund, as well as funds from local government, such as the Shenzhen Guidance Fund.

Compared with the traditional way that local governments' industrial investment, government industrial guidance funds have three distinct characteristics. First, most guidance funds do not invest directly in industrial firms, rather they give their money to private equity funds to invest on their behalf. A PE fund typically has multiple LPs, in addition to government guidance funds. Therefore, by investing in PE funds, government guidance funds can leverage investment from other LPs and guide them into targeted industries. For this reason, the funds are named "industry guidance". Additionally, since government guidance funds invest in other funds, they are also known as "fund of funds" or FoF. Second, by handing government funds to private equity managers, a part of taxpayers' money is managed by private entrepreneurs and subject to market risks. This process involves many institutional reforms and run into many difficulties in practice (see the analysis below). Third, most guidance funds are invested in "strategic emerging industries", such as chips and electronic cars. These funds are not allowed to invest in infrastructure and real estate, which differentiates them from another similar financial tool commonly used in infrastructural projects, i.e., public–private partnership or PPP (see Chapter 3).

In the previous chapter, we introduced urban investment corporations. Local governments cannot borrow directly from banks, therefore urban investment corporations act as financing vehicles. Similarly, governments cannot make direct equity investments in capital markets, therefore it is necessary to set up a company to operate and manage the guidance fund. These fund managing companies fall into 3 broad categories. The first group are wholly state-owned enterprises, such as Beijing Yizhuang State Investment, an investor in BOE. The second group are mixed-ownership companies, such as Shenzhen Capital Group Co. Ltd., which is entrusted to manage the huge Shenzhen Guidance Fund. The largest shareholder of this company is the Shenzhen city government, but it only holds a 28% share. The third category is more like CFLD discussed in the previous chapter. Guidance funds in small cities are small in scale, and local governments have neither the resources nor the expertise to establish special management companies for them, so they simply entrust the funds to private companies, such as Prosperity Investment Group.

The concept of government guidance funds is easy to understand. Outside China, institutional investors have had decades of experience acting as LPs and have established industry associations to share investment and governance experience.[51] But in China, there are three prerequisites for the development of government guidance funds as institutional investors. First, institutional and policy changes need to be made, otherwise local governments won't dare to invest taxpayers' money into the risky equity market. Second, capital markets need to be relatively developed, and there should be a large number of sophisticated GPs available to manage the government funds. In addition, capital markets should be large and liquid enough for these investments to find channels to exit. Third, industrialization and economic development needs to reach a certain stage, so that there are sufficient investment opportunities available in the high-tech and high-risk strategic emerging industries. A large number of high-tech firms would not appear until the economy is relatively developed.

Institutional Conditions Supporting the Rise of Guidance Funds

In 2005, the National Development and Reform Commission and the Ministry of Finance for the first time confirmed that the central and local governments could set up venture capital funds, in order to support startup companies by providing equity investment or by offering financing guarantees.[52] In 2007, the newly revised Partnership Enterprise Law came into effect, and the LP/GP operation model explained above was codified in Chinese law. The first wave of RMB denominated limited partnership funds were soon established. In 2008, the State Council set the policy framework for the establishment of government guidance funds, specifying that their purpose is to *"Leverage up and Amplify the impact of fiscal funds, increase the supply of startup capital, and rectify market failures in the allocation of startup capital"*. The new framework clarified that government guidance funds can operate as funds of funds,

[51] For example, the Institutional Limited Partner Association (ILPA), a membership organization found in 2002 in the US.

[52] In 2005, the National Development and Reform Commission, the Ministry of Science and Technology, the Ministry of Finance, the Ministry of Commerce and the People's Bank of China jointly issued "Interim Measures for the Management of Venture Capital Enterprises".

and that private capital can be used together with government funds in order to increase investment in start-ups. Moreover, guidance funds were required to operate with the principles of *"guided by government, operated by market rules, scientific decision making, and risk prevention"*, which thereby are accepted as basic principles for the operation of government guidance funds across China.[53]

If government money enters a private company in the form of equity, and one day the company goes public, what will happen to the "state owned shares". Is it necessary to transfer 10% of the value to a state social security fund as is often required for the IPO of a state-owned enterprise?[54] If such a transfer is required, neither local government nor any other state-owned investor would be willing to invest. Therefore, in order to incentivize the participation of state-owned capital in venture capital financing, the Ministry of Finance and other departments stipulated that qualified state-owned venture capital institutions and state-owned guidance funds may apply for an exemption to transfer state-owned shares during an IPO.[55]

GP fees are also a potential issue. Although a 2% management fee and 20% performance commission are an international convention, should they apply to manage public money, particularly for such a high percentage of commission? In 2011, the Ministry of Finance and the

[53] In 2008, the General Office of the State Council backed the "Guiding Opinions on the Establishment and Operation of Venture Capital Guidance Funds" issued by the National Development and Reform Commission and other departments.

[54] In 2002, the Ministry of Finance stipulated that state-owned enterprises listed overseas should transfer 10% of the issued shares to the National Council of Social Security Fund for holding. In 2009, the Ministry of Finance, the State-owned Assets Supervision and Administration Commission, the China Securities Regulatory Commission and the Social Security Fund jointly issued the "Implementation Measures for the Transfer of Partial State-owned Shares in Domestic Securities Markets to Enrich the National Social Security Fund", applying to any domestic IPOs that involve state-owned shares, unless otherwise stated by the State Council. According to the regulations, 10% of the actually issued shares at the time of IPO must be transferred to the Social Security Fund, if these shares are held by state-owned shareholder. If the number of shares held by state-owned shareholders is less than 10% of the actually issued shares, all the state-owned shares should be transferred.

[55] In 2010, the Ministry of Finance, together with the State-owned Assets Supervision and Administration Commission, the China Securities Regulatory Commission and the Social Security Fund, jointly issued the "Notice on Exempting State-owned Venture Investment Institutions and State-owned Venture Investment Guidance Funds from the State-owned Share Transfer Obligation".

National Development and Reform Commission clarified that revenue and risk should be shared between government funds and private capital. That GPs, as well-being able to charge a management fee of between 1.5% and 2.5%, could also charge 20% commission on extra investment returns. By explicitly outlining the fee structure, the value created by GPs was recognized and they were no longer treated as a simple investment vehicle.[56]

The above policies provided the institutional framework for government guidance funds, however their explosive development only started around 2014. The spark that led to this sudden growth was a set of reforms in the new version of the Budget Law. Prior to the reforms, local governments often used various special funds from their budgetary revenues to subsidize firms. After the 2014 reform, the State Council strictly limited the budgetary subsidy provided by local governments to firms. Local governments, which had typically used tax rebates or subsidies directly from their annual budget, had to find a new way to spend the money on firms. Since money not spent within 2 years, according to the new Budget Law, might be transferred to the treasury of higher-level government.[57]

By 2015, the basic institutional framework has been set up. And given that local governments needed a new outlet to invest money on firms, industry guidance funds were ready to go. However, for such a new way to invest public money, a more detailed operation guide was needed. Starting from 2015, the Ministry of Finance and the National Development and Reform Commission have issued a series of detailed rules governing the management of guidance funds, providing guidelines for local governments. There are two guidelines which are most important. First, the principle of "benefits and risk sharing" was clarified once again, recognizing the possibility of investment loss for government guidance funds that use public money. Second, it was clarified that although the treasury department of local government provides capital to funds, "(*they)*

[56] In 2011, the Ministry of Finance and the National Development and Reform Commission issued the "Interim Measures for the Management of Emerging Industry Startup Funds Investing Venture Capital Funds".

[57] In 2014, the State Council issued the "Notice of the State Council on Reviewing and Regulating Preferential Policies Such as Tax Refunds", which stipulated that "*without the approval of the State Council, no region or department may provide preferential financial policies for enterprises*." Regarding local government's surplus budget funds, please refer to Article 42 of the 2014 Budget Law.

usually do not participate in the day to day operations of funds". The rules also stipulate the need for local treasury departments *"to help build a good environment for government guidance funds to support industrial development"* and to encourage these government investment funds to operate by market rules.[58]

After 2015, the guidance funds begun to expand rapidly. According to Zero2IPO, in 2013, government guidance funds had roughly 40 billion yuan under management. The number grow to 212.2 billion yuan in 2014, 337.3 billion yuan in 2015 and to over 1 trillion yuan in 2016, increasing more than 20 times in just three years (2013–2016). Many of the best-known industry guidance funds were established during this period, including the famous National Integrated Circuit Industry Investment Fund, also known as the Big Fund. The fund was established by the Ministry of and Information Technology in 2014, and it raised 140 billion yuan just for the first round. Most local government guidance funds were also established during this period.

Financial and Industrial Conditions Supporting the Rise of Guidance Funds

Most government guidance funds operate in the form of "fund of funds", which invest together with private capital in other market-orientated funds. The later invest the money in the equity of private companies. The popularity of this model requires three conditions to be met: a large amount of private capital is ready to be deployed alongside government money, a large number of capable and trustworthy private equity fund managers need to be available, and there must be sufficient channels available to exit investments. The final condition is also the most important and it requires a well-functioning capital market.

In the first decade of the twenty-first century, there were three key policies which laid the foundation for the development of capital markets in China. First, in 2003, the third plenary session of the 16th Central Committee of the CCP passed the "Decision of the Central Committee

[58] In the last two months of 2015, the Ministry of Finance successively issued the "Interim Measures for the Administration of Government Investment Funds" and the "Guiding Opinions on Investing Fiscal Capital into Government Investment Funds to Support Industrial Development".

of the CCP on Issues Concerning Improving the Socialist Market Economy". A year later, the State Council issued "Opinions on Promoting the Reform, Opening and Stable Development of the Capital Markets". These policies laid institutional foundations for establishing a multi-level capital market system and for developing venture capital. Second, the 2005 Split-Share Structure Reform, a landmark reform of capital market, made non-tradable shares tradable.[59] Third, in 2006, the newly revised Company Law came into effect, officially differentiating the shares held by company founders and those held by venture capital investors. After listing in public markets, a founders' shares were subject to a 3-year lock-up period, but venture capital shares could be sold after 1 year, giving more flexibility in terms of exit channels. In the same year, the China Securities and Regulatory Commission formalized its regulation and approval standards and procedures for IPO applications.[60]

During this period, both the Shanghai and Shenzhen Stock Exchanges made many reforms to make available more IPO opportunities. In 2004, the Small and Medium Enterprise Board was launched on the Shenzhen Stock Exchange, which was followed in 2009 by the ChiNext Board. In 2013, the over-the-counter system, the National Equities Exchange and Quotations, expanded nationwide. In 2019, the Sci-Tech Innovation Board opened on the Shanghai Stock Exchange, in which a registration-based system of IPOs was started to replace the traditional application-approval-based system. The expansion of domestic IPO opportunities helped to put an end to the period of companies looking to both raise capital overseas and exit on stock exchanges overseas. After the financial crisis in 2008, RMB-denominated funds started to dominate both venture capital and private equity market in China, and US dollar-denominated funds became less and less important.

As for those private capital that could be invested together with government guidance funds, they might come from the investment departments of large companies or from other institutional investors.

[59] At the time, two-thirds of the shares in China's stock market were not tradable. The reason was to maintain state control of publicly listed state-owned enterprises by making state-owned shares non-tradable. This severely restricted the rights and benefits of shareholders of non-tradable shares, resulting in many distortions. In April 2005, the China Securities Regulatory Commission initiated the reform on this split-share structure.

[60] In 2006, the China Securities Regulatory Commission issued the *Administrative Measures for IPOs*.

Institutional investors have been supported through various reforms in this century and thereby increased their participation in private fund investments. As an example, between 2010 and 2014, a series of regulations from the China Insurance Regulatory Commission allowed insurance funds to start investing in the equity of unlisted companies and venture capital funds.[61]

Therefore, from 2006 to 2014, China's private equity funds developed rapidly, and a large number of market-orientated funds and fund management talents begun to emerge. In 2014, once domestic IPOs begun to take off, the private equity market started to surge. Starting in the same year, the development of government guidance funds and the development of private equity investment began to merge, public funds and private capital begun to mix, and government fiscal resources found a new and market-orientated way of operation. Over time, government guidance funds have gradually become the most important institutional LPs for private equity funds.

The vast majority of government guidance funds ultimately ends up being invested in strategic emerging industries. These industries tend to have three characteristics in common. First, developing these new industries is a part of China's national development strategy. Investing government money into these industries that have been identified as strategically important is supported by the central government, which reduces political risks associated with investing government money. In both the Twelfth and the Thirteenth Five-Year Plan, the State Council made special provisions for the development of new industries and made it one of the top priorities of China's industrial policy. The central government also sets specific targets. For example, by 2015, these strategic emerging industries should account for 8% of national output and to 15% by 2020. By 2030, these industries should become dominant drivers of China's sustainable and healthy economic development, with China being recognized as a globally important manufacturing and innovation center in these industries. These two five-year plans also proposed to support

[61] In 2010, the China Insurance Regulatory Commission issued the *Interim Measures for Equity Investment with Insurance Funds*, which allows qualified insurance companies to directly invest in the equity of non-listed companies or to invest up to 4% of their total assets in equity investment funds. In 2014, the China Insurance Regulatory Commission issued the *Notice on Matters Concerning the Investment of Insurance Funds in Venture Capital Funds*, which cleared the way for insurance funds to invest in venture capital funds.

these new industries by using more and innovative fiscal and financial policies. Particularly, the plans explicitly encouraged the use of government funds to guide and attract private capital, expand investment scale, and promote the rapid development of the emerging industries.

The second common characteristics is that these strategic emerging industries are placed in the frontline of technology, and require vast amounts of investment in R&D and innovation. Innovation by its nature is highly uncertain, and this kind of investment therefore needs shareholders who are able to shoulder large amounts of risk and also be able to help solve various problems for the investee company. From the perspective of companies, government funds not only provide capital but also an access to government networks and resources. From the perspective of government, compared with a simple subsidy that does not need to be paid back, equity investments seek investment returns, which provides a stronger incentive to the investee company, at least in theory.

The third commonality is that many of these strategic emerging industries are still in the early stage of development, and no obvious geographical clusters have been formed. Many local governments therefore see an opportunity to build such a cluster in their region (e.g., Hefei, Chengdu or Wuhan which all invested in BOE). The Thirteenth Five-Year Plan also encourages local governments to develop such industrial clusters, as a way to drive local economic development and transformation. Eventually, many regional clusters of new and innovative industries would support China's future economic development.

Successes and Challenges of Government Guidance Funds

In recent years, many well-known Chinese companies in high-tech sectors, such as new energy, semiconductors, artificial intelligence, biomedicine and aerospace, are backed by government guidance funds. In March 2018, the Office of the United States Trade Representative (USTR) released the "301 Investigation Report" reviewing China's industrial and technology policies.[62] A whole section of the report was dedicated to China's government guidance funds. After the report was

[62] See USTR's "Section 301 Investigation Report", *Findings of the Investigation into China's Acts, Policies, and Practices Related to Technology Transfer, Intellectual Property, and Innovation.*

released, the government funds mentioned in the report received likes from some of their peers. "Great job! Even the Americans know you!"

The effectiveness of the guidance funds of course depends on the successful development of the investee industries. If the industry develops well, then the guidance funds' contribution would be recognized, otherwise they would be seen as a huge waste of public resources. An investment will be always judged by the result, but right now it's still too early to make a judgment about whether guidance funds have been successful. Regardless of the result, however, judging from the current situation, it's fair to say that government guidance funds have faced many difficulties and challenges. Unlike the local government financial vehicles discussed in the previous chapter, the difficulties here are not high debt levels or falling land prices, but instead the institutional difficulties associated with operating a government-owned equity investment fund. There are four key challenges.

The first challenge relates to the contradiction between the obligation of keeping fiscal funds safe and the risk of losing money in equity investment. Although in principle, guidance funds are allowed to lose money, it's still politically risky for managers, who are often government employees, if losses actually occur. Of course, for most government guidance funds, the primary objective is never to seek outstanding financial returns, but to attract more industrial investment and resources. But it is still very important to avoid any financial loss. This leads to the second key challenge.

The second challenge stems from the contradiction between borderless capital and the local nature of government guidance funds. In a mature capital market, institutional investors care about financial return and do not care as much about which location they invest in. On the other hand, the capital for government guidance funds comes from local governments and they are aimed to attract investment to the local economy. They are not willing to invest these local public funds to other places. The previous two chapters already discussed that neither land finance nor tax incentives can alter the underlying fundamental factors that make an area attractive for investment. Local resources, talent pool, geography and prospects for economic development are the key factors. The area surrounding the Yangtze River Delta and the Pearl River Delta, as well as some large inland capital cities, have little problem attracting investment, therefore their government guidance funds can be successful by only investing locally.

However, in other regions, the role of guidance funds in attracting investment is not as successful and may in fact lead to other distortions. In some areas, guidance funds that should be invested in equity have instead been restructured as a debt instrument. For example, equity investors are supposed to share profit and losses with the investee company, but in some areas, guidance funds have agreed with investee companies to let the company repurchase the shares in the future. If the company is successful and makes a profit, the shares can be repurchased on their original value, perhaps plus some low interests (say 2–3% per year). However, even if the company is not successful and loses money, it must also find a way to repurchase the shares from the guidance fund. This is not an equity investment but rather a loan in disguise. As another example, in order to attract other private investors to invest together, government guidance funds may promise to purchase shares from them in the future. In this way, the guidance fund essentially removes any investment risk for the private capital, but creates an implicit liability for the local government. These practices go against the original intention of guidance funds, which is to drive deleveraging across the economy by replacing debt financing with equity financing, and they are explicitly prohibited by the central government.[63]

The third challenge stems from the capital markets themselves. Equity investment, especially private equity investment, is very sensitive to changes in market conditions. A private equity fund usually has multiple investors as its LPs, and a government guidance fund would typically not provide more than 20% of its total capital, or in other words, 80% of the capital needs to come from other sources. So, if for some reason other private capital is not willing to invest, for example due to economic recessions or poor market conditions, then government guidance funds may also have to stay idle without enough investment partners. After 2018, as a part of the deleveraging reform in China, the "New Regulations on Asset Management" were introduced, and as a result, the available private capital shrunk sharply, and many private equity funds were liquidated and

[63] According to the estimates by Jiang et al. (姜超, 朱征星, 杜佳 2018), by the end of 2017, the total amount of various "debt disguised as equity" formed by PPP and government guidance funds was about 3 trillion yuan. In early 2017, the National Development and Reform Commission issued the *Interim Measures for the Administration of Government Industrial Investment Funds*, which explicitly prohibits "*the act of increasing government debt in disguised form, such as "debt disguised as* equity*"*".

shut down. Many government guidance funds therefore have also been unable to attract other capitals to invest jointly into local economy.

The fourth challenge relates to incentive mechanism. Private equity funds often provide high salaries to attract top talents. Government guidance funds, however, come from the state system or state-owned enterprises. Employment might be safe but salaries are hardly competitive. As a result, government guidance funds may not be able attract top investment talents and therefore adopt a fund of funds method of investment, transferring money to more private fund managers to invest. Even so, in order to effectively monitor and communicate with these private fund managers, in a way supervising their behavior so that the government objectives in industrial development are met, it is necessary to keep up to date with current industry practices. This would require government funds to retain some talents and reform their salary structure to be more competitive. The results vary from place to place, in a place like Shenzhen that is more market-orientated and flexible, salaries on working for government funds could be competitive, but in other regions, salaries might be too low to attract and incentivize talents.

Summary

Economic development is always a result of the joint efforts of government, enterprises and society. How these forces would be combined depends on the resources that each of the parties possess. The endowment and distribution of resources at any given time are largely determined by history. In the case of China, the economic reforms of recent decades were born out a planned economy, therefore the government is in possession of a large number of resources which are crucial to economic development, including land, universities and various research institutes, as well as financial institutions such as banks. Therefore, Chinese government is bound to be a key player in industrialization and economic development. In the real world, there is no black-and-white line between the government and the market, and almost all important phenomena are the result of interactions between the governments and the market. To understand this complex and nuanced world, we should try to avoid an overly simple dichotomy the government and the market.

This chapter therefore tries to avoid talking about industrial development and government intervention in the abstract, instead focusing on two specific industry case studies and one particular tool of industrial policy, government industrial guidance fund. The aim is to help the reader understand the complex and multi-faceted nature of the problem. There is no one-size-fits-all model of industrial policies and economic development. Policies must be pragmatic and adaptive to everchanging realities. Specific policy tools also must evolve to reflect the changes in market environment and government capacity. Therefore, when studying economic development, it is more useful to study the real history of developed countries, to understand the specific challenges and their solutions as they develop, rather than to believe some highly ideological and oversimplified development models such as "the Washington Consensus".

From the 1990s until the early twenty-first century, China's infrastructure, legal system, capital and credit markets were all underdeveloped. Therefore local governments and state-owned entities who were more creditworthy used land to leverage up financial resources into rapid urbanization and industrialization. This model is obviously successful, evidenced by China's rapid economic development, but it also led to some serious problems, such as rampant corruption related to land transactions, an urbanization focusing on land development instead of people's quality of life, a lack of quality public services such as healthcare and education, and soaring debt and house prices. Meanwhile, overreliance on investment leads to low disposable income of people, and as a result, domestic consumption is too small to absorb the oversupply of products caused by overinvestment in production capacity. This inevitably results in a high level of exports, causing trade imbalances and conflicts. These are all hot topics in recent years that have occupied the media in both China and overseas, spawning many reforms. Based on the first 4 chapters of introduction of microeconomic environment, the following 4 chapters will discuss these macroeconomic consequences.

Further Readings

There are a lot of Chinese documentaries and books about the development of different industries in China. For English audience, it might be interesting to study industrial investment in a historical context and how it influences the rise and fall of other countries. Industrialization was never a simple market-driven process, national states, empires, government-supported enterprises, and wars all played critical roles. After reading histories of industrialization in various countries, readers may find that China's state-led model is actually not so special or unique at all.

There are many great books on this topic. In particular, I recommend four pieces that explain industrial development by focusing on specific industries or enterprises. Thomas K. McCraw's *Creating Modern Capitalism: How Entrepreneurs, Companies, and Countries Triumphed in Three Industrial Revolutions* (1998) and Sven Beckett's *Empire of Cotton: A Global History* (2019) are masterpieces whose titles are self-explanatory. Joe Studwell's *How Asia Works: Success and Failure in the World's Most Dynamic Region* (2013) tells the success story of Asian countries such as Japan, Korea and China, as well as some failure stories in Southeast Asia. The ideas and structures in this book are crystal clear, and the case studies are easy to understand. For a more recent story of perhaps the hottest industry, Chris Miller's *Chip War: The Fight for the World's Most Critical Technology* (2022) is a great read.

References

Acemoglu, Daron, Ufuk Akcigit, Douglas Hanley, and William Kerr (2016). "Transition to Clean Technology." *Journal of Political Economy* 124.1: 52–104.

Aghion, Philippe, Jing Cai, Mathias Dewatripont, Luosha Du, Ann Harrison, and Patrick Legros (2015) "Industrial Policy and Competition." *American Economic Journal: Macroeconomics* 7.4: 1–32.

Akerlof, George A. (2020). "Sins of Omission and the Practice of Economics." *Journal of Economic Literature* 58.2: 405–418.

Alchian, Armen A. (1950). "Uncertainty, Evolution, and Economic Theory." *Journal of Political Economy* 58.3: 211–221.

Appelbaum, Eileen, and Rosemary Batt (2014). *Private Equity at Work: When Wall Street Manages Main Street*. Russell Sage Foundation.

Bloom, Nicholas (2014). "Fluctuations in Uncertainty." *Journal of Economic Perspectives* 28.2: 153–176.

Cherif, Reda, and Fuad Hasanov (2019). "The Return of the Policy that Shall Not Be Named: Principles of Industrial Policy," *IMF Working Paper.*

Gomory, Ralph E., and William J. Baumol (2000). *Global Trade and Conflicting National Interests*. MIT Press.

Havranek, Tomas, and Zuzana Irsova (2011). "Estimating Vertical Spillovers from FDI: Why Results Vary and What the True Effect Is." *Journal of International Economics* 85.2: 234–244.

Krugman, Paul (1987). "The Narrow Moving Band, the Dutch Disease, and the Competitive Consequences of Mrs. Thatcher: Notes on Trade in the Presence of Dynamic Scale Economies." *Journal of Development Economics* 27.1–2: 41–55.

Krugman, Paul (1992). *Geography and Trade*. MIT Press.

Lane, Nathan (2019). "Manufacturing Revolutions: Industrial Policy and Industrialization in South Korea," *Working Paper*.

Levchenko, Andrei A. (2007). "Institutional Quality and International Trade." *Review of Economic Studies* 74.3: 791–819.

Lin, Justin Yifu (2012). *New Structural Economics: A Framework for Rethinking Development and Policy*. World Bank Publications.

Lin, Justin Yifu (2014). *The Quest for Prosperity: How Developing Economies Can Take Off*. Princeton University Press.

Liu, Ernest (2019). "Industrial Policies in Production Networks." *Quarterly Journal of Economics* 134.4: 1883–1948.

Melitz, Marc J., and Daniel Trefler (2012). "Gains from Trade when Firms Matter." *Journal of Economic Perspectives* 26.2: 91–118.

REN21 (2020). *Renewables 2020 Global Status Report*, Renewable Energy Policy Network for the 21st Century.

Shiller, Robert J. (2020). *Narrative Economics: How Stories Go Viral and Drive Major Economic Events*. Princeton University Press.

Sivaram, Varun (2018). *Taming the Sun: Innovation to Harness Solar Energy and Power the Planet*. MIT Press.

Studwell, Joe (2013). *How Asia Works: Success and Failure in the World's Most Dynamic Region*. Open Road+ Grove/Atlantic.

Yergin, Deniel (2020). *The New Map: Energy, Climate, and the Clash of Nations*. Penguin Press.

Yip, George S., and Bruce McKern (2016). *China's Next Strategic Advantage: From Imitation to Innovation*. MIT Press.

Young, Alwyn (1991). "Learning by Doing and the Dynamic Effects of International Trade." *Quarterly Journal of Economics* 106.2: 369–405.

Translated References (in Chinese)

Gong, Yongfeng, and Jie Lin (2020). "'De-globalization' Is Difficult to Shake the Dominant position of China's Photovoltaic Industry Chain," CITIC Securities. (in Chinese)

Jiang, Chao, Zhengxing Zhu, and Jia Du (2018). "The Scale of the Potential Debt of Local Government," Haitong Securities. (in Chinese)

Lin, Yifu, Hemao Wu, and Yiqing Xing (2010). "'Wave Phenomena' and Formation of Excess Capacity." *Economic Research Journal* 10: 4–19. (in Chinese)

Liu, Shouying, and Jidong Yang (2019). "The Evolution and the Policy Selection in China's Industrial Upgrading: Based on Product Space Perspective." *Journal of Management World* 6: 81–94+194–195. (in Chinese)

Lu, Feng (2016). *Photonic Change: An Enterprise and Its Industrial History*. Contemporary China Publishing House. (in Chinese)

Lu, Feng (2019). *Towards Self-reliance and Innovation: Finding the Source of Chinese Power*. China Renmin University Press. (in Chinese)

Lu, Feng (2020). *New Fire: Towards Independent Innovation 2*. China Renmin University Press. (in Chinese)

Yuan, Jiancong, Tao Xu, Zhe Wang, Chong Ao, and Chao Li (2020). "New Materials Industry Panel Materials Series Report," CITIC Securities. (in Chinese)

Zhao, Ting, and Zhao Chen (2019). "Comparative Advantage and Central, Local Industrial Policies in China." *The Journal of World Economy* 10: 98–119. (in Chinese)

Zhu, Yue (2019). "The Power of Cycle and the Edge of Growth: 15-year Review and Outlook of the Photovoltaic Industry." Industrial Securities. (in Chinese)

Macroeconomic Consequences

The first part of the book introduced how local governments in China promote economic development. The first key feature of this model is that in the process of urbanization, local governments put more efforts in acquiring and developing more lands instead of in improving conditions for new residents of cities. While driving rapid urbanization and industrialization, the model has clear side effects. Public services are insufficient. House prices have skyrocketed, leading households to carry more and more debt. At the same time, the gap between wealthy urban areas and poorer rural areas has widened. Chapter 5 will analyze these problems and introduce how governments try to combat them by initiating sweeping reforms on the land market and the labor market.

The second feature of the model is that local governments need to compete to attract investment, and in doing so, they tend to focus on investment scale and speed over long-term sustainable development. The advantage here is that industrialization takes place rapidly, and the downside is that it has greatly increases the debt burden in the economy. Governments, firs and households have all taken on lots of debt, leading to increasing financial risks. Chapter 6 will look at structural reforms of deleveraging and reducing overcapacity across the economy.

The third feature of this model is that it focuses on investment and production at the expense of consumption. This has developed China into the world manufacturing powerhouse, led to rapid economic growth and expanded foreign trade greatly. The problem, however, is that the economic structure is imbalanced. Too many resources are transferred to the sectors where investment are concentrated, i.e. corporate sector and government, while the share of national income going to households is too low. Consumption is therefore too low to sustain long-term economic development. Additionally, any productive capacity that cannot be consumed within China has to be exported abroad, which can exacerbate trade conflicts with other countries. Chapter 7 will analyze these issues and discuss reforms introduced after the 19th National Congress of the CCP, which are determined to move the economy to a new development model of *"dual circulation"*: to make the domestic market the main driving force of the economy and to make the domestic and international markets mutually reinforcing each other.

CHAPTER 5

Urbanization and Imbalances

After teaching for a long time, I have developed a keen understanding about the mentality of students at different stages. University freshmen are free from the worries of careers and adult life, they like to explore questions in more detail and ask why things happen the way they do. By the final year of university, students are more anxious and need to think more about what they are going to do with their lives. The predicament faced by most students is that the city with desired jobs is too expensive to live in, but less expensive cities do not have desirable jobs. Chasing dreams in big cities is too difficult, but returning to hometowns is too embarrassing. They see high rise buildings being developed everywhere, but still can't afford a place to live. Why is housing so expensive? Why do the students have such a low sense of belonging? Is it really necessary to fly the nest and fly alone away from their parents and family? These problems are all related to the economic development model driven by local governments.

It takes a lot of capital to build the infrastructure necessary for urban development. Using land to leverage up capital is an effective way to finance the process. By selling state-owned urban land, local government can accumulate enough capital to promote rapid industrialization and urbanization. This system of state-owned urban land enables local governments to monopolize the supply of urban land, thereby being able to turning this latent public wealth into the huge capital necessary to

X. Lan, *How China Works*,
https://doi.org/10.1007/978-981-97-0080-6_5

urban development. However, there is a downside, local governments' financial resources become highly dependent on land prices, real estate and housing prices. Housing prices are linked to land prices, land prices are linked to fiscal revenues, and fiscal revenues are linked to infrastructure investment. Therefore local economic growth, local government's fiscal health, banking system and real estate industries are combined into a complex intertwined relationship, where they either rise together or fall together.

This land-driven urbanization model distorts the real purpose of urbanization, which is to create a better life for people. Land prices are driven by housing prices, but housing prices must be paid by people, and mortgages must be extracted from people's income. Therefore, the capitalization of urban land is essentially the capitalization of the future income of homeowners. It is people's income that supports house and land prices. If we leave people out of the picture and ignore the fact that urbanization should eventually serve people, raise their income and create a better living and working environment for them, then urbanization will go astray.

In 1980, China's urban resident population accounted for less than 20% of the total population. By 2019, the number exceeded 60%. In just 40 years, 500 million people moved to cities, a miracle of urbanization. However, if we look at household registration, the registered urban population in 2019 was only 44% of China's total population, a 16-percentage-point gap from the urban resident population. That means there's more than 200 million people who reside in urban areas but do not have a local household registration (*Hukou*), and therefore can only have a very limited access to local public services such as public education, since these services are provided based on registered population. This leaves a huge difference between supply and demand of public services in the cities with large number of immigrants, that's why they have a low sense of belonging. It's therefore difficult for urban immigrants to settle down and raise a family in the city, which also creates a phenomenon of *"left behind"* children, women and elderly living in rural areas when adult men migrate to cities to work. In recent years, a series of reforms have been introduced to change the status quo and make urbanization more migrant-friendly.

The first section of this chapter analyzes the relationship between house prices and the supply and demand for land. It will also discuss the heavy household debt burden brought about by house prices. The second section analyzes regional imbalances, which roots in the limitations that exist in terms of the movement of people and land. It will also look at recent reforms in the land transfer and household registration systems, which have taken a high priority during recent years. The third section will analyze the rise in income inequality in China, which is also related to house prices and the reforms of the land and labor markets.

Section 1: House Prices and Household Debt

The 1994 tax sharing reform discussed in Chapter 2 was a watershed moment for many major economic developments in China, including urbanization. Prior to 1994, the fiscal contracting system was in place, which promoted the development of township and village enterprises (TVE) that were one pillar of industrialization. Most peasants did not have to leave their hometowns to a city for a factory job, instead choosing to join local TVEs, urbanization therefore didn't happen on a large scale. After the tax sharing reform, TVEs started to decline and the tide of migrant workers moving from rural to urban areas started to swell. Figure 5.1 shows that the urban resident population began to increase quickly after 1995. Then land finance gradually became the main driver of urbanization. The key to the success of this urbanization model is rising house prices. House prices can be affected by many factors in the short term, but in the long term are mainly affected by supply and demand. In both developed and developing countries, house prices are closely linked to demographics as young people forming households are the main buying force. In China, most young people flow into economically developed cities where land supply is tightly regulated. This leads to a mismatch between housing supply and demand, so prices rise.

House Prices and the Supply and Demand for Land

The effects of industrial agglomeration are very strong in a modern economy, and economic activity is increasingly concentrated in large cities. As incomes rise and living standards improve, people compete for buying urban homes. Whether this increasing demand pushes up prices, it depends on the elasticity of supply of housing and residential land. If the supply of residential land is tightly regulated, house prices will rise quickly. Although for any city, the given amount of land is more or less fixed, the percentage of land used for residential housing can be changed.

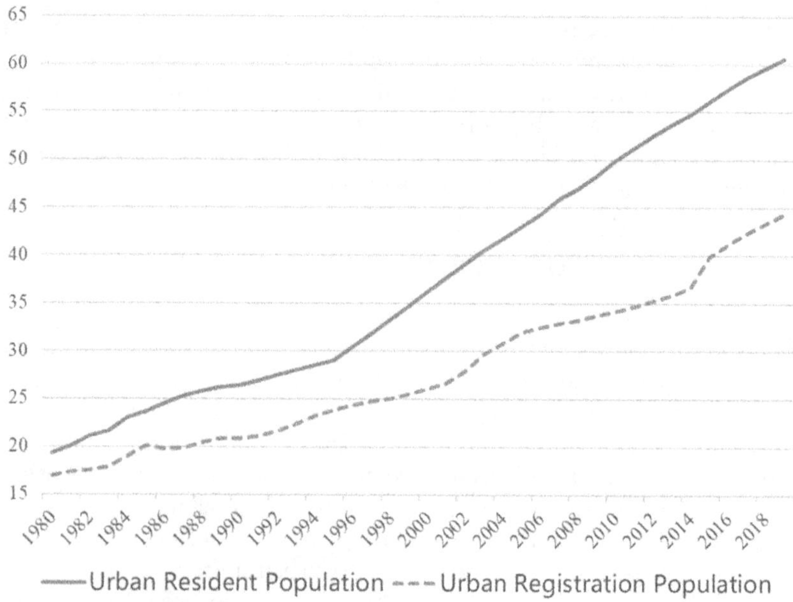

Fig. 5.1 Percentages of urban population in the total population (*Source* WIND and National Bureau of Statistics of China)

The designed density and number of houses contained on a given plot of land can also be increased.[1] These adjustments are all affected by policy. Even though land ownership is private in a country like the US, urban construction and land use planning are usually also subject to government regulation. San Francisco, as an example, has particularly strict control on new housing construction, and as a result house prices were high even in the 1990s. During the real estate boom leading up to the Great Recession in 2008, the city's housing construction metrics didn't increase, and

[1] A floor-area ratio can be calculated as the ratio of a buildings' area compared to the area of the land it occupies. The higher the ratio, the larger the buildings' area and the more people it can accommodate. For a given piece of land, a higher floor-area ratio will make the land more valuable. Brueckner et al. (2017) find that in places with more restrictions on real estate development, the higher the correlation between the floor-area ratio and land price.

house prices soared. Another example is Atlanta, where housing construction policies are more flexible, so despite a large influx of people, house prices have remained relatively stable.[2]

China's urbanization has progressed quickly, urban residents' income has also grown rapidly, so demand for housing and house prices has risen. According to the National Bureau of Statistics, since housing was first commercialized in reforms starting in 1998, the average price of commercial housing increased by 4.2 times in the following two decades. However, the level of increases varies widely across the country. Before reforms in 2015, which sought to compensate the resettlement of people living in shantytowns with cash instead of a new apartment (will be discussed more in Chapter 6), house prices in small cities increased only by about the same amount as average per capita incomes. Conversely, in large cities, house prices rose faster than per capita incomes, with the largest cities rising particularly fast. In the 10 years leading up to 2015, house prices in Beijing, Shanghai, Guangzhou and Shenzhen quadrupled, with an average annual growth rate of 13%.[3]

The main reason for this regional difference in house prices is the imbalance between supply and demand for land. In big cities that experienced a large population influx, the growth in supply of residential land is much lower than the growth in population. Between 2006 and 2014, the urban population increase in large cities (with a population over 5 million) accounted for nearly 40% of the total urban population increase, but the residential land increase in these cities accounted for only 20% of the national increase. Given this mismatch, house prices in these cities naturally rose fast. In smaller cities with a population less than 3 million, and especially less than 1 million, the increase in residential land is actually greater than the increase in the urban population, therefore house prices do not rise. In terms of the geographical distribution, the growth rate of the urban population in Eastern China is 10% faster than the growth rate of residential land, while in the western and northwestern regions,

[2] The examples from San Francisco and Atlanta come from Glaeser and Gyourko (2018).

[3] The data on housing prices and per capita disposable income of various cities are from Fang et al. (2015).

the growth rate of residential land has outpaced the growth rate of urban population.[4]

China implements a strict regulation on urban land construction quotas. Each year, new quotas are allocated by the central government to provinces, who then allocate them to cities and counties with the province. Quotas cannot be traded across provinces, so eastern China, facing large population inflows, cannot use permits that have been granted to the west, facing large population outflows. In the 10 years following 2003, in order to support the development of western regions and control the population size of large cities, the issuance of land use quotas not only did not favor the east and large cities, but rather proactively favored the west and small and medium sized cities. In 2003, the supply of land in the western regions accounted for less than 30% of the total supply of new construction land, but by 2014 it had risen to 60%. In 2002, China's urban constructed areas located in small and medium sized cities account for roughly half of the national total, but by 2013 it had risen to 64%.[5] The flow of land was clearly not geographically aligned with the flow of population, so the gap between housing prices in different regions increased.

As we can see, the policy of giving more housing construction permits to western regions did little to halt the flow of population to the large cities in the east. Not only have house prices in these large cities soared, but so have admission bars of colleges located in these cities. Although house prices and living costs in the west are lower, young Chinese are still willing go to the east where house prices are higher, because of more job opportunities and other amenities available. Many western cities, with an oversupply of cheap land at disposal, were eventually left only with empty houses, empty industrial parks and a large pile of debt. Many investors, who took advantage of cheap lands and generous government subsidies in the west, did not choose to reinvest their windfall profit and help further develop the local economy, instead they bet their money in the huge real estate boom in eastern cities.

Construction land permits cannot be traded across provinces, and it's therefore hard to increase the national efficiency of land use. Although

[4] Data on regional urban population and land come from Ren, Xia and Xiong (任泽平, 夏磊, 熊柴 2017).

[5] The data come from Han and Lu (韩立彬和陆铭 2018), who analyze the relationship between the land supply and house prices across different regions in China.

competition for attracting investment among local governments is typically fierce, often using land as a means of attraction, this competition can hardly continuously improve land use efficiency. The demand for land in highly developed areas is high and the price of land is high, so more land use quotas should have been flown to these areas to meet the rising demand, which would have reduced the pressure of price rise. But because land use is constrained by administrative boundaries and government policies, it is underdeveloped regions that are able to continue to supply a large amount of land at very low prices (sometimes even free). This mismatch clearly needs to be corrected. In 2020, the central government proposed a reform to the cross-regional allocation of land use permits, including the possibility of a cross-regional trading system for permits.[6]

House Prices and Household Debt: Lessons from Europe and the US

For a typical household, the largest amount of debt they will take during their lifetime comes from buying a house. The higher the house price, the larger the mortgage and the burden of debt. Rising house prices across various countries is mainly a result of supply and demand mismatches that we discussed in the previous sector. First, the demand for housing continues to rise in the process of urbanization, and second, the supply of land and mortgages is limited by political factors.

In the West, house ownership has become popular only relatively recently. Before World War II, most people did not own their own houses. Even in the US, where there are fewer people and more land, the homeownership rate between 1900 and 1945 was only about 45%. The rate only started to rise after World War II. The same was true for the UK. Before World War II, the homeownership rate in the UK was 30% and it only begun to rise after the war, reaching 70% prior to the global financial crisis.[7] Because most people in the UK and US rented house for a long time, their economists like to used rent control as an example when describing the principles of supply and demand. I first learned about rent control in 1998 when going through a textbook by Joseph Stiglitz.

[6] In April 2020, the Central Committee of the CCP and the State Council issued the *Opinions on Improving the Systems and Mechanisms for Market-Based Allocation of Production Factors.*

[7] Figures for the US are from Spader, McCue and Herbert (2016). Figures for the UK are from Ryan-Collins, Lloyd and Macfarlane (2017).

Although the argument was easy to understand, rent control was very remote from my experiences, because few people I knew at the time rented homes. In China at the time, peasants were provided with a piece of land to build their house, and most urban workers were provided with an apartment by their employers. So in China, that everybody is talking about urban house prices is also a relatively new phenomenon.

The rising rate of homeownership in Europe and the US has two important consequences. For renters, a house is merely a place to live, but for homeowners it is the most important asset they own. As the number and price of houses have continually climbed, house property has become the main component of national wealth. For example, house property rose from a 36% to 57% in national wealth in the UK, from 28 to 61% in France, 28% to 57% in Germany, and 38% to 42% in the US.[8] The second important consequence is that there are more and more homeowners and therefore more and more people benefit from rising prices. In order to please these homeowning voters, the government is reluctant to let house prices fall. Meanwhile, people without homes also want to buy a house as soon as possible to catch up with the wealth generated by rising house prices, so the government acts to help finance more house purchase, by lowering thresholds of home loans, such as down payments and interest payments.

In the US, house prices and electoral politics are also closely linked. Income inequality in the US has grown rapidly since the 1970s and 1980s, causing many political problems. However, fundamental reforms related to education or taxation face great political resistance and therefore not effective in the short term. Lending money to poorer people to allow them to buy homes, on the other hand, not only helps to alleviate their dissatisfaction but also gives them a shot at realizing the American dream. It also helps to stimulate house price growth, increasing the wealth of homeowners. This in turn can help to drive up their consumption, creating more employment and stimulating economic growth. So, prior to

[8] House property as a share of national wealth rose sharply across Europe, which was related to the economic recovery and reconstruction after World War II. In the US, this share rose by a much smaller amount, in part because the US became a superpower after the war, so the denominator of national wealth increased enormously. Data on the composition of national wealth across countries come from Piketty and Zuckerman (2014).

the global financial crisis of 2008, the government uses two government-sponsored agencies, Fannie Mae and Freddie Mac, to support the poor to take out mortgage loans. The two agencies purchased mortgage loans from commercial banks, which in essence lending money to banks to issue more mortgages.[9] In 1995, the Clinton administration stipulated that home loans issued to low-income people should be at least 42% of total assets of Fannie and Freddie. In 2000, the last year of Clinton's presidency, that rate rose to 50%.[10] In 2004, the Bush administration increased the ratio further to 56%. At the time, the two agencies were also happy, since loans to the poor were very profitable and there didn't seem to be too many risks involved. Furthermore, the down payment requirements for purchasing a house were also becoming lower and lower. Prior to the 2008 financial crisis, many mortgages were even issued with no down payment at all, which sparked a speculative frenzy. From 2002 to 2007, US house prices rose by an average of nearly 60%, according to the Case-Shiller Home Price Index. After the crisis, house prices fell 27% from the highest point in 2007 through to 2012 before gradually recovering. They only succeeded to return to the previous high nine years later in 2016.

Falling house prices and falling income would increase household debt burdens, which in turn would depress consumption. Consumption, which accounts for around 70% of US GDP, plummeted during the global financial crisis, pushing the economy into a deep recession. Areas that prior to the recession experienced higher house prices also experienced the sharper drops in consumption, higher unemployment, and more severe recessions.[11] The same situation replayed itself in Europe as most European

[9] Fannie Mae and Freddie Mac are not a state-owned enterprise, but rather private enterprises with close ties to the US government. They are "government-sponsored enterprises" and enjoy various government preferential policies, while at the same time assisting the government to undertake certain policy tasks. For example, Fannie and Freddie can obtain lines of credit directly from the US Treasury, which is almost equivalent to an implicit government guarantee for their debt, although the government has no legal obligation to guarantee it.

[10] The data come from Rajan (2010).

[11] The traditional theories on business cycles pay great attention to the role of investment. Although the proportion of investment in GDP is relatively small in developed countries, it is far more volatile than consumption and is often the main driver of business cycles. Over time, economists have paid more and more attention to the impact of consumption on the economic cycle, particularly the consumption decline related to a heavy household debt. Mian and Sufi (2014) analyze debt and consumption of US households.

countries also experienced a decades long rise in house prices before 2008. The higher the price rise, the heavier the debt burden of households, and the lower consumption caused by the crisis.[12]

Real estate is often referred to as the "mother of the business cycle" because of its inherent mismatch between supply and demand. On the one hand, banks can create almost unlimited new purchasing power through mortgages, on the other hand, the supply of urban land is often limited. This contradiction often leads to cycles of asset bubbles and bursts and is at the heart of real estate and financial instability. Additionally, real estate is not only connected to banks and other financial sectors, but also to household wealth and consumption, so it has a great impact on the overall economy.

House Prices and Household Debt: The Situation in China

In the 10 years after 2008, house prices in China rose rapidly. The total value of mortgages became larger and larger, and the debt burden of households more than tripled (Fig. 5.2). At the end of 2018, household debt accounted for 54% of GDP, which was still lower than the 76% of the US, but close to that of Germany and Japan. According to the aggregate data of credit and loans from the People's Bank of China (the central bank), 53% of household debts are home loans, and 24% are various types of consumer loans (e.g., car loans).[13] But these statistics may underestimate the debt associated with buying a home, since some consumer loans are used as a down payment for buying a home, a practice that is in violation of regulations but not uncommon. In addition, the central bank's aggregate data do not include informal lending outside of financial sectors, for example lending within families or friends.

The denominator of the debt burden in Fig. 5.2 is GDP, and this ratio is often used to do comparisons between countries, however it underestimates the real debt burden of households. Money for debt repayment

[12] A research report by the San Francisco branch of the Federal Reserve (Glick and Lansing 2010) shows that in the 10 years before 2008, housing prices and household debt in major European and American countries were highly positively correlated, and for more indebted countries, the greater the decline in consumption after the crisis.

[13] The remaining 23% are various operating loans. Chinese statistics divides the whole economy into three sectors, government, household and corporation. But the household sector also includes various unincorporated enterprises, such as self-employed businesses, so household loans also include their business operating loans.

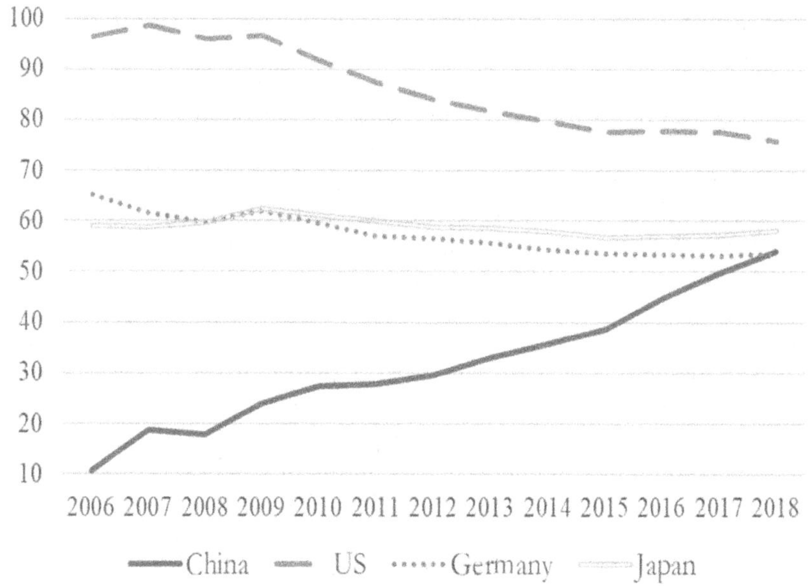

Fig. 5.2 Percentages of household debts over national GDP (*Source* IMF Global Debt Database)

cannot come from an abstract number such as GDP, instead it must use real money accruing to households. In 2019, the Survey and Statistics Department of the People's Bank of China surveyed the income and debt of more than 30,000 urban households across China. Nearly 60% of households are in debt, and the average debt-to-income ratio is 1.6, in other words the debt burden is 1.6 × the annual household disposable income. This burden is not low and is in fact close to the US. In 2000, the US household debt-income ratio was about 1.5, it soared to 2.1 prior to the financial crisis in 2008, then dropped back to 1.7 afterward.[14]

According to this 2019 survey by the People's Bank of China, mortgage loans accounted for 76% of urban household debt. On the asset side, the main asset held by urban residents was their house. Real estate

[14] The data on China come from a report by the People's Bank of China (中国人民银行调查统计司 2020). The US data come from the Federal Reserve's Quarterly Report on Household Debt and Credit.

accounted for 70% of total household assets, with 60% being in the form of residential housing while 10% in the form of shops or business real estate. If we compare the wealth of Americans, 72% of total household wealth is held in financial assets and only 28% is held in real estate.[15] So, we can see that the key assets for Chinese households are housing assets, whereas the key assets for American households are financial assets such as stocks and bonds. This difference can help us to understand some important policy differences between the two countries, for example China paid much more attention on the housing market instead of the stock market.

To summarize, when looking from an international perspective, the overall debt level of Chinese urban residents is already not low, and is still rising rapidly. The main cause is the rapid rise in house prices. Rising household debt has already begun to affect consumption. Take buying a car as an example, which is the most expensive consumer good aside from housing, and it plays an important role in the macroeconomy, accounting for roughly 10% of total retail sales in China. Cars are typical luxury goods and its income elasticity of demand is very high, meaning when income increases, demand for cars increases more, and when income decreases, demand decreases more. As household debt increases, the disposable income after mortgage debt repayments decreases. Once the overall economic situation deteriorates, demand for cars would greatly decrease. China's car market has experienced many years of 2-digit growth, and the number of private cars in 2018 was more than 14 × larger than 2005. However, starting from 2018, China-US trade war fears started to mount, and the future economic outlook became more uncertain, so sales of cars began to fall. From 2018 to the end of 2019, the year-on-year value of car sales declined every month, and when the coronavirus pandemic struck in 2020, sales fell 80% year on year in February and 40% in March. After which many cities introduced policies to stimulate automobile consumption and support the car industry.

House Prices and Household Debt Risk

According to the 2019 survey by the central bank, the average level of individual household total assets in Beijing (not deducting for liabilities such as mortgage loans) is 8.93 million yuan (roughly 1.3 million

[15] The data on the composition of US household wealth come from the 2019 financial account composition published by the Federal Reserve.

USD). In Shanghai, it's 8.07 million (1.17 million USD), which is more than 6 or 7 times greater than provinces such as Xinjiang or Jilin, where the numbers are only 1.28 million (190,000 USD) and 1.42 million (210,000 USD), respectively. Most of this difference comes from different house prices across regions, which have acted to increase intra-regional wealth inequality. In addition, cities with higher house prices tend to also have higher house vacancy rates. In other words, even though many people cannot afford a house, many houses stand vacant, presumably owned by richer people. According to the 2019 survey report of the central bank, the wealthiest 10% of households owned 49% of total urban household wealth, while the poorest 40% owned only 8%.[16]

Rising house prices not only increase the debt burden on households, but also widen the gap between the haves and have-nots, thereby stimulating poorer people to borrow and consume, something known as trickle-down consumption which is also common in developed countries.[17] During the period from 2014 to 2017, the savings of the bottom 50% of Chinese were essentially zero or even negative.[18] Since 2015, the use of consumer loans has surged, such as credit cards as well as those provided by financial technology companies such as Ant Group or JD Digits. According to the People's Bank of China, from 2016 to 2018, the total value of outstanding credit card balances increased by nearly 30% annually. In 2019, credit card-related risks started to materialize, and banks had to slow down lending.

Among those households carrying debt, low-income households face a particularly heavy debt burden. The average debt-to-income ratio of urban households in China is 1.6, while among households earning less than 60,000 yuan per year (roughly 8,700 USD), the ratio is closer to 3. The bottom 20% of households in terms of total assets are also more likely to carry riskier private loans.[19] In 2020, the IPO of Chinese fintech giant, Ant Group (what was to be the largest IPO in history), was suspended,

[16] Zhang, Jia and Yang (张川川, 贾坤, 杨汝岱 2016) show the positive relationship between housing prices and vacancy rates across Chinese cities, arguing that both are affected by income inequality.

[17] Trickle-down consumption leads to poor people consuming more by borrowing, see Bertrand and Morse (2016).

[18] The data on saving are from Gan, Zhao and Sun (甘犁, 赵乃宝, 孙永智 2018).

[19] A report by the People's Bank of China (中国人民银行调查统计司 2020) pointed out that among the 20% of households in debt with the lowest value of assets, informal

and at the time there were many articles on social media discussing the sharp rise in consumer debt and "indulgent consumption" of the younger generation. This kind of debt-driven consumption cannot be sustained, because the borrowed money is consumed away instead of being invested to form a higher human capital and future income, so the debt burden only becomes heavier over time.

If household debt remains high, then it's hard for the economy to weather economic downturns, particularly those triggered by falling house prices. The wealth of low-income households is almost entirely held in housing and most of the wealth is backed by mortgage loans, which makes this group particularly vulnerable to falling house prices. During the mortgage crisis in 2008, one out of every four mortgages was insolvent, and the wealth of many poor people was completely wiped out. Between 2007 and 2010, the net worth of the poorest 20% of Americans dropped from an average of $30,000 to almost nothing. The richest 10% saw their net worth drop by roughly 10%, from an average of $3.2 million to an average of $2.9 million. But even this small drop was short-lived. By 2016, the stock market and the housing market had rebounded and the real net wealth (after inflation) of the richest 10% was 16% higher than prior to the crisis. But for the bottom 50%, real wealth was cut in half and returned to 1971 levels, 40 years of wealth accumulation had been wiped out.[20]

Although the rise in house prices and subsequent rise in mortgage debt in China will also lead to many economic problems, it is unlikely that a mortgage and financial crisis on the scale of the global financial crisis would break out. Firstly, China's mortgage loans have a higher deposit ratio, with an average down payment of at least 30%. This is much higher than the US where a down payment could be as low as zero. The higher deposit ratio means that households are less willing to default on their mortgages (and lose their down payments) unless house prices drop by a sum greater than the value of the down payment. So the risks of lending banks are low. At the end of 2018, the non-performing loan

and private loans accounted for nearly 10% of their total debt. The data on the debt-to-income ratio of households with an annual income of less than 60,000 yuan come from another report of the People's Bank of China (中国人民银行金融稳定分析小组 2019).

[20] The figures here are Mian and Sufi (2014) and Kuhn, Schularick and Steins (2020).

ratio of household mortgage loans in China was only 0.3%.[21] Secondly, the Chinese financial system is far less complicated than the US system, and mortgage loans are not moved around in packages of risk-magnifying financial derivatives. At the end of 2019, the total amount of residential mortgage-backed securities (RMBS) in China accounted for only 3% of total mortgage loans, compared with 63% in the US. In fact, this 63% number doesn't include various derivates products, such as CLOs, that might be based on the underlying RMBS.[22] Thirdly, due to strict capital controls, foreign funds and international hot money rarely participate in the Chinese housing market. So, unlike in the US, a mortgage crisis was amplified by multiple times in the global financial markets and spread throughout the world, a mortgage crisis in China, even if there is one, is likely to stay within the country's borders.

In order to reduce the risk to the economy posed by higher household debt, the most important step is to curb the trend of rising house prices. After that, the fundamental solution is to increase household income, especially for low- and middle-income groups. This can be done in part by encouraging them to work in regions and industries that could offer more opportunities and higher wages. The regional gap in economic development and income levels can be an opportunity for low-income people to migrate and seek for better opportunities, rather than an obstacle to population mobility.

Section 2: Factor Market Reform

The final report issued at the end of Nineteenth National Congress of CCP in 2017, concluded that "*the major contradiction in modern Chinese society is the divergence between people's need for a better life and the current imbalanced and insufficient economic development*". It is the first time this major contradiction has been redefined since 1981, when the Sixth Plenary Session of the Eleventh Central Committee concluded that "*the major contraction to be solved is the divergence between the people's*

[21] The data are from the People's Bank of China (中国人民银行金融稳定分析小组 2019).

[22] Data on RMBS in China come from the WIND database. The US data here also include commercial real estate. Data on the total mortgage data are from the Federal Reserve, and the total MBS data are from the Securities Industry and Financial Markets Association.

growing material and cultural needs and the backward state of the economy". This 2017 statement suggests that the fundamental direction of Chinese economic policy has changed.

During the past 40 years, the income inequality in China has widened significantly. During the same period, income inequality in many developed countries has also widened. However, compared with more developed countries, income inequality in China has two different dimensions. The first is the inequality between urban and rural residents, and the second is the inequality between different regions. In 2018, the per capita disposable income of urban residents was 2.7 × that of rural residents. Meanwhile, the per capita income of rich provinces like Beijing and Shanghai was 3.5 times that of Guizhou, Gansu and Tibet. These two dimensions are both related to restricted population mobility.

Population Mobility and Income Inequality

The most obvious way for low-income people to increase their income is to work in economically developed cities, which can provide a decent income for low-skilled jobs such as couriers or housekeepers. However, if people cannot move freely and they have to stay in rural or economically underdeveloped areas, the income gap between people and regions will continue to widen. To this day, China's population mobility is still limited, and the land-driven urbanization and development model used by local governments is one of the key reasons. This model puts an emphasis on land over people, and it spends too little on public services, such as education, medical cares and pensions, to provide immigrants with better living conditions, which in turn restricted their job opportunities in richer cities. This investment-oriented development model also leads to a bias in favor of capital accumulation rather than labor income, which is detrimental to lower and middle-class wage earners. Chapter 7 will discuss the income distribution in more detail. This section will focus more on the population mobility.

Before we go deeper into the analysis, let's first examine what would happen to China's population if people could move freely between regions. The columns in Fig. 5.3a show the proportion of GDP produced by each US state, and the line shows the proportion of resident population in each state. The GDP of different states varies greatly, with California alone accounting for roughly 15% of US GDP, and many smaller states, such as Vermont or Wyoming, have a share well under 1%.

Of course, population size and GDP are positively correlated, and therefore the line representing the share of population in each state shows a similar trend. If a state's share of GDP is roughly 3%, then its population share is roughly equal to 3%. Therefore, despite the large differences in GDP across states, the differences in GDP ***per capita*** across states are small. In other words, the average standard of living across states is similar.

This situation of unequal scale but roughly equal per capita income is very different from the situation in China. Figure 5.3b shows the same information for the different provinces in China. We can immediately see that there is a large difference between the height of both the columns and the line. In economically developed provinces, such as Guangdong, Jiangsu, Zhejiang, Shanghai and Beijing, the line is much lower than the columns, which means the population share of those provinces is much lower than their GDP share. In other words, fewer people are able to enjoy more income, so these places are relatively wealthy. In most other provinces, the columns are much lower than the line, or the GDP share is much lower than the population share, so more people need to share less income, and these provinces are poorer.

In order to reduce the income inequality between regions, it's necessary to equalize the gap in per capita income rather than the gap in total product. Not every city can become Beijing or Shanghai, and it's not possible to equalize the total output for each province. Likewise, it's neither possible nor necessary for every province to replicate the industrial and logistics networks formed by economic powerhouses around the Pearl River and Yangtze River deltas. Modern economies continue to experience rapid agglomeration around key hubs. Even in developed countries such as the US, Europe and Japan, these agglomeration effects are still strengthening.[23] So, the ideal situation is to achieve a balance in per capita incomes between regions. In order to achieve this equilibrium, the most important step is to allow for free movement of labor. Workers' income is not only affected by education and skills, but also by their environment. In China, only 60% of the population lives in urban areas while 40% living in rural areas, but the agricultural economy accounts for only a 10% share of GDP. This means 40% of the population share roughly 10% of the total GDP, and their per capita income is naturally low. Even if some rural residents are in fact engaged in non-agricultural activities, the income per

[23] 24 Lu (陆铭 2016) shows that the economic agglomeration and urbanization of developed economies is still continuing.

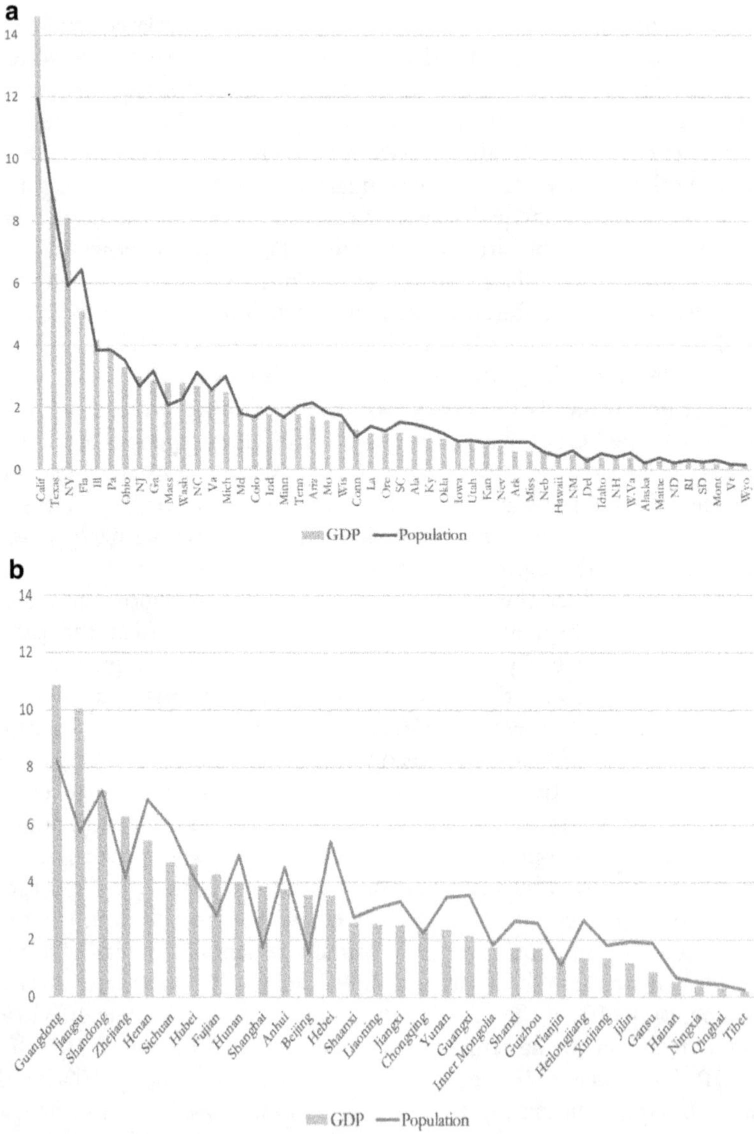

Fig. 5.3 **a** Percentages of Populations and GDPs of US States, 2019; **b** Percentages of Populations and GDPs of Chinese Provinces, 2019 These figures are designed by Lu (陆铭 2016), and I update them with more recent data (*Note*)

capita in rural areas will still be low. One solution to this problem is to encourage more rural residents to migrate to cities to work. Given the larger market size and further division of labor in cities, even low-skilled people could have higher productivity and income. For example, a family running a breakfast stall in the city has a large market to serve and can make enough to feed themselves, they even may also have the chance to develop into a small chain. In rural areas, however, breakfast is most often eaten at home and market demand is therefore small, so there may not be room for such a business. We can find many such examples, housekeeper, delivery men, takeaway businesses, taxi drivers and restaurant waiters, etc. Because of the large market and division of labor, these low-skill jobs are not necessarily low-income jobs in big cities.

These seemingly low-skilled service jobs play a critical role in driving the prosperity of big cities and help support the quality of life of high-income residents. Without quality and affordable services, the cost of living in cities would skyrocket. There is an office building close to my apartment in Shanghai and near the subway station, in recent years many low-income workers have left the area and some of the restaurants have closed down, and the price of the remaining restaurants increased significantly. As a result, more white-collar workers choose to bring meals to work. If a city only wants high-income and high-skilled talents, and tries to drive away low-skilled workers, the results will not be good. The prices for services will increase and incomes of high-skilled workers will gradually be eroded by the increasing cost of living, and the reduced convenience will also lead to a decrease in quality of life. High-skilled workers may end up leaving. In fact, there are barely any successful examples of cities that used administrative planning to limit or control population size. The planned population size in cities that experience inflows is almost always too small, while the planned population size in cities that experience outflows is almost always too large.

Expanding the size and increasing the population density of urban areas can further the division of labor within the city, leading to higher productivity. It can also help to promote division of labor between cities and regions. Some regions may specialize in high-end manufacturing, while others do low-end manufacturing, agriculture or tourism. In an ideal world, each region should develop an economic model that plays to its comparative advantage, leading to an increase in productivity at the national level. Even in places that specialize in agriculture, per capita income can increase, not only because of returns to scale in larger farms, but because the population base would be smaller, with many people moving to other places to find work in more productive industries.

The logic and benefits for allowing more people to enter cities are clear, however in reality there are still many factors to consider. City governments and incumbent residents worry about the pressure that an influx of new immigrants will put on scarce resources, such as housing, public education and healthcare, and they worry that crime may also rise. The concerns are understandable, and it's impossible for any city to expand indefinitely. Free movement of labor means that people will come and go, and if the costs of overcrowding outweigh the benefits of city living, then people will choose to leave. As for public services, such as healthcare and schooling, the best way to resolve the problem is to increase supply rather than to choke demand. People who move to cities to work and earn a living, thereby providing services, not only consuming resources. For example, by the end of 2019, Shanghai had a total of 5.12 million people over the age of 60, accounting for roughly 35% of the population. If there is no influx of younger people to work, then how can the social security and pension system be sustained? Who will provide care for the elderly? However, if the provision of education and healthcare for new migrants is limited, they are unable to settle in the city, and the problem of children and elders left behind in rural areas will continue well into the future.

Reforms on Land Transfers and Household Registration System

While it may be relatively easy to increase the number of hospitals and schools in Chinese cities, increasing the amount of housing available is a much more difficult proposition. Large cities have limited land area and new construction requires permits that are issued according to set quotas. If land use quotas follow population flows, then they would increase in the city experiencing an influx in population, which may alleviate part of the housing problem by increasing house supply. It would also improve the overall efficiency of land use. The first step in increasing the supply of urban land is to allow collective-owned land to be used in urban development. Land in China is broadly divided into two categories (see Chapter 2). The first type of land is owned by the state, usually located in urban areas, and its use rights can be sold on the market, after which the land can be put to commercial use. The second type of land is owned by village collectives, usually located in rural areas, and its use rights are subject to many restrictions. In the past 40 years, ever-expanding cities took in many neighboring villages and townships, so a large amount of originally rural lands become a physical part of urban areas. However, in legal terms, these lands are still owned by collectives instead of the state. Therefore their use rights are still very limited, and cannot be easily put to commercial use. In order to increase the supply of urban land for construction, the most obvious way is to use these collective-owned lands. For example, in the administrative areas of Beijing, 50% of land are collective-owned land, and their average floor-to-area ratio is only 0.3 to 0.4, much less developed and constructed than state-owned land. Similarly, in Shanghai, 30% of land within its administrative boundary is collective-owned and much less constructed.[24]

As early as 2008, the government begun to look for ways to introduce more collective-owned land into the market. The Third Plenary Session of the 17th Central Committee of the CCP approved the *"Decision of the Central Committee of the CCP on Fundamental Issues Concerning Promoting Rural Reform and Development"*. The policy contained some principles to *"gradually establish a unified market for urban and rural construction land…for rural collective-owned land which is acquired legally, land use rights must be transferred in a standard and public way on a standardized and transparent market and, conditional on official planning of land use, should enjoy equal rights and interests as state-owned land"*. However, at that time, city governments continued to have an incentive to limit land supply because they could benefit more under the old land finance model, and these principles were largely put on ice in practice. In the years following 2008, local governments continued to acquire and expropriate rural collective-owned land and expand cities.

In rural China, land is collectively owned and leased to individual household. All the land can be further divided into three broad categories: farmland, homestead and other construction land. Since 2015, 33 pilot counties and cities across the country have begun to trial a new round of reforms on the acquisition of rural land, the access to land market of collective-owned construction land, and institutions related to homestead. Prior to this reform, there were also some small-scale pilots at the local government level. The most famous is the "land certificate" system introduced in the south-western city of Chongqing. Under this system,

[24] 25 The data are from Shao, Tian and Tao (邵挺, 田莉, 陶然 2018).

if a peasant who has moved to the city area and his homestead in the village is idle, he could first turn the homestead back into farmland, after which he could receive a certificate and sell this piece of "land certificate" to a district or county government in Chongqing, in the local land exchange. Once the government had purchased this piece of certificate, they could then expand accordingly the use of construction land for urban development. In the local land exchange, the average price of such a land certificate is about 200,000 yuan per mu (mu is a Chinese unit of area, equal to one fifteenth of a hectare or about 0.16 acre). So the peasant could earn 200,000 yuan if his homestead is one mu large, and the cost of reverting this piece of homestead to farmland is about 20,000 yuan. Of the 180,000 yuan left over money, roughly 85% (or 150,000) could be kept by the peasant and 15% would be paid to the local rural collective. This money could help the peasant to make a new start in the city. Each year, the central government gave Chongqing a land quota of 20,000 mu for building new residential houses. And the system of land certificates could add an additional 20,000 mu into the total land supply. As a result, house prices in Chongqing have been relatively stable as compared to other major cities.[25]

In 2017, the central government proposed that "*in the megacities where the gap between supply and demand of rental housing is largest, pilot projects should be launched to allow the construction of rental housing on collective-owned construction land*".[26] This is an important breakthrough, and it means that city government's monopoly over the supply of urban housing land can gradually be removed. In 2019, the first batch of 13 pilot cities were chosen to take part in the project. The cities selected included megacities such as Beijing, Shanghai and Guangzhou, as well as large provincial capital cities such as Nanjing, Shenyang, Wuhan and

[25] The data on "land certificate" prices are from Huang (黄奇帆 2020), who is a former Chongqing mayor.

[26] In 2017, the Ministry of Housing and Urban-Rural Development and the Ministry of Land and Resources issued *Notice on Strengthening the Management and Regulation of Housing and Land Supply*.

Chengdu.[27] In the same year, an amendment to the Land Administration Law was passed, which for the first time stipulated that the use rights of collective-owned construction land (excluding homestead) could be directly sold or leased, or priced as shares in a corporation, without first being acquired by the state and transformed into state-owned land. In effect, this amendment granted collective-owned land owned the same rights as urban state-owned land. The monopoly on land supply previously held by city governments has therefore ended.

As for homesteads in rural China, which account for roughly 50% of all construction land owned by collectives, fundamental reforms have not begun yet. In cities where urban housing demand is large, homesteads are often illegally sold in private. The 2019 amendments to the Land Administration Law made only some small provisions to the reform of homestead system, allowing village residents who have migrated to a city and become registered urban residents to sell their homestead willingly and to receive compensation according to laws, and encouraging the rural collectives and their members to put empty homesteads to good use. In 2020, the central government launched another pilot reform of the homestead system. All these reforms are experimental and emphasize three bottom lines in practice: the ownership of land must remain public, the total amount of farmland must not be reduced, and the interests of peasants must be protected.

In addition to the reforms of land policy outlined above, a series of reforms on the household registration system (Hukou) have also been introduced to allow people to move more freely. In 2013, the first urbanization work meeting of the Central Committee of the CCP was held, which proposed to drive a *"people-centered form of urbanization"*. In 2014, a report published after China's annual "two sessions" (sessions of the National People's Congress, the national legislature, and of the Chinese People's Political Consultative Conference, the national political advisory body), for the first time, made helping people to become a registered urban resident a government's work goal. At the same time,

[27] In 2019, the Ministry of Land and Resources and the Ministry of Housing and Urban-Rural Development issued the "Pilot Plan for Building Rental Housing on Collective-owned Construction Land", which identified Beijing, Shanghai, Shenyang, Nanjing, Hangzhou, Hefei, Xiamen, Zhengzhou, Wuhan, Guangzhou, and Foshan, Zhaoqing and Chengdu as the first 13 cities to pilot the project.

reforms to the household registration also started. An existing distinction between agricultural registration and non-agricultural registration has gradually been abolished, and a unified household registration for both urban and rural areas has been established.[28] Local governments also started to update their public service delivery plans. Where previously they had planned the supply of public services based only on the registered population in the local area, they now started to consider the actual resident population, registered or not. These public services include public education, healthcare, employment support, state pensions as well as housing. In 2016, the central government required local governments to improve land development plans and based their plans on the inflows and outflows of local population, thereby ensuring sufficient land supply to new immigrants.[29]

China's reform on household registration system has accelerated in recent years. In 2019, the National Development and Reform Commission proposed that *"Cities with a population between 1 and 3 million should completely cancel restrictions on registration. Larger cities with a population between 3 and 5 million should also significantly relax conditions required for registration, cancelling them completely for some critical groups. Megacities with populations greater than 5 million should adjust and improve their point-based registration requirements, significantly increase the total number of permits available, simplify the calculation of the points, ensure the major part of the points are tied to the length of residence and the length of contribution to social security…and allow residents who do not own but rent a local house to be eligible for registration"*.[30] At present, in the most attractive megacities, such as Shanghai and Beijing, the threshold to obtain a local registration permit is still not low. In recent year, some

[28] Under the new and unified system, households who previously had a non-agricultural registration permit are essentially unaffected, and households who previously had an agricultural registration permit can retain the rights and interests related to rural land (such as their rights to lease and operate on rural land, and their rights to use homesteads), and their benefits from social securities can be gradually converged to the level of urban residents.

[29] In 2016, the Ministry of Land and Resources, together with other five central ministries, issued the Implementation *Opinions on Establishing a Mechanism for Linking the Increase in Urban Construction Land and the Newly Registered Urban Populations Transferred from Agriculture.*

[30] Quoted from *The Key Tasks for the New Form of Urbanization in 2019,* issued by the National Development and Reform Commission.

megacities have begun to operate a "war for talent" by making registration easier for those with a college degree, even by providing additional housing subsidies or other perks to attract talents to the city. But these preferential policies do not apply to low-education rural migrants. Since 2020, some large provincial capital cities, such as Nanchang (the capital of Jiangxi province), Kunming (the capital of Yunnan) and Jinan (the capital of Shandong), have completely abolish any prerequisites for registration, including those on education level or the length of contribution to social security.

Within any country, the movement and commercialization of products will naturally lead to the movement and commercialization of production factors. If agricultural products can be bought and sold freely, and peasants can move to work in cities, the use rights of rural land should eventually be able to transact on the market. Dividing lands and people into different categories or forms of registration and grant different rights accordingly is very inefficient and distortionary, which cannot be expected to sustain in the long run in a market economy. As times goes by, these distortions left over from history would continue to grow, such as the social problems caused by left-behind women, children and elderly. Eventually they would become too huge for the society to bear.

The center of urbanization should be people not land. Putting people first is necessary for reducing the level of income inequality both between regions and between people. To truly help low-income groups, it's necessary to increase their mobility and freedom of choice, helping them to leave poor places behind for places with more opportunities and higher wages. In this way, their human capital can become more valuable. At the same time, as land previously controlled by peasants is allowed to transact, their physical capital can also become more valuable.

In April 2020, the Central Committee of the CCP and the State Council issued their "*Opinions on Building a More Market-Based Allocation Mechanism for Production Factors*". The document comprehensively outlined the future direction of reforms on production factors including land, labor, capital and technology. Regarding land, the document emphasized the need to "*establish and improve a unified market for urban and rural land development…to formulate and issue guidelines for the entry of collective-owned land into urban land markets*". Regarding labor, the document emphasized the need to "*Deepen reform of the household registration system. Improve points-based applications for registration in megacities…Relax or abolish restrictions on household registration in all except the largest cities, and experiment a household registration system based on place of permanent residence. Further, develop a mechanism for linking basic public services such as education, employment services, and health-care to the resident population rather than the registered population. Public resources should be allocated according to the size of the resident population"*. The general direction of reform is to allow market forces to play a greater role in the allocation of production factors, to allow resources to move more freely and to improve efficiency in terms of resource utilization.

Section 3: Economic Development and Income Inequality

During China's process of urbanization and rapid economic development, the gap between the rich and poor is greatly widened. This section will approach the problem from three perspectives. First, more than one billion Chinese have been lifted out of poverty in just 40 years, greatly reducing inequality among the 7 billion people around the world. Second, due to rapid economic growth, although the income gap between the rich and poor is widening, the level of income of poor Chinese has been rising rapidly, so they have paid less attention to inequality. Accordingly, here comes the third perspective: if economic growth starts to slow down, people will start paying more attention to inequality, and the gap between the rich and poor could start to trigger social conflict.

Income Inequality

The rise of China has led to a dramatic reduction in global inequality. According to the World Bank's definition of extreme poverty (income less than \$1.90 per day), the number of people living in extreme poverty has fallen from 1.9 billion in 1981 to 700 million in 2015 (Fig. 5.4), a fall of 1.2 billion people. This is a remarkable achievement, especially given that the world's population has increased by 3 billion during the same period. However, if we don't count China, the number of people living in extreme poverty fell by only 300 million over the same period. In the years between 1981 and 2008, the number of poor people in the world outside China remained more or less unchanged. It can therefore be concluded that achievements in global poverty reduction come mainly from China.[31]

The rise of China has completely changed the global income distribution. In 1990, there were 5.3 billion people in the world, of which 40% of the poorest half lived in China, while in the richest 20%, there were barely any Chinese, the vast majority being either Europeans or Americans. By 2016, the global population was nearly 7.4 billion, of which only 15% of the poorest half were Chinese, while about 22% of the richest half were Chinese. Since China accounts for 19% of the world population, their proportion among the poorest half is relatively low and their proportion

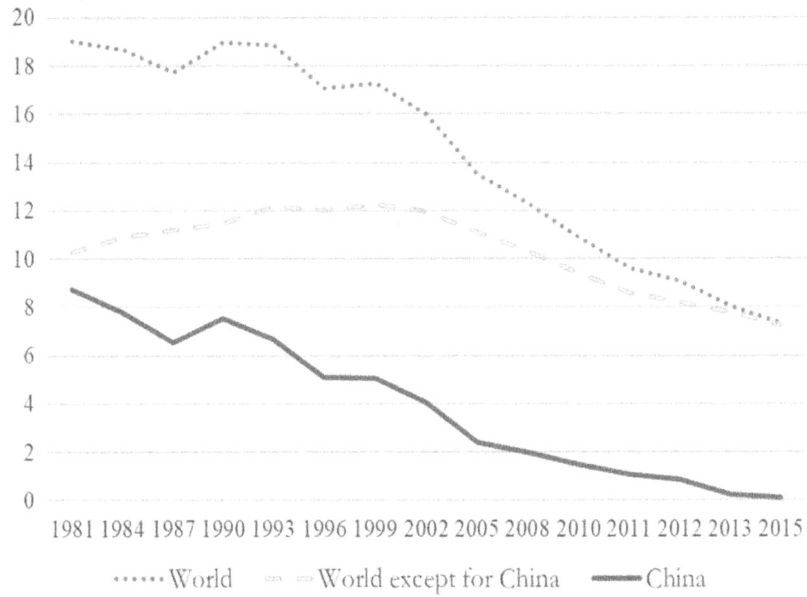

Fig. 5.4 The World Population in Extreme Poverty (a hundred million) (*Source* World Bank. The definition of extreme poverty is income less than $1.90 per day)

[31] The extreme poverty line of US$1.9 per day, as defined by the World Bank, was equivalent to 2,441 yuan per year after adjusting for purchasing power parity in 2011. In 2011, the minimum rural poverty line set by the Chinese government was 2,300 yuan per year, but the urban poverty line was set at a higher level than the World Bank line.

among the richest half is relatively high.[32] In addition, China accounts for the largest national proportion of the global middle class.

China's economic reform broke down the egalitarianism that was present during the planned economy period, and income inequality started to widen. A common indicator used to measure income inequality is the Gini coefficient, which is a number between 0 and 1. A higher Gini Coefficient indicates a higher level of income inequality. In the early 1980s, China's Gini Coefficient stood near 0.3, but by 2017, it had risen to 0.47.[33] According to income data released by the National Bureau of Statistics, by 2019, the top 20% of people earned 48% of total income, while the bottom 20% only earned 4%.

Although income inequality is widening, the absolute income of nearly everybody has been rising too. This is the result of the rapid economic growth, with the benefits being widely shared. From 1988 to 2018, both urban and rural areas in China experienced per capita increases in real income (after inflation) of roughly 8–10 times. People's income, in all income groups, has been rising rapidly. Taking urban residents as an example, although the real income of the top 20% has increased fastest, roughly 13 × in 30 years, the real income of the middle 40% and bottom 40% has also increased by 9 × and 6 × respectively.[34]

Economic growth by its very nature is accompanied by improvements in productivity and the continuous emergence of new economic opportunities. Although growth in and of itself does not necessarily reduce income inequality, it can curb the intergenerational transmission of inequality. If the income of each generation is much higher than the previous generation, then younger people's own labor income would be more important wealth inherited from their parents. For most of the 1970s generation (born between 1970 and 1980 in China), labor income and hard work are the main source of wealth because their parents were generally poor and did not save much. The drastic changes in the economy at the time required the 1970s generation to acquire new skills and leave their hometowns to seek for new opportunities and foster new

[32] A cross country distribution of the global population by income level can be found in a report by the World Inequality Lab (2017).

[33] The data for the Gini coefficient are from Li and Zhu (李实和朱梦冰 2018).

[34] The average annual rate of real income growth is 6.2% for the urban low-income groups, 7.6% for the middle-income group and 8.9% for the high-income group.

connections. The existing family networks in their hometowns generally being of little use.

However, for the generations born in the 1980s and 1990s, parents' wealth and network started to have a much bigger impact on their children's income.[35] One reason is that wealth inequality started to widen in the parents' generation, and income from assets rather than labor started to take a larger share of total income. The most important reason for this is the growing importance of real estate in the economy. In large cities across China, the growth in house prices has outpaced the growth in labor income.[36] Physical assets, such as a housing and money, are different from human capital in that they can be passed entirely from generation to generation. The children of super smart people may not necessarily be as smart. Education itself has many uncertainties, and genetic traits such as cognitive ability are subject to the law of the regression to the mean, so it is likely that children of exceptional parents will be more average than them. However, physical assets are not affected by such laws, 1 million yuan of parents is still 1 million yuan of children, so is a 100 square meter house.

Inequality in wealth is usually much larger than inequality in annual income. Wealthy people tend to be able to accumulate more wealth, to have an access to more investment options, they could obtain higher risk-adjusted returns on their assets. As mentioned above, according to the National Bureau of Statistics, in 2019, the top 20% of the income distribution accounted for 48% of total income, whereas the bottom 20% accounted for only 4%. In terms of wealth, this gap is even bigger. According to the 2019 survey from the People's Bank of China, the wealthiest 20% of urban households accounted for 65% of total urban household wealth, while the poorest 20% held only 2%.[37] In coastal and richer provinces, asset appreciation has been faster, and the impact that parent's wealth has on their children's income is greater than in western

[35] Fan, Yi and Zhang (2021) study the impact of parents' income on children's income in China.

[36] For detailed data on house price and income growth across Chinese cities, please see Fang et al. (2015).

[37] The data are from a report by the People's Bank of China (中国人民银行调查统计司 2020).

provinces.[38] When economic growth slows down and new opportunities become fewer, competition among young people will become more intense, while parents' wealth and resources will play a more important part in determining children's life outcomes. As income growth slows, Chinese society's tolerance for inequality is likely to decrease and risks of social instability could rise.

Tolerance for Income Inequality

While income inequality cannot be completed eliminated, a society may find it hard to bear the issues that could arise from extreme levels of inequality. For this reason, income inequality must be controlled within an acceptable range. Many factors can impact people's tolerance for income inequality, and the most important one is economic growth, because lower economic growth tends to hit the poorer parts of society first. Imagine there are two groups of people in a queue, the first queue is full of rich people and the second queue is full of poor people. To start with, the rich queue is advancing faster than the poor queue, but since the poor queue is still moving forward, people are willing to be patient. But if the poor queue comes to a standstill and the rich queue is still moving forward, albeit more slowly, then the people in the poor queue will quickly lose patience. This phenomenon is called the "tunnel effect" and it describes the anxiety experienced in a tunnel when one lane of traffic moves and the other is at a standstill.[39]

As we mentioned before, since 1988, the real income of the wealthiest urban residents in China has increased by 13 × while the incomes of lower- and middle-income groups have increased by 6 × and 9x. Therefore, as the economic pie has grown, high-income groups have captured a larger slice, however since everyone has a much larger piece of pie than before, this result can be tolerated. The situation in the US is different. Since the 1970s, the income of the richest 10% saw their incomes increase

[38] In coastal provinces, the correlation between the income of those children born in the 1980s and their parents is higher than that of those born in the 1970s; however, in inland provinces, the correlation does not change much between the two generations. This finding comes from Fan, Yi and Zhang (2020).

[39] This effect was proposed by the influential late economist Albert Hirschman (Hirschman 2013). He also discusses factors that influence tolerance for inequality, such as population homogeneity and family ties.

2.5x, while the income of the middle 40% has increased only modestly by 35%. As for the poorest 50%, the real income has not increased at all. As a result, American society has become increasingly intolerant of the gap between rich and poor. The global financial crisis of in 2008 greatly reduced the wealth of the poor and further widened the wealth gap, triggering movements such as "Occupy Wall Street". During Donald Trump's term from 2016 to 2020, the political and social divisions in the US only became more serious.

Another factor that affects tolerance for inequality is the homogeneity of populations. Before the economic reform, the vast majority of Chinese people led a similar life, either working together on collective farms in rural areas, or working together in state-owned factories or governments in urban areas. In this scenario, if some people start to get rich after the reform, then it may bring hope and inspirations to others. "Since everyone is similar, maybe I also have a chance of becoming rich" goes the thinking. In the 1990s, many people left their original jobs and started to do business, getting rich in the process. Although a certain level of envy started to creep into people's thinking, they still believe that they could become rich if they try, "I could go and start a business too if I wanted, but I just don't want to". But if income inequality is mixed with other factors such as race, caste or gender, then people will feel very differently. These factors cannot be changed through effort, and so are more prone to cause anger and despair. In recent years, racial conflicts in the US have increased, and one of the fundamental reasons is the poverty of black people. The median income of a black household is less than 60% of the median income of a white household, and the gap has persisted through generations. A white person who is born into poverty (parents' income is the lowest 20% among their generation) still has a 10.6% chance of becoming rich (children's income is the highest 20% among their generation), and only a 29% chance of continuing to be poor. But for a black child born into poverty, the chance of becoming rich is only 2.5% and the probability of continuing in poverty is as high as 37%.[40]

Family relationships also have a strong influence on people's tolerance for inequality. In places with strong family ties, children usually take the responsibility of caring for parents. Provided that children have the chance of climbing up the social ladder and being well paid, then tolerance for

[40] The data come from Chetty et al. (2020).

inequality will be relatively high because the younger generations will catch up later in this long race. A children's income level compared to their parents is mainly affected by economic growth. Looking at China, most children born in the 1970s and 1980s have a higher income than their parents. If the parents' income fell into the bottom 40% of the income distribution of their generation, the probability that the children's income exceeded their parents was close to 90%. Even if the parents' income was in the middle 40% of their generation, the chance that the child's income will exceed their parents was still 70%. This situation is similar to America's post-war golden generation, where the probability of people born in 1940s and 1950s having an income surpassing their parents was close to that of Chinese people born in the 1970s and 1980s. However, once we get to people born in the 1980s in the US, the probability that children's income exceeds parents becomes much lower. If the parents are in the lower 40% of the income distribution of their generation, the probability of the children's income surpassing their parents is only 60%, and if the parents are in the middle 40%, then the probability is only 40%.[41]

To summarize, the relationship between economic growth and income inequality is complicated. There is one famous curve in economics known as the "Kuznets Curve", which claims that inequality first rises and then falls with economic growth. The curve became famous in the 1950s, but in fact only applies to a short period after World War II in Europe and the US. If we expand the time period, we can see that a single "Kuznets curve" no longer fits the data, instead we see series of ups and downs of inequality over time, or "Kuznets waves".[42] There are many factors that can lead to these ups and downs, economic and political, internal as well as external. There are no mysterious economic forces that can inevitably reduce inequality, and the idea that those who get rich first will help others to get rich later is never guaranteed. Policy and politics

[41] The probability that children's income exceeds that of their parents is called "absolute mobility". Estimates of absolute mobility in China come from Fan, Yi and Zhang (2020); estimates for the US are from Chetty et al. (2017). At the time of writing this book in 2020, The Chinese generation born in the 1990s has just entered the labor market and as a result their incomes have not yet stabilized, so data have yet to be collected.

[42] Piketty (2014) analyzes the ins and outs of the theory of "Kuznets curve". Milanovic (2016) describes the ups and downs of "Kuznets waves".

matter a lot. Increasing inequality can be a huge risk to a society and can end very badly. It must therefore be treated with care.[43]

Summary

China's urbanization can roughly be divided into three stages. The first stage, taking place before 1994, was the rise of township and village enterprises (TVE), with peasants continuing to work in their place of birth. During this stage urbanization happened slowly. The second stage is after the 1994 reform of the tax sharing system and before 2012, TVEs declined and countryside migrant workers started to move to the city. During this stage, the urbanization of land was treated higher in priority than the urbanization of people, and funds from land finance helped support large-scale urban infrastructure construction, but less money was spent on public services that new urban immigrants desperately need. The third stage started after the 18th National Congress of the CCP in 2012, which commenced a series of reforms shifting the center of urbanization from land to people.

Urbanization and industrialization reinforce each other. Industrialization is one of the main driving forces between each stage of urbanization. Before 1994, industrial capacity and infrastructures were both weak, so small-scale TVEs had a chance of meeting local demand for simple products. At the same time, rural land reforms freed redundant labor from farming, which provided lots of workers for TVEs. By the mid-to-late 90s, exports of industrial products begun to grow rapidly. In 2001, China entered the World Trade Organization. To compete in the global market, Chinese enterprises must grow in scale, become more efficient and stay close to port regions in the East to reduce logistics costs. Therefore, manufacturing industries quickly congregated in the coastal regions, attracting a large number of migrant workers moving with them. Although today China has come to be known as "the World's Factory", manufacturing capabilities require constant upgrading if they are to stay competitive. Industrial agglomeration has become even more important than before, as different parts of a supply chain moving to the same place in order to save on logistics and other costs, as well to share knowledge

[43] Stiglitz (2012) discusses the various costs of inequality. Scheidel (2017) points out that historically widening inequalities rarely end well, often ending in massive violence and catastrophes.

and technology. So industries are still concentrated in coastal regions and some inland large cities. Industrial clustering in these places helps to drive rapid growth in local service industries, which help to absorb more new migrant workers from countryside or small cities. This new generation of migrated workers have adapt to city life, and by the second generation, countryside migrants no longer have the skills or desire to engage in farm work, they therefore choose to stay in cities. For this reason, urbanization needs to be people-centered and focus on providing sufficient public services such as housing, healthcare and education.

In the process of urbanization, local governments have been burdened with a heavy debt load, and soaring land and house prices have also left households with large debts. Over time, these debts have led to significant macroeconomic and financial risks. In recent years, China's government has put a lot of emphasis on so-called supply-side reforms aimed at "deleveraging" as well as preventing and reducing financial risks. So, what exactly are these risks? How do they affect the economy? And what specific reform measures have been put in place? This will be the topic of the next chapter.

Further Readings

All my knowledge on China's land reforms and urbanization are from sources in Chinese, so I am not able to recommend English readings on this topic. On the growing inequality in many countries, which has been one of the most popular research topics of recent years in economics, there are many excellent papers and books. For serious readers, Thomas Piketty's epic bestseller *Capital in the 21st Century* is a great book. It is a long book, but it contains a lot content and fascinating information, and the authors' ideas are wide-ranging. Even just reading the first two sections can teach you a lot about economic development.

References

Bertrand, Marianne, and Adair Morse (2016). "Trickle-Down Consumption." *Review of Economics and Statistics* 98.5: 863–879.

Brueckner, Jan K., Shihe Fu, Yizhen Gu, and Junfu Zhang (2017). "Measuring the Stringency of Land Use Regulation: The Case of China's Building Height Limits." *Review of Economics and Statistics* 99.4: 663–677.

Chetty, Raj, David Grusky, Maximilian Hell, Nathaniel Hendren, Robert Manduca, and Jimmy Narang (2017). "The Fading American Dream: Trends in Absolute Income Mobility since 1940." *Science* 356.6336: 398–406.

Chetty, Raj, Nathaniel Hendren, Maggie R. Jones, and Sonya R. Porter (2020). "Race and Economic Opportunity in the United States: An Intergenerational Perspective." *Quarterly Journal of Economics* 135.2: 711–783.

Fan, Yi, Junjian Yi, and Junsen Zhang (2021). "Rising Intergenerational Income Persistence in China." *American Economic Journal: Economic Policy* 13.1: 202–230.

Fang, Hanming, Quanlin Gu, Wei Xiong, and Li-An Zhou (2015). "Demystifying the Chinese Housing Boom." *NBER Macro Annual* 30: 105–166.

Glaeser, Edward, and Joseph Gyourko (2018). "The Economic Implications of Housing Supply." *Journal of Economic Perspectives* 32.1: 3–30.

Glick, Reuven, and Kevin J. Lansing (2010). "Global Household Leverage, House Prices, and Consumption," *Federal Reserve Bank of San Francisco Economic Letter*.

Hirschman, Albert O. (2013). "The Changing Tolerance for Income Inequality in the Course of Economic Development." *The Essential Hirschman*, Ed. by Jeremy Adelman: 74–101. Princeton University Press.

Kuhn, Moritz, Moritz Schularick, and Ulrike I. Steins (2020). "Income and Wealth Inequality in America: 1949–2016." *Journal of Political Economy* 128.9.

Mian, Atif, and Amir Sufi (2014). *House of Debt: How They (and You) Caused the Great Recession, and How We Can Prevent it from Happening Again*. University of Chicago Press.

Milanovic, Branko (2016). *Global Inequality: A New Approach for the Age of Globalization*. Harvard University Press.

Piketty, Thomas (2014). *Capital in the Twenty-First Century*. Harvard University Press.

Piketty, Thomas, and Gabriel Zucman (2014). "Capital Is Back: Wealth-Income Ratios in Rich Countries 1700–2010." *Quarterly Journal of Economics*: 1255–1310.

Rajan, Raghuram G. (2010). *Fault Lines: How Hidden Fractures Still Threaten the World Economy*. Princeton University Press.

Ryan-Collins, Josh, Toby Lioyd, and Laurie Macfarlane (2017). *Rethinking the Economics of Land and Housing*. Zed Books.

Scheidel, Walter (2017). *The Great Leveler: Violence and the History of Inequality from the Stone Age to the Twenty-First Century*. Princeton University Press.

Spader, Jonathan, Daniel McCue, and Christopher Herbert (2016). "Homeowner Households and the U.S. Homeownership Rate: Tenure Projections for 2015–2035," *Working paper*.

Stiglitz, Joseph E. (2012). *The Price of Inequality: How Today's Divided Society Endangers Our Future*. WW Norton & Company.
World Inequality Lab (2017). *World Inequality Report 2018*.

Translated References (in Chinese)

Gan, Li, Naibao Zhao, and Yongzhi Sun (2018). "Income Inequality, Liquidity Constraints and China's Household Savings Rate." *Economic Research Journal* 12: 34–50. (in Chinese)
Han, Libin, and Ming Lu (2018). "Supply-Demand Mismatch: Solving the Puzzle of China's Housing Price Divergence." *The Journal of World Economy* 10: 126–149. (in Chinese)
Huang, Qifan (2020). *Analysis and Reflection: Huang Qifan's Fudan Economics Courses*. Shanghai People's Publishing House. (in Chinese)
Li, Shi, and Mengbing Zhu (2018). "Changes in the Income Gap of Residents in the 40 Years of China's Economic Transformation." *Journal of Management World* 12: 19–28. (in Chinese)
Lu, Ming (2016). *Great State Needs Bigger City*. Shanghai People's Publishing House. (in Chinese)
Ren, Zeping, Lei Xia, and Chai Xiong (2017). *Real Estate Cycle*. People's Publishing House. (in Chinese)
Shao, Ting, Li Tian, and Ran Tao (2018). "China's Urban Dual Land System and Real Estate Market Development: Analytical Framework. *Policy Evaluation and Reform Potential*." *Comparative Studies* 6. (in Chinese)
The People's Bank of China Financial Stability Analysis Group (2019). *China Financial Stability Report 2019*, China Financial Publishing House. (in Chinese)
The People's Bank of China Statistics and Analysis Department (2020). *Survey Report on the Assets and Liabilities of Urban Households in China*. (in Chinese)
Zhang, Chuanchuan, Kun Jia, and Rudai Yang (2016). "Dwelling Narrowness in 'Ghost Town': Income Inequality and the Housing Bubble." *The Journal of World Economy* 2: 120–141. (in Chinese)

CHAPTER 6

China's Debt Problem

Imagine there exists a young couple. Both work in the financial industry in Shanghai and their income is high. Just a few years after graduation from university, their combined household after-tax income has reached 50,000 yuan per month. The couple are feeling optimistic about their future and they begin to have talks about marriage and housing. After discussing for some time, they decide to get married and buy a house. Their parents spent most their lifetime savings to help the newlywed with the downpayment, and the couple take out a mortgage worth several million yuan and with a monthly payment of 30,000 yuan. Living costs in Shanghai are very high, and after paying their mortgage and feeding themselves for a month, the couple do not have much money left over. However, the future is still bright. With a few years of hard work, the couple's income could double, and the burden of the mortgage would be lower. Moreover, house prices have been rising and buying a house is an investment in the future with a significant expected return.

But accidents will always happen. Starting from 2018, the financial industry in China started to run into troubles. The husband's company goes bankrupt and he is temporarily unemployed. The wife's company also experience difficulties and her year-end bonus shrink to none, resulting in a large drop in income. The total household income has now dropped to 20,000 yuan per month, but the mortgage still stands at 30,000 yuan. Their parents are not able to help much anymore, after

X. Lan, *How China Works*,
https://doi.org/10.1007/978-981-97-0080-6_6

all most their lifetime savings have been used toward the mortgage down payment, and at most they can help to pay the mortgage for a few more months. The husband therefore cannot be too picky when looking for his next job. By the end of 2019, he successfully found a decent job with a stable income, but lo and behold, the coronavirus pandemic arrived.

When people are feeling optimistic, they tend to underestimate the risk of borrowing too much. When risks start to materialize, they can be left with heavy debt burdens and little room to maneuver. As we can see from the above story, even if house prices do not fall, households with large debt burdens face at least three risks. First, it's the rigidity of debt. If you happen to be lucky and make a fortune from your work, your debt will not increase with your wealth. But likewise, if you run into financial trouble, your debt will also not decrease. Second, income can vary a lot. There are a countless number of factors that can have an impact on a person's income, and so many shocks could happen in the macroeconomy, his industry, his company, his boss, his team, his family members and himself. No-one can guarantee that their income will only rise and not fall over the coming decades, when they must pay mortgage every month. Even if your income doesn't decrease, but instead stays the same, there will still be risks involved with taking on large amounts of debt. Every month both the principal and the interest on the mortgage loan needs to be repaid, and it's a lot of pressure to bear. A third risk arises from changes in other household spending, what if the couple run into something and they need extra money? What if their parents suddenly fall ill and need to pay for medical care? What if they have a child?

We can see that if the debt burden is too high, risks might become overbearing. By the end of 2018, China's total debt-to-GDP ratio had already reached 258% (Fig. 6.1) which is on a par with the US at 257%, larger than Germany (173%) and other developing countries such as Brazil (158%) and India (123%). Furthermore, China's debt burden has been growing faster than all these countries. In the past 10 years, China's total debt has increased by 5.5 times, and even though its GDP growth has been strong, total GDP has only increased 2.8 × during the same period. China's debt-to-GDP ratio has therefore doubled in the short period of just 10 years, which has aroused concern both inside China and abroad. Many Chinese government policies in recent years have focused on "supply-side" reforms, which aim to tackle the debt burden and deleverage the economy.

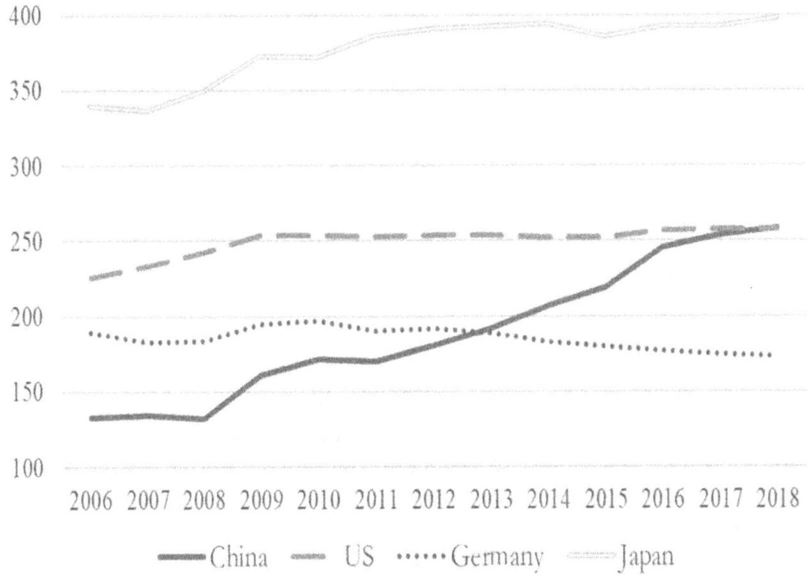

Fig. 6.1 Percentages of total debts over national GDP (*Source* IMF Global Debt Database)

Whether the debt to GDP ratio is an appropriate measure of debt burden is still open to debate. If interest rates are zero or even negative, and nominal GDP continues to rise, then the debt problem may be less serious, at least for the public debt since the government can roll over their debts indefinitely.[1] But for individuals and firms, rapid rising debt could be very risky. Chapter 5 has already examined the risks associated with household debt; this chapter will focus on the risks associated with firms and banks.

Sections "Section 1: Debt and Recession" and "Section 2: Why Is There so Much Debt? Lessons from Europe and the US" of this chapter explain general economic principles related to debt. These sections talk

[1] Furman and Summers (2020) discuss this problem for more details. Blanchard (2022) is a broader yet very accessible review of the fiscal problems in a low- or zero-interest environment.

more about the situations in the US and Europe, and show the similarities between them and China. Although China's debt problem indeed has some unique features, it can still learn from the lessons from the US and Europe. Section "Section 3: Debt Risks in China" analyzes the causes, risks and consequences of China's debt burden. Whether for households and firms or for governments, the debt problem is all related to the development model driven by local governments. Section "Section 4: Solve the Debt Problem" discusses how to repay the existing debt and curb the increase of new debt.

Section 1: Debt and Recession

Debt is vital for the functioning of an economy. Before a company can sell its products and receive payments, it needs to build factories, purchase equipment and pay wages. A company therefore requires a loan from a bank in order to get started. Likewise, most people rely on mortgage loans to purchase a house, otherwise it would take a lifetime of work before they could afford it. Governments also need to borrow money, otherwise they wouldn't be able to invest in infrastructure projects that take years if not decades to receive payback.

Debt acts to link many sectors of the economy together, therefore problems arising in any given sector can be transmitted to other sectors and resulted in a systematic crisis. Banks lend to both individuals and to companies, if someone does not repay their mortgage, then the bank has to write off the loan and suffer a loss. If this happens at a large scale, the bank may need to reduce its lending, then firms that rely on banks for credit will be unable to get loans and need to shrink their businesses and lay off people, thereby leading to more mortgage defaults. The bank will therefore suffer more loss and reduce credit further, hurting even more companies. We can therefore see that debt can create vicious cycles affecting all sectors of an economy. If all sectors are heavily indebted, there will be few places that can act as shock absorbers, and small events may trigger a large-scale crisis. Once a debt crisis breaks out, it usually spreads rapidly, for two reasons.

Firstly, in a heavily indebted economy, asset prices tend to fall rapidly. Once debt burdens become too large for income to cover repayments obligations, assets must be sold. If lots of assets are sold in distress at the same time, then prices will plummet. This kind of "*fire sales*" is not uncommon and was a prominent issue during the subprime mortgage crisis that occurred in the US in 2008 and 2009.[2] The mortgage burden of many American households was heavy, and people had to sell their houses to repay their debts. As a result, house prices dropped by around 20% in less than a year. A similar situation occurred in China in 2011 and 2012, when the "Wenzhou Gang of House Speculators", a group of people from Wenzhou (an eastern city) who borrowed heavily to speculate on houses fell short of money, lots of houses were put on the market for sale at the same time, and Wenzhou house prices fell by 30%.[3] In 2013 and 2014, many companies in the coal industry in Inner Mongolia, Shanxi and Shaanxi (three northwestern provinces) collapsed, this was once again a result of debt. Coal barons had borrowed heavily to expand when coal prices soared, but after the coal price fell, they were unable to service their debts and had to sell luxury cars and real estate at substantial discounts in order to repay their creditors.

The second reason that debt crises spread rapidly relates to the supply of credit. As asset prices fall, banks are less willing to issue credit, which can cause more problems. Lending often requires collateral, such as a home for a mortgage loan or a coal mine for a loan to a coal producer. As the value of collateral collapses, banks would reduce lending, and businesses or households that are unable to refinance their debts would run into troubles. From 2004 to 2008, the Irish economy was overheating and credit grew at an average annual rate of 20%. By 2009, the subprime mortgage crisis in the US had spread to Ireland, causing a crisis in the banking industry. From 2009 to 2013, the average annual growth rate of credit slowed to just 1.3%, which resulted in many companies not being able to access capital to refinance their debts.[4] Similarly, during the Wenzhou crisis mentioned above, some people fled the city to avoid paying their debts and a crisis of trust broke out. Even people with good credit histories could no longer borrow money. Debt crises can therefore spill over into sectors that are only modestly indebted, and the chain effect would cause regional, national or even worldwide recessions.

[2] This behavior of selling financial assets at low prices in order to repay debts is called a "fire sale". Shleifer and Vishny (2011) is a concise introduction to this topic.

[3] The most frequently used indicator to measure US housing prices is the Case-Shiller index, which stood around 180 in early 2008 and fell below 150 by 2009. According to Armstrong-Taylor (2016), Wenzhou's housing price index fell from 120 in January 2011 to 85 by January 2012.

[4] The data for Ireland are from Turner (2017).

The liabilities of one sector of the economy must be the assets of another sector. The process of accumulating debt or "leveraging" is therefore also a process of business transactions occurring between people that helps to drive economic prosperity. A debt crisis or "deleveraging" is a process whereby business activity decreases, leading to periods of recession. As an example, if house prices fall and people begin to feel poor, they will reduce consumption. Sales revenue of companies will be lower, making it difficult for companies to repay their debts. Heavily indebted companies are likely to miss payments and even go bankrupt, leaving banks with bad debts and less willing to issue new loans. Then even financially healthy companies are likely to tighten their belts and spend less. In an extreme scenario, prices and wages will fall due to the low demand, and this deflation would make the money owed more valuable, so real debt burdens would be even higher.[5]

The most important component of the economy in developed countries is consumption. In the US, consumption accounts for roughly 70% of total GDP. During the financial crisis in 2008, consumption dropped sharply and was the main driver of the ensuing recession. States with higher house prices prior to the crash had the highest debt burdens, and they tended to be the places where consumption declined the most, leading to deeper recessions. In Europe, countries where house prices increased the most prior to 2008 also had heavier household debt burdens and witnessed the greatest decline in consumption during the recession.[6]

Recessions that result from debt also tend to exacerbate inequality, since debt problems tend to hit the rich and poor on a different scale. This has to do with the nature of debt, that is, the law gives priority to creditors' claim over debtors' assets. Even an indebted company or an individual goes bankrupt, their assets must be liquidated first to repay

[5] This downward spiral is often called the "debt-deflation cycle" and was first named by American economist Irving Fisher, who used it to explain the Great Depression from 1929 to 1933. This theory was later developed by the Japanese economist Richard Koo, which became known as the "balance sheet recession" and was used to explain Japan's recession in the early 1990s and later the Great Recession after the US subprime mortgage crisis (Koo 2011). Eggertsson and Krugman (2012) elaborate further on this line of thought.

[6] Mian and Sufi (2014) provide a detailed account of the debt and consumption of US residents. Glick and Lansing (2010) show that house prices in major European and American countries in the decade before 2008 were highly positively correlated with household debt, and countries with more debt had a greater decline in consumption during the crisis.

debt. Taking mortgages as an example, poorer people face a heavier burden when borrowing money because their income is low and less stable. If house prices fall, they need to withstand the loss first, and liquidate their assets to repay as much as possible the debt before entering bankruptcy, only after that, any left over debt loss would be borne by the bank or its creditors and shareholders, who are usually richer than the mortgage borrowers. In other words, debt tend to concentrate risks on people who are least able to take them. One example is Spain. In many countries, people who cannot repay mortgage can declare bankruptcy, and their houses would be foreclosed, then the debt obligation ends. In Spain, however, even after declaring bankruptcy and home foreclosure, mortgage borrowers can only be freed from paying mortgage interests, but mortgage principal still must be repaid. Non-payment will result in fines and put people on the list of "untrustworthy people", making life difficult. During the financial crisis, these strict laws led to widespread social unrest with locksmiths and police refusing to comply with bank requests to evict people from their houses. These "unescapable" debt even after bankruptcy became so heavy a burden that in the five years following the financial crisis, the economic recession in Spain was one of the worst.[7]

Section 2: Why Is There so Much Debt? Lessons from Europe and the US

Debt is a part of human nature. People want to satisfy their desires as soon as possible, and they are usually optimistic about the future and overestimate their ability to repay when borrowing money. Human nature is perpetual, however, while debt cycles fluctuate a lot. And every cycle must therefore be also driven by some factors other than human nature. These factors could make people feel more optimistic and want to borrow more, and at the same time, these factors could also increase the supply of credits, make borrowing easier and cheaper.

Since the 1980s, the political and economic environment in Europe and the US has helped to stimulate people's demand for owning a house (discussed in Chapter 5). But one of the premises of buying a house is that banks are willing to lend, otherwise people don't have the funds necessary to realize their demand. If the demand for credits increases but

[7] The Spanish example is from Mian and Sufi (2014).

its supply does not, then interest rates will rise to suppress the demand. The number of loans and the amount of debt therefore may not necessarily increase. From a slightly different perspective, debt of households and companies are also the assets of banks. In order to understand debt, we must therefore first come to understand what causes banks to lend out so much in the first place.

The Supply of Credits and Bank Deregulation

Increases in capital are often preluded by a relaxation in financial supervision. As a result, banks become bigger and bigger, issue more and more credit to the economy, while financial innovation such as securitization and derivatives increases the scales and risks in the financial system.

The wave of global financial liberalization begun with the disintegration of the Bretton Woods system in the 1970s. Under the Bretton Woods system, national currencies were pegged to the US dollar and the US dollar was pegged to gold in a fixed ratio. To maintain this fixed exchange system, all countries needed to maintain sufficient foreign exchange reserves in order to intervene in markets and prevent exchange fluctuations away from the pegs. The scale of international capital flows therefore could not be too large, otherwise it could lead to large fluctuations in exchange rates, requiring large and expensive interventions, thereby potentially depleting a country's foreign exchange reserves. In order to prevent large international capital flows, it is necessary to limit domestic bank lending, otherwise entities that borrow more money could import more or invest more abroad, both of which will result in increased international capital flows.

After the disintegration of the Bretton Woods system, developed countries implemented floating exchange rates and liberalized cross-border capital flows and cross-border trade. Households and companies could borrow from both domestic and foreign banks, and therefore limiting the amount of credit issued by banks domestically no longer made sense. Developed countries therefore started to relax restrictions on banks and financial institutions, and a wave of financial liberalization took off around the world, but this rapid growth in credit also brought many banking crises. Between 1980 and 2010, there were a total of 153 banking crises around the world, an average of five per year. Under the Bretton Woods system running from 1945 to 1970, there were only two banking crises in total. Prior to World War II and throughout the nineteenth century, the frequency of banking crises was also highly correlated with the volume of international capital flows.[8]

Banks are a core part of the financial system, and financial crises are typically accompanied by banking crises. There are at least four reasons for this. First, banks are large in scale and highly leveraged.[9] The assets of the US banking system accounted for 60% of US GDP in 1950, but prior to the global financial crisis in 2008, banks' total assets had already exceeded GDP. Meanwhile, bank capital to asset ratio held fallen to only 5%. Put simply, US banks were using $5 of capital to do $100 of lending, and the "leverage ratio" reached 20x. In principle, a loss of mere 5% of lending is large enough for banks to lose all their capital.[10]

The second risk lies in the fact that most money borrowed by banks is short term, for example easy access deposits, whereas most of the money being lent out to businesses and households is long term. This so-called maturity mismatch between the maturity of banks assets and liabilities gives rise to liquidity risks. If depositors suddenly decide to withdraw their money all at once, then the banks will be in big trouble because they are unable to meet the demand while the money it has lent out can't be immediately retrieved. This kind of risk led to the introduction of government deposit insurance, which aimed to reduce the risk that people would demand their money at the same time. But this type of risk has not been eliminated. Modern-day banking is increasingly complex and no longer involves simply taking deposits and making loans. Many liabilities come from money market funds, hedge funds or other institutions that may not be covered by the deposit insurance system. Therefore, if

[8] Reinhart and Rogoff (2009) count the number of banking crises in major countries in the past 200 years and found that the frequency of crises is highly positively correlated with the scale of international capital flows.

[9] Mervyn King, former Governor of the Bank of England, has an excellent and insightful book on bank risk (King 2016).

[10] According to a report from the Bank of England (Haldane et al. 2010), the leverage ratio (total assets/Tier 1 core capital) of major commercial banks in the US in 2007 was about 20 times (such as 21 times for Bank of America). For investment banks, it was around 30 times (for example Lehman Brothers at 28 times). In Europe, Deutsche Bank's leverage was 52 times, and UBS's was 58 times.

institutional clients lack confidence or have an urgent need for liquidity, a bank run could still occur.[11]

The third risk relates to real estate. Bank credit is most often linked to real estate, therefore the price of land and housing can have a significant impact on banks. Due to the high level of leverage and business risks, banks typically require collateral when making loans to households or businesses. Land or housing is often the best collateral, since they are fixed and not easy to hide or move. Compared to other physical assets that can only be used for some specific purpose (such as a machine), land and houses have a wide range of potential uses and tend to be more stable in value. Banks therefore like to lend to real estate companies and to make residential mortgage loans. For example, in 2012, 79% of all bank loans made in the UK were linked to residential or commercial property, and nearly 65% of the total was residential mortgage loans. In the US, nearly 70% of total bank loans are linked to mortgage and real estate. On average, over 60% of bank loans made in the US and Europe are linked to mortgage and real estate. Therefore, the housing cycle tends to coincide and fluctuate with the bank credit cycle. Since both the banking industry and the real estate industry are highly leveraged, their mutually reinforced cycles have a large impact on business cycles.[12]

Furthermore, the value of land rises and falls along with the economic cycle. In boom times, land prices rise rapidly, before declining again during recessions. The willingness of banks to offer credit also rises and falls along with the value of land, which acts as the main collateral. When land value rises, the value of the collateral rises, and the banks' profits also rise. With a higher safety margin and more capital at hand, banks are willing to lend more, to even less qualified borrowers, which increases the risks. During recessions, this process reverses, and banks become less willing to lend, and it becomes much harder for households and businesses to access credit. This process can lead to the overheating of the economy, as banks continue supplying easy credit when

[11] The largest category for this type of fund is "repo", which can be understood as a short-term collateral loan. Gorton (2010) provides a concise and excellent introduction to this important business.

[12] Data are from Turner (2017) and Jordà et al. (2016). In addition, Knoll et al. (2017) point out that house prices began to accelerate after the disintegration of the Bretton Woods system in the 1970s. Growing at a much faster rate than the rate of per capita GDP growth, which may be related to the financial deregulation that allowed a large amount of funds entered the real estate market.

the economy runs well, likewise it can exacerbate economic downturns as banks refuse to lend when companies and households need credit most. In early 2000s Ireland, a large amount of bank credits poured into the real estate industry, housing price soared and real estate investment rose from 4 to 9% of GDP by 2008. Employment in the construction industry also increased rapidly. Once the financial crisis of 2008 struck, the real estate industry collapsed, and many companies were in urgent need of capital to keep operating. However, the growth in bank credit essentially stopped, dropped from 20% per year during the boom years to 1.3%. Many companies had to close down and the unemployment rate rose sharply.[13]

The fourth and final risk associated with banks is that banks transmit risks to other parts of the financial sector. For example, banks may package mortgage loans together and sell the portfolio to other financial institutions as residential mortgage-backed securities (RMBS). By doing this, banks reduce their own credit risk and also free up capital to increase lending. But there is a problem, if credit risk is going to be passed to someone else, then banks' incentive to perform effective credit analysis is reduced. When banks can easily sell their loans, whether the borrowers can repay their loan matters less. During the 2008 financial crisis, the credit quality of many US mortgage loans was very low, and borrowers were simply unable to repay the money they owed. In some cases, people applied for mortgages using the name of their pets and still succeeded. Hence the 2008 financial crisis also became known as the "subprime mortgage crisis".

As the number of transactions between banks and other financial institutions increased, the size of the entire financial sector has grown dramatically, and it has become the largest sector in the economy. Before the financial crisis, the value added generated by the financial industry accounted for 8% of US GDP.[14] However, the increased financial activity didn't necessarily improve the efficiency of capital allocation. Instead, excessive levels of short-term or short-sighted transactions brought increased risk and unnecessary costs to the economy. Funds and

[13] Data for Ireland are from Turner (2017). The pro-cyclical nature of bank credit is also reflected in interest rate movements. In bad times, interest rates tend to rise quickly too. Gertler and Gilchrist (2018) describe the movement of various interest rates and the behavior of financial institutions during the 2008–2009 global financial crisis.

[14] Figures are from Haldane et al. (2010).

resources got captured in the financial sector without helping to grow the size of the real economy. An arms race in talent and technology between financial companies occurred while they dealt with each other and tried to outsmart their opponents, with many talented scientists and engineers finding work in the financial sector, giving up potentially more productive careers.[15] After the financial crisis, the financial sector invoked anger and criticism across society, and spawned movements such as Occupy Wall Street.

Inequality Between Countries and Within a Country

Financial liberalization has opened the door to more debt, however it is difficult to increase the total level of debt without more funds being made available in the financial sector. In the case of the US, there are two primary sources of funds. Firstly, some countries, such as China, have lent large sums of money to the US. Secondly, inequality in the US has increased dramatically and wealth has become more concentrated. Since the rich spend a smaller fraction of their wealth, they have more savings available to be lent out to other parts of society.

East Asian countries, including China, lend money to the US as a result of trade imbalances. In 2018, the bilateral trade deficit between China and the US was $400 billion, which means that the US needs to borrow $400 mn from the world in order to pay for the excess imports from China. The main creditors are China and other East Asian countries such as Korea and Japan. These countries suffered a large loss during the 1997 Asian Financial Crisis, so after that, they greatly increased their US dollar reserves, and invested heavily in US treasuries and other related securities, i.e., lending money to the US. This phenomenon was called "*the global savings glut*" by former Federal Reserve Chairman Ben Bernanke. Bernanke argued that this inflow of money into the US drove down US interest rates, which in turn led to speculation in real estate, triggering the global financial crisis in 2008.

The European Union also lends money to the US, and many EU countries were among the hardest hit during the financial crisis. In fact, some of the largest overseas holders of "toxic" financial assets during the crisis were not from Asia, they were European banks. The flow of money from

[15] Philippon and Reshef (2012) document how the financial sector sucks up highly educated talent in the US.

Asia to the US is related to trade imbalance, but trade between the US and Europe is more or less balanced, so Europe lends money to the US and vice-versa. Even though the total amount of capital flows is very large, the value of funds flowing in each direction is more or less equal, so the "net flow" is small. This type of balance, in fact, is also risky. Money simply flows backward and forward, increasing the transaction amount and value of financial assets, making the financial system more fragile. For example, a German bank may issue US dollar-denominated bonds in order to borrow dollars in the US, this money may then be spent purchasing mortgage-backed securities in the US and the money therefore flows back to the US. The liabilities and assets from the transaction are both denominated in US dollars, just the same as an American bank. The only difference is that the physical location of the bank is in Germany. Prior to the financial crisis, trans-Atlantic capital flows were far larger than trans-Pacific capital flows. In fact, during the financial crisis, many emergency loans provided by the Federal Reserve ended up being given to European banks.[16]

There are other reasons why international capital tends to flow to the US instead of other countries. The US dollar is the worlds' most important reserve currency and financial assets denominated in US dollars are the most popular form of investment. Global funds allocate a significant portion of assets to the US and this provides another reason why the US government can borrow money at the low cost from the world. However, large net inflows of capital act to exacerbate the US trade deficit since dollars can only be obtained by other countries by selling goods and services to the US. In order to preserve the dollar's status as the leading international reserve currency, the US needs to run a trade deficit that provides the world with a sufficient supply of dollars. However, persistent trade deficits lead to the accumulation of debt, and this situation may eventually challenge the dollar's status as global reserve currency. This situation is known as the "Triffin Dilemma". The global economic imbalances that we see today are therefore a combination of trade imbalances

[16] Avdjiev et al. (2016) disaggregated aggregate financial capital flows between continents, rather than focusing only on the volume of net flows. The close linkages between transatlantic financial institutions have complex causes and consequences, which is very detailed and brilliantly discussed in Tooze (2018).

and capital flow imbalances necessitated by the status of the dollar as the global reserve currency.[17]

Capital inflow from abroad is not the only source of the loanable funds in the US, another source is the domestic income inequality. If most wealth is concentrated in a small group of rich people, the supply of loanable funds will increase, while the demand for credit will also increase because poor people need to borrow money to survive. Imagine a country that has only two person. The country produces 100 units, and each person needs to consume 50 to live. If the distribution of the products is equal, the total consumption will be equal to the total production, and there will be zero saving and zero debt. However, if person A earns 100 and B earns 0, A will spend 50 and save 50 while B must borrow 50. Both the saving rate and the debt level of the country will be 50%.

In most developed countries, the widening gap between the rich and poor has been accompanied by rising levels of debt.[18] Taking the US as an example, in 2015, the richest 10% earned nearly half of all total income, up from 35% 40 years ago. In other words, for every 100 dollars produced, the richest 10% took 35 dollars with the remaining 65% going to the bottom 90%, but today the value going to the richest 10% has increased to 50 dollars. The richest therefore sliced an extra 15% of income from the total pie. This income transfer to the richest is huge. Compared to it, the "huge" bilateral trade deficits between the US and China in 2018 only accounted for less than 2% of American GDP.

This inequality becomes even more alarming when looking at disparities in wealth instead of income. In 2015, the richest 10% of Americans owned 78% of all wealth.[19] However, the rich cannot spend all their money, and their consumption therefore represents a much lower share of their income than those lower down the income distribution. This results in a great deal of excess savings that needs to be managed by the financial system. The excess savings of the top 1% of Americans over the past 40 years is as large as the excess savings pouring into the US from abroad

[17] This theory was proposed for the Bretton Woods system and for the gold standard before it. Whether it can be directly applied to the current US trade deficit is still controversial. It also cannot be assumed that if the Renminbi wants to become an international currency, then China's current trade surplus must become a deficit.

[18] Mian et al. (2020a) examine the link between income inequality and rising debt in developed countries.

[19] Data on income and wealth inequality come from Kuhn et al. (2020).

("the global savings glut", called by Bernanke).[20] In theory, excess savings from the wealthy can be used to invest both at home and abroad, however most of this capital stayed in the US, being lent to domestic companies, the US government or residents. When we further examine the data in the decades prior to the global financial crisis, investment of US companies actually decreased while government borrowing remained relatively stable, therefore most of the money was lent to households lower down the income distribution, becoming their debts.

The main purpose of this borrowing was to purchase houses, so the surplus money flowed into real estate through financial intermediaries such as banks. Before the financial crisis, nearly 70% of US banking loans were mortgages or other real estate-related loans. Therefore, most banks did not direct large amounts of funds to the real economy or convert the money into productive assets, instead they served as intermediaries to lend rich people's money to poorer people to buy houses. This expansion of real estate finance therefore didn't necessarily increase the efficiency of capital allocation, and it led to increased risks in the financial system.

This phenomenon of financial resources moving from the real economy to the financial economy has also caused concern in China. At the 2019 Bund Summit conference in Shanghai, Guo Shuqing, Chairman of the China Banking and Insurance Regulatory Commission, emphasized the need to improve the efficiency of capital allocation and to solve the problem of capital moving from the real to the financial economy. He also outlined plans to clear up so-called idle-funds within the financial system. Moreover, he described the problem of financialization of the real estate sector where "*some real estate developers borrowed too much from limited credit resources, reduced the efficiency of capital allocation, and promoted real estate speculation*".

Insufficient Investment of the Real Economy

Debt is not a problem in and of itself. If money borrowed can be put to productive use, and the investment can increase future output and

[20] Put simply, money from of the wealthy is lent to the not so wealthy. This is easy to understand in theory, but it is not easy to prove. It is necessary to get rid of the fog of financial intermediaries and figure out the detailed flow of funds. The analysis that the savings of the richest 1% in the US became the debt of the poorest 90% can be seen in Mian et al. (2020b).

income, then debt repayment will present no problem. Likewise, if debt flows to companies which use it to invest in a productive manner, rather than into real estate and financial speculation, debt may not lead to higher asset prices and bubbles. Yet over the past 40 years, the average share of investment as percentage of GDP in major developed economies has fallen from 28% in the 1970s to 20% today.[21] One reason is that many large companies have relocated investment to developing countries such as China, and manufacturing supply chains as a whole have also relocated offshore. The manufacturing industry is investment-heavy, so the decline in manufacturing has naturally contributed to the decline in investments' share of GDP. At the same time, with the development of the IT industry, machines have become much smarter and must rely on software and related services to operate, so the relative value of physical equipment has also declined. A lot of investment has therefore gone into so-called intangible assets and service industries, which are more dependent on human capital and ideas than physical capital. Since the development of service industry requires the agglomeration of people, the demand for housing and social spaces in specific locations (such as various types of commercial real estate) also increased.[22]

Another reason for the decline in physical investment is a weakening of competition in developed economies. Over recent decades, industry concentration has been increasing and top companies have been becoming larger and larger. This is not necessarily bad in theory. If superstar companies beat their rivals through fair competition and continue to move ahead and innovate after occupying the market, investment and productivity will continue to rise. However, the reality is that in the US, higher industry concentration and larger companies often lead to a decline in investment and productivity.[23]

[21] Data come from Mian et al. (2020a).

[22] Haskel and Westlake (2018) pointed out that, from 1990 to 2014, the price of capital equipment relative to the price of products and services fell by 33%. They refer to developed countries as "capitalism without capital", a form of capitalism that places greater emphasis on intangible assets and talent, which may lead to stagnant productivity and income inequality.

[23] Philippon (2019) writes a wonderful book analyzing the US economy's drift away from the free market and its declining competitiveness.

An influx of capital increased the supply of funds, combined with a lack of business investment reducing the demand for funds, led to the long-term real interest rate in developed economies falling steadily for 40 years, close to zero today.[24] In other words, it is difficult to find assets that could deliver a safe and stable long-term returns, which led to all kinds of short-sighted speculation, various financial innovations and real estate bubbles spread in countries around the world. After the financial crisis, the Federal Reserve drove low short-term interest rates to zero too and maintained that low rate for a long period. This encouraged large companies to borrow money to acquire smaller competitors, which further increased industry concentration and reduced competition. The low-interest rate environment also pushed a lot of money into the stock market, driving up share prices. Since the richest 10% of people hold 90% of stock market, this pushed up the gap between rich and poor even further.[25]

This situation also aroused the vigilance of China's policymakers. In 2019, Yi Gang, the governor of the People's Bank of China, pointed out that "*In the absence of economic growth, the central bank can provide liquidity to the banking system, however commercial banks cannot make loans due to the insufficient demand for funds, then liquidity will flow into asset markets. Loose monetary policy is overall beneficial to asset owners, and super-loose monetary policy may exacerbate wealth inequality, solidify structural distortions, and make crisis' more serious and harder to adjust*".[26]

Section 3: Debt Risks in China

The rapid rise in China's debt levels began in 2008. When the financial crisis that started in the US spread around the world, exports from China declined rapidly. In order to prevent a severe economic downturn, the Chinese central government unleashed a large stimulus package. At the same time, many restrictions and controls on local government borrowing and investment were removed, leading to a huge increase in investment in infrastructure and real estate. A period of sustained investment led

[24] Data come from Mian et al. (2020a).

[25] Data are from Kuhn et al. (2020). 90% of the wealth of the wealthy is in stocks, a proportion that has changed little since 1950.

[26] See Yi's article (易纲 2019).

to rising house prices and increasing debts at local government, real estate companies and also among individual homeowners. Other companies, such as state-owned enterprises, also borrowed heavily given the easy financial conditions. This wave of borrowing led to overcapacity and declining returns on investment. As a result, debt grew faster than GDP and China's overall debt-to-GDP ratio increased.

In comparison with other developing countries, China's external debt levels are very low, and most debts are denominated in Chinese RMB currency. It is therefore unlikely that there could be a sovereign debt crisis caused by external debt, such as the one witnessed in Greece around 2011. According to China's Balance of Payment Report, issued by the State Administration of Foreign Exchange (SAFE), China's external debt balance accounted for only 14% of GDP at the end of 2019 (the internationally recommended safety limit stands at 20%). Moreover, China's foreign exchange reserves account for 2.6 times the amount of short-term external debt (with the internationally recommended safety limit being 1 times). This means that there are sufficient funds available to repay debt in any crisis. In addition, even China's foreign debt is often denominated in RMB (up to 35% of total external debt), so the default risk is very small.

An Introduction to China's Debt Accumulation: 2008–2018

Figure 6.2 depicts how the debt-to-GDP ratio in China increases over time, and this process began in 2008. In 2008 and 2009, China responded quickly to the global financial crisis, launching a 4 trillion-yuan stimulus plan. The plan included 1.18 trillion yuan spent by the central government (including the disaster relief and recovery funds after the 2008 Sichuan earthquake), and 2.82 trillion-yuan spent by local governments. In order to ensure efficient implementation of the stimulus plan, and to help local governments raise money, the central government relaxed restrictions on local government financing vehicles (see Chapter 3), cut interest rates, and lower bank reserve requirement ratios. Stimulus funds eventually found their way into either infrastructure or real estate, and investments in these two areas increased rapidly. For example, local governments, cooperated with the Ministry of Railways, borrowed a lot in order to build high speed railway at home, which resulted in fixed asset investment in railways increasing from 250 billion yuan in 2007 to 700 billion yuan in 2009 and 850 billion yuan in 2010.

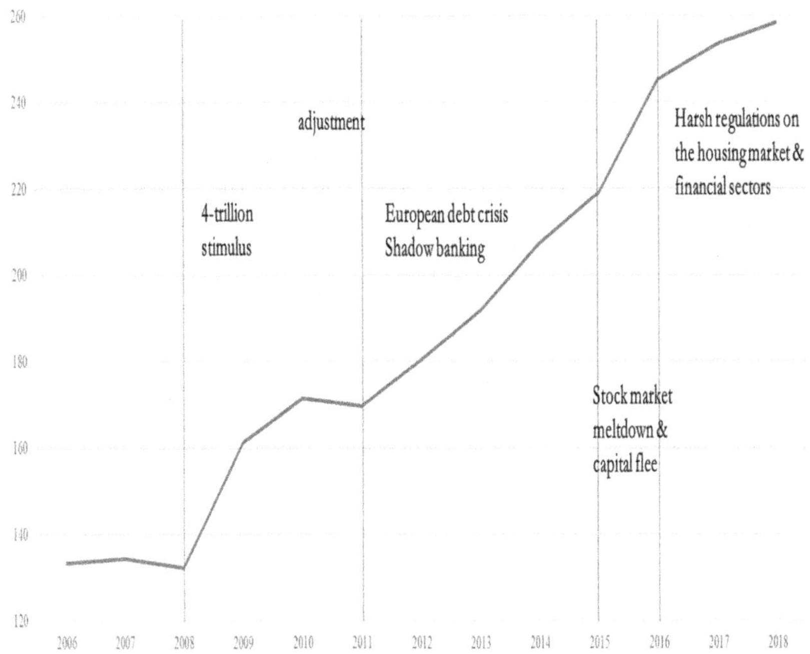

Fig. 6.2 Percentage of Chinese debts over national GDP (*Source* IMF Global Debt Database)

However, by 2010 and 2011, the Chinese economy was already starting to show signs of overheating. Coupled with a rise in the price of food staples such as pork, inflation started to rise, and monetary policy was tightened as a result. In mid-2011, the European sovereign debt crisis broke out and China's export-orientated manufacturing industry started to run into trouble. In 2012, the central bank once again cut reserve requirements and interest rates, and eased restrictions on bond issuance by local government financing vehicles. Issuance of urban investment bonds more than doubled in one year. Also starting from 2012, the "shadow banking" system begun to expand in China, which further directed funds to local government financing vehicles, leading to a rapid increase in infrastructure investment in 2012. The overall debt level therefore started to climb fast again after 2012.[27] During this period, the central government began to try to strengthen control and supervision over the real estate industry.

In 2015, China suffered a stock market crash, and the problems of overcapacity and excess real estate development caused by overinvestment in the previous years started to emerge. At the end of 2015, the Federal Reserve started to exit from quantitative easing and raise interest rates. This external environment, combined with some domestic forces such as the anti-corruption campaign, led to a significant depreciation of the Chinese RMB against the US dollar, and a large amount of capital begun to leave China. In reaction, the Chinese central bank once again cut interest rates and reserve requirements, the Ministry of Finance helped to replace bonds issued by local government financial vehicles with bonds issued by local governments (see Chapter 3), and the central government once again relaxed its controls on the real estate industry. The house price started to rise rapidly again across the country. At the same time, the shadow banking industry, which had only recently taken off, also begun to transform: trust and entrusted loans shrunk rapidly after stricter supervision was enforced, while "wealth management products" issued by banks took off, and funds flowing into the local government financing vehicles and real estate industry did not decrease. The overall debt burden therefore continued to grow after 2015.

In 2016, the process of removing real estate inventory in smaller cities came to an end, thanks to the huge monetary compensation to the displaced and resettled residents of urban shantytowns. By the end of the year, the central government first made the proposition that "housing is made for living not for speculating" and started to comprehensively tighten real estate regulation. It was also in 2016 that serious reforms to industrial overcapacity also begun to take effect and the profit margins of industrial and manufacturing enterprises gradually started to recover. The PPI (producer's price index), a widely watched gauge that measures the price change of manufacturing products, turned positive for the first time after a continued decline for five years.

In the first half of 2018, the central bank and four government ministries issued "new asset management regulations" to place stricter

[27] For details on "shadow banking", see the subsection "Bank Risk" later in this chapter.

control on the shadow banking industry, attempting to reduce the financial risks that had accumulated over years. Overall credit issuance started to shrink, and private companies run into difficulties raising money. In the second half of the year, the US-China trade war started in earnest and economic growth continued to slow. By the end of 2018, China's total debt to GDP ratio reached 259%, with 54% consisting of household debt, 51% of government debt, and 154% of corporation debt. Among government debts, 17% was owed by the central government and 34% by local governments (Fig. 6.3).[28] In Chapters 3 and 5, I have discussed the local government and household debts respectively and will not repeat them here. In the remainder of this chapter, I will focus on corporate debt and the risks of creditor banks.

China's Corporate Debt

As can be seen from Fig. 6.3, the level of household debt in China is at similar levels to that of developed countries. The level of government debt is lower than developed countries, but the level of corporate debt is much higher. In 2018, corporate debt in the US and Germany accounted for 75% and 58% of GDP, but the figure was as high as 154% in China. One of the reasons is that capital markets in China are less developed and corporate financing is dominated by debt financing (i.e., bank loans) and equity financing accounts for a very low proportion. By the end of 2018, the total amount of corporate debt was 140 trillion yuan but domestic equity financing stood at only 7 trillion yuan.[29]

[28] Many people think that local government debt should include not only debt explicitly issued by the local government, but also the debt of affiliated state-owned enterprises, particularly the debt of local government financing vehicles. In that case the debt burden of local governments would be more than 34%. However, if these "hidden" debts are counted as local government debts, they cannot be counted a second time as corporate debt, so such disputes regarding accounting do not affect the estimation of the overall debt level.

[29] In Fig. 6.3, total corporate debt is calculated as a percentage of GDP. The companies included in the graph exclude financial firms, which is an international convention when calculating macro debt burdens. Debt in the figure refers to the total amount of debt borrowed by the corporate sector from the financial sector (such as banks), and it excludes debts that arise between corporates (e.g., receivables arising from business transactions). The total amount of domestic stock financing of non-financial enterprises in China comes from the "Statistics of Social Financing Stock" issued by the People's Bank of China.

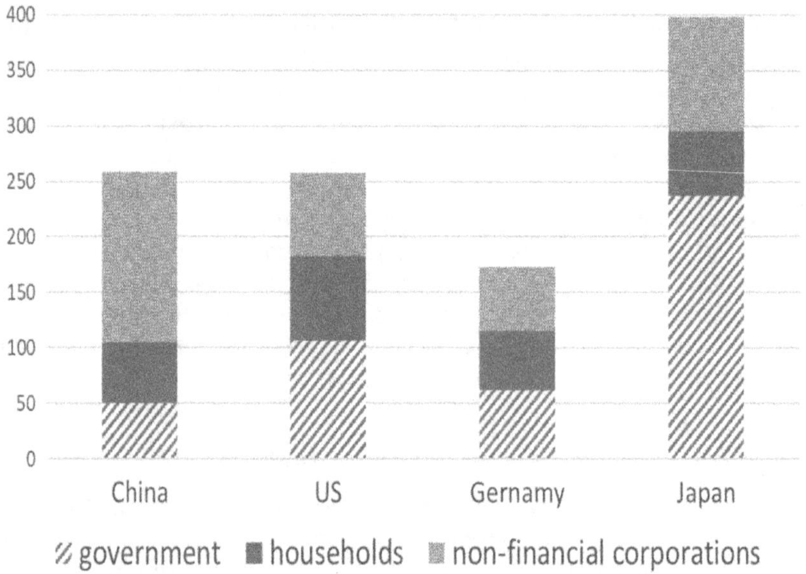

Fig. 6.3 Debt compositions, percentages over national GDP in 2018 (*Source* IMF Global Debt Database)

The first issue to be aware of when discussing corporate debt in China is local government financing vehicles. This type of debt represents roughly 40% of GDP and is mainly invested in infrastructure with very low rates of return (about 1% on average). Since we have discussed this type of debt in detail in Chapter 3, I will not repeat here.

The second issue to be aware of is the phenomenon called "state enterprise advance, private sector retreats" in recent years. After 2008, state-owned enterprises (SOEs) expanded rapidly, but these companies are typically much less efficient than private companies. According to the China Fiscal Yearbook published by the Ministry of Finance, in decade before 2008, the total assets of SOEs increased by 1.6 times, however in the decade after 2008, their total assets increased by 4.4 times and their total liabilities increased by 4.7 times. Consequently, SOE debt as a proportion of GDP increased from 78 to 144%.[30] Worryingly however,

[30] This ratio cannot be directly compared with the ratio of 154% of corporate debt in GDP shown in Fig. 6.3. The corporate debt in this figure is the total external debt of the

total profits of SOEs during the same period actually dropped from 4.2% of GDP to only 3.9%, and operating income dropped from 72% of GDP to 65%.[31]

The above data on SOEs are widely used, but these data and related research have many problems and it is difficult to know the real situation of all state-owned companies.[32] Fortunately, the data for state-owned industrial enterprises are much clearer, since the National Bureau of Statistics records detailed data in this area. According to this dataset, from 2008 to 2017, the assets and liabilities of state-owned industrial enterprises did not expand significantly relatively to GDP, instead staying relatively stable. Therefore, there was no obvious evidence of the expansion of state-owned industrial enterprises. SOEs in China have long been recognized to have higher debt to asset ratios and lower profit margins than private enterprises, and after the 4 trillion-yuan stimulus plan, the gap in profit margins between SOEs and private companies became larger, and the gap did not started to shrink until 2013. This change was not driven by SOEs but by private companies. After the 4 trillion-yuan stimulus, the margins of private firms expanded rapidly, falling back only after 2012. One possible

company as a whole, including only bank loans and bonds; but the 144% here also includes debts between companies such as accounts receivable. These debt between companies cancels each other out when calculating the total external debt of the company as a whole. If only the debt of a subset of companies is calculated, such as state-owned enterprises, the debts between companies should also be included. There are two sets of data on state-owned enterprises, one is from the SASAC, and the other is from the Ministry of Finance. The latter set covers a wider range because many state-owned enterprises are not under the control of the SASAC. This section discusses only non-financial corporations because the corporate debt statistics in Fig. 6.3 include only non-financial corporations.

[31] For corporate data, the most comparable variable to GDP should be total value added, but the total value added of state-owned enterprises is difficult to estimate, and each estimation methodology has its own flaws. According to Zhang's estimate (张春霖 2019), the proportion of the value added of state-owned enterprises in China's GDP has not changed much in the past 10 years.

[32] For example, 45% of all SOE assets in 2017 were categorized as either "social services" or "associations and others", and these two types of enterprises have negligible operating income. The Ministry of Finance does not elaborate on exactly what businesses these are. For another example, in terms of asset size, at least 24% of state-owned enterprises in 2017 were categorized as infrastructure enterprises, including local government financing vehicles. Obviously, the contribution of such enterprises to the economy should not only be based on their own return on assets, but also on their contribution to or spillover effects on the growth of other sectors, but these contributions are difficult to estimate.

reason is that with lots of funds available, many large private companies deviated from their main businesses and begun to speculate in land and real estate, which benefited them in the short term as house and land prices rose, but ultimately led to a decline in the overall efficiency of capital use.[33]

Inefficient or even loss-making SOEs or private enterprises should ideally be allowed to go bankrupt, otherwise they need to rely on year-round support to keep going. By extracting external credit that could have gone to more efficient uses, these "zombie companies" reduce the efficiency of credit allocation, burdening the whole economy and pushing up the overall debt burden. In response to the increasing prevalence of this situation, reforms in recent years have included promoting mixed ownership of SOEs, placing restrictions on local government interventions, increasing financial supervision and restricting funding, promoting market-oriented reforms and more competition in the allocation of production factors such as land, labor and capital, and improving bankruptcy laws and giving local government less room to interfere in debt restructurings, in the event they favor local indebted at the expense of their creditors (e.g., the bankruptcy case of SDK discussed in Chapter 4).

The third issue to be aware of is related to real estate companies. Real estate is one of China's core industries, not only is the industry itself very large, but it also drives many related industries such as steel, glass, furniture and home appliances. Taking 2013 as an example, the output from real estate and related industries accounted for 15% of GDP, and these industries grew fast and accounted for 30% of China's GDP growth in the year.[34] Real estate development requires a large amount of capital to purchase land and fund construction. It also has a long investment cycle, with many projects taking several years to complete. The industry therefore relies heavily on debts, and the asset-liability ratio is

[33] For more information regarding the expansion and declining efficiency of private enterprises, including industrial enterprises, after the "4 trillion" plan, readers can refer to Bai et al. (2016). Driven by the real estate boom and rising house prices,. during the period from 2007 to 2015, Chen et al. (2018) show that domestically listed non-real estate companies purchased many commercial real estate and residential buildings, with the total value of purchases accounting for 30% of their total investment.

[34] This kind of estimation is very complicated and involves calculating the input and output of various industries related to real estate. The estimation results here come from Xu et al. (许宪春等人 2015).

discussed above also apply to China. The first risk is the financial deregulation and the expansion of the banking industry. The 4 trillion-yuan stimulus plan launched in 2008 was not only a fiscal stimulus, but also a financial stimulus. The reserve requirement ratio and the benchmark interest rate were both cut sharply by China's central bank. As a result, the ratio of total bank credit to GDP rose from around 1.2 × in 2008 to 2.14 by 2016.

The second risk is that banks prefer issuing loans with land or real estate as collateral. I explain this with two small examples. Imagine a bank lends Mr. Zhang 1 million yuan to purchase a house. The bank is betting that Zhang's future income will be sufficient to repay the loan, however the future holds many uncertainties. Zhang may lose his job or encounter health problems, and he may be unable to repay the loan, so the bank asks Zhang to use the house as collateral. The house makes for good collateral, since it cannot be easily moved or disappear, and there should be a ready set of buyers in case the house needs to be sold. Without the collateral, risks of Zhang are essentially risks of the bank. With the collateral, risks are shared by both Zhang and the bank. Zhang also had to pay 300,000 yuan as a down payment on the house, which is equivalent to borrow only 700,000 with a collateral worth 1 million. The bank therefore has quite a large margin of safety when making the loan. Now let's look at business loans. The bank loans 5 million yuan to an entrepreneur named Mr. Li. The loan is used to purchase equipment that can produce products to be sold into the market. The 5 million repayment is expected to come from the operating income generated by Li's business in the coming years. But for use as collateral, the equipment is too specific. It needs knowhow to operate and not many people would be willing to buy it. In case Li has problems with his loan, the equipment cannot be sold as easily as the house. Even if it can be sold, the price is likely to be heavily discounted, with the bank recovering only a fraction of its value. In this case the risk to the bank is much larger than in the prior example. However, if Li's company has a government guarantee, or the company is a SOE with an implicit government guarantee, the risk to the bank will be much smaller.

Therefore, if there is more good collateral available (such as house and land), or more firms with government guarantees, then banks will have an incentive to expand lending. In a financial system that is dominated by banks, such as the one that China has, an increase in the amount of land that can be collateralized by local government financing vehicles, an influx of people moving to cities and buying houses, or an increase in the amount of implicit local government guarantees given to companies, will all stimulate credit expansion. Credit expansion is therefore influenced both by loose monetary policies and by the increasing demand for credits, and it is inseparable from the local governments' land finance and the real estate industry.

The third risk is that any problems of banks will be transmitted to other areas of the financial sector, and one important channel is shadow banking. The shadow banking system makes loans like regular banking, but their activities are not recorded on a bank's balance sheet and are therefore not subject to bank regulation. Banks are the core of any financial system, and these huge and highly leveraged banks also manage the savings of nearly all households, so of course they are heavily regulated. Imagine a scenario where a real estate company is willing to borrow money at a rate of 10% and a bank is willing to lend the money, but there is a problem, China's bank regulations limit the amount of money that can be lent to real estate companies and the loan cannot be made. The bank may therefore create a so-called wealth management product that attracts household savings at a rate of 5%, entrusting the money to a trust company. Then the trust company lends the money to the real estate company. In this so-called bank-trust cooperation, the wealth management product created by the bank is not recorded as bank deposits, and the money entrusted to the trust company is not recorded as bank loans, so the entire transaction is not recorded in the balance sheet of the bank and is therefore not subject to bank regulations. This is a form of shadow banking.

Many companies need to borrow money, and many people want to purchase wealth management products from banks because they pay higher interests than deposits, so the shadow banking industry in China has boomed in recent years. Even though Chinese regulators have tried to keep up with this growth, banks have proved adept at finding ways around any new regulations. For example, asset management companies may emerge in between the bank and the trust, helping to channel more funds. As a result, the transactions between financial firms increased a lot, and the scale of the entire financial industry got larger and more complex, with more and more interlinkages. Around the year 2000, the financial industry in China accounted for roughly 4% of GDP, by 2015 it had already doubled to 8%, which is equivalent to the level of the US prior to the global financial crisis. However, the financial industry in the US only reached this level because the Wall Street is the center of the global finance, taking in funds from across the world, whereas China's capital markets are largely isolated from the global financial market. When looking from this perspective, China's financial industry is obviously too large for its economy. As funds are transferred back and forth within the financial sector, incremental layers of fees are added, which eventually results in higher interest rate and costs of the final borrowing companies. More resources therefore are shifted from real business sectors to the financial sector, and various speculative bubbles emerge. Further problems are also present, for example while wealth management products are not on the bank's balance sheet and therefore in principle, their owners may suffer a loss. But if problems arise, people will still hold the bank responsible and are likely to protest to get their money back. In fact, banks indeed covered the loss of these wealth management products and gave money back to the investors. This type of implicit guarantee creates an additional risk for banks and the entire financial system.[39]

Most of the shadow banking businesses in China are dominated by banks and simply act as an extension of banking activities, so it is sometimes also called "the shadow of baking". This is different from the Western world, where shadow banking is mainly driven by non-bank financial firms. In China, the business of shadow banking is also much simpler, with less securitization of assets and without derivatives, and foreign capitals are rarely involved, so supervision costs are also lower. New capital market regulations launched in 2018 managed to shut down many channels through which money flows to the shadow banking sector. This put a squeeze on real estate companies and local government financing vehicles. But other non-real estate private enterprises were also left without financing after the new regulations. In summary, these new regulations have exposed many problems of China's financial sector.

Section 4: Solve the Debt Problem

To tackle a debt problem in any country, the solution must include two parts: repaying existing debts and curbing issuance of new debt. These require reforms of the political and economic system that encourages debt.

[39] Zhu (朱宁2016) explains this so-called rigid bubble phenomenon.

Repaying Existing Debt

For debtors, repayment is a simple matter of arithmetic. Either income needs to be increased or expenditures need to be cut. If neither can be achieved, one needs to sell assets in order to pay for the debt. If all of these actions are still not enough to repay the debt, the debtor may have to default, causing losses of the creditor. Since the main creditors in most economies are banks, a large wave of defaults can therefore cause damage to the financial system.

If borrowed money can be put to good use through investing in high-quality assets that generate higher income, then the debt burden will not be a problem. However, if an investment fails, or the borrower simply squanders the money with no hope of generating higher income, and debt repayment has to rely on squeezing expenditure, then households need to spend less or businesses need to cut costs or lay off staff. Likewise, governments may need to impose austerity and cuts in public services in order to make debt repayments. However, the expenditure of one person is the income of another, if someone reduces spending, then another person receives less income and may also need to reduce their spending, and everyone ends up cutting down and the aggregate demand falls. This can cause the economy to shrink, and national income would be lower. Indeed, even if the absolute value of debt is reducing, but if incomes fall faster than debt, then the overall debt burden will actually rise. This process is very painful, life is lived on a tight budget, products are hard to sell, and prices fall. As money becomes more valuable, real debt burdens become heavier. Moreover, if assets are sold to repay debts, then asset prices are also likely to be lower, which lowers the value of bank collateral and brings more risks into the system.

Taking local governments as an example. They borrow money to engage in real estate development and urbanization, this can not only help to bring investment into the area, but also lead to an increase in land prices and increased incomes of local residents. Debt burdens will not be a major problem while incomes are rising. However, once the economy starts to go down, tax revenues decrease and land price falls. Since public expenditures are difficult to cut, debt burdens are likely to increase. Other government assets, such as state-owned enterprises, may need to be sold to repay debts. Over the past few years in China, pressures on public finances have been growing and the central government has tightened many local government financing channels, so the reform of

SOEs that tries to attract more private capital into SOEs has accelerated. For example, in 2019, the Zhuhai City State-Owned Assets Supervision and Administration Commission sold 15% shares of Gree Electric, while the Wuhu City State-Owned Assets Supervision and Administration Commission sold 40% shares of Chery Automotive.

Paying off debts makes life difficult for debtors, while defaulting on debts makes life difficult for creditors. So, the whole process of debt repayment can be very painful, which may drive the economy into a recession. In contrast, issuing additional money can be another way to reduce debt burdens, something that seems less painful with no-one obviously losing out. There are roughly three ways that central banks can pump additional money into the economy. The first method is to increase money supply and reduce interest rates, which has been the main method of major central banks prior to the global financial crisis. Low-interest rates help to reduce interest payments and can also act to stimulate investment and consumption in the economy. If the economy grows as a result and real incomes rise, then debt repayment will become less of a burden. Even if real incomes do not increase, extra money can help to maintain a positive level of inflation. As price rises over time, the debt burden will gradually decline in real terms since money borrowed becomes worth less and less.

The second method is quantitative easing (QE): central banks inject more money into the economy by purchasing various assets across the economy. This has become a mainstream practice in developed countries after the financial crisis. In a crisis situation, many people sell assets to pay off debts and asset prices tumble. When central banks step in to purchase assets, it helps to support assets prices and at the same time injects liquidity into the economy, relieving the pressure of repaying debts. From an accounting perspective, this newly issued money is a central bank's liability, and this QE operation simply moves the liabilities of other sectors to the balance sheet of the central bank, so the balance sheet of the central bank will expand rapidly. Provided that the assets purchased are denominated in the home currency, the central bank can theoretically print unlimited amounts of money to buy. This operation in practice may not drive up inflation, since the money is used to pay down debt and there is no immediate increase in spending, which does not necessarily put pressure on prices. After the 2008 financial crisis, both the US and the EU carried out large-scale QE without experiencing significant inflation.

The main problem with QE is that it is difficult to get money into the hands of those lower down the income distribution, therefore the effect on consumer spending may be limited, but its effect on wealth inequality may be large. Since QE leads to an increase in asset prices, it will benefit asset owners who tend to be wealthier than average. After the 2008 global financial crisis, the US maintained low-interest rates and pursued QE for many years, and stock markets soared and house prices rebounded from crisis lows. But for poor people who already lost their home during the crisis and do not own any stock, they could not benefit from the situation and may feel unhappy with this wealth flowing to rich people (see Chapter 5). QE therefore has political consequences that show up in elections or protests. After the COVID outbreak reached the US in 2020, the Federal Reserve opened the floodgates again and the size of the central banks' balance sheet expanded by more than 60% in 3 months. The pattern of economic recovery later looked like the letter "K": rich people went up while poor people went down.

The third way that central banks can increase the supply of money into the economy is to monetize debt. In this method, the government issues debt that is directly purchased by the central bank with newly issued money. This operation of "debt monetization" removes the financial system from the process of monetary policy transmission. In the decade after the global financial crises, interest rate was cut to zero and QE seemed to reach its limit, but the economic recovery was still slippery. With the onset of the COVID outbreak, fierce debates broke out in the US about whether to use this third method of supplying money to the economy, and "Modern Monetary Theory or MMT", the economic theory that supports this approach broke into the public's eye.

The core of "deficit monetization" is to replace interest bearing debt with zero-interest debt, and to replace the financial market as a channel for resource allocation with an administrative system of government budget revenues and expenditures. In theory, if the private sector is struggling but government is strong in both finance and administrative capacity, then "deficit monetization" may work out. However, if the government is strong in both finance and administrative capacity, but still needs to turn to this extreme solution of "deficit monetization", then it means the external environment must be very difficult and unpredictable. In this case, the effects of "deficit monetization" cannot be known from theory alone, and we should look at historical experiences to find more evidence. Historically, countries that engage in "deficit monetization" did not ended well. It tended to cause hyperinflation, and soaring prices would damage currencies and countries' credibility, plunging countries into chaos. Indeed, this consequence is well documented in economics textbooks and is well known to the proponents of MMT. However, they argue that the cause of hyperinflation in history was not the increase in money supply itself, but rather the conditions at the time, such as revolutions or wars, which led to a destruction in productive capacity and weakened governments. Had productive capacity and governments been normal, "deficit monetization" would have helped to stimulate the economy. This brings us back to a fundamental question, if conditions are normal and governments are capable, then why would we ever arrive at the need to monetize the fiscal deficit? Can monetize deficits really solve the root cause of the problems? How should these newly issued money be used? Who should benefit and who should suffer?

The Nationalist government that led China until 1948 tried this kind of deficit monetization and ruined the economy. After the war against the Japanese ended in 1945, the Nationalist government needed a lot of money to fight in the civil war against the communists and much of it came from fiscal deficits. The fiscal deficit of the first half of 1948 was 780 times larger than the deficit of the whole year of 1945. At the same time, nearly all the newly printed money by the central bank was used directly by the government. The amount of new money in the first half of 1948 was 194 times larger than the amount of the whole year of 1945. Prices begun to spiral out of control. The price level in August 1948 was 5.58 million times that of early 1946. People gave up using government currency and turned to bartering or gold instead. In August 1948, the Nationalist government introduced a new currency and tried to stabilize the currency, but the government's credibility had been lost. Only 8 months later, prices denominated in this new currency rose by 112 times. A historian Ji Xianlin said that, professors at Tsinghua University at the time had to run to buy rice immediately after receiving their salaries, and the price would be higher for those who run slowly.[40]

Monetary policy in modern-day China is cautious. The State Council and the central bank have made clear on many occasions that they will not flood markets with liquidity, nor will they debase interest rates to

[40] The price figures in this paragraph are calculated based on the data in the book by Kia-Ngau Chang (Chang 1958), a famous banker in the Republic of China. The story about Ji Xianlin comes from Zhou (周其仁 2012).

zero or engage in QE policies.[41] There are two main reasons for this stance. Firstly, the government is afraid that low-interest rates will stimulate further housing market speculation. Since 2018, President Xi has laid out the principle that houses should be for living and not for speculation. Secondly, China's slowing economic growth and a rising debt burden is a structural problem that can't be solved by loose monetary policy. It is more a problem with the way how local governments promote economic growth.

Curbing New Debt Issuance

After understanding the causes that lead to various types of debt being issued, it is not difficult to begin developing some basic principles for controlling new debt issuance. House prices must be controlled, local governments' land finance activities must be managed, government implicit credit guarantees must be eliminated to prevent excessive borrowing by state-owned enterprises. However, even with a perfect understanding of the causes of debt, it is still very difficult to deal with the consequence. After all, the causes are from the past, but the consequences are about the present and the future, while the whole situation has changed over time. It's similar to an obese person who ate too much, and diet is absolutely necessary in order to regain health. However, suddenly stopping eating or doing things in an extreme way can only lead to even worse problems than obesity.

On the other hand, the past cause that led to the present debt problems also has its reasons, sometimes the debt was simply used as a last resort. The immediate cause for many of China's current debt problems was the 2008 financial crisis. During that time, China encountered wave after wave of bad shocks, with export orders plummeting. If the governments' stimulus had been too small, no-one knows what the consequences might have been. Although looking back, many people think the "4 trillion" stimulus plan may have been too much, we can never know what might have happened had it been less.

As for the implicit or explicit guarantees that governments issue to companies in order to help them borrow, they are not necessarily bad things either. In the early stages of economic development, there were

[41] At the end of 2019, the governor of the central bank, Yi Gang, published an article to explain the goals and concepts of China's monetary policy (易纲 2019).

many promising projects with high returns. However, due to underdeveloped financial markets and high levels of uncertainty, it was difficult to mobilize sufficient investment. Government guarantees were therefore the only means by which these projects could be made possible. However, as China's market economy has developed, the number of projects that can deliver guaranteed high returns has decreased. Investment decisions have become more difficult and faced more uncertainties, and companies also have more channels to finance themselves on the financial market. If governments continue to intervene too much, then funds will inevitably be channeled to low-quality projects and inefficient enterprises, which will result in excess capacity and crowd out resources of other firms. As returns on investment get lower, the contribution of investment to economic growth would become smaller, and debt burdens and the risk of default would become higher.

In fact, China's debt problem is a product of its export- and investment-driven economic system. After 2008, net exports dropped significantly, leading to a drop in GDP, and domestic investment was required to pick up the slack (see Fig. 7.4 and the next chapter for a detailed explanation). Regardless of whether this investment goes into infrastructure or real estate, they are both driven by local governments who control land and local banking systems. Various debts that results, no matter what forms they take, are all a response to governments' credit. The debt risks, although appearing on the balance sheet of creditor banks, are eventually the risks of government. In recent years, China has carried out a series of major economic and financial reforms that seek to tackle this debt problem. These included controls on house prices, new regulations for the asset management industry, restrictions on local governments' land finance, reforms of state-owned enterprises, as well as the anti-corruption campaign. These reforms have been effective in reducing the amount of new debt issued, but the economic transformation that moves China away from the old investment- and debt-driven growth model has still not been completed. Therefore, a reduction in debt may slow down this type of growth, but it cannot automatically make the system more efficient, economic growth therefore declines.

Another way to limit debt growth is to reform capital markets. The reforms should reduce the dominant role of the indirect financing provided by bank loans, and increase direct financing channels such as equity. By using more equity financing, the debt burden can be reduced, and the efficiency of capital markets can be improved. Equity has different properties from debt. First, shareholders share the risk of company performance. Second, equity can also be more easily sold through stock markets, and stock prices can exert pressure on company management. Even bonds, as another type of debt finance, are more flexible than bank loans since they can be sold on open markets.

China's capital market reforms have progressed slowly and the root cause is not difficult to understand. Financing and investment are two sides of the same coin; whoever invests must bear the investment risk, and the financing system must channel resources and risks to these investors. If the investment is made by government or state-owned entities, the risk should naturally be borne by them. The current financing system does exactly that, and it concentrates risks on government, because banks risks are eventually government risks. Take 2018 as an example, according to the Natural Bureau of Statistics, private enterprises accounted for 62% of fixed asset investment in China, with governments and SOEs accounting for the remaining 38%. But this ratio greatly underestimates the role of government, since many private investments are launched only with the support of the governments' industrial policies. In the real estate sector, 40–50% of the total investment is used to purchase land from governments. The risks corresponding to these investments are eventually borne by governments or government-controlled financial institutions. According to a calculation by Yi Gang (governor of the central bank) in 2018, 72% of the risks associated with financial assets in China are borne by governments or related financial institutions. In 1995 and 2007, this proportion was 74% and 70% respectively. We can see that the figure has not changed much over years, demonstrating the slow progress of reforms on the capital market.[42]

Investment made by government and SOEs therefore always go hand in hand with financing made by state-owned banks. This system has played a key role in China's past economic growth. However, if these investment decision-makers do not change, and if the power of decision-making is not delegated to markets, then it's not possible to transform the financial market, shifting the risks borne by governments and banks to a decentralized set of investors, because it would be violating the simple principle of "whoever makes the investment decision should bear the

[42] The data are from a paper by Yi (易纲 2020).

investment risks". Therefore, without significant reforms on the investment sectors, the progress on the reforms of capital markets is naturally slow. Moreover, even once these reforms are achieved, they are not a panacea. America's financial system is much more decentralized than China's, however financial catastrophes still happen on Wall Street from time to time. It is still unknown what the end game is for China's financial system. What proportion of financing will eventually come from indirect bank loans and from direct equity? What would be the future role of various state-owned financial enterprises, such as commercial banks, policy banks, and social security funds?

To summarize, the main risks associated with China's financial system are not those associated with speculations on the finance market, rather they are risks associated with government finances and resource misallocation. Although this system is not a new one, debt burdens and risks have increased in recent years mainly because this system cannot continue to promote economic growth. Indeed, the pace of credit and debt growth has been faster than both inflation and economic growth. So the overinvestment has crowded out resources for consumption, leading to overcapacity and overproduction in some industries and overinvestment in real estate in some areas, accompanied with corruption and lower government efficiency. It is clear that this kind of debt-fueled growth cannot continue, and the reforms in recent years have tried hard to change the situation, to make the market play a greater role in allocating resources, especially in the markets of production factors, such as land and capital.

Summary

This chapter analyzes the debt problem in China. It focuses mainly on corporate and bank-related risks, which, combined with government and household debt risks discussed in the previous chapters, can help outline the overall debt situation. China's debt problems do not have a simple root in fiscal or monetary policy, rather they are a result of the overall economic system that has driven China's growth over the past decades. Therefore, the "deleverage" process must be accompanied by a series of structural reforms. The direct causes of China's debt problem, however, are the 2008 financial crisis and the European sovereign debt crisis a few years later. The effects of these crises on the global economic system are large and far-reaching. These events greatly reduced demand for Chinese products and led the government to stimulate the economy through its 4 trillion-yuan stimulus plan. While helping stabilize the economy both for China and for the world, the stimulus also led to overinvestment in real estate and excess productive capacity that exacerbated the country's debt burden.

Overinvestment in productive capacity can be understood from three perspectives. The first is a decline in production efficiency. From a macro perspective, this decline in efficiency leads to GDP growth slower than debt growth, and the ratio of debt to GDP rises. From a micro perspective, overcapacity manifests itself in excessive investment by local governments, and they continue injecting capitals to "zombie companies" to survive. The allocation of resources is distorted, and the level of debt grows for both firms and local governments. In addition, the land finance system of local governments rely too much on rising land prices and the prosperity of real estate development, which pushes up house prices and the debt burden of households, as well as the risks in the banking system.

The second perspective to look at excess capacity is the international imbalance. While Chinese local governments pay great attention to investment, production and corporate taxation, relatively little attention is given to consumption, household income, and people's livelihoods. This leads to an imbalance in the economic structure, and the income distribution is biased toward capital while against labor. The share of labor income is therefore lower and domestic consumption is not sufficient to absorb all products. Excess productive capacity must therefore be exported. China is different from neighboring countries such as South Korea and Japan in that its size is huge, so its internal imbalance would have a large impact on the global economy and lead to international imbalance. China can therefore easily become drawn into trade conflicts with other countries.

The third perspective to examine excess capacity is industrial upgrading and development. Given there is too much productive capacity in China, competition in the manufacturing industry is fierce, which causes prices and costs to continually decrease. This affects low-end manufacturing industries both in other countries and in China. To survive and maintain a competitive advantage, Chinese companies must continually innovate and climb up on the value chain. Therefore, the quality and technology of China's manufacturing industry are constantly improving, moving up fast on the value chain. This has helped to drive technology innovation and to improve basic scientific research, which further impacts the international division of labor that was previously dominated by developed countries.

Starting from Chapter 3 until the end of this chapter, the book has analyzed the first perspective in detail and also laid a foundation for understanding the second and third. The next chapter will discuss China's impact on the international economic system. From this perspective of international economic conflicts, I will re-examine the structural imbalances in China's domestic economy.

Further Readings

Over the past 10 years, there have been many good books reflecting on the 2008 global financial crisis from the perspective of debt. *House of Debt: Why the Great Recession Happened and How to Avoid It (2014)* written by University of Chicago economist Amir Sufi and his Princeton colleague Atif Mian is a popular book on the American real estate industry and debt problems. For the general reader, the book may be too narrow in focus, but for students of economics, it will make for excellent reading to clearly understand the macro problems using microeconomic data. The book *Between Debt and the Devil: Money, Credit and Fixing Global Finance (2017)* written by British economist Adair Turner is a more comprehensive and popular book on the debt crisis. *The End of Alchemy: Money Banking and the Future of the Global Economy (2016)*, written by former Governor of the Bank of England, Mervyn King, is another well-written book and uses King's insights from his time at the Bank of England to examine the financial and banking systems. *Crashed: How a Decade of Financial Crises Changed the World (2018)*, written by Columbia University Economic Historian Adam Tooze, comprehensively and meticulously records the changes in the world's economic structure that occurred in the decade following the global financial crisis. Another book is written by Ray Dalio, the famous founder of the hedge fund Bridgewater. His book *Principles for Navigating Big Debt Crisis (2018)* is not restricted by the frameworks of mainstream economic theory and is therefore more concise and direct.

There are many discussions and studies on China's debt problems, but most of them are either academic literature or industry reports. There are few comprehensive and systematic books that are written for a general audience. *Debt and Distortion: Risks and Reforms in the Chinese Financial*

System (2018) written by Paul Armstrong Taylor, a Professor at the Johns Hopkins Institute in Nanjing, is good as an introductory primer. *China: The Bubble that Never Pops (2020)*, written by Bloomberg chief economist Thomas Orlik, reviews the causes and consequences of China's debt crises since the time of the reform and opening up. The author admits frankly that the history of China's economic development is also a history of the failure of predictions that China would collapse.

Banks are the core of the financial system and they are also the eye of the storm in financial crises. Understanding the risks posed by banks requires an in-depth understanding of banks' business models, which is the most interesting part of research published on financial crises in recent years. Although it is interesting to analyze the crisis from a macro perspective, only by deeply understanding the details of a banks' business, we can truly comprehend their complexity. Although the content is relatively specialized, there are two books that provide a concise introduction. One is *Slapped by the Invisible Hand: The Panic of 2007 (2010)*, written by Gary Gorton of Yale University, and the other is *The Fall of the House of Credit: What Went Wrong in Banking and What Can Be Done to Repair the Damage? (2009)* written by Alistair Milne. The Oscar-winning movie, *The Big Short*, also contains many details on the lead up to the financial crisis. Although the film is based on real people and real events, the protagonists are not the ones who made the most money from shorting the crisis. Rather Gregory Zuckerman's book, *The Greatest Trade Ever: The Behind the Scenes Story of How John Paulson Defied Wall Street and Made Financial History (2010)*, is a riveting account and read almost like a novel.

Regarding the risks and reforms of China's banking system, two investment bank economists, Carl Walter and Fraser Howie, wrote a very approachable book *Red Capitalism: The Fragile Financial Foundation of China's Extraordinary Rise (2012)*, which is well worth a read. *Dealing with China: An Insider Unmasks the New Economic Superpower (2015)* written by former President of Goldman Sachs and US Treasury Secretary Hank Paulson contains many anecdotes and stories from the authors' experience as a witness to China's economic rise.

References

Armstrong-Taylor, Paul (2016). *Debt and Distortion: Risks and Reforms in the Chinese Financial System*. Palgrave Macmillan

Avdjiev, Stefan, Robert N. McCauley, and Hyun Song Shin (2016). "Breaking Free of the Triple Coincidence in International Finance." *Economic Policy* 31.87: 409–451.

Bai, Chong-En, Chang-Tai Hsieh, and Zheng Song (2016). "The Long Shadow of a Fiscal Expansion". *Brookings Papers on Economic Activity*, Fall: 129–165.

Blanchard, Olivier (2022). *Fiscal Policy under Low Interest Rates*. MIT Press.

Chang, Kia-Ngau (1958). *The Inflation Spiral: The Experience in China 1939–1950*. MIT Press.

Chen, Ting, Laura Xiaolei Liu, Wei Xiong, and Li-An Zhou (2018). "Real Estate Boom and Misallocation of Capital in China," *Working paper*.

Eggertsson, Gauti B., and Paul Krugman (2012). "Debt, Deleveraging, and the Liquidity Trap: A Fisher-Minsky-Koo Approach." *Quarterly Journal of Economics* 127.3: 1469–1513.

Furman, Jason, and Lawrence Summers (2020). "A Reconsideration of Fiscal Policy in the Era of Low Interest Rates." *Brookings Working Paper*.

Gertler, Mark, and Simon Gilchrist (2018). "What Happened: Financial Factors in the Great Recession." *Journal of Economic Perspective* 32.3: 3–30.

Glick, Reuven, and Kevin J. Lansing (2010). "Global Household Leverage, House Prices, and Consumption," *Federal Reserve Bank of San Francisco Economic Letter*.

Gorton, Gary B. (2010). *Slapped by the Invisible Hand: The Panic of 2007*. Oxford University Press.

Haldane, Andrew, Simon Brennan, and Vasileios Madouros (2010). "The Contribution of the Financial Sector: Miracle or Mirage?" *A Technical Report at the London School of Economics*.

Haskel, Jonathan, and Stian Westlake (2018). *Capitalism Without Capital: The Rise of the Intangible Economy*. Princeton University Press.

Jordà, Òscar, Moritz Schularick, and Alan M. Taylor (2016). "The Great Mortgaging: Housing Finance, Crises and Business Cycles." *Economic Policy* 31.85: 107–152.

King, Mervyn (2016). *The End of Alchemy: Money, Banking, and the Future of the Global Economy*. WW Norton & Company.

Knoll, Katharina, Moritz Schularick, and Thomas Steger (2017). "No Price Like Home: Global House Prices, 1870–2012." *American Economic Review* 107.2: 331–353.

Koo, Richard C. (2011). *The Holy Grail of Macroeconomics: Lessons from Japan's Great Recession*. John Wiley & Sons.

Kuhn, Moritz, Moritz Schularick, and Ulrike I. Steins (2020). "Income and Wealth Inequality in America: 1949–2016." *Journal of Political Economy* 128.9.

Mian, Atif, and Amir Sufi (2014). *House of Debt: How They (and You) Caused the Great Recession, and How We Can Prevent it from Happening Again.* University of Chicago Press.

Mian, Atif R., Ludwig Straub, and Amir Sufi (2020a). "Indebted Demand," *NBER Working Paper* No. w26940.

Mian, Atif R., Ludwig Straub, and Amir Sufi (2020b). "The Saving Glut of the Rich and the Rise in Household Debt," *NBER Working Paper* No. w26941.

Philippon, Thomas (2019). *The Great Reversal: How America Gave Up on Free Markets.* Harvard University Press.

Philippon, Thomas, and Ariell Reshef (2012). "Wages and Human Capital in the US Finance Industry: 1909–2006." *Quarterly Journal of Economics* 127.4: 1551–1609.

Reinhart, Carmen M., and Kenneth S. Rogoff (2009). *This Time Is Different: Eight Centuries of Financial Folly.* Princeton University Press.

Shleifer, Andrei, and Robert Vishny (2011). "Fire Sales in Finance and Macroeconomics." *Journal of Economic Perspectives* 25.1: 29–48.

Tooze, Adam (2018). *Crashed: How a Decade of Financial Crises Changed the World.* Penguin.

Turner, Adair (2017). *Between Debt and the Devil: Money, Credit, and Fixing Global Finance.* Princeton University Press.

Translated References (in Chinese)

Ren, Zeping, Lei Xia, and Chai Xiong (2017). *Real Estate Cycle.* People's Publishing House. (in Chinese)

Xu, Xianchun, Hai Jia, Jiao Li, and Junbo Li (2015). "On the Role Played by Real Estate in the Growth of China's National Economy." *Social Sciences in China* 1: 84–101+204. (in Chinese)

Yi, Gang (2019). "Maintain Prudent Monetary Policy & Keep Yuan Stable." *Qiushi* 23. (in Chinese)

Yi, Gang (2020). "Revisiting China's Financial Asset Structure and Policy Implications." *Economic Research Journal* 3: 4–17. (in Chinese)

Zhang, Chunlin (2019). "Understanding China's SOE Sector Expansion." *Comparative Studies* 6. (in Chinese)

Zhu, Ning (2016). *China's Guaranteed Bubble.* China CITIC Press. (in Chinese)

Zhou, Qiren (2012). *Lessons from Currency: Exchange Rate and Currency Series Review.* Peking University Press. (in Chinese)

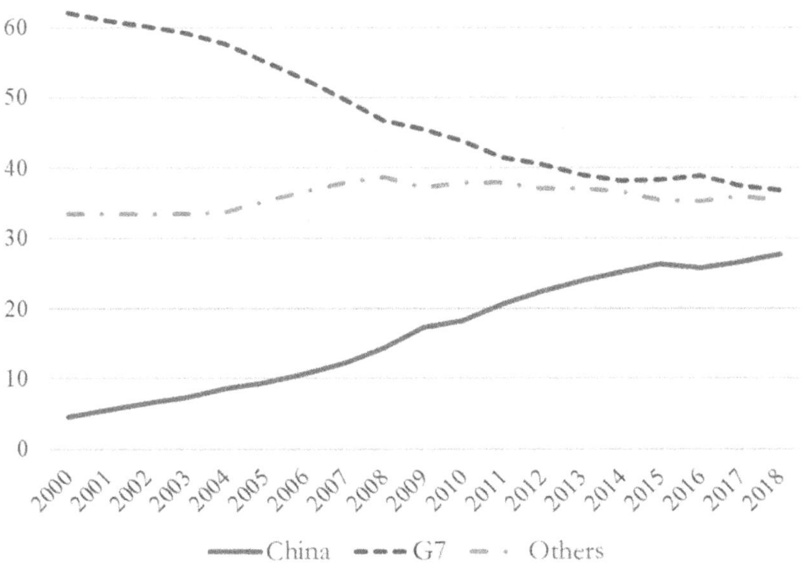

Fig. 7.1 Regional composition (%) of the global manufacturing output, value added (*Source* World Bank. G7 includes Canada, France, Germany, Japan, Italy, UK and US)

development model pursued by local governments. This also has a huge impact on foreign trade. The second section uses the US-China trade war as an example to discuss the impact of China's economy on foreign countries. With these in the background, in 2020, China's central government proposed the "dual circulation" strategy, to promote "the formation of a new development model in which domestic market is the main driving force of the economy, with the global market and the domestic market reinforces each other". The third section of the chapter analyzes the conditions and related reforms necessary for this strategy to succeed.

Section 1: Low Consumption and Excess Production

The most prominent feature of China's economic imbalance is insufficient consumption. In 2018, household consumption accounted for 44% of China's GDP. If we make a comparison to the US, the ratio is close to

70%; and in the EU and Japan, 55%.[2] In the period from 1980 to 2010, the proportion of consumption (counting both household and government consumption) as a share of GDP in China actually dropped from 65 to 50% before gradually resuming to 55% (see Fig. 7.2). The proportion of household consumption as a share of GDP dropped from 54% in the 1980s to 39% by 2010, recovering to 44% by 2018. The gap between the total consumption and household consumption is accounted for by government consumption, which has been relatively stable at around 11% of GDP.

Household consumption is equal to income minus saving. The following equation helps to lay out the relationship between these

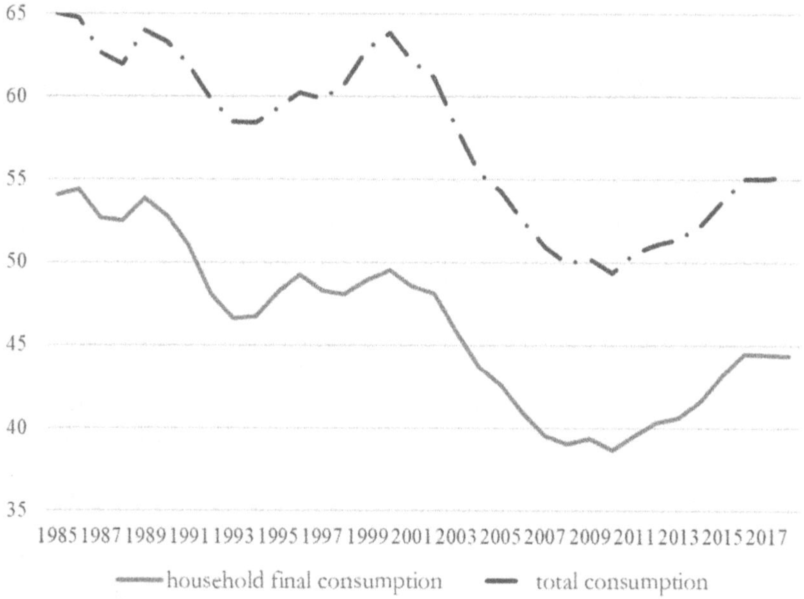

Fig. 7.2 Consumption as a percentage of Chinese GDP (*Source* China Statistical Yearbook 2020)

[2] Here I use "actual final consumption expenditure", the expenditure after considering various government transfer payments, which is higher than the consumption expenditure directly calculated from the GDP (expenditure method).

variables:

$$\frac{\text{Consumption}}{\text{GDP}} = \frac{\begin{pmatrix}\text{Disposable}\\ \text{Income}\end{pmatrix} - \begin{pmatrix}\text{Household}\\ \text{Saving}\end{pmatrix}}{\text{GDP}}$$

$$= \frac{\begin{matrix}\text{Household}\\ \text{Disposable}\\ \text{Income}\end{matrix}}{\text{GDP}} \left(1 - \frac{\begin{matrix}\text{Household}\\ \text{Saving}\end{matrix}}{\begin{matrix}\text{Household}\\ \text{Disposable}\\ \text{Income}\end{matrix}}\right)$$

So when we observe that the proportion of consumption in GDP declines, there are two possible scenarios. Either the share of income available to households in GDP has declined, or households choose to save a larger part of their income and the savings rate increases. In China, both happened. As we can see from Fig. 7.3, from the 1990s to 2010, the ratio of household disposable income to GDP dropped from 70 to 60%, before gradually bouncing back to 65%. Meanwhile, the household savings rate has increased from 25% in the early twenty-first century to 35%, before gradually falling back more recently. These rises and falls are closely related to the local governments' model of developing economy, which has a big impact on the macroeconomy.

High Household Savings Rate

The average savings rate of Chinese households is very high. During the 1990s, it reached a peak of between 25 and 30% compared to a level of 6%-7% in the US. In major European countries such as Germany and France, the level was 9%-10%, and in Japan was relatively higher at 12%-13%. How do we explain the differences across countries? Culture and habit are one explanation, even language and subconscious behavior may have an effect, therefore Chinese people have always tended to be thrifty and save more money. A few years ago, there was an eye-catching study looking at the relationship between languages spoken around the world and savings rates. Many languages (such as English) have tenses, so grammar needs to be changed when speaking about the past, present or future, which gives people a sense that the future is not the same as the

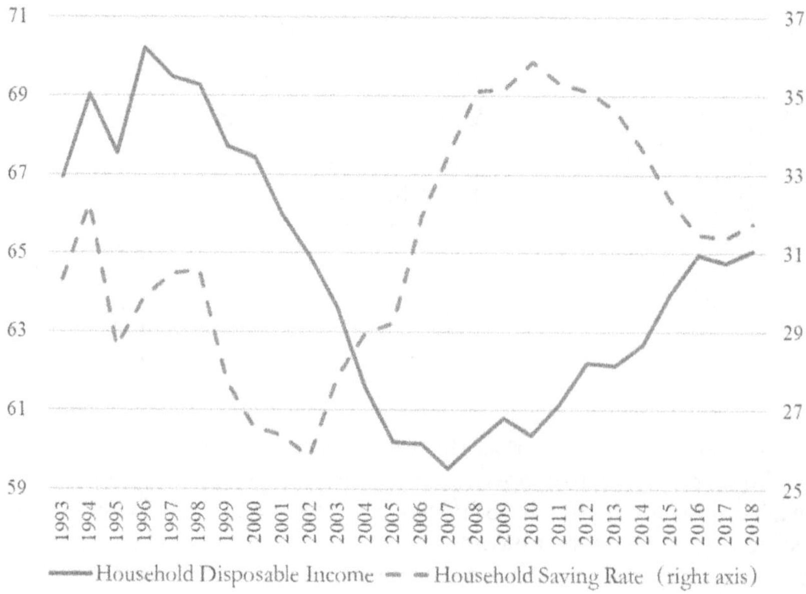

Fig. 7.3 Household disposable income as a percentage of GDP, and household savings as a percentage of disposable income (*Source* China Statistical Yearbook 2020)

present, so why worry about the future? Just live for the present. People who speak languages with this kind of grammatical structure therefore tend to save less. However, there are also many languages (such as Chinese) that don't have explicit tenses. The way we talk about the past, present and future are the same, and people who speak these languages tend to save more.[3]

There are other fancy theories that try to explain differences in savings rates, but factors such as language, culture and habit that remain unchanged for long periods of time cannot explain the ups and down in China of recent years, so we must start with a thorough analysis of the economic environment. The most popular explanation for China's high

[3] See the paper by Chen (2013).

savings rate relates to the combined effects of the one child policy, insufficient government welfare spending and rising house prices.[4] After the one child policy came into effect, the proportion of children in China dropped rapidly and the proportion of the working age population increased. Working age people tend to save more, so along with these demographic changes, China's savings rate increased. After the number of children in the population decreased, the tradition that children care for elders in their old age started to become less relevant and effective, and people must save more for their retirement. Although parents have also increased their spendings on children, leading to a rise in certain expenditures such as education, the reduction in the number of children has overall reduced children-related expenditures and had the effect of raising the savings rate. At the beginning of the twenty-first century, the children under the one child policy in the 1980s started to enter the workforce, and being the only child in their families, they had to save money to buy a house, get married, raise their children, as well as take care of multiple parents and even grandparents. As a result, the overall savings rate has climbed once again.[5]

Several main elements in this process are all related to local government. The first is the rise in house prices, which is closely related to the local governments' model of urban development and land finance (see Chapters 2 and 5). In areas where land supply is limited and house prices rise rapidly, households need to save money for down payments and mortgage repayments, so savings rates naturally rise and consumption falls. Although rising house prices help to increase the wealth of homeowners, which theoretically will increase consumption through a so-called wealth effect, most homeowners only have one house and their ability to turn the increased house value into spendable money is limited. The level of their consumption is therefore mainly restricted by income, and the wealth effect driven by rising house prices is insignificant. So, on the

[4] Zhang et al. (2018) summarize various studies explaining changes in China's savings rate.

[5] İmrohoroğlu and Zhao (2018), Choukhmane, Coeurdacier and Jin (2019) discuss the Chinese tradition of "raising children for old age", as well as the impact of factors such as family planning on the savings rate.

whole, rising house prices has the effect of lowering consumption and increasing savings.[6]

Secondly, China's local governments' development model spent more resources on constructing infrastructure and attracting business investment at the expense of investment in public services, so expenditure on such as public education and public healthcare remain insufficient (Chapter 5). Moreover, due to government policies and regulations, the market supply of private education and medical care is also limited, and the price of such services in the private market is very high. Therefore, households must increase savings for these expenditures. This has also caused a somewhat unique phenomenon, namely the savings rate of the elderly in China is also high. Generally speaking, people have a higher savings rate when they are young and working, and a lower savings rate when they are elderly and retired. However, the savings rate of the elderly in China is also very high, since they may need to cover the housing expenses of their children, the educational expenses of the third generation and their own medical expenses. In addition, in the past, local governments' supply of public services is based on the size of the local population of registered household (*hukou*), without considering other non-registered residents. So it is difficult for non-registered migrant workers to take their wives and children to live with them since public healthcare and educational resources are not open to them. This means non-registered workers tend to spend little on housing or durable goods, and the money they earn is saved and sent back home. The large population of these workers therefore also contribute to the rising savings rate.[7]

[6] Chen and Yang (陈斌开和杨汝岱 2013) analyze the impact of land supply and house prices on urban residents' savings in various regions and find that house prices were the main driving force behind the increase in savings. Wan, Yan and Fang (万晓莉, 严予若, 方芳 2017) estimated that the wealth effect of rising house prices on consumption is very small, and the main factor affecting consumption is income.

[7] Zhang et al. (2018) compare the spendings on public education, medical care and pensions between China and other countries. Chamon and Prasad (2010) show the high savings rate of the elderly in China, arguing that the high expenditure of urban residents on education and medical care is the main reason. Chen, Lu and Zhong (陈斌开, 陆铭, 钟宁桦 2010) analyze the problem of low consumption of urban migrants.

Low Share of National Income Going to Households

Insufficient consumption among Chinese households is not only caused by the high savings rate, but also by low income. Since the beginning of the twenty-first century, the percentage of China's national income going to households has been continually falling. At the lowest point, the share had dropped by 10 percentage points and then rebounded by 5 percentage points (see Fig. 7.3). During the process of economic development, this pattern of falling and then rising is not uncommon. In the early stage of development, the process of industrialization is capital intensive and the share of capital income is naturally higher than in the prior agricultural society. Compared with agriculture, which relies on primitive animal or human labor, machines and heavy equipment of manufacturing relies can boost labor productivity and labor income, but the proportion of labor income relative to capital income would decline. In the middle to late 1990s, China's industrialization process started to accelerate at great pace, and a large number of peasants moved into industry and the share of labor income relative to capital income began to decrease. In addition, within the industrial sector, compared with private firms, state-owned enterprises have more responsibility to stabilize employment and wages, and they hire more people with higher wage. Therefore, the fundamental reform of the SOEs starting in the mid-to-late 1990s that led to millions of laid-off workers also reduced labor's share of national income.[8] Later, with the development of the economy, service industries would grow fast, in which labor/capital ratio is typically much higher than in manufacturing, then labor's share of national income would gradually rise.

In the process of this structural reform, China's local governments further accelerated the rise in capital's share and the fall of labor's share of national income. The second to fourth chapters of this book introduce the methods used by local governments to attract investment and provide financing to businesses. In this process, the emphasis is placed on enterprise, production, and the scale of investment. In order to attract large industrial projects, local governments are willing to provide various types of support such as subsidies, cheap land, discounts on loans and tax

[8] Economic development will lead to changes in the industrial structure and in the share of national income going to labor. Readers can refer to Luo and Zhang (罗长远和张军 2009) and Bai and Qian (白重恩和钱振杰 2009). The latter also estimates the impact of the SOE reform.

incentives, which help to stimulate capital investment while reducing the relatively demand for labor. Although China's manufacturing industry is still labor intensive compared with developed countries, it is somewhat overly capital intensive considering the huge labor force in China. After joining the WTO, tariffs on imported capital goods were reduced and capital investment increased. At the same time, industrial agglomeration in the southeast coastal provinces has triggered large labor migration. But policies related to household registration and land have led to a fast rise in house prices and labor costs. Combined with restrictive policies regarding public healthcare and education, migrant workers found it is difficult to live a settled life, so labor shortages occurred from time to time. As a result, companies are further inclined to invest more in capital and use less labor.[9]

Of course, even if the price of capital relative to labor falls, then the decision to substitute capital for labor still depends on the suitability of capital as a replacement for labor in the production process. Nowadays, as technology continues to advance, machines are becoming smarter and smarter and they are capable of undertaking an ever-increasing array of tasks. Therefore, if the price of capital assets and machinery drops, labor is likely to be substituted.[10] As an example, China is the largest user of industrial robots, accounting for 30% of the world's industrial robot market in 2016. An important reason is the rising cost of labor.[11]

From the perspective of income receivers, as the share going to households decreases, the share going to the government and firms must increase. Similarly, from the perspective of expenditure, as the proportion of household consumption decreases, the expenditure share of government and firms must increase, and the vast majority of these expenditures

[9] Lu (陆铭 2016) analyzes the institutional causes of this "over-capitalization". Yu and Liang (余淼杰和梁中华 2014) point out that after joining the WTO, the cost of using capital goods and technologies dropped, which stimulated firms to replace labor with capital.

[10] There is a concept in economics called "the elasticity of substitution between capital and labor". If the elasticity is greater than 1, then when the relative price of capital falls, firms will use more capital and less labor, resulting in a decline in the share of labor income. Chen and Chen (陈登科和陈诗一2018) point out that this elasticity of substitution is greater than 1 in China's industrial firms. Karabarbounis and Neiman (2014) show that the decline in the labor share caused by the decline in the relative price of capital goods is a global phenomenon.

[11] Chen et al. (2019) discuss the use of industrial robots in China.

are related to investment. Therefore, money that used to go to households has been transferred to the government and firms and invested in infrastructure, such as roads, high-speed rail, factories and machinery, while spending on consumer goods such as automobiles and household appliances has seen a relative decrease. Another part of the expenditure comes from foreign countries, so a decrease in the share of domestic consumption within China not only corresponds to an increase in investment, but also corresponds to an increase in exports as a share of GDP. So, for many years, China's economic growth has been driven by two key pillars, investment and exports, while domestic consumption growth has been relatively sluggish.

All this leads to the question of how we should evaluate this economic development model. Firstly, it should be noted that we are talking in relative terms and not in absolute numbers. China's economy has been growing rapidly and although the proportion of income going to households has decreased, the absolute value of this income has been increasing fast. So, consumption and investment are both rising rapidly, just at different speeds.

From the perspective of economic growth, an increase in the share of income going to capital also means an increase in the amount of capital per person, which is necessary for increasing productivity and industrialization. In just a few decades, China has completed the industrialization that took other countries centuries, so a period of fast capital accumulation is necessary. The same was also true for the UK, US, Japan and South Korea. Many readers will be familiar with the Enclosure Movement that took place in Britain during the process of industrialization, as well as the process of primitive accumulation of capital described by Marx. Indeed, one of the core issues that has returned to the fore in studies of the history of capitalism in recent years is the "compulsion" process of capital accumulation, which saw the exploitation of colonies by European countries and the use of slave labor in the US.[12] During the so-called East Asian Miracle where countries such as Japan and South Korea achieved rapid industrialization, people's hard work, high savings, high investment and capital accumulation are also well known in the world. China is of course

[12] Sven Beckert's book (2015) is one of the masterpieces of this "New Capitalist History". But some inaccuracies and exaggerations in the book have also drawn criticism from economic historians, see for example an excellent paper of Olmstead and Rhode (2018).

no exception, in addition to hard work, various institutional factors also act to accelerate capital accumulation. For example, during the planned economy period, the state-monopoly of grain purchasing and selling, and the use of higher prices of industrial products and lower prices of agricultural products, helped move more resources from agricultural sectors into the industrial sectors. In order to reduce the cost of capital for firms and stimulate investment and industrialization, banks lowered the interest rate on loans. But to keep the viability of the banks' business, the interest rate on household savings must be cut, so banks can earn profits between low interests rate of loans and even lower interests rate of deposits. This "financial repression" further reduces household income. To achieve a certain level of deposits, household must save more. The savings rate therefore rises, while at the same time consumption falls.[13]

If we proceed solely from the logic of economic growth, starting from a lower level of GDP, poorer countries should grow faster than richer countries. On the other hand, even if larger rich countries such as the US only tries to grow by 1%-2% each year, the required amount of additional output is huge in absolute terms, which is not an easy task. In theory, if poor countries kept growing faster than rich countries over long periods of time, then these countries would eventually converge at a similar same level of development. In reality, however, this kind of converge does not happen, except in one sector, which is manufacturing. Countries with low manufacturing productivity have tended to make rapid progress in productivity growth, while countries with high levels of productivity have tended to grow slowly in productivity.[14] So the learning effect of the manufacturing industry is particularly strong, and the latecomers tend to learn fast. Indeed, over time, the manufacturing productivity of late-developing countries has converged with the levels of developed countries. But why is the global economy as a whole not converging? One critical reason is that most poor countries are not able to mobilize and invest more resources in manufacturing, so they are

[13] Regarding the "Asian Miracle" and "Chinese Miracle" models of intense capital accumulation and heavy investment (actually, to a considerable extent, the general model of industrialization), there are two books that have made systematic, in-depth, vivid and popular descriptions and analysis. One by Joe Studwell (2013), and another is from Lin, Cai and Li (2004).

[14] Rodrik (2013) describes and analyzes the phenomenon of "convergence" in global manufacturing productivity.

not able to kick off the industrialization and maintain its momentum for a long period of time.

Therefore, in the early stage of economic development, shifting resources from household consumption to invest in infrastructure and factories can effectively promote economic take-off and industrialization, in turn increasing productivity and per capita income. Moreover, at the beginning of the process, the infrastructure and industrial base are in very poor conditions, so any investment could be very useful and profitable. The key is to increase investment and accelerate capital accumulation. However, when capital markets and legal institutions are not well developed, it is difficult for private firms to borrow and invest. Government and its affiliated entities such as SOEs, on the other hand, could be more effective in mobilizing more resources to invest, so they naturally dominate the investment in infrastructure and industrial development.

But when economies reach a certain level of development, this state-led investment-driven growth becomes unsustainable. Four types of problem tend to emerge. First, infrastructure and industrial networks have been well developed, and obvious great investment opportunities disappear and investment becomes more difficult. Therefore, the system of investment decision-making and resource allocation needs to adapt. Local government led investment may no longer be the most suitable approach. This problem has been elaborated previously in Chapters 3 and 6 and I won't repeat it here. Second, due to the low share of income going to households, consumption is insufficient and much of the new productive capacity cannot be absorbed domestically. Either the country needs to find a way to export abroad or much of the productive capacity will be wasted, which leads to low returns on investment. Debt burdens therefore tend to get heavier, which brings a series of risks that we have discussed in Chapter 6. Third, the decline in the share of labor income and the increase in the share of capital income widens the gap between the rich and the poor, since capital is often concentrated in the hands of a few. The inequality may grow exceedingly large and society will start to lose tolerance, something that we discussed in Chapter 5. Fourth, due to insufficient domestic consumption, excess production capacity must be exported abroad, which can lead to global trade imbalances and aggravate trade conflicts (we will discuss more in the next section).

Against this backdrop, the report of the 19th Congress of the CCP re-defined the main contradiction of China's society, *"the contradiction between the people's ever-growing need for a better life and unbalanced and inadequate development*". The "unbalanced" here refers to inequalities between different regions, between rural and urban areas, and between rich and poor. It also refers to structural imbalances in the economy, such as excess investment and insufficient consumption. The "inadequate" here includes the fact that household income share is low, so is people's sense of gain.

In response to the low share of national income going to households, the 19th Congress of the CCP proposed to "*improve the quality of employment and the level of household income*". The Congress proposed the following reform framework, "*Break down institutions and mechanisms that hinder the free flow of labor and talent in society, so that everyone has the opportunity to realize their own personal development through hard work. Improve the coordination and discussion of government, trade unions and companies, to ensure strong and harmonious labor relations. Stick to the principle of income distribution according to work, improve income distribution according to factor input, achieve a more reasonable and orderly income distribution. Ensure that the path to riches is through law-abiding hard work, build a strong middle-class, increase income of low-income earners, regulate excessive levels of high income, and eliminate illegal income. Household income and economic growth should grow in proportion, so should labor income and labor productivity. Broaden the channels for households to earn more labor income as well as capital income. Improve the governments' redistribution mechanism. Accelerate the equalization of basic public services and narrow the gaps in the income distribution*".

If people spend a fixed proportion of their income on consumption, then in order to increase the share of consumption in China's GDP, it is not enough to make household income and GDP grows "in proportion". Household income must grow faster than GDP, then the share of national income accruing to households can increase, leading to a rise in consumption as a share of GDP. In November 2020, Liu He then a Vice Premier on the State Council and a leader in economic management, published an article in the *People's Daily* titled "*Accelerating the Construction of a New Development Model of Mutually Reinforcing Domestic-International Dual Circulation, Led by the Domestic Circulation*", arguing that China "*must adhere to the target of common prosperity, reduce income inequalities, expand the size of the middle-class, strive to grow household income at a rate faster than economic growth*".

To implement the above principles put forward at the 19th Congress, China's economy needs a vast series of specific reforms. Chapter 2 introduces the reforms in public expenditures, which requires that local governments spend more on public services and people's welfare. Chapter 3 introduces the reforms to the evaluation of government officials, which requires officials to pay more attention to expenditures on public services and solve the problems related to the "unbalanced" and "inadequate" development. Chapter 5 introduces reforms to factor markets, with the aim of increasing labor income and reducing the debt burden on households by stabilizing house price, which together would lead to more consumption. Here we can talk about another reform, which is the reform of transferring the shares of state-owned enterprises to social security funds.

When looking at changes in the distribution of national income, a decrease in the share of household income typically corresponds to a rise in income retained by corporates. In order to increase the proportion of household income, it is necessary to transfer the money retained by companies to households. The profit margin of privately-owned firms is typically higher than state-owned enterprises (SOEs), so they retain more income. However, these retained income are all spent on financing investment, and they are still not enough, so private firms also borrow a lot. So for private firms, their "net savings" are actually negative. For SOEs, they invest less, so even though their gross savings are less than privately firms, their "net savings" are positive. With these money in hands, SOEs, however, pay out a lower portion of their profits as dividends to shareholders than private firms.[15] In 2017, the state council proposed that 10% of the government-owned equity of SOEs be transferred to the social security fund. In 2019, this reform accelerated, which required SOEs owned by the central government complete the transfer by the end of 2019, and that local SOEs complete the transfer by the end of 2020.[16] This reform is very complicated, since it involves the transfer of trillions

[15] Zhang et.al. (2018) estimate the savings rate and dividend rate of state-owned and private enterprises in China. The increase in the corporate savings rates or retained profits is also a global phenomenon, which can be witnessed by the huge amount of cash on Apple's balance sheet. There have been many studies on this topic, see Chen, Karabarbounis and Neiman (2017) and Karabarbounis and Neiman (2019).

[16] In 2017, the State Council issued the *Implementation Plan for Transferring Part of State-Owned Capital to Social Security Funds*. In 2019, five departments including the Ministry of Finance, the Ministry of Human Resources and Social Security, the State-Owned Assets Supervision and Administration Commission, the State Taxation Administration, and the Securities Regulatory Commission jointly issued the *Notice on*

of RMB and countless conflicting interests, but it has to be done. After all, in the 1990s when the social security reform started, retired SOE employees were treated as if they had contributed enough to the social security fund so they could receive pension. But they had not contributed enough. So even at the beginning, there was a huge gap between income and expenditure of social security funds. This gap should be filled using assets of SOEs. By the end of 2019, the transfer of 1.3 trillion yuan from central SOEs had been completed, and in 2020, the transfer from local SOEs was still in progress.

Overcapacity, Debt Risk and External Imbalances

In an open economy, internal imbalances will always be accompanied by external imbalances. Products produced domestically that are not consumed within the country need to be exported. GDP consists of three components, consumption, investment and net exports (exports minus imports). After China joined the WTO in 2001, the proportion of investment and net exports increased sharply (Fig. 7.4). At the same time, the proportion of consumption dropped sharply (Fig. 7.2). This economic structure is fragile and unsustainable for a few reasons. First, demand from foreign countries is greatly impacted by foreign political and economic conditions, and it is out of China's control. Second, the proportion of investment cannot stay at such a high level of 40% for too long. Investment that exceeds consumption is likely to become overcapacity and being wasted. As a comparison, the proportion of investment in GDP in developed countries such as the US and Europe is only about 20–23%.

Although from an accounting perspective, investment can increase GDP, if the assets formed through investment cannot lead to higher productivity, higher income and in turn higher consumption in the future, this kind of investment is wasted because it will not increase any real wealth. If the government borrows money to build a road and many people use it, reducing commuting and logistics costs, and therefore increasing productivity, then it is a good investment. But if the government keeps digging up and repairing the same road for no reason or builds a road to a place that no-one needs to go, then the debt used

Comprehensively Rolling Out the Work of Transferring Part of State-owned Capital to Enrich Social Security Funds.

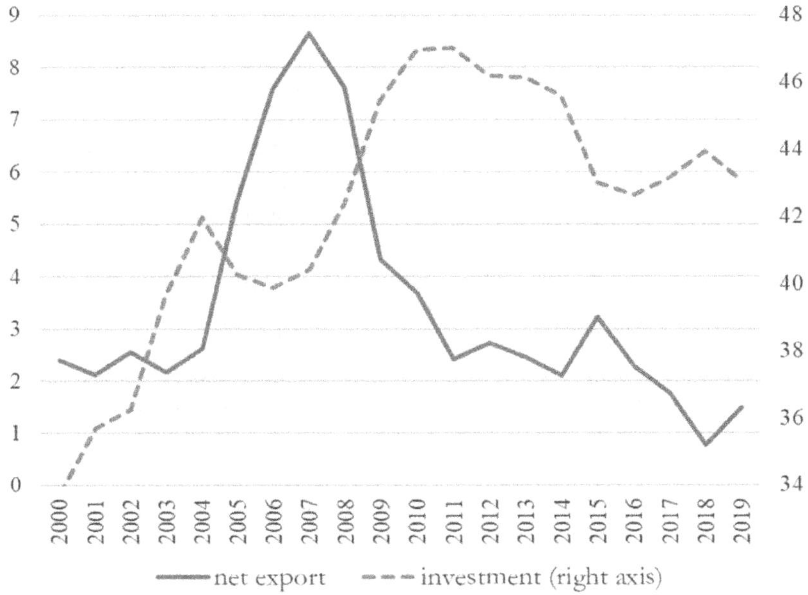

Fig. 7.4 Net Export and Investment, as a Percentage of GDP (*Source* China Statistical Yearbook 2020)

to build the road will not be recovered. Revenues generated from these investments will be worth less than the construction cost, so debt burdens increase. Although GDP increases temporarily during the construction of the road, the real resources are wasted. Indeed, such instances are not uncommon in China. Many losses that have not yet been realized for now will eventually realize somewhere in the future.

China's imbalance between investment and consumption is not a new problem. As early as 2005, household income as a share of GDP had dropped to a low point (see Figs. 7.2 and 7.3). At the time, the government was already aware of the problem. In 2007, Premier Wen Jiabo pointed out that *"there are huge problems in China's economy, and these structural problems are unstable, unbalanced, uncoordinated, and unsustainable"*. For example, *"there is an mismatch between investment and consumption, and economic growth relies too heavily on investment and exports*".[17] However, when the global financial crisis struck in 2008, China's exports plummeted, and the 4 trillion-yuan stimulus had to be launched, which led to a further increase in investment as a share of GDP, going from 40 to 47% (Fig. 7.4). Although the incremental investment helped to plug the gap in GDP left by the drop in net exports and stabilize economic growth, it also exacerbated the structural problems in the economy. In 2011, with the onset of the Eurozone debt crisis, there was still no room to move away from the investment-led model. As a result, during the period from 2007 to 2012, consumption and household income as a share of GDP hardly changed, while the savings rate of households also failed to decrease (Figs. 7.2 and 7.3). Due to the insufficient demand from both the domestic and foreign markets, the incentives for companies to invest in the real economy was limited, and much of the stimulus money therefore flowed into real estate and infrastructure, driving up land and house prices and the overall debt burden (Chapters 3–6). It was not until after the 18th CCP Congress in 2012, that systematic supply-side reform begun to be implemented to tackle the problem.

Given that the proportion of consumption is too low, even the super high level of investment cannot absorb all the products produced domestically, so the surplus must be exported abroad. As a result, China's exports have been consistently higher than its imports, which means there are other countries whose imports are greater than their exports. In this bucket, the US is the main player. Due to China's vast scale, its impact on international trade flows is huge, and related economic adjustments can be painful.

Of course, domestic and international imbalances are two sides of the same coin. Domestic imbalances can lead to international imbalances and vice versa. For China, the problem is domestic consumption being less than production and the surplus being exported. At the same time, consumers in countries like America spend much more than its production. They purchase many products from China and pay a high price, so many Chinese manufacturing resources are shifted from satisfying domestic demand to capturing this overseas market, which further aggravates the domestic imbalance between consumption and production. Between the 9/11 terrorist attack in 2001 and the global financial crisis in 2008, the US government spent trillions of dollars fighting its "war on

[17] See Wen Jiabao's answer to questions from Chinese and foreign journalists, after the closing of the Fifth Session of the Tenth National People's Congress (March 2007).

terror", meanwhile American housing market soared, and the increasing wealth stimulates more consumption. These demands drove the imports from China. As a result, the US accumulated a huge external debt, with one of the largest creditor countries being China. At the same time, this served to further enhance China's internal imbalances. After the financial crisis, both China and the US embarked on a painful process of economic adjustment and rebalancing. For China, the adjustments include supply-side reforms, factor market reforms and the "dual circulation" strategy focusing on the domestic market. In the US, the adjustment process is accompanied by protectionism and political polarization.

Therefore, trade issues are never just about trade, and the root cause of trade conflicts lies not in trading itself. In an open world, significant changes in domestic economic structures also have an impact on international trade. The different distributions of economic resources between households, companies and governments will lead to changes in the proportion of production and investment relative to consumption, thereby affecting the internal and external balance of the economy. It is often said that diplomacy is an extension of domestic politics, and from a macroeconomic perspective, foreign trade imbalances is also an extension of structural imbalances in domestic economies.

Section 2: US-China Trade War

The balance of a country's internal economic structure has a direct impact on its balance of payments account. China's domestic production capacity is larger than domestic consumption, so its exports are greater than its imports, and its current account (which can be understood as a summary of exports and imports during the year) is in surplus. Conversely, domestic production in the US is not enough for domestic consumption, and imports are therefore greater than exports, and the current account is in deficit. Figure 7.5 depicts the balance of payments from 1990 to the present. Some countries have surpluses (above the black line and greater than zero) and some countries have deficits (below the black line and less than zero). Logically, the aggregate global balance should be zero after all countries cancel each other out. But in reality, due to false reporting for tax evasion or transportation delays, the aggregate global balance is roughly 0.3% of global GDP.

Figure 7.5 has two notable features. First, the imbalances in the 1990s were not severe, less than 0.5% of global GDP. The imbalances enlarged

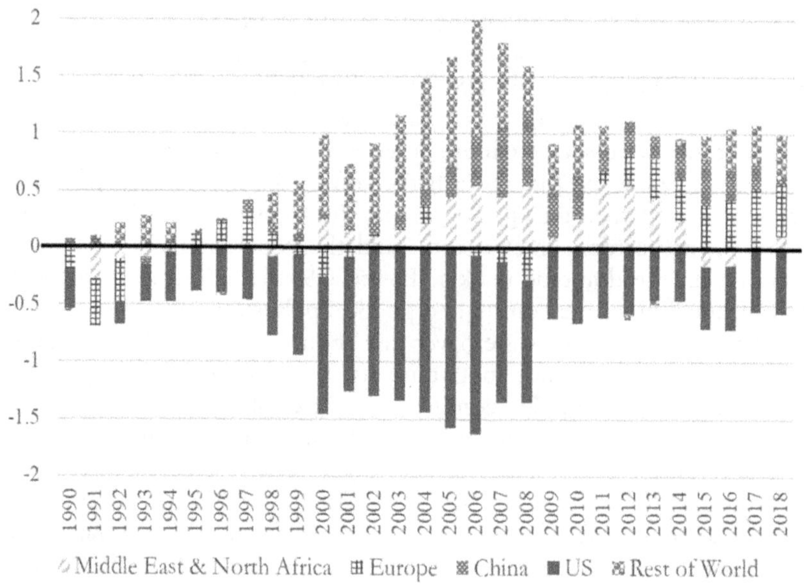

Fig. 7.5 The balance of current account, as a percentage of global GDP (*Source* WIND Database)

at the beginning of the twenty-first century and reached a peak before the global financial crisis, accounting for roughly 1.5%-2% of global GDP. After the crisis, the imbalance dropped to less than 1% of global GDP. Second, the global current account deficit is almost entirely composed of the US, while most of the surplus is composed of China, Europe and the Middle East. After joining the WTO in 2001, China has developed rapidly, and its share of the global trade surplus has increased rapidly. China's rapid development also led to a global super cycle in commodities such as oil. Consequently, oil prices soared, and the trade surplus of the Middle East also increased. After the financial crisis, US consumer spending decreased and at the same time, an energy revolution occurred in the US, with shale oil and shale gas coming onto the market in vast scale. This had a dramatic effect on global energy markets and the US changed from being a net importer of oil and gas to one of the world's most important oil and gas producers and exporters. The prices of oil and gas plummeted, which led to a decrease both in the US's current account deficit and in the current account surplus of countries in the Middle East. Finally, in 2017, China surpassed Canada and became the biggest importer of US oil.[18]

The US is able to absorb other countries exports because of its economic power and the US dollar being the world's reserve currency. The US imports more than its exports every year, which is equivalent to continuously borrowing resources from abroad. The US is therefore the world's biggest debtor country. However, these foreign debts are almost all denominated in US dollars, so in principle, the US can print money to repay these debts and is therefore unlikely to default. In other words, provided that the world still trusts the value of the US dollar, the US can continuously exchange US dollars for the real products and resources of other countries. This is truly is an "exorbitant privilege" that other countries do not have.[19] When looking at the total trade deficit of the US, the deficit with China is one that has continued to grow. In the early 2000s, China represented roughly 25% of the US's total deficit, and in recent years the share has grown to 50–60%. So, although the US has trade conflicts with many countries, the one with China has always been of primary concern.[20]

Shocks on Employment and Politics

During recent trade conflicts between China and the US, the most frequently mentioned topic by American politicians and media is that China is taking jobs away from American workers. The main argument and evidence proposed goes as follows: during the 1990s, the proportion of manufacturing employment in the US labor force was relatively stable. However, after China joined the WTO in 2001, Chinese goods flood into the country and one factory after another moved overseas.

[18] Changes in the international oil market have always captured people's imagination, with various conspiracy theories and geopolitical analysis. But the most important factor behind these ups and downs is still market supply and demand. Wang (王能全 2018) analyzes the ups and downs of the oil market in recent decades. This great reference book includes clear facts and detailed data.

[19] There are many works on the origin and impact of this dollar privilege. Eichengreen (2011) is a popular book.

[20] Data on the US trade deficit and the bilateral trade balance between China and the US come from the US Bureau of Economic Analysis and the Census Bureau.

The share of manufacturing employment therefore begun to decrease sharply. Regions that were more severely impacted by this shock saw manufacturing employment fall more sharply.[21]

When looking at the data, it seems that this argument is valid. The middle part of the two black lines in Fig. 7.6 demonstrates that, during the 1990s, the portion of manufacturing employment in the US work age population was stable at 15%. After 2001 it begun to decline fast, dropping to 11% prior to the global financial crisis. But what's really striking is when we look at the areas outside the two black lines, we can see that US manufacturing employment has been falling going way back to the 1970s, and it continuously fell from 26% to less than 10%. Even if the 4% decline in the early 2000s was all to do with the trade with China, this so-called China Syndrome discussed in American academia and media would not be a big deal in this long-term trend of decline. Further, from 1970 to 2013, the portion of US value added by the manufacturing industry has remained stable at roughly 13%.[22] Although there are fewer people employed in manufacturing, the overall output has not decreased, which is clearly the result of technological progress and higher productivity improvements. There is nothing special about this, just that machines replaced workers. Advances in agricultural technology also reduced the number of farmers dramatically, but agricultural output did not drop either. Furthermore, the low prices of products imported from China helped to cut the cost of the sectors that use these products, thereby helping to expand these sectors (including both manufacturing and services) and increase their employment. So, although it is true that many workers lost their jobs due to factory closures, the overall employment in the US has not worsened by US-China trade.[23]

However, we live in an age of populism and anti-globalization sentiment and there is little chance for arguments such as the one above to

[21] Autor, Dorn and Hanson (2013) is a very influential paper.

[22] This is the proportion after adjusting for price changes, and the data come from Rodrik (2016).

[23] Imports from China stimulate employment in many sectors, especially those that use Chinese goods as inputs. For detailed analysis and evidence, see Wang et al. (2018) and Bloom et al. (2019).

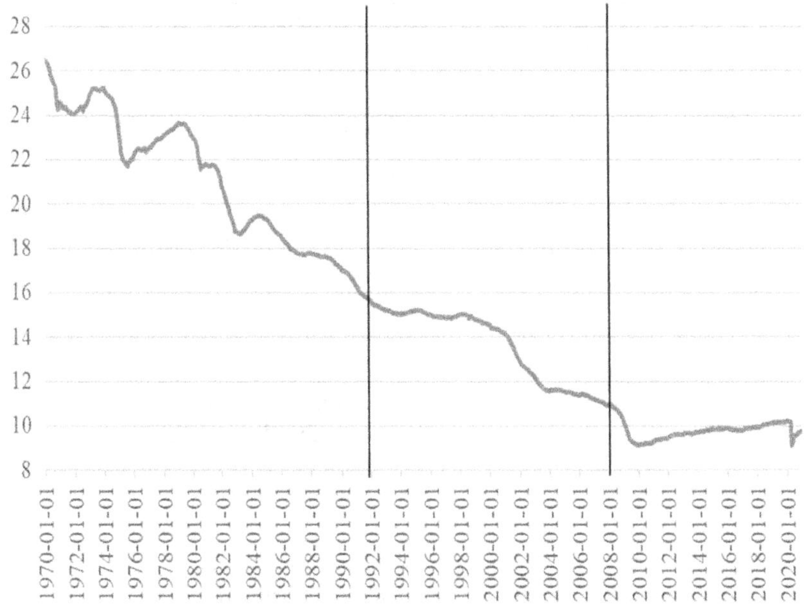

Fig. 7.6 Employment in manufacturing in the US, as a percentage of working age population (*Source* Federal Reserve Economic Data, St. Louis FED)

find an audience. There are many reasons for unemployment, such as technological progress, changes in market and poor corporate management, but globalization is the current curse and trade protectionism has been labeled as the cure. A recent experiment conducted using a large-scale online poll is illustrative. The experimenter showed the subjects a piece of news, saying that an American company had made some business adjustments, without mentioning any layoffs. The article did not give any reason for the business adjustments, but 20% of Trump supporters still stated that trade protection would be a good solution. If the article is adjusted to mention layoffs, but also explicitly state that the adjustments and layoffs were caused by changes in market and poor management, not trade conflicts, then the number suggesting trade protection as a solution among Trump supporters rises to 30%. If we adjust further and make clear that the layoffs are caused by international trade, then the number rises to 50%. In this final scenario, even if a candidates' political inclination is to the center, or even to Cliton, they will still increasingly suggest trade protectionism as an answer. These sentiments are not only reflected in opinions, they will affect voting results.[24]

Technology Shocks

The rise of China's manufacturing industry and the impact of US-China trade on US employment is not that important in a bigger picture. In contrast, the rise of China's technology and its challenges to the US is more fundamental, which may lead to continued trade conflicts. Although manufacturing now only accounts for a single digit share of US employment, manufacturing industries are still a key foundation for technological innovation, with 60%-70% of US R&D spending and company patents coming from manufacturing companies.[25] In recent years, we also see the US trying to contain China's technological development, for example, through bans on certain technologies. This is a new front in the traditional trade war and may last for a long time.

Figure 7.7 depicts some fundamental changes of China relative to the US. The first is the total value added of manufacturing. In 1997, China's manufacturing value added was equivalent to only 14% of the US, but by 2010, it had already grown to surpass the US, and by 2018, was equivalent to 176% of the US. The second line looks at technological innovation, measured by the number of international patent applications. The data come from the Patent Cooperation Treaty system of the World Intellectual Property Organization. In 2019, for the first time since the system begun operation in 1978, the US lost its top spot, being surpassed by China. The third line looks at basic science, measured by the number of scientific research articles. This so-called nature index only includes papers published in 82 internationally recognized top-quality journals across different fields in science and engineering, and the proportion of authors from each country is then calculated. In 2012, the number from China was equivalent to 24% of the US and only slightly higher than that of Germany and Japan. By 2020, China's publications were equivalent to 69% of the US, 3 times larger than Germany and 4.4 times larger than Japan.

[24] The experimental results come from Di Tella and Rodrik (2020). Autor et al. (2020a) shows that those regions that are more exposed to trade shocks are more polarized in voting and political inclination.

[25] The data come from Autor et al. (2020b).

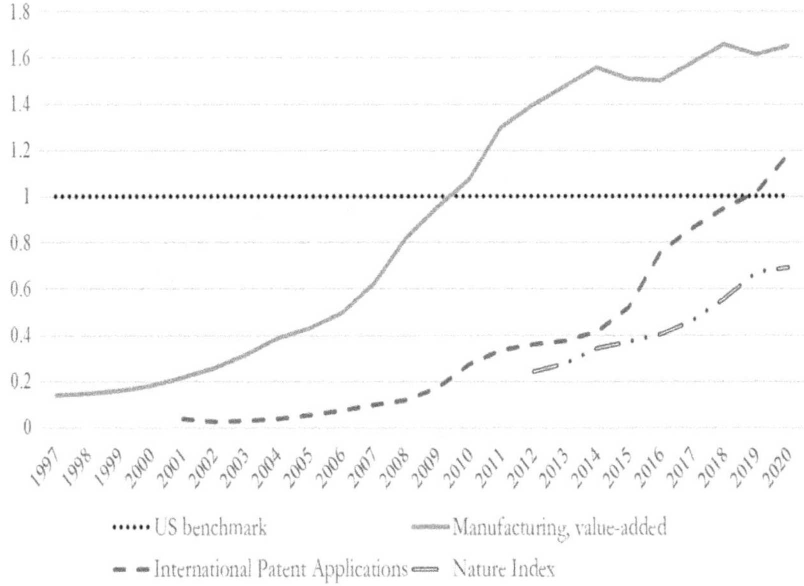

Fig. 7.7 Manufacturing, technology and scientific research, china relative to the US (US = 1) (*Source* Manufacturing data are from the World Bank. Patent data are from the World Intellectual Property Organization. Nature Index is from the website of Nature)

These indicators are about quantities, not quality. But in science and technology, there must first be a large quantity as the base before any quality can be produced. In addition, the data in Fig. 7.7 represent the flows of new patents and new papers, not their stock. If we were to look at the accumulated stock of knowledge and knowhow in science and engineering, we would find that China is still a long way behind the US. It is like a young worker whose salary finally reaches a high level after years of hard work, but compared to those executives who have earned a high salary for decades, this young guy's wealth is still low. But the fact that the young worker already earned a high salary proves that he has acquired the capability to earn money, with this strong momentum and continued hard work, it is only a matter of time before she accumulates wealth. Nowadays, people's recognition of the quality behind "Made in China" is dramatically different from 10 years ago, but this change takes time. The same is true for basic science and technology.

For countries at the forefront of scientific innovation, the invention and application of new technologies usually starts with scientific theories and experiments in the research lab, then being patented and applied to commercial scenarios, before finally reaching large-scale industrial production. But for late-developing countries, this order of innovation is often reversed: it starts from manufacturing products invented by developed countries, learning related technology by doing, accumulating experiences and knowhows, trying to adapt technology according to their market needs, then creating some new patents. Once sales grow and its technology gets closer to the frontiers of developed countries, the company will have more resources to invest in R&D and to promote more basic and general-purposed scientific research. In 2010, China passed the US in terms of manufacturing value added, and in 2019, it surpassed the US in terms of the number of international patents applications. According to the current growth rate of scientific papers, China will surpass the US by 2025 (Fig. 7.7).

So, for late-developing countries, manufacturing industry is often the basis for technological progress. There is no technological leader in the world that is (at least was) not a manufacturing powerhouse. Using the manufacturing industry to capture a share of the global division of labor is also a good development strategy because manufacturing has a strong learning effect and encourages agglomeration of supply chains. Over the past 10 years, the continued upgrading of China's manufacturing industry has been self-reinforcing. It attracts many foreign companies to set up factories in China, while domestic upstream and downstream producers and suppliers have also developed rapidly, and the effect of collaboration and innovation across the supply chain is very strong. The largest category of exports from China is electronics and communication technology (e.g. mobile phones). In 2005, the amount of value created overseas in these exports accounted for 43% of the products' final value, but by 2015, this number had dropped to only 30%, demonstrating China's continued industrial upgrading.[26]

Let me use Apple's iPhone as an example. Many years ago, there was a saying among media commentators and industry analysts. A "Made in

[26] The data come from the TiVA database of the Organization for Economic Cooperation and Development (OECD).

China" iPhone sold for hundreds of dollars, but the value contributed by mainland China was equivalent to only two or three dollars in assembly costs. In recent years, I still see this number being cited, even though it is a long way from the current reality. Apple publishes a list of its top 200 suppliers each year, and these companies account for 98% of all the money spent by Apple on raw material, manufacturing and assembly. In the 2019 edition of the list, there are a total of 40 companies from mainland China and Hong Kong, including 30 mainland companies, some of which are listed.[27] In China's A-shares market, the concept of "Apple Supply Chain" has long existed. Such companies include Lens Technology (making glass of iPhone), Ofilm (making camera modules), Goertek (making acoustic units) and Desai Battery. Although it is difficult to estimate the precise added value contributed to an iPhone by Chinese industry, judging from the prices of various parts and components estimated in some industry reports, Chinese (including Hong Kong) companies contributed roughly 20% of the value of an iPhone's hardware.

In theory, US-China trade does not necessarily hurt US technological innovation. Although some weaker American companies may lose their advantage when competing with China, causing their profits to decrease and R&D spending to drop, many large companies can benefit from trade with China. By moving manufacturing sector to China, they can locate closer to the world's largest and fastest growing consumer market. This can theoretically increase profits that can then be funneled back into R&D spending in the US, enhancing their innovation capability and comparative advantage. America's overall ability to innovate would not be affected.[28] In recent years, however, in the US political sphere and also in the media, a conservative mentality has taken hold and the policy of containing China's technology sector may continue. If the world's largest market and the world's strongest innovation center gradually split apart, it will be a huge loss to both countries and to the world. After all, China still has a long way to go in terms of the quality of its basic scientific

[27] For the specific list and a brief introduction of the companies, please refer to the Wechat blog by Ning Nanshan titled "The Changes of the Global Electronics Industry: An Analysis of the Top 200 Suppliers of Apple in 2019".

[28] Aghion et al. (2018) provides a theory for this argument.

research and the efficiency of scientific commercialization. Likewise, for US companies, it is impossible to replace a market of the size and scale of China. Indeed, without Chinese market, it would be difficult for US companies to sustain the current level of profitability and R&D spending, then their technological progress may slow down. Moreover, even though America's strategy of impeding China's technological development may cause short-term setbacks in some Chinese sectors, Chinese companies will find many new chances of replacing American products with their less advanced technology. They will gain market share in China, and their increased revenues will help to drive R&D spending. Then their technology will improve fast and gain even more market share. Eventually, this continued industrial upgrading will lead to a complete replacement of American technology with domestic technology. But the premise of this process is of course that China's domestic market can continue to grow, and that domestic consumption can continue to increase, only then can China truly realize its "dual circulation" strategy.

Section 3: Rebalancing and the Strategy of Dual Circulation

China's economic development has largely benefited from globalization. With the help of a huge amounts of investment and export growth, it has grown into an industrial powerhouse and the world's second largest economy in just a matter of decades. In 2019, China's GDP was equivalent to the world's total GDP in 1960 (after adjusting for inflation). However, China's past development model is not sustainable and as we have seen above, both the domestic economy and international trade have become unbalanced. As a result, the geopolitical situation is also becoming more complex. Therefore in 2020, China's central government proposed a new development model of "dual circulation", which means having domestic consumption as the main driving force, and making the domestic and international market reinforce each other. This is a transformation in China's development strategy.

In this chapter, we have noted that the key to this strategic transformation is to increase household income and consumption. Although the central government is still emphasizing supply-side structural reforms, supply and demand sides of the economy are not two separate things, but two perspectives to look at the same thing. For example, to adjust production capacity from the perspective of supply is also to adjust the level of investment expenditure from perspective of demand, and to upgrade industrial structures from the perspective of supply is also to upgrade the level of income and consumption from perspective of demand. In December 2020, the Central Economic Work Conference proposed that *"China must firmly grasp the principle of supply-side structural reform, focus on demand-side management. Make breakthroughs in key areas, while overcoming current shortcomings to better connect production, distribution, with consumption. Form a higher-level dynamic balance that allows demand to drive supply and supply to foster demand"*.

In order to continue increasing household income, it's necessary to continue promoting urbanization by encouraging people to move to cities, particularly large cities. Although the manufacturing industry is the main driver of technology progress and productivity growth, when looking at the experience of developed countries, we can see that the manufacturing industry cannot continue to create large employment. With globalization and technological progress, the degree of standardization in manufacturing continues to increase, and many processes can be completed by machines and robots. High-end manufacturing is very capital intensive and requires few workers since most processes are automated. In the US, even though the manufacturing industry has continued to grow, the number of jobs it provides has not (Fig. 7.6). Therefore, in order to increase people's income and provide more employment, it must rely on the development of service industries, which can only occur in densely populated cities. Not only does the number of traditional shops and restaurants grow with population density, but so does the supply of new jobs such as express delivery workers, takeout businesses, and ride hailing. If urbanization is to continue, the level of public expenditures on urban residents must increase to make people live more comfortably in cities. This requires reforms of factor markets, such as reform of land markets and reform of the Hukou (residence permit) system, which we have discussed in Chapter 5.

In order to drive up household income and consumption, more resources need to be transferred from the government and firms to households. Reform should focus on local governments and their role in the Chinese economy. Their investment and production impulse should be curbed, and more public expenditures should be spent on projects that would improve people's livelihoods, such as public services. Making this change would bring about four important changes. First, increasing spending on public services can help to move away from the existing urbanization model which prioritizes land over people. This would help to make China's cities more people-orientated, and comfortably settled people would save less and consume more. Second, by increasing spending on public services, the spending on building more production capacity would decrease. At the current stage of economic development, investment in manufacturing has become very complicated, and government investment has become increasingly risky and wasteful, which seriously reduces resources that can be used by households. Furthermore, investment in production is difficult to reverse, and once local governments become involved, it would be difficult to leave without suffering a huge loss (Chapter 3). Even after local firms have lost their market and competitive advantage, local governments may have to keep injecting new sources into them, reducing the overall level of economic efficiency (Chapter 4). Third, the "dual circulation" strategy requires continued technology progress, and the core of innovation is people. Local governments must spend more on public education and medical services, which can be considered as investments in "human capital". This will increase China's economic performance over the long run. Fourth, increasing spending on people's livelihoods and curbing investment may also reduce local government's dependence on land finance, restrict its use of land to leverage borrowing, reduce its dependence on land price, thereby help to stabilize house price, which also preventing further growth in household debt levels that suppress consumption (Chapter 5).

Another way to increase household income is to allow them to earn more from their assets. There need to be more financial channels through which households can invest and share in the benefits of economic growth, which requires reform of capital markets and financial institutions. However, as discussed in Chapter 6, financing and investing are two sides of the same coin, and if the investment is still dominated by the government and state-owned enterprises, the financial system will always find ways to concentrate both more resources and more risks in them, so it's hard to reform the system and allow a wider range of investors to participate.

The strategy of "dual-circulation" emphasizes not only "rebalancing" and the expansion of domestic market, but also the need to continue opening to the world. Exports can create more employment and revenues in manufacturing sectors, but imports can also help to create employment and revenues in service sectors, such as trade, warehousing, delivery, transportation, financing and after-sales service. As China continues to develop and productivity continues to grow, the RMB should also appreciate over time. As a result, the purchasing power of Chinese will increase, which will allow them to have more consumption choices and a higher standard of living. This will also increase the attractiveness of China's market to the world.

In the real world there is no such thing as an abstract and perfectly functional market. After any market is established, it takes time to gradually improve its efficiency and expand its scale. A well-functioned market is the result of economic development, not a prerequisite. China has a large population and huge territory, establishing a unified national marketthat allows free flow of factors and goods is a huge task and will take many years to complete. It is not easier than globalization, only in a smaller scale. It would take years for institutions and regulations to adapt. Over recent decades, China has invested heavily in infrastructure such as high-speed rail and internet connectivity, which provides the foundation for a unified national market and makes some institutional breakthroughs. In the future, China needs to continue promoting market-orientated reform of labor markets, capital markets and land markets, and it needs to further open up to the world. The production-orientated local governments need to become service-orientated. Then the potential of China's consumer market would be realized, and the country would step into the circle of high-income countries.

Summary

This book discusses how China's local governments promote economic development. It starts by looking at microeconomic mechanisms and ends by analyzing macroeconomic phenomena. In summary, this development model has three key characteristics. First, in the process of urbanization, local governments put more importance on land and land use than on people's livelihoods. Second, local governments place a high value on investment scale and industrial expansion as they compete to attract investment. Third, a higher emphasis is placed on investment and production than on consumption. Chapters 5 and 6 analyze the costs and benefits associated with the first two characteristics and related reforms, and this chapter analyzes the third characteristics. The benefit associated with it is that foreign trade can quickly be expanded, and the integration into the global economy promotes rapid economic growth. But the cost is an unbalanced economic structure. Domestically, resources are transferred to governments and firms, and the share of household income and consumption is low, which is not conducive to long-term economic growth. Internationally, exporting excess production capacity causes trade conflicts.

Rebalancing economic structures is never easy and is often accompanied by painful domestic adjustments and international conflicts. After the global financial crisis in 2008, the global economy entered a period of major adjustment, and China became the main driver of global economic growth and the worlds' second largest economy. At the same time, China has become a major protagonist in the global economy for the first time in nearly a century, which has put pressure on the economic system previously dominated by the US and Europe, and difficulties and challenges are sure to follow. In fact, to long-term China observers, China's economic reforms has continually been undergoing huge challenges over the past 40 years, most of those years have been difficult and there have been several major crises. That's why I like to joke with my students that in reality, economic growth is a life and death process. Standing on the sidelines, you can only see a great picture of economic progress, and it is easy to ignore the turbulence that has been going on beneath the surface.

As for conflict between existing and rising economic powers, this has been a norm throughout history. For new powers to rise, they have to effectively imitate and learn from more advanced countries, while at the same time adapting to their own unique circumstances, which means its development path will be different from those advance countries in many aspects. While imitating and learning is often criticized and labeled "copying" by existing powers, it is the different development path and associated different thoughts that are really hard for existing powers to accept.[29]

The future is always unknown. And for observers of China's economy, it's necessary to train a perspective of development. First, it's important to keep in mind that the target of development is not the process of development. The current practice in developed economies may not work for a developing China. Second, the situation keeps changing, and what worked for China in the past may not work today. If reforms don't continue, then policies and experiences that proved effective in the past

[29] Gerschenkron (1962) elaborates on the conflict brought about by these similarities and differences.

may become burdens or even traps today. In pursuing development, we must continuously reexamine the facts, insist on specific analysis of specific issues and put aside ideologies, be pragmatic in solving problems in practice and find a development path that works for China. In the next chapter, we will discuss more about this.

Further Readings

Economic forces are very powerful, and changes in the international economy can have fundamental effects on political relations between countries. However, to get a thorough understanding of international economics, a knowledge of basic concepts such as current accounts and exchange rates is necessary. Therefore, some of the recommended readings below may require a certain level of background knowledge, but I have attempted to choose popular yet accurate books. I believe those readers who care about these phenomena will be able to understand.

International economic phenomena often occur in chains, with one event leading to another, and shocks and related adjustments coming in waves. If we look back today at the decade following the global financial crisis, we can see that the world has undergone a profound transformation. The economic factors driving these changes have been documented in the book I recommended in Chapter 6, which is *Crashed: How a Decade of Financial Crises Changed the World (*2018), written by Columbia University's economic historian Adam Tooze. But how did this crisis happen? If we put the 2008 crash in a global perspective, we must reach to another major event with far reaching influence, which is the Asian financial crisis of 1997–1998. Andrew Shen, the former Chairman of the Hong Kong Securities and Futures Commission (SFC) wrote a book, *From Asian to Global Financial Crisis: An Asian Regulator's View of Unfettered Finance in the 1990s and 2000s (2009).* This great book discusses the changes in the global economic and financial system from 1997 to 2008. Then, how about prior to 1997? If we go back to the 1970s and 1980s, the situation was different again and free market thoughts was sweeping the world. *Changing Fortunes: The World's Money and the Threat to American Leadership (1992),* co-authored by Paul Volcker, former Chair of the Federal Reserve, and Toyoo Gyohten, former Vice Minister of Japan's Ministry of Finance, is also a great read. The authors have personally experienced a series of historical events, such as the oil crisis of the 1970s, the disintegration of the Bretton Woods system, the Latin American debt crisis, and the Plaza Accord. Their deep thinking and narrative details of the period are unmatched. If we look from a more macroeconomic perspective and over a longer historical period, Barry Eichengreen's book, *Globalizing Capital: A History of the International Monetary System (3rd edition in 2019),* explains the evolution of the international monetary and financial system over the past 100 years, and related various political and economic events.

There are two books by Michael Pettis, a professor at Peking University's Guanghua School of Management, which explain the causes and consequences of international imbalances from various perspectives. The first is *The Great Rebalancing: Trade, Conflict and the Perilous Road Ahead for the World Economy (2013)* and the second *Trade Wars are Class Wars: How Rising Inequality Distorts the Global Economy and Threatens International Peace (coauthored with Matthew Klein, 2020).* Although I don't agree with every analysis contained within these books, most of the difference in opinion would be in respect to the importance of particular issues. I think some things are not as important as he emphasized, but I agree with the way he analyzes the balance of payments crisis from multiple different angles.

The Great Convergence: Information Technology and the New Globalization (2017) written by Richard Baldwin provides a good background on globalization, and it is concise and easy to read. Baldwin divides globalization into three phases, the globalization of goods, the globalization of information, and the globalization of people. The book contains many interesting analyses of how global value chains developed. Of course, globalization has also impacted the political systems of many countries, and Dani Rodrik's book *The Globalization Paradox: Democracy and the Future of the World Economy (2011)* introduces the idea of a trilemma between deep international economic integration, national sovereignty and democratic politics. The book includes many intriguing arguments and explains that all three cannot be had at the same time. In addition, the 2019 Oscar best documentary, *American Factory,* tells the story of Fuyao Glass, a Chinese company opening a new factory in the US. It clearly shows how the "made-in-China" shock affects American industries and workers, but it also shows many difficulties of moving manufacturing industry back to the US.

As for the impact of China's rise on the US and the rest of the world, there have been an overwhelming number of books published on the subject just in recent years. From "*China Rules the World*" to "*Thucydides*

Trap", and to various versions of how China is destined to collapse, there have been authors with many different backgrounds, theories from many different perspectives, and predictions of many different possibilities. Here I would like to recommend one small book, *China Reconnects: Joining a Deep-Rooted Past to a New World Order (2019),* written by Chinese historian Wang Gungwu. Professor Wang's life experience is difficult to replicate. He studied in Nanjing during the Chinese Civil War and later worked and lived in Southeast Asia, the UK and Australia. He worked as Vice-Chancellor of the University of Hong Kong for an eventful decade from 1986 to 1995, before returning to Singapore. Throughout his life, he has combined his intense study of Chinese history with his unique experience living through many historic events. He published this valuable book at age 89 to talk about his thinking and observations. His deep thoughts on many issues are far more valuable than those random observations prevalent in today's media.

References

Aghion, Philippe, Antonin Bergeaud, Matthieu Lequien, and Marc J. Melitz (2018) "The Impact of Exports on Innovation: Theory and Evidence," *NBER working paper* 24600.

Autor, David, David Dorn, and Gordon Hanson (2013). "The China Syndrome: Local Labor Market Effects of Import Competition in the United States." *American Economic Review* 103.6: 2121–2168.

Autor, David, David Dorn, Gordon Hanson and Kaveh Majlesi (2020a). "Importing Political Polarization? The Electoral Consequences of Rising Trade Exposure." *American Economic Review* 110.10: 3139–3183.

Autor, David, David Dorn, Gordon H. Hanson, Gary Pisano, and Pian Shu (2020b). "Foreign Competition and Domestic Innovation: Evidence from US Patents." *American Economic Review: Insights* 2. 3: 357–374.

Bai, Chongen, and Zhenjie Qian (2009). "Factor Income Share in China: The Story behind the Statistics." *Economic Research Journal* 3: 27–41. (in Chinese)

Beckert, Sven (2015). *Empire of Cotton: A Global History.* Vintage.

Bloom, Nicholas, Kyle Handley, Andre Kurman, and Phillip Luck (2019). "The Impact of Chinese Trade on US Employment: The Good, The Bad, and The Debatable," *Working Paper*.

Chamon, Marcos D., and Eswar S. Prasad (2010) . "Why Are Saving Rates of Urban Households in China Rising?" *American Economic Journal: Macroeconomics* 2.1: 93–130.

Chen, M. Keith (2013). "The Effect of Language on Economic Behavior: Evidence from Savings Rates, Health Behaviors, and Retirement Assets." *American Economic Review* 103.2: 690–731.

Chen, Peter, Loukas Karabarbounis, and Brent Neiman (2017). "The Global Rise of Corporate Saving." *Journal of Monetary Economics* 89: 1–19.

Cheng, Hong, Ruixue Jia, Dandan Li, and Hongbin Li (2019). "The Rise of Robots in China." *Journal of Economic Perspectives* 33.2: 71–88.

Choukhmane, Taha, Nicholas Coeurdacier, and Keyu Jin (2019). "The One-Child Policy and Household Savings," *Working paper.*

Di Tella, Rafael, and Dani Rodrik (2020). "Labour Market Shocks and the Demand for Trade Protection: Evidence from Online Surveys." *Economic Journal* 130.628: 1008–1030.

Eichengreen, Barry (2011). *Exorbitant Privilege: The Rise and Fall of the Dollar and the Future of the International Monetary System.* Oxford University Press.

Gerschenkron, Alexander (1962). *Economic Backwardness in Historical Perspective: A Book of Essays.* Belknap Press of Harvard University Press.

İmrohoroğlu, Ayşe, and Kai Zhao (2018). "The Chinese Saving Rate: Long-Term Care Risks, Family Insurance, and Demographics." *Journal of Monetary Economics* 96: 33–52.

Studwell, Joe (2013). *How Asia Works: Success and Failure in the World's Most Dynamic Region.* Open Road+ Grove/Atlantic.

Karabarbounis, Loukas, and Brent Neiman (2014). "The Global Decline of the Labor Share." *Quarterly Journal of Economics* 129.1: 61–103.

Karabarbounis, Loukas, and Brent Neiman (2019). "Accounting for Factorless Income." *NBER Macroeconomics Annual* 33.1: 167–228.

Lin, Justin Yifu, Fang Cai, and Zhou Li (2004). *The China Miracle: Development Strategy and Economic Reform* (Revised Edition). The Chinese University of Hong Kong Press.

Olmstead, Alan L., and Paul W. Rhode (2018). "Cotton, Slavery, and the New History of Capitalism." *Explorations in Economic History* 67: 1–17.

Rodrik, Dani (2013). "Unconditional Convergence in Manufacturing." *Quarterly Journal of Economics* 128.1: 165–204.

Rodrik, Dani (2016). "Premature Deindustrialization." *Journal of Economic Growth* 21.1: 1–33.

Wang, Zhi, Shang-Jin Wei, Xinding Yu, Kunfu Zhu (2018). "Re-examining the Effects of Trading With China on Local Labor Markets: A Supply Chain Perspective," *NBER Working Paper 24886.*

Zhang, Longmei, Ray Brooks, Ding Ding, Haiyan Ding, Hui He, Jing Lu, and Rui Mano (2018). "China's High Savings: Drivers, Prospects, and Policies," *IMF Working Papers.*

Translated References (in Chinese)

Chen, Dengke, and Shiyi Chen (2018). "Capital-Labour Relative Price, Substitution Elasticity and Labour Income Share." *Journal of Management World* 12: 73–97. (in Chinese)

Chen, Binkai, Ming Lu, and Ninghua Zhong (2010). "Household Consumption Constrained by Hukou System." *Economic Research Journal* 45.S1: 62–71. (in Chinese)

Chen, Binkai, and Rudai Yang (2013). "Land Supply, Housing Price and Household Saving in Urban China: Evidence from Urban Household Survey." *Economic Research Journal* 1: 110–122. (in Chinese)

Lu, Ming (2016). *Great State Needs Bigger City*. Shanghai People's Publishing House. (in Chinese)

Wang, Nengquan (2018). *The Era of Oil*. China CITIC Press. (in Chinese)

Wan, Xiaoli, Yuruo Yan, and Fang Fang (2017). "Housing Price, Housing Wealth and Household Consumption: Evidence from Aggregate and Survey Data about China." *China Economic Quarterly* 2: 525–544. (in Chinese)

Yu, Miaojie, and Zhonghua Liang (2014). "Trade Liberalization and China's Labor Income Share: An Empirical Analysis Based on Manufacturing Trade Enterprises Data." *Journal of Management World* 7: 22–31. (in Chinese)

Zhang, Jun and Changyuan Luo (2009). "Labor Income Share and Economic Development: An Empirical Study Based on Chinese Industry-level Data." *Social Sciences in China* 2009.4: 65–74. (In Chinese)

CHAPTER 8

Government and Economic Development

There are many jokes about economists and most economics students will know at least a few. Economists often laugh at themselves as well and for a period of time the annual meeting of the American Economic Association set up a talk show to give economists the chance to let off steam and mock the profession. One of the jokes goes like this: a physicist, a chemist and an economist are adrift on an isolated island. While sitting at the shore, they find a can of food that floated in from the sea. On discussing how to open the can, the physicist suggests that they can use pressure exerted from rocks to break it open. The chemist chimes in and suggests that they can use heat from a wood fire to heat the can, so it expands and bursts. Finally, the economist gives a solution, "suppose we had a can opener…".

Of course, any theory will need a set of assumptions, otherwise it can't be expressed clearly. Many assumptions will be different from the reality, but whether these differences are enough to make a theory unacceptable is another matter. It should be judged based on the theory as a whole. The real problem comes when stepping outside the classroom and applying economic theories to real-world problems and policies. Then it is absolutely necessary to be practical and to consider the feasibility of any plan suggested. Therefore, there is often a huge gap between theoretical research and application. Alan Blinder, an economist at Princeton University and one-time Vice-Chairman of the Federal Reserve, once invented a "Murphy's Law of Economic Policy". On areas where economists have

X. Lan, *How China Works*,
https://doi.org/10.1007/978-981-97-0080-6_8

the highest level of understanding and consensus, they tend to have the smallest policy impact; while on areas where economists have least consensus and are most divided, they tend to have the biggest policy impact.

One of the great advantages of using a market-based economic theory to analyze China's economy is that it becomes easy to detect various "distortions" and "misallocation". But there is still a long way to go from identifying a problem to proposing an adequate solution. It is necessary to understand historical and present causes of any problems and to grasp the pros and cons of any solution. In the real world, there are no reforms that everyone would support, and there are no distortions that no-one would benefit. So, the pros and cons in every situation are different. Taking the hypothetical perfect market as a baseline for thinking and making judgements is just one possible approach among many. If we start from a different benchmark, the way of thinking may be completely different. As economic historian, Alexander Gerschenkron remarks, quoted at the beginning of this book: *"A rigid conceptual framework is no doubt useful in formulating questions, but at all times it evokes the peril that these questions will be mistaken for answers. There is a deep-seated yearning in the social sciences for the discovery of one general approach, one general law valid for all times and all climes. But these attitudes must be outgrown. The overestimate both the degree of simplicity of economic reality and the quality of scientific tools".*

The reason why less developed countries lag behind is precisely because they lack the same resources that more developed countries possess, particularly well-functioned market institutions. So, when developing countries begin the process of industrialization and modernization, they must organize and mobilize resources in a different way to developed countries. The key to success lies in whether they can find such a way that fits with their own unique circumstances and is able to drive a continued economic growth. One of the current fundamental reforms in China is to "let the market play a decisive role in the allocation of resources". Looking forward to the future, this is the guide of reform and development; but looking back over the past decades, market-orientated reforms and achievements have been the result of coordination and mutual efforts of the economy, the government and the society. Without doubt, China's market-orientated transformation has been strongly supported and driven by the government. If we go back to 1980, even the most ardent promoters of the market economy then would be hard-pressed to imagine the depth and breadth of subsequent reforms. This book tries to introduce specific practices in the process of China's economic development, which is obviously not a set of models copied from Europe and the US. I believe readers can judge for themselves the pros and cons of China's model.

As a development economist, I understand the complex way in which markets and development interact, and there is no simple one-way causality. Indeed, an effective market-economy system is the result of continuous reform and construction. And whether this market-economy system is a prerequisite for economic development depends on the stage of development. In the early stages of China's development, market-based institutions were lacking, and government played a dominant role in helping to drive economic take-off and to cultivate many market-based institutions. However, with the development of the economy and the continuous improvement of institutions, the role of the government also needs to adapt.

Emphasizing the role of government is certainly not the same as advocating for a planned economy. A soviet-style planned economy has two key characteristics. The first is solely relying on planning, thereby not allowing a price mechanism nor private enterprises to exist. The second is that it is essentially closed and therefore participation in international trade and globalization is limited. In China, these two factors have long ceased to exist, therefore to consider China as a planned economy is off the topic.

The first section of this chapter summarizes and refines one of the key themes of this book that is the competition among Chinese local governments to attract investment. The second section discusses government capacity building as well as the changing role of government in China's economy. It summarizes the pros and cons of a production-orientated government and explains the necessities to transition to a service-orientated government. The third section summarizes another key perspective of the book: we must distinguish between the economic development process and development goals. When studying development, we should neither overestimate the replicability of experiences of developed countries, nor overestimate the replicability of our own past successes in the future. We must therefore be courageous enough to seek the truth from facts and to insist specific analysis of specific issues. We must be pragmatic in considering and solving problems and continue to promote economic reforms step by step.

Section 1: Local Government Competition

The guiding principle of economic development is to mobilize people and resources and make the best possible use of them. To achieve this goal, we must rely on competition. The starting point for China's economic reform was a planned economy. The government not only directly controlled a large amount of resources, but also indirectly affect the allocation of resources with its policies, so the government's role in the economy naturally persists, even after a long period of continued market reforms. In order to increase the overall efficiency of the economy, it is therefore necessary to introduce competition into the government system. In theory, there are two approaches that can be taken. The first is based on reforms at the central government level. China's central government is divided into ministries and commissions based on their functions. And resources across the country are mobilized by these ministries in Beijing. Competition can be introduced between ministries when the central government set annual and multi-year plans, during which these ministries must compete for more planned resources. For example, during the planned economy period, there were 8 ministries responsible for industry that competed for limited resources. This kind of top-down competition was copied from the Soviet Union. The second approach is to promote competition between local governments. In this model, goals are set by the central government and then delegated to local governments. Meanwhile, local governments is given sufficient authority to mobilize resources to achieve the goals, while having enough flexibility to adapt to differing regional conditions. This method is more of a bottom-up style of competition between regions.[1]

Even during the planned economy period, these two models always coexisted in China, and the balance between centralization and decentralization of power was continually changing. Mao Zedong did not believe completely in the Soviet model. In his famous 1956 article, "On the Ten

[1] The first model of competition is also known as the "U-shaped" (unitary) model, and the second is known as the "M-shaped" (multi-divisional) model, both of which are common in corporate governance. A "U-shaped" company divides departments by function, such as production, sales, purchasing and so on. An "M-shaped" company is divided into several sub-brands or business divisions, each of which forms a system and is highly independent from each other. Maskin, Qian and Xu (2000) use these structures of corporate governance to study the relationship between the central and local governments in China.

Major Relationships", Mao noted that *"Our territory is so vast, our population is so large and the conditions are so complex that it is far better to have the initiative come from both the central and the local authorities than from one source alone. We must not follow the example of the Soviet Union in concentrating everything in the hands of the central authorities, shackling the local authorities and denying them the right to independent action"*.

After the reform and opening up period, the power of local governments continued to expand. "Local authority" and "local government competition" became the key model of competition within China's government system. Chapters 1 and 4 of the book describes this system in detail. This kind of competition is not only a simple competition for resources, but also a competition between local policies, the business environment and even models of development. Local authority is conducive to local policy experiments and innovations because these experiments are designed to be local. If it succeeds, it might become a national policy. But if it fails, the risks and costs of failure could be limited to local areas and will not impact the whole country. For example, when the first batch of four special economic zones (Shenzhen, Zhuhai, Shantou and Xiamen) were established in 1980, there was significant political resistance. The name "special economic zone" was carefully chosen over the name "special zones" to ensure that only economic experiments, not political experiment, were carried out. At the time, Deng Xiaoping said to Xi Zhongxun (Xi Jinping's father) that *"[The party center] has no money. So we will give you a policy that allows you to charge ahead and cut through your own difficult road"*.[2]

In order to engage in regional competition during industrialization, regions should start at a more or less similar level, otherwise resources will quickly gather in those regions that have a strong industrial advantage and it will be difficult for disadvantaged regions to compete. During the planned economy period, China's industrial sectors were dispersed geographically, which helped to lay the foundation for regional competition during the later period of reform and opening-up. An important reason for this scattered distribution is the "*Construction of Third Front*" that began in 1964. At the time, the geopolitical situation of China was tense and in order to better prepare for any potential military conflict, the central government decided to move industry away from big cities where

[2] The story of the special economic zones is detailed in Vogel (2011). Xu (2011) explains how regional competition promotes local policy innovation and experimentation.

they had previously been concentrated. Thereby requiring that *"all new construction projects should be located at the Third Front and close to mountains, arranged according to the principal of dispersal and concealment. They should therefore not be concentrated in a few big cities. Important factories, universities, research institutes in the First Front cities should be completely or partially relocated to the Third Front"*.[3] During the following 10 years, China invested 40% of its industrial capacity in the Third Front regions, mostly in provinces in the west or the mid-west, such as Yunnan, Guizhou, Sichuan, Chongqing, Ningxia, Gansu, Shaanxi, Jiangxi, Hubei and Hunan. By the end of the 1970s, the industrial fixed assets of the Third Front regions had increased by 4.3 times, the number of employees had increased by 2.5 times and total industrial output had increased by 3.9 times.[4]

The Third Front movement not only led to the development of factories and research institutions, but also infrastructure. The program established a comprehensive although somewhat less developed production system in the central and western provinces, which completed transformed the geographic distribution of China's industry. These broadly distributed industrial technology and knowledge created the environment for the later nationwide development of local township-village enterprises and private firms. These small firms were not only able to produce simple industrial products to meet the demand of local populations, but also worked in joint operation with local state-owned enterprises to produce more complex products that could be used in the industrial supply chains. They soon would grasp more advanced industrial technology and become larger and more efficient. In a backward and vast country where infrastructure had not been developed and regions were essentially isolated from each other, this technology spillover was only possible because of the Third Front movement. After the reform of the township-village enterprises in the mid-to-late 1990s, most of them became private firms, with their technical foundation originating from the state-owned factories constructed during the Third Front movement.[5]

[3] See the report submitted by Li Fuchun, Luo Ruiqing and Bo Yibo to Mao Zedong and the Party Central Committee on August 19, 1964.

[4] See Bo (薄一波 2008) and Yan (严鹏 2018).

[5] Fan and Zou (2019) analyze the positive impact of the "Construction of Third Front" on the long-term development of local industrial firms across China, especially of local private firms.

Chapter 4 introduced another important function of township-village enterprises, namely training peasants to become factory workers. This transformation of farm laborers into factory laborers is one of the critical steps in industrialization. It involves not only a change in work content, but also in way of thoughts and living habits. It is not easy for peasants to leave the land and learn to become reliable and disciplined workers who can operate factory machinery. It is therefore far from given that a large population can automatically become the demographic dividend of an industrial economy. And in many countries with a large and poorly educated population, qualified industrial workers are actually in short supply. [6] All over China, small township-village enterprises thrived within a geographically dispersed system of industry and associated knowledge, and the fact that these enterprises were located in rural areas helped peasants to leave agricultural work but not have to leave their home. These enterprises became perfect places to transmit industrial knowledge and train peasants to become factory workers. In addition, through the efforts of selling locally produced industrial products, the newly trained industrial workers acquired experiences in commerce and expanded their connections with the outside world. When China's industrialization accelerated in the late 1990s and early 2000s, there was a ready-made industrial workforce who were familiar with factories and ready to leave home to work.

China's decentralized system might be less efficient than a nationally integrated and well-functioned market economic system. But from the perspective of development, this non-existent system is not a valid comparison. China's territory is vast, with customs and cultures varying greatly between regions. At the beginning of the reform and opening up period, China's infrastructure was underdeveloped and people across the country were not connected. Economic development also occurred in fits and starts, with large differences between regions. The only possible way forward was to gradually integrate the independently developed regions into a national system. During this period of great social reform, people

[6] Gershenkron (1962) pointed out although many underdeveloped countries have a large population, they are extremely short of qualified industrial workers. *"industrial labor, in the sense of a stable, reliable and disciplined group that has cut the umbilical cord connecting it with the land and has become suitable for utilization in factories, is not abundant but extremely scarce in a backward country. Creation of an industrial labor force that really deserves its name is a most difficult and protracted process"*.

need time to adjust and adapt to the new situation. Whether the reform occurs fast or slowly makes a huge difference for the people who live through it. For the reform to succeed, sufficient time and resources must be given for people to adapt. If we only consider economic efficiency derived from an economic model, then these resources and time left for the adaptation, whether they were designed by the government or spontaneously developed by the society, would be seen as distortions or misallocations since they seemed not to serve the goal of maximization of efficiency. However, this type of "maximization" is nothing but a theoretical construction. Everyone knows that industry is much more productive than agriculture, but it is a very difficult process for hundreds of millions of peasants to leave the land and move to factories, even though such a change may lead to an increase in their income. It would take generations of time, accompanied with conflicts and adaptions. Radical reforms often only lead to failure and societal unrest.

Another key ingredient for Chinese industrialization is to assess and promote local government officials based on their economic performance. Local government leaders must therefore compete not only for economic resources on the market, but also for political promotion. This system of competition has three main characteristics.[7] First, political incentives of government leaders are linked to economic performance through political promotion. The exact mechanisms of GDP growth or economic performance are assessed in the promotion of local officials remains controversial, but no-one denies that economic development is the main priority and political achievement for local government officials. Second, the behavior of local officials is constrained by market competition. Though government policies can have a great impact on a company, its success is ultimately decided by its performance in the domestic market or even in the global market, which is often out of control of local government. In order to win, local government officials therefore must incorporate economic factors, such as market competition when into their decision-making and resource allocation, and they must consider the economic costs and benefits of specific policies. In addition, key factors of production, such as capital and labor, can flow between regions. If a local government acts recklessly and harms the

[7] Zhou (周黎安 2018) elaborates on the pros and cons of this competition system of "government plus market". Much of the content in this paragraph is taken from this paper.

regional business environment, resources would flee to other regions. Third, local economic performance can provide timely feedback to works and policies of the local government. On the one hand, local governments have an information advantage over the superior government in dealing with local issues (Chapter 1). On the other hand, if one region succeeds economically, then the officials from that region are likely to be promoted, which can help to spread knowledge and lessons of what works and what doesn't. Since economic performance has been a critical aspect of officials' performance and promotion for many years, senior officials at all levels of government are likely to have significant experience in dealing with economic matters. Most major leaders of the central government have extensive experiences in economic matters since they have worked as local leaders for many years, which benefits the overall economic development in a country where the government controls a large amount of resource.

This system of "dual competition" both on the market and in the government can help us understand how China grows so fast as a whole. However, in reality, the way this system operates varies greatly from place to place. After all, this type of competition between officials or governments is not real market-based competition. There are three key differences. First, there is no real elimination mechanism. Even if a regional government fails to push for progress, it will not go bankrupt the same way a business would. Officials with poor performance may face fewer chances for promotion, but as long as they do not break the law or political rules, they will not lose their jobs or suffer personal loss because of bad investment decisions or poor local economic conditions. Second, the vast majority of market-based competition can be viewed as a positive-sum game and there is possibility for win–win cooperation, which can lead to overall market size expanding with more for everyone. In contrast, promotion of officials is a zero-sum game. With a limited number of positions available, the promotion of one official means the loss of another official. This can lead to malign forms of competition between regions, such as local protectionism or policies of "starve your neighbor". Third, competition between companies tends to last over long time periods and there is strong continuity in the market. Whereas for government officials, terms are limited, and officials need to get things done before their tenures end. Moreover, new officials would not be assessed by the debt level left by the previous officials. This can lead to short-termism in decision-making. Officials tend to over-borrow and over-invest to drive

GDP growth as fast as possible, ignoring the long-term debt sustainability and risks.

These differences highlight the costs of this system of "dual competition", and this system could encourage corruption (Chapter 3). Additionally, governments are not companies, and they cannot take economic performance as their only objective, they must also provide multiple public services to people and to the society. In the early stages of industrialization and urbanization, the primary goal of governments is economic growth, which is aligned to the goal of companies, so they can act as strong partners to promote growth together. At the current stage, priorities of government should be shifted to public services. Government should invest more resources into healthcare, education and social security. This type of service-oriented government should change its previous production-oriented way of interacting with private sectors.

Section 2: The Development and Transformation of Government

The development of a society is a process involving all parties, enterprises and markets, as well as governments, and the development of these entities reinforces each other. In general, the richer the country, the larger, not smaller, the share of government as a part of the overall economy, something known as "Wagner's Law". As countries and people get richer, their demand for various public services would become larger, and governments must spend more on healthcare, education, unemployment insurance and pensions. In recent decades, globalization and technological change have also led to various economic shocks, and governments need to provide more insurance functions.[8] One of the common features of economically underdeveloped countries is that their government is too weak to provide a stable environment that can foster economic growth, and some of them cannot even keep the streets safe. Economic prosperity, social stability and state capacity are three pillars of a country's prosperity, and they usually develop together.[9]

[8] Rodrik (1998) explains the positive correlation between globalization and "big government".

[9] Besley and Persson (2011) constructs a theoretical framework that connects these three pillars. The contents in the following paragraphs on taxation capacity and legal capacity are inspired by their work.

Take the rule of law as an example, even though mainstream economics considers the protection of property rights to be a prerequisite for the development of a market economy, in reality the ability to protect property rights can only be gradually improved during the process of economic development. In other words, for already developed countries, the protection of property rights is a prerequisite for further economic development, whereas for developing countries, effective property rights are more likely to be the result of further development. Writing laws of property rights is easy, but it will be of no use if a government's ability to catch and prosecute criminals is weak. Likewise, for commercial disputes, an effective legal system requires a large number of professional lawyers and judges, as well as professional financial personnel and financial infrastructure capable of tracing and freezing assets. Without them, court judgements and orders are just pieces of useless paper. However, all these hard and human assets require long time investment and accumulation. As mentioned in Chapter 4, complex products and industrial chains involve many entities trading with each other, and the business relationships are often complex and money involves are often huge, which is not possible without an effective legal system or more broadly, a good overall environment for contracts to be respected and for business to proceed smoothly. From 2000 to 2018, the complexity of China's export commodities rose from 39 to 18th in the world, and one of the underlying reasons is the improvement in China's business environment.[10] As mentioned previously, China's ranking in the World Bank's "Ease of Doing Business" rose from 89th in the world in 2010 to 31st in 2020.

For developing countries, the relationship between the market and the government is not as simple as one step forward and one step back, rather it is a question of whether the government can create a framework and space for the market to operate. This requires investing a large amount of resources and it takes a long time. If the government does not do that, a lively market economy and so-called entrepreneurship will not somehow spontaneously appear by magic.

In any country, there is a great deal of government regulation that exists outside the formal legal system. After all, litigating a lawsuit is time-consuming and costly. Not only is the cost of litigation high, but

[10] The measure of product complexity comes from the "The Atlas of Economic Complexity", a project run by the Center for International Development at Harvard University.

a losing party can continue to appeal, which can make a case even more protracted. Amending the law is not a trivial matter either, and it takes a long time to gather support and to find the right opportunity window for making a change. In contrast, government regulations and policies have greater flexibility and can serve as a supplement to the legal system. For example, in the US at the end of the nineteenth century, industrialization and railway construction were advancing rapidly, but they were also accompanied by a lot of work-related accidents, high death rates and constant lawsuits. The powerful and resourceful companies would continuously appealed court decisions, and around 40% of cases never paid any compensation whatsoever. Even when compensation was paid, the average amounts were very small, less than 8-months wages. This injustice helped to spur the rise of government regulation. Before accidents happen and lawsuits are carried out, the government put in a place a series of safety inspections and regulations that helped to prevent risks.[11]

For effective regulation, government must also have sufficient resources and capability to enforce them. And as societies and economies develop, the relative importance of regulation and the rule of law continues to evolve. The total investment made by the society in ensuring the rule of law is constantly increasing, and the related legal infrastructure is constantly improving. Meanwhile, citizens and firms are becoming wealthier and can afford high litigation costs, which can also increase the demand for the rule of law. Therefore, over the time, the rule of law and a country's legal system will become more important than government regulation. This is the result of overall political and economic development, and it cannot be achieved overnight.

Whether it be protecting national security, constructing infrastructure or providing social security, governments have to spend money, and an effective government must have enough money. But taxation is never an easy task, the capacities for tax collection and inspection needs a long time and lots of investment to build up. Take personal income tax for example, the government must be able to track the income of each individual, verify deductible expenses and pursue and punish any tax evaders. This requires powerful systems to track and process information. Even in developed countries such as the US and Europe where personal income

[11] For the rise and current situation regarding government regulation in the US and its relationship with the rule of law, see Glaeser and Shleifer (2003) and Mulligan and Shleifer (2005).

taxes is the largest source of tax revenues, it is difficult to collect them in full. Rich people in particular have many ways to evade or minimize their tax payments. For example, President Trump, who was very rich when he entered the White House, only paid $750 in income tax in 2016 and 2017. And after the tax reforms he enacted in 2018, the average rate of personal income taxes for America's richest 400 billionaires dropped to only 20%, which is lower than someone below the median income level. Taking Meta founder Mark Zuckerberg as another example, he owns 20% of Meta's shares and the company reported a profit of 20 billion dollars in 2018. So, in theory, Zuckerberg's income should be equal to $4 billion, but since Meta didn't payout profits as a dividend, Zuckerberg's income is zero as long as he does not sell his shares. At a corporate level, Meta transferred a large share of its profits to a tax haven in the Cayman Islands, meaning the level of corporate tax paid was also low.[12]

Since personal income tax is not easy to collect, the tax systems of developing countries are largely different from developed countries. In China, value added tax (VAT) is the largest portion of tax income, accounting for 40% of the total tax revenue in 2019, followed by corporate income tax with a 24% share. In comparison, personal income tax accounts for less than 7%. Compared with personal income tax, VAT is much easier to collect. First, there are invoices which can act as proof that a transaction has taken place, and second, buyers and sellers have conflicting interests, so they can supervise each other. The seller prefers that the invoiced amount can be lower so that less tax can be paid, while buyers hope that the invoiced amount is larger so that more tax can be deducted as cost. The two sets of invoices for buyers and sellers can therefore be compared against each other, reducing the risk of counterfeiting. But in reality, fake invoices and fake bills are not uncommon in China. Especially at the end of the twentieth century and early in the twenty-first century, illegal invoices were rampant across the country. In a 2001 audit, the number of invoices suspected of violating laws was as high as 8.5%.[13] However, after the completion of the "Golden Tax Project-Phase II" in

[12] Data on taxation of America's wealthy and the example of Mark Zuckerberg come from Saez and Zucman (2019).

[13] The data come from a speech by Jin Renqing, then Director of the State Administration of Taxation, at the 2002 Conference of the Construction of National Taxation Information System.

2003, the VAT invoicing system was made fully electronic, including anti-counterfeiting, certification, auditing and inspection systems, then the problem of false invoices was gradually eliminated and tax revenue from VAT increased significantly.[14] Up to today, the "Golden Tax Project-Phase III" has already completed, and anyone who has recently used China's Individual Income Tax APP to file their annual tax return in 2020 should be impressed by the details and accuracy of the income information in the system. It is not difficult to appreciate that such an effective tax system represents a capability that requires long-term investment.

We can see from the above examples that both the quality of government services and the amount of government revenue are constantly changing. Indeed, an effective government or an efficient market does not come into existence naturally, and they are the result of continuous investment and development. The nature and performance of a market economy is constrained by government resources and government capacity, while the role of the government must also constantly evolve and adapt to meet the needs of different stages of economic development.

In the early stages of economic development, markets are often imperfect or even absent, and governments may become supplements or substitutes for market activity. Economically underdeveloped countries lag behind precisely because they lack the well-functioned markets and efficient institutes of resource allocation. And creating and developing such institutes is precisely the goal of, not a prerequisite for, economic development. For less developed countries, the key to economic development in to find a way to mobilize and allocate resources to promote economic growth without the help of well-functioned markets. Then the economic development could provide more resources to the government, which can be used to create and improve a market economy. For example, developed countries have well-functioning capital markets and legal systems that can allocate resources into the hands of trustworthy entrepreneurs, and then create more wealth. At the beginning of the reform and opening up period, China's capital markets and legal systems were very weak, and people tended to distrust or even despise private enterprises and self-employed individuals. These conditions limited the feasible ways of fostering economic growth at the time.

[14] Fan et al. (2020) estimate the impact of the "Golden Tax Project-Phase II" on VAT revenue.

Therefore, in the process of industrialization and modernization, economically less developed countries must use different methods of organizing and mobilizing resources as compared to developed countries. In China one of these methods has been called "the whole nation system", where the whole nation, including public and private sector, works together to achieve certain goals such as technological independence. Another method is to concentrate available resources in certain areas critical for the country's development. In many ways, these methods are not unique to China. Developed countries now were developing countries in the past, and most of them had to overcome many of the same problems and at the time government allocation of resources played a critical role. However, due to differences in terms of history, society and political circumstances, different governments had different ways of allocating resources and different relationships with market institutes, and we should be careful not to generalize too much. The decentralized regional competition combined with centralized coordination, or the "dual competition" in both the market and the government, is a specific feature in China's development.

Of course, not all government interventions are successful. Take the popular trade protection of infant-industries as an example. Some countries, such as South Korea, raise tariffs on imports to protect domestic industrial firms, while promoting exports and using competition in the international market to force them to improve efficiency. With the rapid development of domestic firms, tariffs and protection can gradually be reduced and eliminated. A group of world leading companies, such as Samsung and POSCO, were developed under this system. However, there are also countries in Latin America and South East Asia where it has proved hard to ween domestic companies off government support and tariff protection. There protection policies produced a group of rent-seeking companies and inefficient monopolies, which harms economic development. In a larger and more complex country such as China, both successful and failed cases are common. Some companies and industries become outstanding when competing internationally, while some companies are busy cheating and rent seeking to win government subsidies. The difference in results stems from differences in political and economic conditions across countries and regions. The strength of government lies not only in its ability to provide resources and support firms, but also in its ability to say no when necessary.[15]

Throughout the process of economic development, it is necessary to continuously mobilize land, labor, capital and other resources to produce things that meet the needs of society. Under a planned economy system, these resources can be mobilized, but the output cannot meet the needs of society, and a cycle of positive reinforcement between supply and demand cannot be formed, so the overall productivity remains low. Market reforms in China was started as a way of meeting society's needs. In 1981, the Sixth Plenary Session of the Eleventh Central Committee of the CCP proposed that *"the main contradiction to be resolved in China is the contradiction between the ever-growing material and cultural needs of the population, and underdeveloped levels of production"*. During the subsequent reforms, due to the absence of a well-functioned market and legal system, it was difficult for private companies to overcome various coordination difficulties and uncertainties. As a result, the government and state-owned enterprises played a leading role in investing and driving the process of urbanization and industrialization. The achievements made under this model are clear for all to see, and at the same time it has helped to promote the establishment and continued improvement of China's market economy.

However, this model cannot last forever, and successful experience in the past does not necessarily translate into present or future success. A well-functioning government should not only be able to extract resources, but also be able to continually adapt and upgrade itself in the process of development. Once the economy develops to a certain stage, markets will have become well-functioned, the legal system will have been developed, private companies will have controlled a large amount of resources and the concept of a market economy will have been widely accepted by the population. By the time we reach this stage, if the economy is still primarily led by the government and state-owned enterprises, the overall efficiency will be greatly reduced. Investment, financing and production will all require more decentralized decision-making. Therefore, if market-based reforms

[15] Bardhan (2016) summarizes and discusses the successes and failures of trade protection and industrial policies in various countries. He particularly emphasizes the problem of "time inconsistency" in the protection commitments of infant industries. That is, the protection is designed to be removed after some time, but the removement often fails when the time comes.

are to succeed in the long run, then the current production-oriented government must become service-oriented.

As mentioned in Chapter 7, in order to change China's unbalanced economic structure, the key is to transfer more resources from the government and state-owned enterprises into the household sector, and to reduce government spending on investment and increase spending on public services. In developed countries, government expenditure tends to accounts for a larger share of GDP, and the majority of this spending is on public services. If we take the OECD countries as an example, average government spending on healthcare, education, social security and pensions accounts for 24% of GDP, while the number for China is only 13%.[16] As countries get richer, people's demand for these types of public services increases. At the same time, fluctuations and cycles are a part of the nature of market economies, and the resulted unemployment and inequality need to be managed by the government. If we take inequality as an example, an effective income redistribution policy requires not only taxing the rich, but also spending more on the poor and on improving public welfare.

Urbanization is an irreversible process. China's current reforms on its land and household registration system recognize this irreversibility. In the face of shocks during the process of economic development, returning to the countryside is one option for urban migrants but it is rarely an effective long-term solution. It is necessary to develop stabilizing mechanisms within cities by increasing expenditure on healthcare, education and housing, which helps to provide more security for people in the face of economic fluctuations.

Increasing expenditure on public services is also in line with China's current stage of economic development. As China's manufacturing sectors continues to upgrade their technology, they inevitably use more machines and less people. Employment becomes increasingly dependent on the services sector. The development of the service sector in turn is dependent on urbanization and population density.[17] If the share of the service

[16] The data come from Zhang et al. (2018).

[17] The development of the service industry cannot be separated from population density. The main reason is that most services (such as restaurants or barber shops) cannot be traded at distance and instead transactions need to happen face to face. Zhong, Lu and Xi (钟粤俊, 陆铭, 奚锡灿 2020) analyze the positive correlation between population density and the development of the service industry across regions in China.

sector in GDP increases, the Chinese production-oriented government must become more service-orientated. There are two reasons for this. First, as compared to large and standardized industrial firms, firms in service industry are usually smaller and more flexible, so they can meet the non-standardized and local demands. In this kind of industry, the power of the government to consolidate resources and make large investments is not very useful. Second, service-oriented governments also needs to invest a lot, but in humans instead of capital goods or infrastructures. The core of a service-orientated economy is human capital, which needs to be developed through government spending on healthcare and education that serve to make people more productive, thereby raising the overall level of human capital. But since service industries tend to be diversified and market-orientated, the required government investment should be more indirect. They should focus on raise the level of general-purpose human capital, rather than supporting specific firm projects.

The bottleneck of increasing expenditure on public services is a lack of local government revenue. The first chapter of the book analyzes the factors that determine the division of power within China's government, and it shows that the majority of public service expenditure must come from local governments instead of the central government. In 2019, China's local governments accounted for 96% of public expenditure on education, healthcare and social security, while the central government accounted for only 4%. Through the mechanism of transfer payment, the central government has effectively equalized the level of expenditure on basic public services across China (Chapter 2), but this does not change the fact that local governments are still responsible for using these expenditures. After many reforms of the tax system (Chapter 2), China still lacks a major tax that 100% goes to local government, such as state or city property tax in the US. The model of land finance, as we have seen, is not sustainable. If local governments are to increase spending on public services and welfare, it is necessary to once again reform the overall tax system, shifting more tax revenue to local governments. One of the mostly discussed reforms in recent years has been introducing a real estate tax. Although this would definitely be a tax accruing to local governments, the impact of this reform would be very significant. Even though the idea has been discussed for many years, it has not moved forward in any substantial form.

Section 3: Development Goals and the Development Process

Mainstream economics is a set of theories that explain the operation of markets through a price mechanism. On many core issues, these theories do not incorporate factors such as politics, society and history. The differences between countries therefore are essentially ignored. For many developing countries, however, the most important issue is not how a well-functioned market works, rather it is how they can build such a market from scratch and improve it gradually. So, in developing countries, the capabilities, objectives and methods used to consolidate and mobilize resources is vastly different from developed countries. Of course, even between developing countries, the specific development pathway followed by different countries also differs greatly.

Increasing productivity is always at the heart of economic development, for developed countries that are already using the most advanced technologies, the key to increasing productivity is to continue innovating and making breakthroughs. The well-functioned market economy of developed countries is a system of decentralized decision-making, in which competition and price mechanisms help to continuously experiment and select the winners from this innovation. For developing countries, however, the key to increasing productivity lies not in frontier innovation, but rather in learning to apply the existing technologies and management techniques of developed countries. They must mobilize and invest resources to support and accelerate the learning process. This model of "organizational learning" requires a different way of allocating resources from the model of "mass innovation". Indeed, Chinese economists studied the difference between the two models 20 years ago. Although developing countries have a so-called latecomer advantage when it comes to learning and imitating the technologies of developed countries, the advantage of this "organizational learning" cannot last forever. When a country's technology and productivity reach a certain level, this model of learning and imitating must transform to one driven by experiment and innovation. If the transformation fails, the economy may struggle to develop further, and the latecomer advantage could become the latecomer disadvantage.[18]

[18] For discussions of the "latecomer advantage" and the "latecomer disadvantage", see Sachs, Woo and Yang (2000) and Lin (林毅夫 2003). Stiglitz and Greenwald (2015)

Throughout the book, I have continually emphasized that the process of economic development is not the same as the goal of economic development. Indeed, copying more developed countries will not solve many problems faced by China. Likewise, things that worked in the past in China may not work again in the future, so this book not only discusses the past accomplishments of China, but also tries to explain current obstacles and reforms needed. I personally believe that there are many modes of economic development, just as countries imitate in different ways, they can innovate in different ways too, and the American and European model of innovation may not be the optimal model for China.

Not only are there differences between developing and developed countries, but the development models used by developing countries are also different.[19] From a macroeconomic perspective, these models may look similar, for example, capital accumulation, exports-oriented strategy, active industrial policies, exchange rates manipulation and financial repression are all typical policies. But across different countries and circumstances, the specific ways to implement these policies differ greatly. Effective development policies must conform with the historical, political and social conditions of a given country. No country is a blank sheet of paper on which any beautiful picture could be drawn from scratch. What can or cannot be done differs greatly across countries. The Chinese political and economic system described in this book has three crucial components: local governments with a large amount of resources and a large freedom of acting, a powerful central government with a strong ability to coordinate and control, and a well-organized bureaucratic system with strong human capital. These three "institutional endowments" originate from the special history of China and may not necessarily be present in other developing countries.

Not only do social conditions and development paths differ across countries, but within a country as large as China, the development path followed by each province can also differ. At the beginning of the first chapter, I mentioned that Guangdong, Zhejiang, Jiangsu, Shandong and Henan would all rank inside the top 20 countries by GDP if their

systematically explain the relationship between learning and economic development and discuss how a series of policies that are considered "distortions" in mainstream economics could promote economic growth, including industrial policy and trade protection.

[19] Rodrik (2007) elaborates on this point.

economies were counted separately, and each one of them is equivalent to a European country in terms of economic size. If the economic histories of a European country can fill many books, the unique development paths of China's provinces is obviously also worth studying and recording.[20] It is a pity that the current trend in academic economics is to pursue one-size-fits-all theories, and scholars do not pay much attention to studies on specific countries or specific cases. This kind of study would be labeled as anecdotal and unscientific. I do not like this attitude and fashion. Although I have learned a lot studying abstract and theoretical development economics, I am more interested in real-world practices, this book has therefore introduced many real-world case studies and policies.

The political and social realities of each country determine what kind of economic policies are possible. Take industrialization and urbanization, which are undoubtedly the key to economic development, as examples. Superficially, these two issues look similar across countries, and they are a process of industrial production and infrastructure building. But if we look deeper, the process of industrialization and urbanization is essentially a process of turning peasants into urban factory workers, and the way to achieve this varies greatly by country. In China, the feasible policy choice is constrained by three institutions: the collective ownership of rural land, the state ownership of urban land and the household registration system. As a result, China's industrialization is inseparable from the development of township and village enterprises, and China's urbanization is inseparable from land finance. I think these country-specific development pathways are the most interesting issues of studying economic development.

Viable policies are constrained not only by the institutions in place, but also by entrenched interests. Policies must be designed with the interests of the various stakeholders and power brokers in mind. Policies must be able to improve economic efficiency without incurring huge damage to decision-makers and powerful interest groups, otherwise the policies can

[20] In fact, let alone provinces, even Chinese cities are large enough. There are about 95 Chinese cities with a population over 5 million, larger than Norway. Their development stories and models also have their own unique characteristics. There are not many in-depth studies in city-specific development stories, however. Interested readers can refer to Zhang and Liu (2019) on the Zhejiang Model. Zhang et al. (张军 2020) is a collection of papers on the Shenzhen Model. Zhang et al. (张燕生等 2001) is a research reports on the Foshan model, and Shi et.al. (史晋川等 2002) is a research report on the Wenzhou model.

be very difficult to implement.[21] Real-world economic policies are therefore the result of compromises made between various interests, behind which lie the unique political systems and agendas of different countries. This process of compromise depends on the ability to align differing incentives, while also being subject to the specific culture of each country. For example, there is an important concept in political economy called "elite capture", and the classical example of elite capture is politicians being controlled by local interest groups, who then pursue their own interests rather than the good of the people. In China, these conflicts between local and national interests have a long history, and the way to combat the problem has been to build and develop a set of institutions, as well as cultivating a national ideology and developing a unified education system for bureaucrats (see Chapter 1).

Another example is the conflict between free trade and protectionism. The concepts and theories supporting free trade are some of the most convincing in economics, but however convincing the theories, they are often constrained by real-world interests. Anyone who has studied economics knows that comparative advantage and free trade can provide overall benefits for an economy. But benefiting the whole does not mean benefiting everyone. Theoretically speaking, free trade should be pursued anyway even when many individuals suffer, because the overall economic gain far outweighs any loss. Provided some compensation is taken from the winning party and offered to the losing party, everyone should be happy with the outcome. But in reality, how much compensation? In what form and to whom? These questions often involve complex political battles. Compensation may be delayed or insufficient, or even never comes, and as a result someone will benefit more and more, and someone will suffer more and more. Although gains from trade may improve the average level of welfare, those who suffer do not live a statistically-average life. They are real people and they will resist and seek ways to protect their own interests. This is the basis for protectionism.[22]

Finally, compared with the neoclassical economics that mainly studies well-developed markets, the economics treating development as a process includes two special topics, the sequence of development and the pace of development. In reality, these two questions often overlap, but for

[21] A collection of papers written by Qian (2017) elaborates on this point.

[22] Rodrik (2018) illustrates the conflict between trade theory and real interests.

researchers, the sequence relates more to industrial structure and the pace relates more to stability or gradualism.

The goal of a reform is different from its process. Even if all parties agree on the intention and purpose of a given reform (highly unlikely), there may be different views on how it should be carried out and in what sequence. It is never easy to decide where to start and in which order things should be done. At every step, someone will benefit and someone will suffer. Those who suffer may choose to fight and resist any change that harms their interests. Even if the end is clearly seen and understood, it may not be achieved, since there are always many pitfalls and obstacles that need to be overcome. In the middle of the twentieth century, just after the World War Two, a large number of emerging economies appeared, which helped to promote the rise of development economics. At the time, research was focused on the sequence of development or structural transformation, however later this research paradigm gradually declined. In the past 10 years, a research center led by Professor Justin Yifu Lin of Peking University has begun to pay more attention to issues of structural transformation. Their line of research has come to be known as "new structural economics", which extends the basic logic of comparative advantage to explain the sequence of development and the process of structural transformation. This can be considered the third generation of development economics. Even though many aspects of this paradigm remain controversial, it is definitely an important school of thoughts.[23]

Economic development must alter old ways of living and redistribute benefits accruing during the process, therefore it is bound to be accompanied by contradictions and conflicts. One of the most important roles for government is to regulate the pace of change. The speed of social change has a huge impact on those who live through it, and people need time to adapt to a new environment. People are not machines, and they cannot update or adjust immediately, therefore sufficient time and resources should be spent helping people to adapt and ensuring social stability. The various buffers or stabilizers built into this kind of gradualist reform often reduce efficiency and slow down the overall reform process, so they are often labeled as "distortion" or "misallocation", but without them most reforms are doomed to fail.

[23] Lin (2012) introduces the basic framework of New Structural Economics, and it also includes many scholars' discussions on this theory and Professor Lin's response.

Economic development is a continuous process. The most important question at the moment is not when and whether China's GDP will surpass the US, but rather whether China has built up the necessary environments and foundations for its next stage of development. Can industrial upgrading and technological progress continue? And can the hundreds of millions of people still living in the countryside continue to be urbanized? Can inequality between rich and poor be controlled within an acceptable range? At this stage, what would be the next fundamental reform and what specific polices would be used? Therefore, each chapter of the book seeks to introduce relevant policies and reforms currently being implemented so that readers can understand how policymakers are considering the present problems and how they are trying to solve them. Some economic historians said at the beginning of their book on the rise of the US: "In successful economies, economic policy has been pragmatic, not ideological. It has been concrete, not abstract".[24]

Summary

Economics is an interpretation of real-world economic phenomena. Phenomena are complex and variable, and accidental factors and luck play an important role. What happened in the past was never inevitable and what happens in the future will always be uncertain. In spite of this, economic research is still valuable. Lessons and factors can be extracted from past events, and interpretations and analyses of these factors can be insightful and inspiring. But what factors? What lessons? How to interpret? The answers to these questions are inseparable from the environment where these events took place. Of course, any well-developed theory is logically consistent within itself, but in order for applying the theory in practice, we must look beyond the theory itself to investigate its validity and usefulness in in different scenarios and environments. We may find differing results depending on the time, the place or the people.

Extracting and interpretation of relevant factors essentially involves repeatedly asking *"what is important?"* in a certain context. The answer requires making comparisons, and these comparisons must be carried out both across time periods and across regions or countries. Researchers should not only have a deep understanding of their own country's history

[24] See Cohen and Delong (2016).

and present context, but they should also understand the present and history of other countries in their comparison group. It is easy to compare data and some superficial phenomena, but to really understand the data-generating-process and phenomena-generating-mechanisms takes a lot of work. These understandings are much more useful. The most important aim of development economics is to understand the process by which development happens, and it is therefore always necessary to understand the initial conditions and path dependency. History is powerful, and we should respect its influence and continuity, and be suspicious of simply applying foreign theories onto domestic phenomena without any modification.

In any case, the main function of economic research is to discover and raise questions, and specific solutions can only be explored and found in practice. The role of academics in asking questions should neither be exaggerated nor be belittled. The real world is complicated, and there are too many factors that cannot be incorporated in logic and theory alone. So the solution given for any specific problem must be constantly re-examined, re-evaluated, adjusted and modified in practice. But discovering and asking the right questions is always the first step in any successful solution. And asking the right question is often inseparable from exploring right solutions, and it requires a deep understanding of the problem in hands. So, whether for a theorist or for a practitioner, seeking truth from facts and insisting specific analysis of specific issues are two types of morale that would never be outdated.

Further Readings

Developing a comparative perspective to problems requires a lot of reading, that is why I include a section of "further readings" at the end of each chapter. I personally enjoy reading about economic history, so I dedicate this very last section to economic history. Many great books have been written in this field, and the following are three popular introductory books. These books are concise, but they introduce many important phenomena and raise many important questions. The first, *Global Economic History: A Very Short Introduction* written by Robert Allen (2011), the second, *Why Europe? The Rise of the West in World History 1500–1850* written by Jack Goldstone (2009), and the third, *Global Capitalism: its Fall and Rise in the Twentieth Century* written by Jeffry A. Frieden (2007). These books can act as a starting point for readers to do further exploration in economic history. I often read and re-read books of Karl Polanyi, Alexander Gerschenkron, Eric Hobsbawm and Joel Mokyr. Even though they are old books, I sometimes find myself reading them anew. Readers familiar with these authors may see their influence in my writing of this book, particularly from *Economic Backwardness in Historical Perspective* (Gerchenkron 1962) and *The Great Transformation: The Political and Economic Origins of Our Time* (Polanyi 1944).

Chinese economics students often know a lot about present-day American economic theory, but they know a little about the process of development experienced in America. There are two good books that focus on the US. The first is *Concrete Economics: The Hamilton Approach to Economic Growth and Policy* by Stephen Cohen and Bradford DeLong (2016). This book emphasizes the role of government in the development of the US economy. The US government was very pragmatic and willing to use all kinds of policies to promote economic development, such as industrial policy, trade protectionism and manipulation of exchange rate. It was this pragmaticism and problem-solving attitude that created today's America. By reviewing this history, the authors criticize the free market ideology that has swept through the US and the world since the 1980s. The second is *Ages of American Capitalism: A History of the US* by Jonathan Levy (2021). From reading this long book, readers may find a great deal of similarities in economic development of the US and China, particularly how to capitalize various resources, including lands, to build infrastructures and expand the economy, and how to promote technology progress with mass production.

During the writing of this final chapter, Ezra Vogel, a renowned historian of East Asia passed away. His masterpiece *Deng Xiaoping and the Transformation of China (2011)* is clearly written, meticulous in its research, and easy to read. I have been living in the great era of the reform and opening-up of China, and this book records its difficult start. It is my final recommendation here.

References

Alexander, Gerschenkron (1962). *Economic Backwardness in Historical Perspective: A Book of Essays*. The Belknap Press of Harvard University Press

Bardhan, Pranab (2016). "State and Development: The Need for a Reappraisal of the Current Literature." *Journal of Economic Literature* 54.3: 862–892.

Besley, Timothy, and Torsten Persson (2011). *Pillars of Prosperity: The Political Economics of Development Clusters*. Princeton University Press.

Cohen, Stephen S., and J. Bradford DeLong (2016). *Concrete Economics: The Hamilton Approach to Economic Growth and Policy*. Harvard Business Review Press.

Fan, Jingting, and Ben Zou (2019). "Industrialization from Scratch: The 'Construction of Third Front' and Local Economic Development in China's Hinterland," *Working paper*.

Fan, Yi, Junjian Yi, and Junsen Zhang (2020). "Rising Intergenerational Income Persistence in China." *American Economic Journal: Economic Policy* 13.1: 202–230.

Glaeser, Edward, and Andrei Shleifer (2003). "The Rise of the Regulatory State." *Journal of Economic Literature* 41.2: 401–425.

Lin, Justin Yifu (2012). *New Structural Economics: A Framework for Rethinking Development and Policy*. World Bank Publications.

Maskin, Eric, Yingyi Qian, and Chenggang Xu (2000). "Incentives, Information, and Organizational Form." *Review of Economic Studies* 67.2: 359–378.

Mulligan, Casey and Andrei Shleifer (2005). "The Extent of the Market and the Supply of Regulation." *Quarterly Journal of Economics* 120: 1445–1473.

Qian, Yingyi (2017). *How Reform Worked in China: The Transition from Plan to Market*. The MIT Press.

Rodrik, Dani (1998). "Why Do More Open Economies Have Bigger Governments?" *Journal of Political Economy* 106.5: 997–1032.

Rodrik, Dani (2007). *One Economics, Many Recipes: Globalization, Institutions, and Economic Growth*. Princeton University Press.

Rodrik, Dani (2018). *Straight Talk on Trade: Ideas for a Sane World Economy*. Princeton University Press.

Sachs, Jeffrey, Wing Thye Woo, and Xiaokai Yang (2000). *Economic Reforms and Constitutional Transition*, CID Working Paper.

Saez, Emmanuel, and Gabriel Zucman (2019). *The Triumph of Injustice: How the Rich Dodge Taxes and How to Make Them Pay*. W.W. Norton & Company.

Stiglitz, Joseph E., and Bruce C. Greenwald (2015). *Creating a Learning Society: A New Approach to Growth, Development, and Social Progress*. Columbia University Press.

Vogel, Ezra F. (2011) *Deng Xiaoping and the Transformation of China*. Belknap Press of Harvard University Press.

Xu, Chenggang (2011). "The Fundamental Institutions of China's Reforms and Development." *Journal of Economic Literature* 49.4: 1076–1151.

Zhang, Qi, and Mingxing Liu (2019). *Revolutionary Legacy, Power Structure, and Grassroots Capitalism under the Red Flag in China*. Cambridge University Press.

Zhang, Bing, Xiaolan Chen, and Huanxiu Guo (2018). "Does Central Supervision Enhance Local Environmental Enforcement? Quasi-experimental Evidence from China." *Journal of Public Economics* 164: 70–90.

Zhang, Yansheng, and Geng Xiao (2001). *Government and Market: China's Experience*. China CITIC Press.

Translated References (in Chinese)

Bo, Yibo (2008). *Review of a Number of Major Decisions and Events*. History of Chinese Communist Party Publishing House. (in Chinese)

Lin, Yifu (2003). "Backward Advantage or Backward Disadvantage: A Discussion with Yang Xiaokai." *China Economic Quarterly* 4: 989–1004. (in Chinese)

Shi, Jinchuan (2002). *China Regional Economic Development: A Case Study of Wenzhou*. Zhejiang University Press. (in Chinese)

Yan, Peng (2018). *A Brief History of China's Industry (1815–2015)*. Publishing House of Electronics Industry. (in Chinese)

Zhang, Jun, Haichao Fan, Zhiwei Xu, and Longfei Zhou (2020). "Structural Decline in the GDP Growth Rate: The Impact of the Official Assessment Mechanism." *Economic Research Journal* 5: 31–48. (in Chinese)

Zhou, Li-An (2018). "'Bureaucratic & Economic Markets' and China's Growth Story." *Chinese Journal of Sociology* 2: 1–45. (in Chinese)

Zhong, Yuejun, Ming Lu, and Xican Xi (2020). "Agglomeration and Service Industry Development: Based on the Perspective of Population Spatial Distribution." *Journal of Management World* 11: 35–49. (in Chinese)

Epilogue

Writing a book requires some illusion of self-importance. If I didn't firmly believe that this book is important, I wouldn't be able to get it finished. But once I've finished, there is no need to continue this illusion any more. The comments and discussions of China's stellar economic story will be endless, and this book is just my few rough sketches. Writing such a book constantly reminds me of the parable of the blind men and an elephant, and there is simply too much I don't know. What Keynes said in *A Treatise on Probability*, I feel the same way:

> In writing a book of this kind the author must, if he is to put his point of view clearly, pretend sometimes to a little more conviction than he feels. He must give his own argument a chance, so to speak, not be too ready to depress its vitality with a wet cloud of doubt. It is a heavy task to write on these problems; and the reader will perhaps excuse me if I have sometimes pressed on a little faster than the difficulties were overcome, and with decidedly more confidence than I have always felt.

During the past 40 years, China's nominal GDP has increased by 242 times, and the average person has gone from earning 20 to 30 yuan per month to earning 4,000 to 5,000 yuan per month. If you happened to move a bit too slow, you might have gotten left behind by the rapid changes. People from outside China, no matter how much knowledge and how many theories one has, will not have personally experienced the

X. Lan, *How China Works*,
https://doi.org/10.1007/978-981-97-0080-6

ups and downs, manias and panics, joys and sorrows of this momentous era.

I was born in 1980 and grew up in a small town in Inner Mongolia. I have worked and lived in Beijing, Dalian, Shanghai, Shenzhen and Wuhan for extended periods of time. Except for the years spent studying and living in the US, I have never left China. Although I could fill a few more books discussing the problems and troubles that I have seen, my experience and what I have seen have prevented me from becoming pessimistic about China. I could use many different theories to try to analyze and explain this optimism, however my optimism does not need the support of theories. It is a simple belief, a belief that China will become better. This belief does not come from my academic training, but rather from the writings of Sima Qian, DuFu and Su Shi, and from an admiration for the hard work and pragmatic attitudes of the Chinese people. This belief may bias the way I see things and the way I process information, and I accept this bias and do not intend to change it.

Of course, no-one knows what the future holds. Even if we are only looking 50 or 60 years ahead, it is still a span of time that no-one can predict. So having belief is important. In 1912 when Pu Yi abdicated the throne, and until the reform and opening up period, China went through so many chaos and upheavals that it made people feel like many centuries had passed, but there were only 66 years. Deng Xiaoping was actually born two years before Pu Yi.

Therefore, this book has no grand conception or framework, and makes no predictions. Instead, I have focused on introducing the current situation as it is. If it can help readers to understand some of things around them, to understand some backgrounds in the political and economic news, to see some opportunities in opaque languages in government documents, by which one can make life a bit better or just better engage in a conversation about China, then that is enough.

References

Acemoglu, Daron, Ufuk Akcigit, Douglas Hanley, and William Kerr (2016). "Transition to Clean Technology." *Journal of Political Economy* 124.1: 52–104.

Aghion, Philippe, Antonin Bergeaud, Matthieu Lequien, and Marc J. Melitz (2018) "The Impact of Exports on Innovation: Theory and Evidence," *NBER working paper* 24600.

Aghion, Philippe, Jing Cai, Mathias Dewatripont, Luosha Du, Ann Harrison, and Patrick Legros (2015) "Industrial Policy and Competition." *American Economic Journal: Macroeconomics* 7.4: 1–32.

Aghion, Philippe, and Jean Tirole (1997). "Formal and Real Authority in Organizations." *Journal of Political Economy* 105.1: 1–29.

Akerlof, George A. (2020). "Sins of Omission and the Practice of Economics." *Journal of Economic Literature* 58.2: 405–418.

Alchian, Armen A. (1950). "Uncertainty, Evolution, and Economic Theory." *Journal of Political Economy* 58.3: 211–221.

Alesina, Alberto, and Enrico Spolaore (2003). *The Size of Nations.* MIT Press.

Allen, Robert C. (2011) *Global Economic History: A Very Short Introduction.* Oxford University Press.

Anderson, Benedict (2006). *Imagined Communities: Reflections on the Origin and Spread of Nationalism (revised edition).* Verso.

Ang, Yuen Yuen (2020). *China's Gilded Age: the Paradox of Economic Boom and Vast Corruption.* Cambridge University Press.

Appelbaum, Eileen, and Rosemary Batt (2014). *Private Equity at Work: When Wall Street Manages Main Street.* Russell Sage Foundation.

X. Lan, *How China Works*,
https://doi.org/10.1007/978-981-97-0080-6

Armstrong-Taylor, Paul (2016). *Debt and Distortion: Risks and Reforms in the Chinese Financial System.* Palgrave Macmillan

Autor, David, David Dorn, and Gordon Hanson (2013). "The China Syndrome: Local Labor Market Effects of Import Competition in the United States." *American Economic Review* 103.6: 2121–2168.

Autor, David, David Dorn, Gordon Hanson and Kaveh Majlesi (2020a). "Importing Political Polarization? The Electoral Consequences of Rising Trade Exposure." *American Economic Review* 110.10: 3139–3183.

Autor, David, David Dorn, Gordon H. Hanson, Gary Pisano, and Pian Shu (2020b). "Foreign Competition and Domestic Innovation: Evidence from US Patents." *American Economic Review: Insights* 2. 3: 357–374.

Avdjiev, Stefan, Robert N. McCauley, and Hyun Song Shin (2016). "Breaking Free of the Triple Coincidence in International Finance." *Economic Policy* 31.87: 409–451.

Bai, Chong-En, Chang-Tai Hsieh, and Zheng Song (2016). "The Long Shadow of a Fiscal Expansion". *Brookings Papers on Economic Activity,* Fall: 129–165.

Baldwin, Richard (2017). *The Great Convergence: Information Technology and the New Globalization.* Harvard University Press.

Bardhan, Pranab (2016). "State and Development: The Need for a Reappraisal of the Current Literature." *Journal of Economic Literature* 54.3: 862–892.

Beckert, Sven (2015). *Empire of Cotton: A Global History.* Vintage.

Bertrand, Marianne, and Adair Morse (2016). "Trickle-Down Consumption." *Review of Economics and Statistics* 98.5: 863–879.

Besley, Timothy, and Torsten Persson (2011). *Pillars of Prosperity: The Political Economics of Development Clusters.* Princeton University Press.

Blanchard, Olivier (2022). *Fiscal Policy under Low Interest Rates.* MIT Press.

Bloom, Nicholas (2014). "Fluctuations in Uncertainty." *Journal of Economic Perspectives* 28.2: 153–176.

Bloom, Nicholas, Kyle Handley, Andre Kurman, and Phillip Luck (2019). "The Impact of Chinese Trade on US Employment: The Good, The Bad, and The Debatable," *Working Paper.*

Brueckner, Jan K., Shihe Fu, Yizhen Gu, and Junfu Zhang (2017). "Measuring the Stringency of Land Use Regulation: The Case of China's Building Height Limits." *Review of Economics and Statistics* 99.4: 663–677.

Cai, Hongbin, Yuyu Chen, and Qing Gong (2016). "Polluting Thy Neighbor: Unintended Consequences of China's Pollution Reduction Mandates." *Journal of Environmental Economics and Management* 76: 86–104.

Chamon, Marcos D., and Eswar S. Prasad (2010) . "Why Are Saving Rates of Urban Households in China Rising?" *American Economic Journal: Macroeconomics* 2.1: 93–130.

Chang, Kia-Ngau (1958). *The Inflation Spiral: The Experience in China 1939–1950*. MIT Press.

Chen, M. Keith (2013). "The Effect of Language on Economic Behavior: Evidence from Savings Rates, Health Behaviors, and Retirement Assets." *American Economic Review* 103.2: 690–731.

Chen, Peter, Loukas Karabarbounis, and Brent Neiman (2017). "The Global Rise of Corporate Saving." *Journal of Monetary Economics* 89: 1–19.

Chen, Shuo, Xinyu Fan, Zhitao Zhu (2020). "The Promotion Club," *Working paper*.

Chen, Ting, Laura Xiaolei Liu, Wei Xiong, and Li-An Zhou (2018). "Real Estate Boom and Misallocation of Capital in China," *Working paper*.

Cheng, Hong, Ruixue Jia, Dandan Li, and Hongbin Li (2019). "The Rise of Robots in China." *Journal of Economic Perspectives* 33.2: 71–88.

Cherif, Reda, and Fuad Hasanov (2019). "The Return of the Policy that Shall Not Be Named: Principles of Industrial Policy," *IMF Working Paper*.

Chetty, Raj, David Grusky, Maximilian Hell, Nathaniel Hendren, Robert Manduca, and Jimmy Narang (2017). "The Fading American Dream: Trends in Absolute Income Mobility since 1940." *Science* 356.6336: 398–406.

Chetty, Raj, Nathaniel Hendren, Maggie R. Jones, and Sonya R. Porter (2020). "Race and Economic Opportunity in the United States: An Intergenerational Perspective." *Quarterly Journal of Economics* 135.2: 711–783.

Cheung, Steven N.S. (2014). "The Economic System of China." *Man and the Economy* 1.1: 1–49.

Choukhmane, Taha, Nicholas Coeurdacier, and Keyu Jin (2019). "The One-Child Policy and Household Savings," *Working paper*.

Cohen, Stephen S., and J. Bradford DeLong (2016). *Concrete Economics: The Hamilton Approach to Economic Growth and Policy*. Harvard Business Review Press.

Cunningham, Edward, Tony Saich, and Jesse Turiel (2020). "Understanding CCP Resilience: Surveying Chinese Public Opinion through Time." *Harvard Kennedy School Ash Center Policy Report*.

Dalio, Ray (2018). *Principles for Navigating Big Debt Crises*. Simon and Schuster.

De Soto, Hernando (2003). *The Mystery of Capital: Why Capitalism Triumphs in the West and Fails Everywhere Else*. Basic Books.

Di Tella, Rafael, and Dani Rodrik (2020). "Labour Market Shocks and the Demand for Trade Protection: Evidence from Online Surveys." *Economic Journal* 130.628: 1008–1030.

Eichengreen, Barry (2011). *Exorbitant Privilege: The Rise and Fall of the Dollar and the Future of the International Monetary System*. Oxford University Press.

Eichengreen, Barry (2019). *Globalizing Capital: A History of the International Monetary System* (3rd edition). Princeton University Press.

Eggertsson, Gauti B., and Paul Krugman (2012). "Debt, Deleveraging, and the Liquidity Trap: A Fisher-Minsky-Koo Approach." *Quarterly Journal of Economics* 127.3: 1469–1513.

Fan, Haichao, Yu Liu, Nancy Qian, and Jaya Wen (2020). "Computerizing VAT Invoices in China," *NBER Working Paper* 24414.

Fan, Jingting, and Ben Zou (2019). "Industrialization from Scratch: The 'Construction of Third Front' and Local Economic Development in China's Hinterland," *Working paper*.

Fan, Yi, Junjian Yi, and Junsen Zhang (2020). "Rising Intergenerational Income Persistence in China." *American Economic Journal: Economic Policy* 13.1: 202–230.

Fang, Hanming, Quanlin Gu, Wei Xiong, and Li-An Zhou (2015). "Demystifying the Chinese Housing Boom." *NBER Macro Annual* 30: 105–166.

Frieden, Jeffry A. (2007). *Global Capitalism: Its Fall and Rise in the Twentieth Century*. WW Norton & Company.

Fukuyama, Francis (2011). *The Origins of Political Order: From Prehuman Times to the French Revolution*. Farrar, Straus and Giroux.

Furman, Jason, and Lawrence Summers (2020). "A Reconsideration of Fiscal Policy in the Era of Low Interest Rates." *Brookings Working Paper*.

Gerschenkron, Alexander (1962). *Economic Backwardness in Historical Perspective: A Book of Essays*. Belknap Press of Harvard University Press.

Gertler, Mark, and Simon Gilchrist (2018). "What Happened: Financial Factors in the Great Recession." *Journal of Economic Perspective* 32.3: 3–30.

Glaeser, Edward, and Joseph Gyourko (2018). "The Economic Implications of Housing Supply." *Journal of Economic Perspectives* 32.1: 3–30.

Glaeser, Edward, and Andrei Shleifer (2003). "The Rise of the Regulatory State." *Journal of Economic Literature* 41.2: 401–425.

Glick, Reuven, and Kevin J. Lansing (2010). "Global Household Leverage, House Prices, and Consumption," *Federal Reserve Bank of San Francisco Economic Letter*.

Goldstone, Jack A. (2009). *Why Europe? The Rise of the West in World History 1500–1850*. McGraw-Hill Higher Education.

Gomory, Ralph E., and William J. Baumol (2000). *Global Trade and Conflicting National Interests*. MIT Press.

Gorton, Gary B. (2010). *Slapped by the Invisible Hand: The Panic of 2007*. Oxford University Press.

Haldane, Andrew, Simon Brennan, and Vasileios Madouros (2010). "The Contribution of the Financial Sector: Miracle or Mirage?" *A Technical Report at the London School of Economics*.

Hart, Oliver (1995). *Firms, Contracts, and Financial Structure*. Clarendon Press.

Hart, Oliver, Andrei Shleifer, and Robert W. Vishny (1997). "The Proper Scope of Government: Theory and an Application to Prisons." *Quarterly Journal of Economics* 112.4: 1127–1161.

Haskel, Jonathan, and Stian Westlake (2018). *Capitalism Without Capital: The Rise of the Intangible Economy*. Princeton University Press.

Havranek, Tomas, and Zuzana Irsova (2011). "Estimating Vertical Spillovers from FDI: Why Results Vary and What the True Effect Is." *Journal of International Economics* 85.2: 234–244.

He, Guojun, Shaoda Wang, and Bing Zhang (2020). "Watering Down Environmental Regulation in China." *Quarterly Journal of Economics* 135.4: 2135–2185.

Heilman, Sebastian (ed). (2016). *China's Political System*. Rowman & Littlefield Publishers.

Hirschman, Albert O. (2013). "The Changing Tolerance for Income Inequality in the Course of Economic Development." *The Essential Hirschman*, Ed. by Jeremy Adelman: 74–101. Princeton University Press.

Huang, Zhangkai, Lixing Li, Guangrong Ma, and Lixin Colin Xu (2017). "Hayek, Local Information, and Commanding Heights: Decentralizing State-Owned Enterprises in China." *American Economic Review* 107.8: 2455–2478.

Jia, Ruixue, Masayuki Kudamatsu, and David Seim (2015). "Political Selection in China: the Complementary Roles of Connections and Performance." *Journal of the European Economic Association*, 13.4: 631–668.

Jin, Hehui, Yingyi Qian, and Barry R. Weingast (2005). "Regional Decentralization and Fiscal Incentives: Federalism, Chinese Style." *Journal of Public Economics* 89.9–10: 1719–1742.

Jordà, Òscar, Moritz Schularick, and Alan M. Taylor (2016). "The Great Mortgaging: Housing Finance, Crises and Business Cycles." *Economic Policy* 31.85: 107–152.

İmrohoroğlu, Ayşe, and Kai Zhao (2018). "The Chinese Saving Rate: Long-Term Care Risks, Family Insurance, and Demographics." *Journal of Monetary Economics* 96: 33–52.

Karabarbounis, Loukas, and Brent Neiman (2014). "The Global Decline of the Labor Share." *Quarterly Journal of Economics* 129.1: 61–103.

Karabarbounis, Loukas, and Brent Neiman (2019). "Accounting for Factorless Income." *NBER Macroeconomics Annual* 33.1: 167–228.

King, Mervyn (2016). *The End of Alchemy: Money, Banking, and the Future of the Global Economy*. WW Norton & Company.

Klein, Matthew C., and Michael Pettis (2020). *Trade Wars Are Class Wars: How Rising Inequality Distorts the Global Economy and Threatens International Peace*. Yale University Press.

Knoll, Katharina, Moritz Schularick, and Thomas Steger (2017). "No Price Like Home: Global House Prices, 1870–2012." *American Economic Review* 107.2: 331–353.

Koo, Richard C. (2011). *The Holy Grail of Macroeconomics: Lessons from Japan's Great Recession*. John Wiley & Sons.

Kreps, David (2018). *The Motivation Toolkit: How to Align Your Employees' Interests with Your Own*. Findaway World, LLC.

Krugman, Paul (1987). "The Narrow Moving Band, the Dutch Disease, and the Competitive Consequences of Mrs. Thatcher: Notes on Trade in the Presence of Dynamic Scale Economies." *Journal of Development Economics* 27.1–2: 41–55.

Krugman, Paul (1992). *Geography and Trade*. MIT Press.

Kuhn, Moritz, Moritz Schularick, and Ulrike I. Steins (2020). "Income and Wealth Inequality in America: 1949–2016." *Journal of Political Economy* 128.9.

Kuhn, Philip A. (1990). *Soulstealers: The Chinese Sorcery Scare of 1768*. Harvard University Press

Kung, James Kai-Sing, and Lin Yi-min (2007). "The Decline of Township-and-Village Enterprises in China's Economic Transition." *World Development* 35.4: 569–584.

Lane, Nathan (2019). "Manufacturing Revolutions: Industrial Policy and Industrialization in South Korea," *Working paper*.

Levchenko, Andrei A. (2007). "Institutional Quality and International Trade." *Review of Economic Studies* 74.3: 791–819.

Levy, Jonathan (2021). *Ages of American Capitalism: A History of the United States*. Random House.

Li, Pei, Yi Lu, and Jin Wang (2016). "Does Flattening Government Improve Economic Performance? Evidence from China." *Journal of Development Economics* 123: 18–37.

Li, Xing, Chong Liu, Xi Weng, and Li-An Zhou (2019). "Target Setting in Tournaments: Theory and Evidence from China." *Economic Journal* 129.10: 2888–2915.

Lieberthal, Kenneth (2003). *Governing China: From Revolution through Reform* (2nd edition). W.W. Norton & Company.

Lin, Justin Yifu (2012). *New Structural Economics: A Framework for Rethinking Development and Policy*. World Bank Publications.

Lin, Justin Yifu (2014). *The Quest for Prosperity: How Developing Economies Can Take Off*. Princeton University Press.

Lin, Justin Yifu, Fang Cai, and Zhou Li (2004). *The China Miracle: Development Strategy and Economic Reform* (Revised Edition). The Chinese University of Hong Kong Press.

Liu, Ernest (2019). "Industrial Policies in Production Networks." *Quarterly Journal of Economics* 134.4: 1883–1948.

Maskin, Eric, Yingyi Qian, and Chenggang Xu (2000). "Incentives, Information, and Organizational Form." *Review of Economic Studies* 67.2: 359–378.

McCraw, Thomas K. (1998). *Creating Modern Capitalism: How Entrepreneurs, Companies, and Countries Triumphed in Three Industrial Revolutions.* Harvard University Press.

Melitz, Marc J., and Daniel Trefler (2012). "Gains from Trade when Firms Matter." *Journal of Economic Perspectives* 26.2: 91–118.

Michalopoulos, Stelios (2012). "The Origins of Ethnolinguistic Diversity." *American Economic Review* 102.4: 1508–1539.

Mian, Atif, and Amir Sufi (2014). *House of Debt: How They (and You) Caused the Great Recession, and How We Can Prevent it from Happening Again.* University of Chicago Press.

Mian, Atif R., Ludwig Straub, and Amir Sufi (2020a). "Indebted Demand," *NBER Working Paper* No. w26940.

Mian, Atif R., Ludwig Straub, and Amir Sufi (2020b). "The Saving Glut of the Rich and the Rise in Household Debt," *NBER Working Paper* No. w26941.

Milanovic, Branko (2016). *Global Inequality: A New Approach for the Age of Globalization.* Harvard University Press.

Miller, Chris (2022). *Chip War: The Fight for the World's Most Critical Technology.* Simon and Schuster.

Milne, Alistair (2009). *The Fall of the House of Credit: What Went Wrong in Banking and What Can be Done to Repair the Damage?* Cambridge University Press.

Mulligan, Casey and Andrei Shleifer (2005). "The Extent of the Market and the Supply of Regulation." *Quarterly Journal of Economics* 120: 1445–1473.

Naughton, Barry J. (2018). *The Chinese Economy: Adaptation and Growth* (2nd edition). MIT Press.

Olmstead, Alan L., and Paul W. Rhode (2018). "Cotton, Slavery, and the New History of Capitalism." *Explorations in Economic History* 67: 1–17.

Orlik, Thomas (2020). *China: The Bubble that Never Pops.* Oxford University Press.

Paulson, Hank (2015). *Dealing with China: An Insider Unmasks the New Economic Superpower.* Twelve.

Pettis, Michael (2013). *The Great Rebalancing: Trade, Conflict, and the Perilous Road Ahead for the World Economy.* Princeton University Press.

Philippon, Thomas, and Ariell Reshef (2012). "Wages and Human Capital in the US Finance Industry: 1909–2006." *Quarterly Journal of Economics* 127.4: 1551–1609.

Philippon, Thomas (2019). *The Great Reversal: How America Gave Up on Free Markets.* Harvard University Press.

Piketty, Thomas (2014). *Capital in the Twenty-First Century.* Harvard University Press.

Piketty, Thomas, and Gabriel Zucman (2014). "Capital Is Back: Wealth-Income Ratios in Rich Countries 1700–2010." *Quarterly Journal of Economics*: 1255–1310.

Polanyi, Karl (1944). *The Great Transformation: The Political and Economic Origins of Our Time.* Beacon press.

Prendergast, Canice, and Robert Topel (1996). "Favoritism in Organizations." *Journal of Political Economy* 104.5: 958–978.

Qian, Yingyi (2017). *How Reform Worked in China: The Transition from Plan to Market.* The MIT Press.

Rajan, Raghuram G. (2011). *Fault Lines: How Hidden Fractures Still Threaten the World Economy.* Princeton University Press.

Reinhart, Carmen M., and Kenneth S. Rogoff (2009). *This Time Is Different: Eight Centuries of Financial Folly.* Princeton University Press.

REN21 (2020). *Renewables 2020 Global Status Report*, Renewable Energy Policy Network for the 21st Century.

Rodrik, Dani (1998). "Why Do More Open Economies Have Bigger Governments?" *Journal of Political Economy* 106.5: 997–1032.

Rodrik, Dani (2007). *One Economics, Many Recipes: Globalization, Institutions, and Economic Growth.* Princeton university press.

Rodrik, Dani (2011). *The Globalization Paradox: Democracy and the Future of the World Economy.* WW Norton & Company.

Rodrik, Dani (2013). "Unconditional Convergence in Manufacturing." *Quarterly Journal of Economics* 128.1: 165–204.

Rodrik, Dani (2016). "Premature Deindustrialization." *Journal of Economic Growth* 21.1: 1–33.

Rodrik, Dani (2018). *Straight Talk on Trade: Ideas for a Sane World Economy.* Princeton University Press.

Rozelle, Scott, and Natalie Hell (2020). *Invisible China: How the Urban-Rural Divide Threatens China's Rise.* University of Chicago Press.

Ryan-Collins, Josh, Toby Lioyd, and Laurie Macfarlane (2017). *Rethinking the Economics of Land and Housing.* Zed Books.

Sachs, Jeffrey, Wing Thye Woo, and Xiaokai Yang (2000). E*conomic Reforms and Constitutional Transition*, CID Working Paper.

Saez, Emmanuel, and Gabriel Zucman (2019). *The Triumph of Injustice: How the Rich Dodge Taxes and How to Make Them Pay.* W.W. Norton & Company.

Scheidel, Walter (2017). *The Great Leveler: Violence and the History of Inequality from the Stone Age to the Twenty-First Century.* Princeton University Press.

Sheng, Andrew (2009). *From Asian to Global Financial Crisis: An Asian Regulator's View of Unfettered Finance in the 1990s and 2000s.* Cambridge University Press.

Shiller, Robert J. (2020). *Narrative Economics: How Stories Go Viral and Drive Major Economic Events*. Princeton University Press.

Shleifer, Andrei, and Robert Vishny (2011). "Fire Sales in Finance and Macroeconomics." *Journal of Economic Perspectives* 25.1: 29–48.

Sivaram, Varun (2018). *Taming the Sun: Innovation to Harness Solar Energy and Power the Planet*. MIT Press.

Spader, Jonathan, Daniel McCue, and Christopher Herbert (2016). "Homeowner Households and the U.S. Homeownership Rate: Tenure Projections for 2015–2035," *Working paper*.

Stiglitz, Joseph E. (2012). *The Price of Inequality: How Today's Divided Society Endangers Our Future*. WW Norton & Company.

Stiglitz, Joseph E., and Bruce C. Greenwald (2015). *Creating a Learning Society: A New Approach to Growth, Development, and Social Progress*. Columbia University Press.

Studwell, Joe (2013). *How Asia Works: Success and Failure in the World's Most Dynamic Region*. Open Road+ Grove/Atlantic.

Tooze, Adam (2018). *Crashed: How a Decade of Financial Crises Changed the World*. Penguin.

Turner, Adair (2017). *Between Debt and the Devil: Money, Credit, and Fixing Global Finance*. Princeton University Press.

Vogel, Ezra F. (2011) *Deng Xiaoping and the Transformation of China*. Belknap Press of Harvard University Press.

Volcker, Paul A., and Toyoo Gyohten (1992). *Changing Fortunes: The World's Money and the Threat to American Leadership*. Crown.

Wallis, John J. (2006). "The Concept of Systematic Corruption in American History." *Corruption and Reform: Lessons from America's Economic History*. University of Chicago Press: 23–62.

Walter, Carl, and Fraser Howie (2012). *Red Capitalism: The Fragile Financial Foundation of China's Extraordinary Rise*. John Wiley & Sons.

Wang, Gungwu (2019). *China Reconnects: Joining a Deep-rooted Past to a New World Order*. World Scientific.

Wang, Zhi, Shang-Jin Wei, Xinding Yu, Kunfu Zhu (2018). "Re-examining the Effects of Trading With China on Local Labor Markets: A Supply Chain Perspective," *NBER Working Paper 24886*.

Wang, Zhi, Qinghua Zhang, and Li-An Zhou (2019). "Career Incentives of City Leaders and Urban Spatial Expansion in China." *Review of Economics and Statistics*: 1–45.

World Inequality Lab (2017). *World Inequality Report 2018*.

Xu, Chenggang (2011). "The Fundamental Institutions of China's Reforms and Development." *Journal of Economic Literature* 49.4: 1076–1151.

Yergin, Deniel (2020). *The New Map: Energy, Climate, and the Clash of Nations*. Penguin Press.

Yip, George S., and Bruce McKern (2016). *China's Next Strategic Advantage: From Imitation to Innovation*. MIT Press.

Young, Alwyn (1991). "Learning by Doing and the Dynamic Effects of International Trade." *Quarterly Journal of Economics* 106.2: 369–405.

Zhang, Longmei, Ray Brooks, Ding Ding, Haiyan Ding, Hui He, Jing Lu, and Rui Mano (2018). "China's High Savings: Drivers, Prospects, and Policies," *IMF Working Papers*.

Zhang, Bing, Xiaolan Chen, and Huanxiu Guo (2018). "Does Central Supervision Enhance Local Environmental Enforcement? Quasi-experimental Evidence from China." *Journal of Public Economics* 164: 70–90.

Zhang, Qi, and Mingxing Liu (2019). *Revolutionary Legacy, Power Structure, and Grassroots Capitalism under the Red Flag in China*. Cambridge University Press.

Zhang, Zhiwei, and Yi Xiong (2019). "Infrastructure Financing," *Working paper*.

Zhou, Xueguang (2022). *The Logic of Governance in China: An Organizational Approach*. Cambridge University Press.

Zuckerman, Gregory (2010). *The Greatest Trade Ever: The Behind-the-Scenes Story of How John Paulson Defied Wall Street and Made Financial History*. Currency.

Translated References (in Chinese)

Bai, Chongen, and Zhenjie Qian (2009). "Factor Income Share in China: The Story behind the Statistics." *Economic Research Journal* 3: 27–41. (in Chinese)

Editorial Board (2013). *The History of China Development Bank: 1994–2012*. China Financial Publishing House. (in Chinese)

Bo, Yibo (2008). *Review of a Number of Major Decisions and Events*. History of Chinese Communist Party Publishing House. (in Chinese)

Chen, Binkai, and Yinyin Li (2020). "The Influence of Redistribution Policy on Rural Income Distribution—An Empirical Research Based on the Tax and Fee System Reform." *Social Sciences in China* 2: 70–92+205–206. (in Chinese)

Chen, Binkai, Lu Ming, and Ninghua Zhong (2010). "Household Consumption Constrained by Hukou System." *Economic Research Journal* 45.S1: 62–71. (in Chinese)

Chen, Binkai, and Rudai Yang (2013). "Land Supply, Housing Price and Household Saving in Urban China: Evidence from Urban Household Survey." *Economic Research Journal* 1: 110–122. (in Chinese)

Chen, Dengke, and Shiyi Chen (2018). "Capital-Labour Relative Price, Substitution Elasticity and Labour Income Share." *Journal of Management World* 12: 73–97. (in Chinese)

Chen, Shuo, and Lin Zhu (2020). "Market Transformation and Governance Corruption: Based on Individual Evidence of Officials," Fudan University School of Economics Discussion Paper. (in Chinese)

Chen, Xiaohong, Lei Zhu, and Yangjie Wang (2018). "Government Station Effect: Empirical Evidence from the State Land Supervision in China." *China Economic Quarterly* 1: 99–122. (in Chinese)

Dang, Junzhang, and Qinghua Wang (2010), "Analysis on the Risk of Local Governments' Financing Platform." *The Chinese Banker* 4: 11–16+6. (in Chinese)

Fan, Ziying, and Xin Li (2014). "Political Connection of Ministers and the Allocation of Fiscal Transfer." *Economic Research Journal* 6: 129–141. (in Chinese)

Fang, Hongsheng, and Jun Zhang (2013). "Grabbing Hand, Helping Hand and Tax-Exceeding-GDP Growth." *Economic Research Journal* 3: 108–121. (in Chinese)

Fu, Yong, and Yan Zhang (2007). "The Chinese Decentralization and Fiscal Expenditure Structure Bias: The Cost of Competition for Growth." *Journal of Management World* 3: 4–12+22. (in Chinese)

Gan, Li, Naibao Zhao, and Yongzhi Sun (2018). "Income Inequality, Liquidity Constraints and China's Household Savings Rate." *Economic Research Journal* 12: 34–50. (in Chinese)

Gao, Xiang, and Xiaoning Long (2016). "Does Cultural Segmentation Caused by Administrative Division Harm Regional Economic Development in China?" *China Economic Quarterly* 2: 647–674. (in Chinese)

Ge, Jianxiong (2013). *Unification and Division: Enlightenment from Chinese History*. The Commercial Press. (in Chinese)

Gong, Yongfeng, and Jie Lin (2020). "'De-globalization' Is Difficult to Shake the Dominant position of China's Photovoltaic Industry Chain," CITIC Securities. (in Chinese)

Han, Libin, and Ming Lu (2018). "Supply-Demand Mismatch: Solving the Puzzle of China's Housing Price Divergence." *The Journal of World Economy* 10: 126–149. (in Chinese)

Han, Maoli (2015). *Fifteen Lectures on Chinese History and Geography*. Peking University Press. (in Chinese)

Hong, Zheng, Shuonan Zhang, and Lin Zhang (2017). "Economic Structure, Fiscal Capacity and the Local Government's Financial Holding Pattern of City Commercial Bank." *Journal of Financial Research* 10: 83–98. (in Chinese)

Huang, Qifan (2020). *Analysis and Reflection: Huang Qifan's Fudan Economics Courses*. Shanghai People's Publishing House. (in Chinese)

Jiang, Chao, Zhengxing Zhu, and Jia Du (2018). "The Scale of the Potential Debt of Local Government," Haitong Securities. (in Chinese)

Jin, Guantao, and Qingfeng Liu (2010). *The Cycle of Growth and Decline on the Ultrastable Structure of Chinese Society*. Law Press · China. (in Chinese)

Jing, Yuejin, Mingming Chen, and Bin Xiao (2016). *Contemporary Chinese Government and Politics*. China Renmin University Press. (in Chinese)

Li, Ping (2010). *A Concise Illustration of the Fiscal System*. China Financial & Economic Publishing House. (in Chinese)

Li, Shi, and, Mengbing Zhu (2018). "Changes in the Income Gap of Residents in the 40 Years of China's Economic Transformation." *Journal of Management World* 12: 19–28. (in Chinese)

Li, Xuewen, Xinhai Lu, and Weiwen Zhang (2012). "Local Government and Extra-Budgetary Revenue: Issues in China's Economic Growth Model." *The Journal of World Economy* 8: 134–160. (in Chinese)

Lin, Yifu (2003). "Backward Advantage or Backward Disadvantage: A Discussion with Yang Xiaokai." *China Economic Quarterly* 4: 989–1004. (in Chinese)

Lin, Yifu, Hemao Wu, and Yiqing Xing (2010). "'Wave Phenomena' and Formation of Excess Capacity." *Economic Research Journal* 10: 4–19. (in Chinese)

Liu, Kegu, and Kang Jia (2008). *A Review of China's Thirty years of Fiscal and Tax Reform*. Economic Science Press. (in Chinese)

Liu, Shouying (2018). *Land System Reform and Economic Development in China*. China Renmin University Press. (in Chinese)

Liu, Shouying, and Jidong Yang (2019). "The Evolution and the Policy Selection in China's Industrial Upgrading: Based on Product Space Perspective." *Journal of Management World* 6: 81–94+194–195. (in Chinese)

Lou, Jiwei (2013). *Rethinking of Intergovernmental Fiscal Relations in China*. China Financial & Economic Publishing House. (in Chinese)

Lou, Jiwei (2018). "On the Reform of Intergovernmental Function Assignment and Fiscal Responsibility." *Comparative Studies* 4. (in Chinese)

Lou, Jiwei, and Shangxi Liu (2019). *70 Years of Public Finance and Taxation Development in People's Republic of China*. People's Publishing House. (in Chinese)

Lu, Feng (2016). *Photonic Change: An Enterprise and Its Industrial History*. Contemporary China Publishing House. (in Chinese)

Lu, Feng (2019). *Towards Self-reliance and Innovation: Finding the Source of Chinese Power*. China Renmin University Press. (in Chinese)

Lu, Feng (2020). *New Fire: Towards Independent Innovation2*. China Renmin University Press. (in Chinese)

Lu, Ming (2016). *Great State Needs Bigger City*. Shanghai People's Publishing House. (in Chinese)

Luo, Changyuan, and Jun Zhang (2019). "Labor Income Share and Economic Development: An Empirical Study Based on Chinese Industry-Level Data." *Social Sciences in China* 4: 65–79+206. (in Chinese)

Ma, Guangrong, Kaiqiang Zhang, and Bingyang Lv (2019). "Tax Sharing and Local Fiscal Expenditure Structure." *Journal of Financial Research* 8: 20–37. (in Chinese)

Miao, Xiaolin, Ting Wang, and Yueguang Gao (2017). "The Effect of Fiscal Transfer on the Gap Between Urban-Rural Public Services Based on a Grouping Comparison of Different Economic Catching-Up Provinces." *Economic Research Journal* 2: 52–66. (in Chinese)

Ren, Zeping, Lei Xia, and Chai Xiong (2017). *Real Estate Cycle*. People's Publishing House. (in Chinese)

Shao, Chaodui, Danni Su, and Qun Bao (2018). "Growth Performance Evaluation of County Merger under the Chinese Style Decentralization." *The Journal of World Economy* 10: 101–125. (in Chinese)

Shao, Ting, Li Tian, and Ran Tao (2018). "China's Urban Dual Land System and Real Estate Market Development: Analytical Framework. *Policy Evaluation and Reform Potential*." *Comparative Studies* 6. (in Chinese)

Shi, Jinchuan (2002). *China Regional Economic Development: A Case Study of Wenzhou*. Zhejiang University Press. (in Chinese)

Tan, Zhibo, Li-An Zhou, and Yue Zhao (2015). "'County Administrated by Province' Reform, Fiscal Decentralization and People's Welfare: A Difference-in-Differences Estimation." *China Economic Quarterly* 3: 1093–1114. (in Chinese)

Tang, Wei (2019). "Decentralization, Externalities and Border Effects." *Economic Research Journal* 3: 103–118. (in Chinese)

Tang, Wei, and Yuan Wang (2015). "Administrative Boundary Adjustment and Urbanization of Population: Evidence from City-county Merger in China." *Economic Research Journal* 9: 72–85. (in Chinese)

Tian, Yi, and Xu Zhao (2008). *Township Tax: Thirty Years of a Town, a 'Secret' Financial History of a Country*. China CITIC Press. (in Chinese)

Wan Xiaoli, Yuruo Yan, and Fang Fang (2017). "Housing Price, Housing Wealth and Household Consumption: Evidence from Aggregate and Survey Data about China." *China Economic Quarterly* 2: 525–544. (in Chinese)

Wang, Nengquan (2018). *The Era of Oil*. China CITIC Press. (in Chinese)

Wang, Ruimin, and Ran Tao (2017). "The Equalization Effect of China's Intergovernmental Fiscal Transfer: An Empirical Assessment Based on County-Level Data." *The Journal of World Economy* 12: 119–140. (in Chinese)

Wang, Shaoguang (1997). *Bottom Limits of Decentralization*. China Planning Press. (in Chinese)

Wu, Min, Li-An Zhou (2018). "Political Incentives and City Construction: The Visibility of Public Projects." *Economic Research Journal* 12: 97–111. (in Chinese)

Wu, Yi (2018). *Noisy Town: The Deduction and Interpretation of the Political Operation of a Township*. SDX Joint Publishing Company. (in Chinese)

Xi, Penghui, Ruobing Liang, and Zhenfa Xie (2017). "Tax Sharing Adjustments, Fiscal Pressure and Industrial Pollution." *The Journal of World Economy* 10: 170–192. (in Chinese)

Xi, Penghui, Ruobing Liang, zhenfa Xie, and Su Guocan (2017). "Fiscal Stress, Excess Capacity and Supply-Side Reform." *Economic Research Journal* 9: 86–102. (in Chinese)

Xu, Xianchun, Hai Jia, Jiao Li, and Junbo Li (2015). "On the Role Played by Real Estate in the Growth of China's National Economy." *Social Sciences in China* 1: 84–101+204. (in Chinese)

Xu, Yekun, and Guangyuan Ma (2019). "Local Officials 'Turnover and Enterprises' Overcapacity." *Economic Research Journal* 15: 129–145. (in Chinese)

Yan, Peng (2018). *A Brief History of China's Industry (1815–2015)*. Publishing House of Electronics Industry. (in Chinese)

Yang, Haisheng, Shaoling Chen, Danglun Luo, and Guoman She (2014). "Between the Policy lnstability and the Economic Growth: The Empirical Evidence from China's Change in Her Local Officers." *Journal of Management World* 9: 13–28+187–188. (in Chinese)

Yao, Yang, and Muyang Zhang (2013). "Performance of Officials and the Promotion Tournament: Evidence from Chinese Cities." *Economic Research Journal* 1: 137–150. (in Chinese)

Yi, Gang (2019). "Maintain Prudent Monetary Policy & Keep Yuan Stable." *Qiushi* 23. (in Chinese)

Yi, Gang (2020). "Revisiting China's Financial Asset Structure and Policy Implications." *Economic Research Journal* 3: 4–17. (in Chinese)

Yi, Heng, and Hong Zhu (2011). "A Study of Productive Expenditure Bias in County-Level Finance in China." *Social Sciences in China* 1: 88–101+222. (in Chinese)

Yu, Miaojie, and Zhonghua Liang (2014). "Trade Liberalization and China's Labor Income Share: An Empirical Analysis Based on Manufacturing Trade Enterprises Data." *Journal of Management World* 7: 22–31. (in Chinese)

Yuan, Jiancong, Tao Xu, Zhe Wang, Chong Ao, and Chao Li (2020). "New Materials Industry Panel Materials Series Report," CITIC Securities. (in Chinese)

Zhang, Chuanchuan, Kun Jia, and Rudai Yang (2016). "Dwelling Narrowness in 'Ghost Town': Income Inequality and the Housing Bubble." *The Journal of World Economy* 2: 120–141. (in Chinese)

Zhang, Chunlin (2019). "Understanding China's SOE Sector Expansion." *Comparative Studies* 6. (in Chinese)

Zhang, Jun, Haichao Fan, Zhiwei Xu, and Longfei Zhou (2020). "Structural Decline in the GDP Growth Rate: The Impact of the Official Assessment Mechanism." *Economic Research Journal* 5: 31–48. (in Chinese)

Zhang, Jun (2019). *Shenzhen Miracle*. Oriental Publishing. (in Chinese)

Zhang, Wuchang (2019). *Economic Explanation (2019 updated version).* China CITIC Press. (in Chinese)

Zhang, Yansheng, and Gen Xiao (2001). *Government and Market: The Chinese Experience.* China CITIC Press. (in Chinese)

Zhao, Ting, and Zhao Chen (2019). "Comparative Advantage and Central, Local Industrial Policies in China." *The Journal of World Economy* 10: 98–119. (in Chinese)

Zheng, Siqi, Weizeng Sun, Jing Wu, and Yun Wu (2014). "Infrastructure Investment, Land Leasing and Real Estate Price: A Unique Financing and Investment Channel for Urban Development in Chinese Cities." *Economic Research Journal* 8: 14–27. (in Chinese)

The People's Bank of China Financial Stability Analysis Group (2019). *China Financial Stability Report 2019*, China Financial Publishing House. (in Chinese)

The People's Bank of China Statistics and Analysis Department (2020). *Survey Report on the Assets and Liabilities of Urban Households in China.* (in Chinese)

Zhong, Yuejun, Ming Lu, and Xican Xi (2020). "Agglomeration and Service Industry Development: Based on the Perspective of Population Spatial Distribution." *Journal of Management World* 11: 35–49. (in Chinese)

Zhou, Feizhou (2012). *Interest for Interest's Sake: Fiscal Relations and Local Government Behavior.* Shanghai Joint Publishing Company. (in Chinese)

Zhou, Li-An (2016). "Organizational Boundary of Administrative Subcontracting: An Analysis of 'the Separation of Officials and Local Staff and Stratified Mobility'." *Chinese Journal of Sociology* 1: 34–64. (in Chinese)

Zhou, Li-An (2017). *Local Governments in Transition: Officials' Incentives and Governance* (2nd ed.). Truth & Wisdom Press. (in Chinese)

Zhou, Li-An (2018). "'Bureaucratic & Economic Markets' and China's Growth Story." *Chinese Journal of Sociology* 2: 1–45. (in Chinese)

Zhou, Qiren (2012). *Lessons from Currency: Exchange Rate and Currency Series Review.* Peking University Press. (in Chinese)

Zhou, Xueguang (2016). "Between 'Officials' and 'Local Staff': The Logic of the Empire and Personnel Management in the Chinese Bureaucracy." *Chinese Journal of Sociology* 1: 1–33. (in Chinese)

Zhou, Zhenhe (2014). *History of China's Local Administrative System.* Shanghai People's Publishing House. (in Chinese)

Zhu, Ning (2016). *China's Guaranteed Bubble.* China CITIC Press. (in Chinese)

Zhu, Yue (2019). "The Power of Cycle and the Edge of Growth: 15-year Review and Outlook of the Photovoltaic Industry." Industrial Securities. (in Chinese)

Index

X. Lan, *How China Works*,
https://doi.org/10.1007/978-981-97-0080-6

R

S

T

U

V

W

X

Y

Z